INTERNATIONAL TRADE AND BUSINESS LAW REVIEW

Volume X, 2006

Roger Jones and Gabriël A. Moens

International Trade and Business Law Review

Volume X, 2006

INTERNATIONAL TRADE AND BUSINESS LAW REVIEW

Volume X, 2006

Roger Jones and Gabriël A. Moens

Routledge
Taylor & Francis Group
LONDON AND NEW YORK

First published 2007
by Routledge
2 Park Square, Milton Park, Abingdon, Oxon OX14 4RN

Simultaneously published in the USA and Canada
by Routledge
711 Third Avenue, New York, NY 10017, USA

Routledge is an imprint of the Taylor & Francis Group, an informa business

Typeset in Palatino by
RefineCatch Limited, Bungay, Suffolk

Chapter 9, the Twelfth Annual Willem C. Vis International Commercial Arbitration Moot (Problem and Respondent's Memorandum), is reproduced here with the permission of the Director of the Moot, Professor Eric Bergsten.

British Library Cataloguing in Publication Data
A catalogue record for this book is available from the British Library

ISBN10: 0–415–41965–4 (pbk)
ISBN13: 978–0–415–41965–9 (pbk)

CONTENTS

Articles

International Arbitration Moot

Book Reviews

RELIGIOUS MONOPOLIES AND THE COMMODIFICATION OF RELIGION

Shima Baradaran-Robison, Brett G. Scharffs,† and Elizabeth A. Sewell‡*

ABSTRACT

In recent years, there has been an increase in the number of countries in which a dominant church receives state aid and other forms of preferential treatment. Dominant religions and their supporters in the former Soviet bloc and elsewhere often argue that special benefits and protection are warranted based upon the unique history and contribution of the dominant church to the identity, history, and culture of the country, and the interests of the state and its citizens. Because of the distinctive status of religion and its importance to national and cultural identity, special protection, especially against foreign and other outside influence, is argued to be necessary. Although the spiritual realm is treated as being a special situation requiring special protection, the arguments in favour of religious protection curiously resemble arguments made by monopolists and on behalf of protected industries in the economic sphere in favour of protection. This paper compares the arguments in favour of protection made by religious monopolies with arguments in favour of protection by monopolists and protected industries, and concludes that in their pleas for special treatment, dominant religious groups make arguments that closely parallel those made by other types of monopolists and protected industries. Far from resulting in religion being treated as different and special, protectionist arguments result in religion being treated as just another market commodity. We urge that because religious freedom is a fundamental human right, arguments promoting state protection of dominant religions should be viewed with suspicion.

INTRODUCTION

Religious monopolies in various countries have claimed that they should receive state protection,[1] often citing their unique cultural and historical importance. As appealing as these arguments may be, our analysis reveals that the arguments these groups use to secure and support their financial and legal position parallel closely the arguments used by industrial monopolies.

---

* Law Clerk to the Honorable Jay S. Bybee, Ninth Circuit Court of Appeals.

† Professor of Law, J. Reuben Clark Law School, Brigham Young University. BSBA, MA Georgetown University; BPhil Oxford University; JD Yale Law School.

‡ Associate Director, International Center for Law and Religion Studies, J. Reuben Clark Law School, Brigham Young University. BA, JD Brigham Young University.

1 The terms "religious monopoly" or "industrial monopoly" used throughout this paper refer to dominant religions or industries that receive state protection provided to an industry or religion that limits foreign and domestic competition through financial aid, subsidies, tariffs, quotas, non-tariff barriers, and legislative provisions that discourage competition (i.e., religious registration laws, anti-cult legislation, criminal punishment for minority religious speech, and anti-proselytizing provisions in the religious arena).

States protect religious monopolies through elevated status in the public realm,[2] constitutional protection,[3] financial assistance[4] and enacting of unfriendly laws towards minority religions.[5] One commentator argues that the number of European states providing state aid to religious groups has increased in recent years.[6] Religious monopolies make several arguments that state protection best serves the interests of three parties: the religion itself, the state and society, and citizens.[7] The claimed benefits to the state include that the religion is fundamental to state culture, creates social stability, preserves national identity and national security, and prevents domestic dependence on foreign churches. Religious monopolies also argue that protection is necessary to preserve a church because the church is in its infancy or in a stage of recovery and needs financial assistance to maintain its presence and to compete with heavily funded foreign churches. The religious

2 Robert Schott, *State and Church in Sweden, in* STATE AND CHURCH IN THE EUROPEAN UNION 301 (Gerhard Robbers ed., 1996) (pointing out that the government of Sweden has allowed the Church of Sweden to levy a "parochial tax" through the state tax system). *See generally* STATE AND CHURCH IN THE EUROPEAN UNION (Gerhard Robbers ed., 1996) [hereinafter STATE AND CHURCH] (describing heightened privileges for dominant religions in Spain, Italy, Germany, the United Kingdom, Greece, Denmark, Austria, Portugal, Finland, etc.).

3 The Greek Orthodox Church is recognized in the 1975 Constitution as being "The dominant religion in Greece". CONST. GREECE Art 3, ¶ 1 (1975). Islam is recognized as the state religion in Algeria, Bahrain, Djibouti, Egypt, Iran, Kuwait, Malaysia, Mauritania, Morocco, Qatar, and Tunisia. US Dept of State, *International Religious Freedom Report* (2003), http://www.state.gov/g/drl/rls/irf/2003/.

4 Many states provide large state subsidies and indirect state aid for dominant religions. John T.S. Madeley, *European Liberal Democracy and the Principle of State Religious Neutrality, in* CHURCH AND STATE IN CONTEMPORARY EUROPE 13 T.2 (John T.S. Madeley and Zsolt Enyedi eds. 2003) [hereinafter CHURCH AND STATE] (noting that in 1980 Belgium, Denmark, Finland, Germany, Greece, Iceland, Liechtenstein, Luxemburg, Monaco, Norway, Spain, Sweden and Switzerland provided large state subsidies and that Andorra, Portugal, United Kingdom, Italy and Malta provided indirect state aid for religious organizations).

5 Bill Kissane, *The Illusion of State Neutrality in a Secularizing Ireland, in* CHURCH AND STATE 76 (explaining that Irish legislation on divorce, contraception and freedom of expression "had been brought into line with Catholic teaching" as well as the state's "Censorship of Publications Board" usually being "chaired by a priest"). *See also* George Th. Mavrogordatos, *Orthodoxy and Nationalism in the Greek Case, in* CHURCH AND STATE 120 (describing the objection of the Greek parliament to separating church and state in the 2001 constitutional revision). *See also* John Anderson, *Catholicism and Democratic Consolidation in Spain and Poland, in* CHURCH AND STATE 140 (describing the assertion of the Catholic church that "phrasing on issues such as religious education, divorce, and abortion" should not give "offence to the religious sensibility of the Catholic population").

In addition, dominant religions receive special privileges, and influence legislation controlling whether competing religions can build worship houses or proselytize in a certain state. Mavrogordatos, *supra*, at 121 (describing that Greek Orthodox clergy now obtain "productivity bonus[es]" from the state emphasizing the "unquestioned acceptance of the church's status as a special branch of the state and of its civil service") (internal quotations omitted). Mavrogordatos also asserts that currently "construction of *any* religious building still requires permission of the local Orthodox bishop", leading to an absence of Muslim mosques anywhere in Greece except Thrace and Attica. *Id.* The Greek Orthodox church brought about legislation to prohibit "proselytism and blasphemy" as "criminal offences with respect to any recognized religion". *Id.* at 122.

Even dominant religions that do not explicitly admit that they seek privileges from the state may insist that the state "bear in mind and respect the real life of the people . . . and not ignore that a large majority" of citizens belong to their church. John Anderson, *Catholicism and Democratic Consolidation in Spain and Poland, in* CHURCH AND STATE 140 (quoting a 1975 statement by a Catholic Cardinal in Spain).

6 John T.S. Madeley, *supra* note 4 at 16 T.3 (pointing out that Monaco, Belgium, Denmark, Finland, Greece, Iceland, Liechtenstein, Luxemburg, Norway, Spain, Switzerland, Andorra, Portugal, Britain, Italy, Malta, Armenia and Poland now provide limited state subsidies to churches).

7 Of course protectionist arguments also affect would-be competitors of religions but these arguments are beyond the scope of this paper. In addition, sometimes politicians and other state figures, rather than the dominant religion, make the arguments in favor of protection of a dominant religion.

monopoly also argues that state protection benefits the citizens who retain access to their historical church of preference and avoid exploitation by new religions through fraud and manipulation. Religious monopolies in several countries have received state protection including financial aid and protectionist legislation against competing religions by relying on the above rationale.

Dominant churches benefiting from state protection rely on many of the same arguments as industrial monopolies. These industries have also claimed similar benefits to the state, industry, and citizens in order to obtain subsidies and legislation to protect their industries against domestic and foreign competition.

Varying degrees of state protectionism exist, ranging from state-regulated industries to protection of infant and recovering industries.[8] This paper discusses a variety of protectionist practices (including subsidies, tariffs and legislation limiting foreign and domestic competition). These practices result in various levels of state protectionism (whether consisting of a combination of protectionist practices or an individual protectionist practice in an extreme form) which may be harmful to industry, the state and society, and citizens. As with industrial protection, religious protection is best described as a spectrum with some religious monopolies benefiting from many forms of state protection as a "virtual territorial monopoly",[9] while in other states, despite protection, minority religions survive. Recognising that there is a spectrum of protectionism, this paper points out that the same rationale for rejecting protection of industrial monopolies should apply to reject protectionism of religious monopolies.

While several commentators have explored the state of dominant religions in various countries and the challenges facing minority religions, no commentator has documented the remarkable similarity of the rationales for protection of religious and industrial monopolies. A few scholars have applied economic theories

8 The most extreme form of state-regulated industry results in a public monopoly. A legal (or public) monopoly is defined as "[t]he exclusive right granted by government to business to provide utility services that are, in turn, regulated by the government". BLACK'S LAW DICTIONARY 1023 (7th Ed. 1999).

9 *See* Ralph Della Cava, *Transnational Religions: The Roman Catholic Church in Brazil and the Orthodox Church in Russia*, 62 SOC. RELIG. 535 (2001), 2001 WL 20525099 (referring to the Russian Orthodox Church as a monopoly enabled by foreign registration law enacted by the state and the cooperation of local officials). *See also* W. Cole Durham, Jr. and Lauren B. Homer, *Russia's 1997 Law on Freedom of Conscience and Religious Associations: An Analytical Appraisal* 3 *available at* http://www.law.emory.edu/EILR/volumes/win98/durham.html (noting that the "proponents of the [1997] law claim that the legislation was a practical concern" with laws that made it attractive to "all and sundry to establish a religion in Russia and then claim tax exemptions"). However, legislation that "requires all organizations to re-register, and that will operate in many cases to impose a retroactive fifteen-year limitation on the right of many religious associations to maintain or attain full legal entity status, is obviously an overreaction to the reality that some groups may have abused tax exempt status". *Id.*

Iran, unlike many of the other countries discussed, protects Islam as "the official religion of the country" in its constitution. Annual Report of the United States Commission on International Religious Freedom 32, May 2003, *available at* www.uscirf.gov. Not only is Iran virtually a religious monopoly but the government upholds only its own interpretation of Islam. *Id.*

The establishment of dominant religions comes "about as an evolution, rather than through a revolution". E. Kenneth Stegeby, *An Analysis of the Impending Disestablishment of the Church of Sweden*, 1999 B.Y.U.L. REV. 703, 767. Establishing protection of a dominant religion is a process requiring several elements discussed above, including: state financial aid and protective legislation from domestic and foreign competition. Ravi Batra, THE MYTH OF FREE TRADE 5, 61 (1993).

to questions of religious belief or government regulation of religion,[10] but none has explored the relationship of religious protectionism and economic protectionism. This paper examines the similarities in protectionist arguments made in the industrial and religious arenas and asserts that when protectionist arguments are made to protect religious monopolies, religion is treated as a market commodity.[11]

Perhaps the general reticence to apply the seemingly scientific, rationalistic, and utilitarian field of economics to religious belief[12] and the futility of using a utilitarian calculus to assign objective value to various religious traditions would caution against our approach of comparing religious arguments for government protection and industrial protectionism arguments. Modern protectionist arguments in the industrial field often rely solely on economic efficiency arguments, which seem to have no relevance to arguments for religious policy. Indeed, United States industries seeking to defend state protectionism must legally rely on market efficiency arguments, since current antitrust law relies solely on an efficiency-based economic rationale rather than on social and political principles.

Despite these daunting challenges, we argue that there is a significant correlation between economic and religious protectionist arguments. While we do not propose an optimal "efficiency" of religious belief nor an optimally efficient distribution of believers among various religions, we argue that the social and political principles undergirding arguments against state protection are not out of place in the industrial arena. Underlying the efficiency arguments advanced in the industrial sphere are social and political rationales for freedom and individual choice that apply equally in the religious sphere. Early justifications for US antitrust laws relied on such social and political rationales, arguing that monopolies, which benefit from extreme state protection,[13] permit concentrations of power that decrease democracy and individual liberty. We contend that protectionist arguments in the field of religion conflict with these same principles and ultimately treat religion as no more than an economic commodity.

Since religion is a vital human right, arguments promoting state protection of religion should be viewed with suspicion. This paper asserts that despite arguments by both industries and religions that they benefit from state protection, lessons from industry and religion suggest that protection rarely creates the advantages sought. In fact, the interests of the state, industry, and citizens may actually be harmed,

---

10 *See, e.g.*, Michael W. McConnell and Richard A. Posner, *An Economic Approach to Issues of Religious Freedom*, 56 U. CHI. L.REV 1 (1989); Eric A. Posner, *The Legal Regulation of Religious Groups*, 2 LEGAL THEORY 33 (1996); Eli Berman, *Hamas, Taliban, and the Jewish Underground: An Economist's View of Radical Religious Militias*, NBER Working Paper w10004 (Sept. 2003), *available at* http://www.nber.org/papers/w10004; see also Susan Rose-Ackerman, *Altruism, Nonprofits, and Economic Theory*, 34 J. OF ECON. LIT. 701 (June 1996).

11 Although the concern with competition is usually associated with industry, it is also a concern shared by religious leaders vying for state protection and adds further cause for this comparison. *See infra* p 9–*Domestic and international unfair competition*.

12 *See* discussion in McConnell and Posner, *supra* note 10, at 2–3.

13 Extreme state protection may result in a monopoly. Internal enterprises may assert pressure on a state to allow it to achieve a monopoly. One example is a public monopoly, which is a state-regulated and sanctioned monopoly. An example of a public monopoly is the AT&T monopoly. Public monopolies are justified under a "natural monopoly" rationale that asserts that in some industries the cost and barriers of entry are just too high for there to be free competition and allow more than one entity to compete. These types of monopolies more successfully gain state protection through financial aid and legislation.

rather than served by protection. In examining the similarities between industrial and religious arguments in favour of protection, we are not concerned with economic efficiency arguments, but point out that the social and political motivations to oppose state protection also apply to religion.

This paper summarizes the asserted benefits to an industry of state protection. It also notes the remarkable resemblance of arguments in favor of protection of religion with arguments to protect industry. It goes on to explore the claimed benefits to the state and society of protecting industry, and the similarities between the asserted benefits to the state and society of protecting religion with the asserted benefits to industry. It then explains the claimed benefits of protection of industry to citizens. It marks the resemblance between the claimed benefits to citizens of protecting religion with the claimed benefits of protecting industry. This paper recognizes that the stakes in protection are particularly high with religion, so there are additional claimed benefits to citizens. This paper casts doubt on the benefits of state protection, and points out that protection does not serve the interests of the industry or religion, the state and society, or citizens. It emphasizes that state protection may actually harm the industry, in creating inefficiency and poor service in the industrial arena, and possibly oppressive religions, harming society by increasing the concentration of power and decreasing democracy and possibly inciting violence among religious minorities, and harming citizens through decreasing individual liberty and human rights. Later the paper recognizes the acute interests religious monopolies assert for state protection. Finally there is a brief conclusion.

ASSERTED BENEFITS OF STATE PROTECTION TO AN INDUSTRY OR RELIGION

There are a variety of reasons why a particular industry might claim it needs special protection from competition. The basic concern is usually with competition, especially foreign competition. The first type of argument is the "infant industries" and "dying industries" argument that insists a fledgling or struggling industry needs state protection to survive until it is competitive. Dominant religions also rely on this argument to obtain state financial aid and protectionist legislation for fledgling or struggling churches. A second argument is that protection against foreign and domestic competition, including tariffs, subsidies, and non-tariff barriers, is necessary to prevent foreign domination and control. Dominant religions similarly insist upon protection against foreign competition through non-tariff barriers (including foreign religious registration laws) and protectionist legislation (including anti-proselytism laws). A third argument is that a bigger size creates more credibility and safety for an industry, allowing it to better serve its consumers.

Infant industry and dying industry arguments

Both industries and religions benefiting from protection rely on infant industry arguments to obtain state financial aid and protectionist legislation for a fledgling or struggling church or industry.

Industry

Infant industry protection[14] has been used by various countries, in international conventions and even to justify outcomes in certain cases.[15] Infant industries "are those that are unable to withstand foreign competition without some form of protection by the government, but that with time could grow and compete successfully in the global market".[16] Infant industries are protected through government increases in the "domestic prices of imported goods to enable domestic producers which are uncompetitive . . . in the short-run to stay in business . . .".[17]

Infant industry protection was supported by some influential founding fathers as well as recently through United States congressional legislation. Alexander Hamilton supported tariffs and subsidies to protect infant industries of the early colonies.[18] After World War I, tariffs were imposed on imports because Congress "believed that American businesses which had expanded into new markets as a result of the war, needed protection as infant industries from foreign competition".[19] Some of these tariffs are still in place today against certain nations.[20] During tough economic times, President Reagan proposed that Congress amend the Clayton Act to "exempt . . . 'import-injured' industries from the antimerger law for up to five

14 In referring to "infant industry" protection this term also encompasses "dying industry" or "recovering industry" protection, since the three arguments are similar enough for the purposes of this paper.

15 The Warsaw Convention (officially called the "Convention for the Unification of Certain Rules Relating to International Transportation by Air") "emerged due to differences among the world's countries as to liability rules governing air transportation accidents". *See* Tory A. Weigand, *Accident, Exclusivity, and Passenger Disturbances Under the Warsaw Convention*, 16 AM. U. INT'L L. REV. 891, 892 (2001). The parties felt that carrier's liability should be limited, since liability might "threaten the financial security of the infant industry". *Id.* The "infant industry" was the "fledgling international transportation business". *Id. See also* Convention for the Unification of Certain Rules Relating to International Transportation by Air, opened for signature Oct. 12, 1929, 49 Stat. 3000, 137 L.N.T.S. 11, *reprinted in* 449 U.S.C. § 1502 (2000). *See also United States v Jerrold Electronics Corp.*, 187 F. Supp 545, 556 (E.D. Pa. 1960) (taking into account that the television equipment manufacturer was an infant industry in deciding that manufacturer did not violate antitrust laws).

16 Ruth L. Okediji, *Trading Posts in Cyberspace: Information Markets and the Construction of Proprietary Rights*, 44 B.C. L. Rev. 545, 567–68 (2003) (citing John Stuart Mill).

17 Jeffery K.D. Au, *The Hopes and Fears of Foreign Direct Investment: A Comparative Evaluation of FDI regulation in the People's Republic of China and Taiwan*, 2 J. CHINESE LAW 359, 380 n.121 (1988) (noting that "import substitution" strategies like "infant industry" protection are one way of gaining monopoly profits). *Id.* at 380. Infant industry protection also aims to "encourage other domestic producers to enter the [particular] market". *Id.* at 380 n.121.

18 *See generally* Alexander Hamilton, *Report on Manufactures* (1791) *in* THE PAPERS OF ALEXANDER HAMILTON (Harold C. Syrett ed., vol X, 1966). However, there is some indication that Alexander Hamilton preferred subsidies to tariffs. *Id.*

19 Melissa Ann Miller, Note, *Will the Circle be Unbroken? Chile's Accession to the NAFTA and the Fast-Track Debate*, 21 VAL. U.L. REV. 153, 158 n.37 (1996) (noting that after the war, tariffs were increased on "more than one-thousand articles in trade" including "minerals, chemicals, dyes and textiles").

20 Melissa Ann Miller, 21 VAL. U. L. REV at n.37 (nations that do not have "Most Favored Nation" status with the United States are still subject to the Smoot-Hawley Tariff Act which applied tariffs on most imported articles after World War I). Congress has shown some regret after public condemnation for passing the Smoot-Hawley Act, which some commentators say helped cause the Great Depression. *Id.* at 158 n.39; Edward W. Sim, *Derailing the Fast-Track for International Trade Agreements*, 5 FLA. J. INT'L L. 471, 475 (1990) (discussing Congress's embarrassment due to the Smoot-Hawley Act).

years".[21] Even more recently, "the Communications Decency Act of 1996 was ... enacted to protect the infant industry of Internet service providers".[22]

Western European countries have been known to limit antitrust enforcement and even encourage formation of cartels with "dying" industries in times of slow economic growth and rising unemployment.[23] For example, many European state-run airlines have been supported by government subsidies.[24] In 1994, France proposed $3.7 billion in subsidies to Air France, Greece proposed $1 billion to forgive Olympic Airways' debt and Portugal approved $1.1 billion in government aid to TAP Air Portugal.[25] These proposals were intended to save dying industries and as an American Airlines' government affairs director commented "[would] have made it impossible for an [EU] carrier to go out of business".[26] In the United States after World War I, shipping was considered a "sick" industry and subsidies were maintained despite government investigations that subsidy money was used to fund excessive salaries and lobbying fees rather than to "stimulate new construction or modernization".[27] Despite "scandals, though, Roosevelt insisted that ... [s]ubsidization" would continue.[28]

Despite the claimed benefits of infant industry protection, which arguably include increased domestic employment and industry,[29] it is an anticompetitive practice that allows state protection for a certain domestic industry.

Religious analogues

State protectionism often occurs with former religious monopolies that are now struggling.[30] Those advocating protection argue that certain religions struggling

---

21 William F. Shugart II and Jon D. Silverman, et al. *Antitrust Enforcement and Foreign Competition* in CAUSES AND CONSEQUENCES OF ANTITRUST 179 (eds. Fred S. McChesney and William F. Shugart II 1995); Nadine Cohodas, *Reagan Seeks Relaxation of Antitrust Laws*, 44 CONG. Q. WKLY. REP. 187 (1986).

22 Michael L. Rustad and Thomas H. Koenig, *Taming the Tort Monster: The American Civil Justice System as a Battleground of Social Theory*, 68 BROOK. L. REV. 1, 97 (2002) (also noting that "America Online, CompuServe and Prodigy" were three Internet service providers intended to be protected by the Communications Decency Act of 1996). In addition, the Federal Communications Commission, although maintaining jurisdiction to regulate the Internet, has "consistently declined to regulate" Internet services under the same "infant industry rationale". Timothy D. Casey and Jeff Magenau, *A Hybrid Model of Self-Regulation and Governmental Regulation of Electronic Commerce*, 19 SANTA CLARA COMPUTER AND HIGH TECH. L.J. 1, 7 n.27 (2002) (internal quotations omitted).

23 *Trustbusters Busted*, THE ECONOMIST 17 (April 18, 1981) (noting that "the EEC Commission's competition office, which during the first half of the 1970s looked like growing into a fierce watchdog, has become a Chihuahua" allowing European governments to support "lame industries" and allowing the EEC's industrial commissioner Viscount Etienne Davignon to encourage national steel industries to form a classic cartel that plots to reduce production to prop up prices").

24 Patrick Oster, *EU Considers Subsidies to European Airlines*, WASH. POST, July 23, 1994 at F08.

25 *Id.*

26 *Id.* (internal quotations omitted).

27 Ellis W. Hawley, THE NEW DEAL AND THE PROBLEM OF MONOPOLY: A STUDY IN ECONOMIC AMBIVALENCE 236 (1966).

28 *Id.* (in 1935 Roosevelt told Congress that subsidies "would have to continue"). As World War II approached, the US government funded a "large-scale" investment to expand merchant ships. *Id.* at 238. The aviation industry went from enjoying "a blend of subsidies, cartelization, and public controls" to becoming a "publicly regulated monopoly" like "railroads, motor carriers and shipping companies". *Id.* at 244.

29 Okediji, *supra* note 16, at 568.

30 Schott, *supra* note 2, at 295. The argument made to protect struggling industries resembles the infant industries argument. *See* p 5–*Infant industry and dying industry arguments.*

financially from a lack of members need time to recover before foreign religions are allowed to compete with them.[31] Official state religions and formerly dominant churches[32] have been supported by states through financial grants and protectionist legislation under this rationale. Implicitly expressing a desire for protectionism as a struggling industry, one Russian Orthodox leader exclaimed that after the fall of Communism, the Church has been faced with "very severe competition in the missionary field from everyone here, from the Moonies and the new charismatic movements to our Catholic brothers".[33]

"Struggling religion" arguments are more commonly made by dominant churches; however, infant industry arguments have also been used to protect fledgling churches from competition. In late nineteenth century America, the infant industry argument was made in the religious context claiming that theological seminaries should be protected from foreign clergymen.[34]

Similar to infant industries in the industrial sector that received protectionist subsidies and tariffs from the state, "infant" or "struggling" religions also receive state financial aid and protective legislation from foreign competition. In both areas, the state relies on the same "infant" or "struggling" industry or religion rationale. In addition, just as infant industries received government aid to compete in "hard economic times", struggling religions have also received subsidies and protection during difficult economic as well as moral times.[35] Although states protecting infant religions cannot literally raise the price for foreign religions to compete in the country, states have raised the burden of competing in some countries through registration requirements and other legislative limits on minority religions.[36] For example, laws in some states limit proselytizing, expel or limit foreign missionaries, penalize conversion from a dominant religion or refuse to recognize minority religions.[37]

---

31 Harold J. Berman, *Religious Rights in Russia at a Time of Tumultuous Transition; A Historical Theory, in* RELIGIOUS HUMAN RIGHTS IN GLOBAL PERSPECTIVE: LEGAL PERSPECTIVES 303 (Johan D. van der Vyver and John Witte, Jr. eds. 1996).

32 The Church of Sweden is an example where 88% of the population belongs to the Church but only "4% of the population goes to church each week, with almost half of these attending Sunday morning service". Schott, *supra* note 2, at 295.

33 Daniel L. Schlafly, Jr., *Roman Catholicism in Today's Russia: The Troubled Heritage in Religious Liberty, in* NORTHERN EUROPE IN THE TWENTY-FIRST CENTURY 136 (Derek H. Davis ed., 2000).

34 *Parsons Need Protection*, N.Y. TIMES, Apr. 24, 1888, at 9 (American "theological seminaries, which are infant industries just as much as carding machines or iron mills, are turning out annually enough of this form of labor product to supply the home demand and meet the exigencies of missionary service also").

35 In Eastern Europe this has been referred to as a "moral vacuum" among citizens that the dominant church must help fill.

36 For a thorough discussion of how registration requirements can limit religious minorities, see generally W. Cole Durham, Jr., *Facilitating Freedom of Religion or Belief Through Religious Association Laws, in* FACILITATING FREEDOM OF RELIGION OR BELIEF: A DESKBOOK 321 (Tore Lindholm et al. eds, 2004) [hereinafter. FACILITATING FREEDOM].

37 *See* Tad Stahnke, *The Right to Engage in Religious Persuasion, in* FACILITATING FREEDOM, *supra* note 36, at 619 (describing anti-proselytizing legislation); FREEDOM OF RELIGION AND BELIEF: A WORLD REPORT 28–33 (Kevin Boyle and Juliet Sheen eds., 1997) (describing Egyptian discrimination and laws used against religious minorities); *id.* at 73–77 (describing expulsion of foreign missionaries in Sudan and discrimination against minorities); US Dep't of State, *Executive Summary, International Religious Freedom Report* (2003), http://www.state.gov/g/drl/rls/irf/2003/27185.htm (describing anti-proselytizing laws, closure of churches, bans on foreign or minority religions, blasphemy laws, discrimination in employment and education, limitations on formation of new religions or registration of foreign religions, and other forms of state hostility towards minority religions in a variety of countries).

Domestic and international unfair competition

Industrial monopolies benefit from unfair competitive practices such as tariffs, subsidies, and non-tariff barriers. Similarly, states protect religious monopolies from domestic and foreign competition through financial aid subsidies, non-tariff barriers—such as registration requirements—and protective legislation—such as anti-proselytizing laws.

Industry

One essential aspect of achieving an industrial monopoly is obtaining protection from the state against domestic and foreign competition.[38] State protectionism includes tariffs,[39] subsidies, and other non-tariff barriers "designed to restrict or eliminate foreign competition".[40] Government protection can also be more subtle like shifting government policies to protect domestic industries.

Government subsidies allow protected industries to "charge prices below cost-of-production" for their products.[41] This allows industries to gain a competitive advantage against foreign competitors. European airlines, all of which are often run as public monopolies, often benefit from government subsidies.[42]

Tariffs and quotas are often used to limit foreign competitors from succeeding in a domestic market and may be a source of revenue. In the United States, in tough economic times policy makers have argued that American jobs should be protected by restricting imported goods through quotas and exclusion.[43] One commentator asserts that the Sherman Act of 1890 was actually passed in a "political bargain" between big business and opponents of protective tariffs.[44] In exchange for the Sherman Act, "protectionist trade legislation" (known popularly as the "Campaign Contributors' Tariff Bill") was introduced "just three months after the Sherman Act was signed into law".[45] Before World War I, "tariffs were the most important source

38 Dominick T. Armentano, THE MYTHS OF ANTITRUST (1972); William F. Shugart II, ANTITRUST POLICY AND INTEREST-GROUP POLITICS (1990).

39 *See, e.g., Revving up: Latin America's Car Industry*, 339 THE ECONOMIST 7963, 1996 WL 8671917 (April 27, 1996) (describing the Brazilian government increasing and decreasing tariffs on car imports from 20% to 70% depending on domestic economic health).

40 John White, *Privatization in Eastern and Central Europe*, 13 INT'L LAW PRACTICUM 19, 20 (Spring 2000) (noting that "protectionism" can be "achieved through high tariff barriers or other measures designed to restrict or eliminate foreign competition").

41 *Id.* at 20.

42 *The War in the Skies: Airline Regulation*, THE ECONOMIST 66, 1993 WL 12190605 (Aug. 14, 1993) (noting that "dogged politicians on both sides of the Atlantic will remain the biggest obstacle to free trade in air travel"). Public monopolies have also been defended as a method of achieving "global competitiveness". Steven Dov Lando, Note, *The European Community's Road to Telecommunications Deregulation*, 62 FORDHAM L. REV. 2159, 2198 (1994).

43 Bentsen, *Strong Medicine for Trade Deficit*, N.Y. TIMES, Aug. 28, 1985, at A.23; H.R. 380, 100th Cong., 1st Sess. 133 CONG. REC. H–154 (daily ed. Jan. 7, 1987); S. 549, 100th Cong. 1st Sess., 133 CONG. REC. S–1053 (daily ed. Jan. 21 1987).

44 Shugart and Silverman et al., *supra* note 21, at 179 (quoting DiLorenzo 1985).

45 *Id.*

of [United States'] federal revenue".[46] After World War I, Congress set tariffs at the highest level in history under the Smoot-Hawley Tariff Act to "sustain economic prosperity".[47]

Throughout the post-World War I period the aviation industry also received special government assistance and protection.[48] Brazil has been known to use "a restrictive import licensing system and high tariffs to prevent access to [the U.S.] specialty steel market".[49]

Some countries take advantage of protectionist government policies to protect their industries from foreign competition.[50] Japan has been known to use informal non-tariff barriers to protect against foreign competition.[51] These barriers have resulted in a 1987 World Bank study finding that the "industrialized world's most heavily protected market is Japan", despite its rejection of formal trade tariffs.[52] Japan's goal is to increase exports and "expand the international market share of its producers [so] it views protectionist cartels favorably because they strengthen Japanese producers against foreign competition".[53] Japan has been accused of restricting imported steel products that it manufactures itself, which largely prevents US companies from selling products to Japanese

---

46 Carolyn C. Jones, *Taxes and Peace: A Case Study of Taxing Women*, 6 S. CAL. REV. L AND WOMEN'S STUD. 361, 382 (1997) (noting also that "The Republican party's high tariff program won support from business leaders protected from foreign competition").

47 Miller, *supra* note 19, at 158 (noting that the "prevailing attitude of the years immediately preceding World War II was that the United States could sustain and even dramatically increase the effects of the economic boom of the 'roaring 20s' by sharply raising tariffs"). *See also* Smoot-Hawley Tariff Act of 1930, ch. 497, 46 Stat. 590 (1930) *codified as amended at* 19 U.S.C. §§ 1206–1677 (2000).

48 Hawley, *supra* note 27, at 240 (specifically during the 1920s and 1930s).

49 S. 2610, *Using American Antitrust Laws to Assure Fair Int'l Competition: Hearing before the Subcomm. on Antitrust, Monopolies and Business Rights of the Comm. on the Judiciary* 61 (April 30, 1992) [hereinafter *Hearings on Antitrust*] (statement of Paul R. Roedel) (also noting that "Brazilian authorities would not issue licenses for materials such as specialty steel which were already produced in that country" and that "[e]ven if a license would be obtained, the 50 percent import duty and the additional 25 percent tariff on financial operations would have proven insurmountable to US exports").

50 Johnson, *Japan: Who Governs? An Essay on Official Bureaucracy*, 2 J. JAPANESE STUD. 1 (1975) (attributing Japanese economic success to state protectionist practices); Chalmers Johnson, MITI AND THE JAPANESE MIRACLE (1982) (same); Stephen Haggard, PATHWAYS FROM THE PERIPHERY: THE POLITICS OF GROWTH IN THE NEWLY INDUSTRIALIZED COUNTRIES (1990) (same); Alice Amsden, ASIA'S NEXT GIANT: SOUTH KOREA AND LATE INDUSTRIALIZATION (1989) (same). *But see*, Mathew D. McCubbins and Noble, *Equilibrium Behavior and the Appearance of Power: Legislators, Bureaucrats, and the Budget Process in the US and Japan, in* STRUCTURE AND POLICY IN THE US AND JAPAN (Peter Cowhey and Mathew D. McCubbins, eds., 1995) (asserting that state power over Japan's economy has not been the primary cause of Japan's successful economic growth); Samuel Kernell, *The Primacy of Politics in Economic Policy*, in PARALLEL POLITICS: ECONOMIC POLICYMAKING IN JAPAN AND THE UNITED STATES 325, 326 (Samuel Kernell, ed. 1991) ("The Japanese Miracle has occurred in the sectors of the economy where the government has remained relatively uninvolved").

51 David E. Driefke, Note, *The Foreign Commerce Clause and the Market Participant Exemption*, 25 VAND. J. TRANSNAT'L L. 257, 265 (1992); Michael W. Punke, Comment, *Structural Impediments to United States-Japanese Trade: The Collision of Culture and Law*, 23 CORNELL INT'L L.J. 55, 57–58 (1990).

52 Driefke, *supra* note 51, at 266–67 (noting that while the United States insisted on "free trade, throughout the 1980s, Japan openly restricted imports, subsidized exports, and became the world's richest per capita industrial nation"); *see also* Pat Choate, AGENTS OF INFLUENCE 24 (1990).

53 Driefke, *supra* note 51, at 267, 269 (internal quotations omitted) (noting also that the "Japanese manipulate their economic power ... through government-sanctioned cartels" to ... further their overarching national trade goals"); *see also* James Fallows, *Japan: Playing by Different Rules*, THE ATLANTIC, Sept. 1987, at 26.

customers.[54] These Japanese protectionist practices have also been blamed for the downfall of the American "television industry in the 1960s and 1970s".[55]

Subtle government protections may include offering tax incentives or easing antitrust enforcement against select industries.[56] In the United States, President George Bush Sr. "publicly supported measures aimed at easing the antitrust treatment of corporate research joint ventures to spur the development of the new technologies necessary for meeting the challenge of foreign competition".[57,58] Some evidence indicates that the level of antitrust enforcement corresponds to threats by foreign competitors.[59]

Government protections including tariffs, subsidies and non-tariff barriers all decrease competition in an industry and create industrial monopolies.

Religious analogues

States similarly protect religious monopolies from competition through financial aid subsidies, non-tariff barriers—such as registration requirements—and protective legislation—such as anti-proselytizing laws. Many churches are largely funded through state financial contributions.[60] States also protect religious monopolies through non-tariff barriers such as registration requirements that, for example, ban foreign churches from worshiping in Russia without a license. In Russia the 1997 Freedom of Conscience Law "refus[ed] to recognize foreigners' right to form religious groups or religious organizations . . . unless they permanently reside in the

---

54 *Hearings on Antitrust, supra* note 49, at 61 (statement of Paul R. Roedel) (this claim was made by United States steel industry specialists); *see also id.* at 81 (statement of Lloyd Constantine) (the dominance of the Japanese technology industry is due to "coordinated action of the Japanese industry and Government, aided and abetted by the inaction of our own Government and defects in the American law").

55 *Hearings on Antitrust* S. 2610, *supra* note 49, at 1 (statement of Senator Metzenbaum). American experts also accuse the Japanese consumer electronics industry of price-fixing activities in the United States. *Id.* at 133 (statement of Lloyd Constantine).

56 *Party Time: Brazil's Car Industry,* 332 The Economist 7881, 1994 WL 12754080 (Sept. 17, 1994) (noting that in 1992 the Brazilian government "cut taxes on small cars provided the companies [manufacturing these cars] cut the prices . . . to around $7,350).

57 Shugart and Jon D. Silverman et al., *supra* note 21, at 179.

58 Shugart and Jon D. Silverman et al., *supra* note 21, at 181 (noting that some argue that protection of domestic industry results in "public antitrust agencies plac[ing] the protection of selected domestic competitors ahead of the goal of promoting competition"). *Id.* at 187 (also noting that when foreign competition increases, antitrust funding actually increases).

59 William F. Shugart II et al., *Antitrust Enforcement and Foreign Competition, in* The Causes and Consequences of Antitrust: The Public-Choice Perspective 179 (Fred S. McChesney and William F. Shugart II eds, 1995); Andrew T. Guzman, *Is International Antitrust Possible?,* 73 N.Y.U. L. Rev. 1501 (1998) (describing the self interest of US national enforcement of international antitrust laws). Commentators are divided about whether domestic antitrust enforcement decreases when "foreign producers make greater inroads into the domestic economy".

60 Zsolt Enyedi, *The Contested Politics of Positive Neutrality in Hungary,* in Church and State 163 (pointing out that "state finance contributes three quarters of the overall budgets" of Hungarian churches including education and social subsidiaries of these churches). Enyedi also points out that "mainstream churches receive half of their finances from the state and less than a quarter from their members". *Id.*

Russian Federation".[61] Foreign religions who do not "receive the status of a religious association . . . may not engage in liturgical or other religious activities".[62] Islamic states impose even harsher penalties to avoid competition; some Islamic states protect state religions through criminally punishing blasphemy and conversion.[63] Other states rely on protective legislation that places dominant religions in favoured status. In Portugal, the government grants special privileges to the Catholic Church which is ruled under different laws than other denominations.[64] Similarly, the Orthodox Church in Greece is treated "with special interest and in a favorable manner".[65] Other states have separate categories of "recognized and non-recognized" religions, with the dominant religion existing as the "primus inter pares" among the recognized.[66]

Both the Greek and Iranian governments have instituted anti-proselytizing laws to prevent foreign competing churches from gaining support. The Greek laws apply to all churches but are aimed primarily at evangelical Christian churches which are gaining popularity among Greek Orthodox Church members.[67] The Iranian government recently cracked down on "increased proselytizing activities by evangelical Christians *whose services are conducted in Persian*".[68] Government officials have closed evangelical churches and limited meetings to Sundays only, arrested converts, required evangelical church members "to carry membership cards", and face "identity checks by authorities posted outside congregation centers".[69] The

---

61 T. Jeremy Gunn, *Caesar's Sword: The 1997 Law of the Russian Federation on the Freedom of Conscience and Religious Associations* 7, *available at* http://www.law.emory.edu/EILR/volumes/win98/gunn.html. Note also that "[o]rganizations registered in Russia" that have "parent or sister organizations with directive centers located abroad" do not constitute foreign organizations. Durham and Homer, *supra* note 9, at 33.

62 Gunn, *supra* note 61, at 8 (noting that "under this provision, a group of Roman Catholic priests on an official visit to Russia may not legally pray together").

63 Donna E. Arzt, *Heroes or Heretics: Religious Dissidents Under Islamic Law*, 14 WIS. INT'L L.J. 349, 395 (1996). For example, "[i]n Yemen, the 1990 Law on the Press and Publications bans any publication which . . . 'prejudices the Islamic faith and its lofty principles or belittles religions or humanitarian creeds . . . [and which] distort[s] the image of the Yemeni, Arab or Islamic heritage.' " *Id.* In Sudan, "article 126 of the 1991 Sudanese Penal Code officially codifies the death penalty for any non-repenting Muslim who 'advocates the rejection of Islamic beliefs or announces his own rejection of Islam by word or act.' " *Id.* In a case illustrating the potential reach of this law, Sudan's justice minister as well as its government-controlled press attacked a human rights investigator reporting to the UN Commission on Human Rights. The investigator's report described Sudan's slave trade and noted that its criminal code authorizes punishments such as amputation and crucifixion. As a result, the investigator, a Hungarian law professor, was called "satanic" and "an enemy of Islam", "guilty of blasphemy". *Id.* Other examples include Indonesian students who were "convicted in 1992 of blasphemy and publicly defaming Muslims because they engaged in a spontaneous word play involving puns on Quranic verses during a rock concert"; Saudia Arabian newspaper editors who "facetiously questioned the existence of God" through printing a comic strip were sentenced to prison and a penalty of lashes; an Iranian cartoonist and editor were also sentenced for "drawing a soccer player adjudged to resemble the late Ayatollah Khomeini". *Id.* at 397–98.

64 Vitalino Canas, *State and Church in Portugal, in* STATE AND CHURCH, *supra* note 2, at 271 (pointing out also that the Catholic Church's influence is "reinforced by owning a national radio broadcasting channel (Radio Renascenca) and a private television channel").

65 Charalambos Papastathis, *State and Church in Greece, in* STATE AND CHURCH, *supra* note 2.

66 Rik Torfs, *Church and State in Belgium, in* STATE AND CHURCH, *supra* note 2, at 35 (describing the Belgian state as favouring the Catholic Church among all of the recognized religions).

67 *See* notes 263–69 and accompanying text for discussion of Greek anti-proselytism laws.

68 2001 Annual Report on International Religious Freedom: Iran 8, Bureau of Democracy, Human Rights, and Labor, US Dept. of State, Oct. 26, 2001 [hereinafter Annual Report 2001] *available at* www.state.gov.

69 *Id.* at 8.

government also ordered church officials to "inform the Ministry of Information and Islamic Guidance before admitting new members to their congregations".[70]

In both the industrial and religious arenas, the goal of subsidies, tariffs and protective legislation is to give domestic industries a competitive advantage against foreign and domestic competitors. Government-imposed tariffs operate in the industrial arena to increase prices and limit the success of foreign competitors in the domestic market. The closest parallels in the religious arena are outright bans on and registration requirements for foreign religions which limit the number and type of religions that are allowed access to the country.[71] State subsidies to certain industries are also very similar to state financial aid to dominant religions as both help give the entity a financial advantage and ability to compete. Lastly, protectionist legislation, such as anti-proselytism laws,[72] also resembles non-tariff barriers which prohibit imported products that the state manufactures, since anti-proselytism laws also decrease direct competition with a dominant religion.[73] The parallel between Japan's prohibitions on the types of steel that it imports is strikingly similar to the Iranian government's prohibition on proselytizing in evangelical churches which conduct services in Persian. With prohibitions only on churches which conduct services for Persians, the government expresses its fear that Persian citizens (who are primarily Muslim) will convert to Christianity, not that foreigners living in the state will convert from one Christian sect to another. Both the Japanese and Iranian governments seem concerned less with general foreign religious or industrial success than with foreign success at the expense of their industry or their dominant faith.

Credibility and critical mass

In the United States, several arguments touting the benefits of bigger industries began to take hold in the 1920s;[74] arguments included that bigness was inevitable, made for more affordable products and allowed the best companies to survive. The bigger-is-better mentality had never before "dominated the thinking of large groups".[75] Andrew Carnegie noted: "Now, the cheapening of all these good things . . . is rendered possible only through the operation of the law, which may be stated thus: cheapness is in proportion to the scale of production. Every enlargement is an improvement, step by step, upon what has preceded."[76] The philosophers of the 1920s calculated that the elimination of smaller companies in favour of larger, more robust ones allowed fulfilment of "an irresistible trend [in each trade] towards the elimination of all but a few fit survivors".[77] Justice Holmes even demonstrated this idea of inevitability in his dissent in *United States v Northern Securities Co.*,

70 *Id.* at 8.

71 *See* note 120 and accompanying text for discussion of Iranian registration of Evangelical Christians, note 214 about limitations on certain religions and note 9 on Russian registration laws.

72 *See infra* note 263 and accompanying text for discussion.

73 *See* notes 50–53 and accompanying text for discussion about Japanese non-tariff barriers.

74 Hans B. Thorelli, The Federal Antitrust Policy: Origination of an American Tradition 71 (1955). (This occurred because of the "new gains of large-scale production".)

75 *Id.* at 71.

76 *Id.*

77 *Id.* at 71 (internal quotations omitted).

noting that "bigness is inevitable in railroads and that the Great Northern *per se*, or Northern Pacific *per se*, might then just as well be held in violation of law".[78]

In opposing regulations leading to its break-up, American Telephone and Telegraph (AT&T, or "Ma Bell") relied on the argument that its large size created credibility and quality that the United States should be proud of. During congressional debates discussing deregulation, AT&T touted a "grand system" that in "scale and proficiency is unique on the face of the earth".[79] AT&T felt that the size of the system with its link to "149 million telephones" in the United States should discourage Congress's proposed deregulation of the industry.[80] DeButts claimed that the "*quality* of service" was "in jeopardy", not only with "malfunctioning" equipment but "the compromise of the *integrity* of the nationwide switched network".[81] DeButts also attributed the "half-a-billion" successful calls made every day to a "system that is constantly *growing* and changing" and requiring a "unified system of network management" that will serve "the whole system over the long run".[82] In addition, the size and credibility of the AT&T network also caused government officials to oppose divestiture.[83]

Bigger industries, despite their potential benefits to an industry, are a form of state protection if encouraged by a state.

ASSERTED BENEFITS OF STATE PROTECTION TO THE STATE AND SOCIETY

Industrial monopolies, religions and even states often justify protection with four arguments. First, they often argue that protection of certain industries helps maintain social stability through retaining stable employment and services. Religious monopolies claim that protection will maintain social stability by continuing to teach national traditions and upholding national opinion of the dominant church. Second, the state may claim that certain industries, such as steel and aviation, are vital to national security and would threaten societal safety if sacrificed to foreign competitors. A dominant church may similarly assert that national security is weakened without tightened state control over the rights of minority religions through criminal punishment, anti-cult legislation and government investigations. Third, the state may argue that an industry, such as farming, defines the national

78 *Id.* at 74.

79 *Monopolization in the Telecommunications Industry: Hearings before the House of Rep. Subcommittee on Communications of the Comm. on Interstate and Foreign Commerce*, 94th Cong. 19 (Sept. 28. 1976) [hereinafter *Hearings on Communications*] (statement of Chairman deButts). Chairman deButts of AT&T also distinguished his industry from the "automobile business, the merchandising business, the chemical business [and] the steel business", claiming that they only sell a product, but that the telecommunications industry is based on vital service. *Id.* at 30–31.

80 *Id.* at 19 (statement of Chairman deButts).

81 *Id.*

82 *Id.* at 22.

83 Weinberger also testified before the Senate claiming that "the American Telephone and Telegraph network is the most important communication network we have to service our strategic systems in this country. . . . It seems to me essential that we keep together this one communications network we now have, and have to rely on". Peter Temin and Louis Galambos, THE FALL OF THE BELL SYSTEM: A STUDY IN PRICES AND POLITICS 224 (1987) (noting also that "AT&T dropped from the third largest prime contractor to the Defense Department in 1971 to the twenty-fourth in 1981") (internal citation omitted).

identity and culture and must be preserved. Religious monopolies may similarly assert that the best way to preserve national identity and culture is through allowing the dominant church to educate the people and through recognizing an official state religion. Finally, an industry or religion may argue that the country will become dependent on foreign entities if it does not protect a certain domestic industry or religion.

Social stability

Both industries and religions assert that state protection maintains social stability. Industrial monopolies, especially public monopolies, allegedly maintain social stability through consistent employment, prices, and service in an industry. Religious monopolies also allegedly maintain social stability through ideological unity, preserving national traditions, and upholding public opinion of the dominant religion.

Industry

Industry advocates claim that state protected industries[84] are more stable than private industries since they benefit from government regulation. Private industries vary in the number of people they are able to employ, areas they are able to serve and length of operation depending on fluctuating market conditions. Antitrust suits brought by the Department of Justice have been criticized for causing social instability through "destroying business confidence, retarding recovery, and hampering industrial efficiency and stability".[85]

Religious analogues

Religious monopolies assert to provide social stability through political legitimacy. Dominant religions in countries, like the former Soviet bloc where governments struggle to gain "popular legitimacy", provide legitimacy in some nations' establishment of legal and constitutional principles.[86] Social stability is maintained by the dominant church in Greece, for example, as it "provide[s] for harmony within the Christian polity" while the state "secures the legal and political environment for the flourishing of Orthodox Christianity".[87] Bulgaria, Greece, and Moldova have

---

84 One example of a public monopoly was AT&T which controlled "80 percent of the local phone market and . . . more than 90 percent of the long-distance market" and was regulated by the government. Merrill Brown, *ATT Antitrust Case Opens to Attacks by Government*, WASH. POST, Jan. 16, 1981 at D1.

85 Hawley, *supra* note 27, at 444 (this argument was made in the 1930s).

86 Enyedi, *supra* note 60, at 157 (noting also that "politicians [in Eastern Europe] see in churches the potential providers" of legitimacy).

87 Daniel P. Payne, *The Clash of Civilizations: The Church of Greece, the European Union and the Question of Human Rights*, 31 RELIG. STATE AND SOC. 261, 267 (2003) (this symbiotic relationship that provides political legitimacy for the state and preserves the faith-promoting function of the Orthodox church is called "symphonia"). In Denmark, the church and government participate in creating a legal framework consisting of secular and "theologically-founded rule[s]". Inger Dubeck, *State and Church in Denmark in* STATE AND CHURCH 39 (noting that the Danish National Church and the Danish government create a "double norm-system" of legal rules enforced by the "physical power" of the court system and

also attempted to secure social stability through trying to force Muslim or Orthodox break-off groups to integrate with the majority faction. These attempts have been struck down by the European Court of Human Rights.[88] In these cases, states have relied on arguments that "social tension" would result from divided religious loyalties[89] or that pluralism would negatively affect its relations with a dominant religion.[90] Recent legislation in Bulgaria was in part designed to resolve a schism in the Bulgarian Orthodox Church, and has in effect made it impossible for the "schismatic" group to be registered.[91]

Dominant religions also assert to provide social stability through working with the state to restrict some foreign or minority religions. In some countries of Europe, minority religions, especially foreign religions, are deemed to disrupt social stability.[92] New minority religions have particularly been the subject of intense scrutiny in France and Belgium, where government centres and interministerial missions have been created to observe so-called "sects" and combat "deviant sectarian behaviour".[93] In Germany, the growth of some minority religions is perceived as a threat to the dominant church, depriving Germans of "ideological solidarity" and "political stability".[94] Placing restrictions on minority religions, including "cult classification", is a tactic used by the German government.[95] The government denies some churches legal status, depriving them of tax exemption and the opportunity to participate in official state duties.[96] The German government is partly concerned with stability in this classification since a "cult" is granted legal status when "in light of its statute and the size of its membership, it gives every indication of durability".[97] In Russia, minority religious organizations, especially foreign organizations, have been deemed suspicious and to disrupt social stability,

---

"church rule[s] based upon the confessional books or . . . upon the customs or cultural traditions of the religious community" and enforced by sanctions). Statesman Edmund Burke of England claimed that the establishment of the Anglican Church of England was "*essential*" to the state and was "the foundation of [England's] whole constitution". Michael W. McConnell, *Edmund Burke's Tolerant Establishment, in* Religious Liberty in Western Thought 243 (Noel B. Reynolds, W. Cole Durham, Jr., eds. 1996) (Burke also noted that the Anglican Church was a "barrier against fanaticism, infidelity, and atheism" and was a "great national benefit" and "a great public blessing") (emphasis added).

88 *Serif v Greece*, App. No. 38178/97 (Eur. Ct. H.R., 14 December 1999); *Hasan and Chaush v Bulgaria*, App. No. 30985/96, Eur. Ct. H.R. (2000); *Case of Metropolitan Church of Bessarabia and Others v Moldova*, App. 45701/99, Eur. Ct. H.R. (2001).

89 *Serif*, App. No. 38178/97.

90 *Metropolitan Church of Bessarabia*, App. No. 45701/99.

91 *See* Religious Denominations Act, (2002) [Bulgaria], art. 10.

92 For a discussion of stigmatization of minority religions by associating them with "cults" or "sects" in Western Europe, *see* US Dept of State, *Executive Summary, 2003 International Religious Freedom Report*, http://www.state.gov/g/drl/rls/irf/2003/27185.htm.

93 In Belgium, this takes the form of the government-sponsored "Centre for Information and Advice on Harmful Sectarian Organizations". *See* http://www.ciaosn.be/. In France, a Parliamentary inquiry commission published a report containing a list of 172 so-called "sects". *Rapport fait au nom de la commission d'enquête sur les sectes*, Assemblée Nationale, Report No. 2468 (Dec. 22, 1995) and an "interministerial mission to fight against deviant sectarian behavior" has been formed.

94 Davis, *infra* note 98, at 110.

95 *Id.*

96 *Id.*

97 *Id.*

partly because they "challenge the national customs and tradition, morals of society" and "arouse ethnic, racial and religious discord".[98]

Converting members of a dominant religion and criticizing dominant religious leaders are considered to disrupt social stability in Iran. The Iranian government inflicts restrictions and often harsh punishment on minority religious groups who "attempt to convert Muslims".[99] Critics of a dominant church have also been punished for disrupting social stability. For example, a popular Shi'a cleric was sentenced to 18 months in prison for criticizing the Islamic religious leaders for misusing religion, mistaking themselves with Islam and national interests and believing they should be "immune from criticism".[100] Due to these statements, the cleric was charged with "violating Islamic principles", and "disturbing public opinion".[101]

National security

Both industrial and religious monopolies have successfully used national security arguments to obtain protection against foreign competition. Industries, including shipping, transportation, steel, farming and telecommunications, have used a pending war as well as the threat of future war to preserve state subsidies and tariffs. Similarly, religions benefiting from protection, especially in states like Iran where the dominant religion is highly entangled with the state, have argued that any threats to the religious monopoly by minority religions must be punished criminally as a threat to national security. Even in Germany and Russia, the state attributes its opposition to some foreign religious organizations as threats to national security.

Industry

Throughout history, during wartime, industries often "equat[e] business interests with the national interest" and argue for state protection.[102] United States founding

98 Marat S. Shterin and James T. Richardson, *Local Laws Restricting Religion in Russia: Precursors of Russia's New National Law in* Religious Liberty in Northern Europe in the Twenty-First Century 148 (Derek H. Davis, ed. 2000).

99 Annual Report of the United States Commission on International Religious Freedom 18, 31 May 2003, [hereinafter Annual Report 2003] *available at* www.uscirf.gov (noting that Iran "engages in or tolerates systematic, ongoing, and egregious violations of religious freedom, including prolonged detention and executions based primarily or entirely upon the religion of the victims").

100 Annual Report 2001, *supra* note 68, at 9–10. The Shi'a cleric, Hojatoleslam Mohsen Kadivar, made statements "criticizing [religious leaders'] misuse of religion to maintain power". *Id.* He also "observed [in a newspaper article] that [religious leaders] mistake themselves with Islam, with national interests, or with the interests of the system, [believing] that they should be immune from criticism". *Id.* In April 1999, Kadivar was also charged for "advocat[ing] political reform and greater intellectual freedom". *Id.*

101 Annual Report 2001, *supra* note 68, at 10. *Salaam,* the daily newspaper that published these statements and its publisher were also sentenced. *Id.* The three parties were also charged with "endangering national security". In January 2001, the Tehran General Court "ordered closure of an independent journal, *Kiyan,* for "publish[ing] lies, disturb[ing] public opinion and insult[ing] sacred religion". *Id.* Interestingly, the perceived threats by Iran's Islamic government are not just with minority religions but even Shi'a Muslims who criticize the regime. *Id.* at 9.

102 Hawley, *supra* note 27, at 10–11 (documenting that the majority of people believed that "what was good for business, or at least what businessmen thought was good for them, was by definition good for everyone").

father Alexander Hamilton favoured protection of industries partly to "provide protection in time of war".[103] During World War II, the "antitrust campaign became a casualty of the war effort" because it was argued that the "conduct of a war ... called for a carefully planned, highly controlled and well-coordinated economy".[104] In fact, during the war, industries disapproved of the "national defence cases" brought by Thurman Arnold, head of the Antitrust Division of the Department of Justice.[105] Industry defenders claimed that these cases caused "unremitting interference" and "cumulative harassment".[106] Industry arguments led to certain industries receiving "immunity from antitrust action" for "activities as were requisite for the prosecution of the war".[107]

Even in peacetime, national security arguments have been used to justify protection of industry in pre-emptive preparation for war. During the 1930s, the US transportation industry benefited from state protection because of the "contention that the nation's security and prosperity depended upon [it]".[108] In addition farmers, coal operators and oil industrialists avoided "the agitation against monopoly" using arguments that they were special cases that justified creation of "publicly sponsored cartels" due to "national defense and public safety".[109] Industry commentators have also argued that "[r]apid development of the [aviation] industry ... was vital to the national defense".[110] Even after World War I, Roosevelt allowed subsidization of the "merchant marine industry", claiming it "was necessary for national defense and national security".[111] During the antitrust suit against AT&T, in spite of the Sherman, Clayton and Robinson-Patman Acts, politicians opposed state antitrust suits. President Reagan's Secretary of Defense, Caspar Weinberger, wrote a letter to Attorney-General William French requesting that he dismiss the government

103 Besides the arguments that protection of industries would "encourage domestic manufacture", Alexander Hamilton argued that protection would encourage the development of the nation's resources, promote economic and political independence and provide protection in time of war". Mark E. Brandon, *Home on the Range: Family and Constitutionalism in American Continental Settlement*, 52 EMORY L. J. 645, 669 (2003). *See also* Alexander Hamilton, *Report Relative to a Provision for the Support of Public Credit, in* 6 THE PAPERS OF ALEXANDER HAMILTON, *supra* note 18, at 51–168.

104 Hawley, *supra* note 30, at 442.

105 *Id.*

106 *Id.*

107 *Id.* (resulting in the Antitrust Division cancelling "investigations of the steel, shipbuilding, and aircraft industries and postpone[ing] major suits in the petroleum, electrical manufacturing, chemical, and plumbing industries").

108 *Id.* at 234–35 (noting also that the transportation industry claimed that it was a natural monopoly where "capital requirements were large, fixed costs were high, and rivalry was wasteful"). From 1817, American ships "enjoyed a legal monopoly of the coastwise and intercoastal trade". *Id.* at 235.

109 *Id.* at 245–46.

110 *Id.* at 240 (further, the industry argued that "because it was still in the pioneer stage, risky, speculative, and unable to offer assured returns, the industry on its own could never attract the large capital outlays that were necessary for rapid expansion"). The government supported the aviation industry through the Acts of 1925, 1926 and 1930 with several aids and subsidies. *Id.* The aviation subsidy program also became the "subject of a number of abuses" like the shipping subsidies. *Id.*

111 *Id.* at 236.

antitrust suit against AT&T.[112] Weinberger argued that "the unity of Ma Bell's communications network is essential to national security".[113] AT&T also argued that the Justice Department's divestiture plan was "not in the country's best interests".[114] National security arguments have proved especially effective state protection of industries.[115]

Religious analogues

Some religious monopolies, who are especially closely tied with the state, even claim that national security is compromised without state protection. The threat to national security usually results in state limitation of the rights of minority religions through criminal punishment, anti-cult legislation and government investigations.

Under early Islamic law, national security included subjugating unbelievers in the dominant Islamic faith in order to "protect the welfare of the Muslim community against enemies".[116] In many modern-day Islamic countries, such as Iran, and other areas, such as Nepal and some provinces in India, the dominant faith is such an essential part of the nation that it is a crime to convert from the dominant faith.[117] In the case of Sudan, Pakistan, and Iran, apostasy from Islam is punishable by death.[118] Iran also refuses to officially recognize minority religious groups, especially those accused of "espionage" activities with adversary foreign countries.[119] The government is concerned with minority religions, like Baha'i and Judaism, that it perceives to threaten national security. When confronted about why the Baha'i organization is not recognized as a religion in Iran, government officials stated that Baha'is "are not a religious minority, but a [counterrevolutionary] political organization which is

112 *Trustbusters Busted,* THE ECONOMIST 17 (April 18, 1981). Secretary of Defense, Caspar Weinberger adopted a "military view of AT&T" and insisted that it was "an integral part of the national defense". Temin and Galambos, *supra* note 83, at 223. The "defense establishment relied on AT&T for its communications, and the department was leery of changing the integrated network—or, at least, of changing it very rapidly". *Id.* at 223. Weinberger felt that AT&T was "the nation's vital telecommunications system". *Id.* at 229.

113 *Trustbusters Busted, supra* note 112, at 17. The Economist goes on to comment that Weinberger's argument was "horse feathers" and questioned "why on earth will American military muscle be weakened if Western Electric is spun off from AT&T and has to compete on an equal footing with others to supply telephone equipment to the clients of this quasi-monopoly?" *Id.*

114 *The Break-up-AT&T Trial Begins,* BUSINESS WEEK, Jan. 19, 1981, at 84B.

115 National Security arguments are effective because they "deter many critics from asking pointed questions that ought to be posed". *Trustbusters Busted, supra* note 112, at 17.

116 Arzt, *supra* note 63, at 379; *see* Abdullah Saeed, *The Historical Context of the Debate on Apostasy and the Roots of Intolerance, in* FREEDOM OF RELIGION, APOSTASY, AND ISLAM 20–34 (Abdullah Saeed and Hassan Saeed eds, 2004).

117 *See* Nazila Ghanea, *Apostasy and Freedom to Change Religion or Belief, in* FACILITATING FREEDOM, *supra* note 36, at 633, 644–45 (citing laws in Bangladesh, Bhutan, Egypt, India, Indonesia, Iran, Kuwait, Malaysia, Maldives, Morocco, Myanmar, Nepal, Qatar, Saudi Arabia, and Sudan); Annual Report 2001, *supra* note 68, at 3 (Iran).

118 Said Amir Arjomand, *Religious Human Rights and the Principle of Legal Pluralism in the Middle East, in* RELIGIOUS HUMAN RIGHTS IN GLOBAL PERSPECTIVE: LEGAL PERSPECTIVES 305, 342–43 (Johan D. van der Vyver and John Witte, Jr. eds., 1996) (Sudan, Pakistan, and Iran); Annual Report 2001, *supra* note 68, at 3 (Iran).

119 Annual Report 2003, *supra* note 99, at 32.

against the Iranian Revolution and engages in espionage activities for the benefit of foreign entities".[120] In addition several prominent Iranian Jewish professors have been charged with acts of "espionage on behalf of Israel".[121]

Similar, though less restrictive practices occur in Europe. Several Western European nations including the European Parliament,[122] the Netherlands, Sweden, Belgium, and France,[123] have investigated new religious movements. Germany created a "Parliamentary Commission of Inquiry" designed to determine whether "the beliefs and practices of religious groups ... imperil the state".[124] Russians similarly fear that people join foreign religions to be affiliated with a foreign organization rather than because of their religious beliefs.[125] In December 2002, a report was leaked in Russia, attributed to numerous federal government officials, that specifically lists Roman Catholicism, Protestantism, militant Islam, and new "foreign" sects as threats to Russia's national security.[126] The Russian anti-cult movement relies on the premise that foreign religions are "a threat to the Russian national security" in their "appeal to the Russian public and the state".[127] In addition, some Russians believe that foreign religious organizations "use religion as a cover for espionage".[128] The Moldovan government, in refusing to recognize a minority religion, similarly asserted that the church was a "danger to national security and territorial integrity".[129]

---

120 Annual Report 2001, *supra* note 68, at 2, 4 (Baha'is are charged with "espionage" when they send monetary contributions to the Baha'i headquarters located in the state of Israel). They are also associated with former Shah Pahlavi's regime. *Id.* Other broad "restrictions on Baha'is appear to be aimed at destroying them as a community". *Id.* at 4. In 1998, several Baha'i professors "were convicted under Article 498 of the Penal Code and sentenced to prison terms ranging from 3 to 10 years" for establishing a "secret organization engaged in attracting youth, teaching against Islam, and teaching against the regime of the Islamic Republic". *Id.* at 7. Baha'i groups claim that the professors taught "general science and Persian literature courses". *Id.*

121 Annual Report 2001, *supra* note 68, at 8 (espionage on behalf of Israel is punishable by death). In 2000, the defendants were "convicted on charges of illegal contact with Israel, conspiracy to form an illegal organization, and recruiting agents". *Id.* The Iranian Jews charged with espionage included "prominent rabbis, teachers of Hebrew, and their students". *Id.*

122 *Rapporteur's Report on Behalf of the Committee on Youth, Culture, Education, Information and Sport on the Activity of Certain New Religious Movements Within the European Community*, European Parliament Doc. 1–47/84 (1984).

123 *See* Eileen Barker, *Why the Cults?: New Religious Movements and Freedom of Religion or Belief*, *in* FACILITATING FREEDOM, *supra* note 36, at 535, 548–550 (listing and evaluating various government commissions and reports).

124 Davis, *supra* note 98, at 111. Some leaders demonstrate concern that foreign religions will "corrupt ... the spirit" by teaching non-Christian beliefs. Shterin and Richardson, *supra* note 98, at 148.

125 Shterin and Richardson, *supra* note 98, at 148. Some Russians perceive foreign religions as "infectious" and as "totalitarian sects" *Id.* at 155.

126 US Commission on International Religious Freedom, *Report on the Russian Federation* (May 2003), available on-line at <http://www.uscirf.gov/reports/02May03/russia.php3?scale=1024>.

127 Shterin and Richardson, *supra* note 98, at 158. The movement has proven successful with many "bureaucrats and politicians". *Id.* at 159.

128 Brian Gross, Comment, *Russia's War on Political and Religious Extremism: An Appraisal of the Law "On Counteracting Extremist Activity"*, 2003 B.Y.U. L. Rev 717, 720 (also noting that citizens claim that foreign organizations discourage fulfillment of citizens' responsibility). *See also* Lynn R. Eliason, PERESTROIKA OF THE RUSSIAN SOUL: RELIGIOUS RENAISSANCE IN THE SOVIET UNION 68 (1991) (describing Russian fear of the "conspiratorial potential" of foreign religions).

129 *Case of Metropolitan Church of Bessarabia and Others v Moldova*, European Court of Human Rights (First Section), Applic. No. 45701/99, Strasbourg, 13 Dec. 2001, at ¶ 124–25.

National identity, prestige and culture

Both industries and religions claim that national identity and prestige is weaker without state protection. European Airlines and the AT&T telecommunications monopoly both argued that they were a source of national prestige and pride, without which an important national industry would fail. AT&T also connected its successes with the success of the United States. Similarly, both Greece and Sweden claimed that without protection of dominant religions, the nation would lack unity and would be destroyed. In both areas, dominant religions have been protected from competition through a link with the nation's well-being, national identity, and prestige.

Industry

European airlines have been a source of prestige and national identity. In Europe, every big airline has been "at least partially state owned".[130] Several European countries have sustained state protection in the airline industry because of "national prestige".[131] European governments have been more concerned with "preserv[ing] both jobs and prestige" than with obtaining efficient airline carriers.[132]

In the United States, AT&T invoked the country's pride in industrial progress and a successful telecommunications system to argue that AT&T should not face breakup. When threatened with divestiture, AT&T appealed to national identity and pride. One argument AT&T used to defend against divestiture was that it would destroy "the most advanced, efficient, and successful communications system in the *world*".[133] AT&T lawyers also commented that they hoped that "the country" realized that "we can't destroy our successful companies".[134] A few months before the AT&T settlement with the Department of Justice which divested AT&T's 22 local operating company subsidiaries, AT&T Chairman Charles L. Brown commented that it was teaming up two technologies (computer and telecommunication) which would result in the "most promising and most exciting [innovations] in the history of this *nation's industrial progress*".[135] Congressmen also opposed regulation of AT&T claiming that AT&T is a "service system we are particularly proud of in America".[136]

Religious analogues

States justify protectionist measures by claiming that a religious monopoly preserves national identity and culture. Protectionist measures justified by preserving

130 *The War in the Skies: Airline Regulation*, The Economist 66, 1993 WL12190605 (Aug. 14, 1993).

131 *Don't Coddle or Curb Them; The Pain in the World's Airline Industry can be Eased by more American-Style Deregulation, Not Less*, The Economist 18, 1991 WL 4960745, Feb. 23, 1991; *Keep those Flags Flying*, Editorial, Wash. Post, 1994 WL 2433406, Aug. 5, 1994, at A20 (noting that European countries face trouble deregulating because they have "their own national flag carriers and are desperate, for reasons of prestige and sentiment, to keep them aloft").

132 *The War in the Skies: Airline Regulation*, *supra* note 130, at 66.

133 *The Break-up-AT&T Trial Begins*, *supra* note 114, at 84B (emphasis added).

134 *Id.*

135 *Id.* (emphasis added).

136 *Hearings on Communications*, *supra* note 79, at 5 (statement of Wyoming State Representative Roncalio).

national identity may include explicitly recognizing an official state church, religious education in the dominant religion or prohibiting foreign competing religions to enter the country. State protected churches also insist that their religion is inseparable from the national identity and is vital for state "self-preservation".[137]

Defenders of religious protection claim that the culture of a nation is tied to a church and must be preserved. For example, in Greece, Orthodox education in school is defended "solely on national grounds—and not on moral grounds" because the church emphasizes that the "endangered nation" will be destroyed by pluralistic education.[138] Similarly, in Sweden, people worry that in such a diverse nation there are "few other ways besides religion" to base "national unity".[139] In Britain, discussions over the disestablishment of the Anglican Church invoked an Archbishop to defend establishment by claiming "that church establishment was an essential bulwark of British society".[140] He insisted that the church protected and fortified British society.

Often state traditions and national identity are intertwined with a common religious background which defenders argue justifies state religious protection.[141] In Ireland, the preamble to the constitution "suggests that the common good should be evaluated by religious criteria and implicitly identifies the Irish nation with the

---

137 Mavrogordatos, *supra* note 5, at 122, 134. In Russia, "pluralism is perceived as a problem that needs to be restricted, not as a long term source of stability". Durham and Homer, *supra* note 9, at 3.

138 Mavrogordatos, *supra* note 5, at 134 (noting that Greece, Ireland and Israel each suffer from the same issue). Other religions have insisted that their members vote for parties that represent "Christian-national values" demonstrating a link between religion and national identity. Enyedi, *supra* note 60, at 166 (quoting the Calvinist Church in a 2002 Hungarian election). *See also* Payne, *supra* note 87, at 264 (noting that "[i]n the East ... national identity was not separated from religious identity" but "[i]n the West ... national identity was secularized" and noting that in Greece, "Orthodox hierarchs ... are concerned about the loss of Orthodox identity to a homogenous western culture" and quoting Archbishop Christodoulous who in May 2000 "commented that [f]or Greeks, to be an Orthodox Christian is a defining attribute of their identity") (internal quotations omitted); *id.* at 265 (pointing out as well that Greece, Poland, Slovenia and Serbia all have "unique [national origin myths that involve religious identity"). For Greeks, the connection with religion does not end with Greek national identity as Archbishop Christodoulous also noted that the "European Union is a creation of the spirituality of Christianity". *Id.* at 266.

139 Jonas Alwall, *Religious Liberty in Sweden: An Overview*, in RELIGIOUS LIBERTY IN NORTHERN EUROPE IN THE TWENTY-FIRST CENTURY 182 (Derek H. Davis, ed. 2000) (describing the Swedish "effort in trying to impose a Swedish church order" between the seventeenth and nineteenth centuries). In Swedish history, "faith and unity" were "tested and tightened" through external military threats. *Id.* In 1634, the "Instrument of Government" asserted that "[u]nity in religion and the right [to]divine service is the strongest foundation for a rightful, unanimous and lasting government". *Id.* at 182–83. In 1686, Sweden also linked "a person's religious status" to "his citizenship". *Id.* at 183. This concept was reaffirmed by the "Instrument of Government" of 1809, providing "that the state had a responsibility to provide for the citizens' religious care". *Id.* at 185 (internal quotation omitted). In 1951, "a Religious Liberty Act" recognized a citizen's right to "practice his religion freely". *Id.* at 186. In 1974, the "Instrument of Government" held that religious liberty is "the freedom to practice one's own religion either alone or in company with others". *Id.* at 186. It recognized a person's rights vis-à-vis the government alone. *Id.* Even today, the Church of Sweden is such a dominant part of the culture that all burials in Sweden are "the responsibility of" the Church and the Church's principles comprise the religious instruction in the Swedish school system. *Id.* at 194–95.

140 Madeley, *supra* note 4, at 4 (quoting Archbishop George Carey).

141 Schott, *supra* note 2, at 300 "[The] Church [of Sweden's] activities over the centuries have played a very important part in the development of Swedish society. Society has been profoundly influenced by Christianity ... [and] [f]rom the viewpoint of the State today ... there is still good reason for taking a positive view of religious activities, partly in view of their important societal functions".

Catholic religion".[142] Sweden defends preferential policies toward the Church of Sweden with claims that "strong historical ties between the Church and the state could not be altogether disregarded".[143] Defenders of the establishment of the Church of England claimed that the church was "part of the time-honoured constitutional structure of England" rather than necessarily the right church for the citizens.[144] In addition, national identity in Russia is tied to the Orthodox Church which "believes that the nation . . . is still Holy Russia".[145] The Russian Orthodox Church is believed to be "organically linked with Russia's [ethnic and] national identity" and therefore many argue it "must be legally protected".[146] The Russian Orthodox Church also relies on the long-standing culture of the Russian people that includes one thousand years of "worship of God according to the Orthodox way".[147] Many of the Russian Orthodox holy sites are "linked with physical defence of the motherland against the Latin West" which is a vital part of Russian culture and pride.[148] In Post-Communist Russia, the Orthodox Church attempts to resurrect the "spiritual and cultural traditions of Holy Russia" through restoring and rebuilding destroyed churches and monasteries.[149]

Several states have enacted statutes and constitutional provisions recognizing "traditional" or "official" religions.[150] For example, in Belarus a 1996 constitutional

---

142 Kissane, *supra* note 5, at 77. The preamble to the Irish Constitution states: "In the name of the Most Holy Trinity, from Whom is all authority and to Whom, as our final end, all actions both of men and states must be referred, We, the people of Eire, Humbly acknowledging all our obligations to our Divine Lord, Jesus Christ, Who sustained our fathers through centuries of trial . . . and seeking to promote the common good . . . Do hereby adopt, enact, and give ourselves this Constitution". *Id.* at 76–77. Further, this preamble has been cited "in the [Irish] Supreme Court to justify the prevention of a decision rendering unconstitutional certain nineteenth-century statutes criminalizing homosexual conduct between consenting adult males". *Id.* at 77.

143 Stegeby, *supra* note 9, at 733, 747 (the strong historical ties between the state and Church of Sweden also justified the Church maintaining the responsibility of providing burial grounds and maintaining and preserving historical churches and monuments).

144 McConnell, *supra* note 87, at 209 (Edmund Burke contended that "[t]he Anglican Church held its position in England by prescription; it was the embodiment of the religious experience of the English people over a long period of time"). In discussions about disestablishment of the Anglican Church an Archbishop commented that "the church is an essential part of the fabric of the constitution of this country". Madeley, *supra* note 4, at 19, 4 (also noting that "it remains the position of the Labour government that it would not contemplate disestablishment of the Church of England unless the Church itself wished it") (internal quotations omitted). Throughout Europe, Christianity is still the dominant religion. *Id.* at 11.

145 Schlafly, *supra* note 33, at 137. The Orthodox Church also takes on "a unique responsibility for the Russian land and the Russian people". *Id.*

146 Schlafly, *supra* note 33, at 138; Shterin and Richardson, *supra* note 98, at 148. In addition, church leaders insist the renewal of Russia post-Communism relies on the revival of the Orthodox faith. Schlafly, *supra* note 33, at 137 (Aleksii II, patriarch of the Orthodox church claimed that "the revival of Russia . . . is impossible without reviving the Orthodox faith"). Three years later he "linked the cultural identity" of the Russian people with "their spiritual orientation". *Id.* at 137. He also insisted that "with the state's failure to protect the spiritual-cultural identity of the people, the whole burden of the struggle is placed upon the [Orthodox] Church". *Id.* (internal citations omitted).

147 Schlafly, *supra* note 33, at 138.

148 *Id.* at 138. The Orthodox church "reclaim[s], resanctif[ies], and rebuild[s] churches and monasteries closed or destroyed" under Communism to preserve Russian culture. *Id.*

149 *Id.* (internal quotations omitted).

150 Law on the Freedom of Conscience and Religious Organizations, 1991 [Armenia], English translation published in LAWS ON RELIGION AND THE STATE IN POST-COMMUNIST EUROPE 32 (W. Cole Durham Jr. and Silvio Ferrari eds., 2003) (noting in the preamble "Being cognizant of the Armenian Apostolic Church as the national Church of the Armenian people and as an important bulwark for the edification of its spiritual life and national preservation"); Religious Denominations Act, 2002 [Bulgaria], English

referendum changed the wording of Article 16 of the constitution.[151] The former Article 16 provided that "*establishment of any sort of advantages or restrictions* for a religion or denomination in relation to another religion or denomination is *not* allowed".[152] However, the new language states that "[r]elations between the State and religious organizations *shall be regulated by the law* with regard to their influence on the formation of the spiritual, cultural, and *state traditions* of the Belarussian people".[153] The new language no longer prohibits establishment of "advantages or restrictions" on any religion or denomination but actually allows legal regulation of religious organizations "with regard to their influence" on the "state traditions" of the Belarussian people.[154] Under the banner of national identity and "state traditions", the Belarus government passed a revised religious registration law in 2002 that highlights the "defining role of the Orthodox Church in the historical formation and development of the spiritual, cultural and state traditions of the Belarussian people", and also mentions the "inseparability from the general history of the Belarussian people of the Evangelic-Lutheran Church, Judaism, and Islam".[155]

Like in Belarus, Russian religious campaigns against "dangerous cults" have tied "*national identities* along religious lines",[156] often drawing on the wording of the preamble to the 1997 Law on the Freedom of Conscience and on Religious Associations. While the law follows the Russian constitution in guaranteeing protection for all religious groups, the preamble "recognize[s] a special contribution made by Orthodoxy to the formation of statehood in Russia and to the development of her spirituality and culture, and respecting Christianity, Islam, Judaism and other religions as integral parts of the historical legacy of the peoples of Russia".[157]

---

translation published in LAWS ON RELIGION AND THE STATE IN POST-COMMUNIST EUROPE 77 (recognizing in the preamble "the special and traditional role of the Bulgarian Orthodox Church in the history of Bulgaria to establish and develop its spirituality and culture"); Alexander Vashkevich, *The Relationship of Church and State in Belarus: Legal Regulation and Practice*, 2003 B.Y.U.L. REV. 681, 708 (Belarus grants the "Russian Orthodox Church advantages and privileged status over other religious denominations"). Dubeck, *supra* note 87, at 37 (pointing out that Article 4 of the Danish Constitution states that "[t]he Evangelical Lutheran Church is the Danish National Church"); Canas, *supra* note 64, at 261 (noting that "consecutive constitutional amendments, from 1935 (Law 1910) to 1971 . . . recognize the Roman Catholic religion . . . as the traditional religion of the Portuguese nation").

151 Vashkevich, *supra* note 150, at 698.

152 *Id.* at 698 (emphasis added).

153 *Id.* at 699 (emphasis added). Both the old and new Article 16 provide that "[a]ll religious denominations shall be equal before the law". *Id.*

154 *Id.*

155 Law on the Freedom of Religion and Religious Organizations (2002), English translation in LAWS ON RELIGION AND THE STATE IN POST-COMMUNIST EUROPE, *supra* note 150, at 55; *see also* Vashkevich, *supra* note 150, at 704. The biggest concern for Belarus is the missionary work of "Catholic and Protestant organizations" that has allowed "the existing number of Protestant communities [in 2000] to quadruple since 1989". *Id.* at 704. *See* note 9 and accompanying text for discussion of Russian religious registration laws.

156 Enyedi, *supra* note 60, at 157 (emphasis added). "[T]he influx of religious movements from both the West and the East" exert pressure on Russian nationalism which has added to the "deeper wounds [of] Russian *national identity*". Durham and Homer, *supra* note 9, at 3 (wounds to the Russian "psyche" have also resulted from "the collapse of the Soviet Union and the deteriorating economic situation that followed in its wake"). (emphasis added).

157 LAWS ON RELIGION AND THE STATE IN POST-COMMUNIST EUROPE, *supra* note 150, at 279; CONST. ART. XIV [RUSSIA]; *see* Vsevolod Chaplin, *Law and Church-State Relations in Russia: Position of the Orthodox Church, Public Discussion and the Impact of Foreign Experience*, *in* LAW AND RELIGION IN POST-COMMUNIST EUROPE 281 (Silvio Ferrari et al. eds., 2003).

The Orthodox concept of a "nation-church" and the idea that "the people and the Christian community are identical or indissolubly connected" often means that religious minorities are perceived as "serv[ing] foreign gods in their own land", which leads some "to a conclusion that there are 'wicked souls' amongst the people of God".[158] Protection of Russian national identity is a "major source of pressure to impose limitations on foreign-based religious activity".[159] For example, the US Commission on International Religious Freedom has reported that President Putin's January 2000 security policy directive highlights the critical national security need to "counteract ... the negative influence of foreign religious organizations and missionaries".[160]

Foreign dependence

Religious monopolies and industries both invoke fear of foreign dependence in defending state protection. Industries, like AT&T, threatened granting contracts to foreign firms to warn the state that a successful national industry could be overtaken by US competitors. Religions benefiting from state protection similarly express fear that foreign religions invading their territory will capture their followers causing the state to become morally dependent on foreign churches.

Industry

Industry advocates argue that state regulation and protection of industry is the way to "prevent control of the [national] economy by foreign firms".[161] With the threat of break-up, AT&T relied on "heightening fears that foreign manufacturers will be able to make new inroads in the US market".[162] However, it was not just AT&T but also government officials who were concerned about foreign dependence.[163] For example, in 1981 AT&T "awarded a $75 million contract to Fujitsu America Inc., . . . [the California-based] subsidiary of Japan's Fujitsu Ltd., to create a fiber-optics Long Lines link between Boston and Washington, D.C. [because] Fujitsu had submitted the lowest of 17 bids in open competition".[164] However, the "contract created a stir in Washington" and "AT&T withdrew the award—citing 'national interests' and gave the contract to Western Electric".[165] One industry commentator believed that AT&T awarded the contract to Fujitsu to "hold the threat over Congress and the FCC that

158 Chaplin, *supra* note 157, 286–88.

159 Durham and Homer, *supra* note 9, at 4 (commenting that "[f]rom the perspective of internal nationalism, the proliferation of new religious groups is perceived as exacerbating already intense centripetal forces emanating from religious, ethnic and other inter-regional tensions"). Another pressure causing Russian imposed limits on foreign religious organizations are "anti-foreign attitudes" in Russia. *Id.* at 4.

160 US Comm. on Int'l Rel. Freedom, *Report on the Russian Federation* (May 2003), http://www.uscirf.gov/reports/02May03/russia.php3?scale=1024.

161 White, *supra* note 40, at 20.

162 *The Break-up-AT&T Trial Begins*, *supra* note 114, at 84B.

163 *Id.*

164 *Id.*

165 *Id.* (regarding this award to Western Electric, Victor Schnee, President of Probe Research Inc., charged that "[t]hey simply reached into the closet and brought out a foreign skeleton") (internal quotations omitted).

this great new technology is going to the Japanese, just the way autos and steel have done . . . [a]nd they fell for it".[166] Further, he contends that this was a ploy since Western Electric "could easily have submitted the low bid in the first place, aided by subsidies from AT&T".[167]

Even after the famous US antitrust suit against AT&T, commentators noted that the result of the break-off of "local telephone companies rather than Western Electric, the manufacturing arm of the Bell system" may have been influenced by American concern with foreign competitiveness. AT&T had contended that its break-up would "crush one of the few internationally competitive companies the US has left . . . [and would cause AT&T to] end up pleading for protection against the very foreign competition that the Bell System now trounces".[168] After the AT&T "break-up", Western Electric still enjoyed "roughly two-thirds of each year's telephone equipment sales in America . . . [with even higher shares] of switching apparatus".[169] During the break-up, policy makers feared competition from international competitors like "Canada's Northern Telecom, Japan's NEC, Hitachi and Fujitsu".[170]

Industry advocates insist that without state protection a nation will become dependent on foreign countries.

Religious analogues

Religious monopolies claim that without state protection, foreign churches will invade church territory and society will become dependent on foreign churches. A dominant state church may assume it has *sole* "spiritual rights" to the state.[171] The Russian Orthodox Church has complained that foreign religions proselytize on the "canonical territory" of the Church.[172] In recent years, the Russian government has denied an increasing number of visas to foreign religious workers and expelled foreign-born Catholic bishops, in an attempt to limit the influx of foreign religions and implement the policy of "one city one bishop", which allows "only one bishop—from the Russian Orthodox Church—in any city".[173] Domestic religions are often threatened by "[t]he appearance of financially-robust foreign religious groups" threatening "financially-ailing" domestic churches and that foreign religions are "purchasing souls at the expense of [a state's] culture".[174] Archpriest Vladimir Kharitonov of Russia said that his "chief anxiety" was "the invasion of Russia by various cults, and new religions".[175] Church commentators have insisted

166 *Id.* (comment by Richard Moley, a Vice President at ROLM Corp., Santa Clara, a leading manufacturer of digital PBX (private branch exchange) systems).

167 *Id.*

168 *Id.*

169 *Stripping Ma Bell*, THE ECONOMIST 13, Jan. 16, 1982.

170 *Id.*

171 Gross, *supra* note 128, at 720.

172 Schlafly, *supra* note 33, at 155.

173 *Report on the Russian Federation*, *supra* note 160.

174 Gross, *supra* note 128, at 720 (demonstrating Russian citizens' threat from foreign religions as "betrayal of "Russian-ness".

175 Schlafly, *supra* note 33, at 136.

that domestic churches cannot compete with foreign-funded religions.[176] Protestant and Catholic groups in Russia have been charged with being foreign spies[177] and using humanitarian aid to entice people away from "the Russian state, national traditions, and culture".[178] Foreign religions proselytizing in Latin America have also been accused of being "in the service of foreign powers",[179] for fear that they are invading not only church territory but the state's independence. One Latin American Roman Catholic cardinal described the majority of Protestants in his country as "here on the initiative of the United States".[180] In Belarus, the government has tightened controls over entrance of foreign clergy,[181] and in Sweden its limits on religious liberty have extended to the country's immigration policy.[182]

ASSERTED BENEFITS OF STATE PROTECTION TO CITIZENS

Industry and religious advocates claim that state protection benefits citizens. First, industrial monopolies insist that consumer access, availability, and service improve due to state protections because government regulations keep the rates down and provide for service to broader segments of the public. Second, industrial monopolies insist that regulation by the state protects consumers from fraud and manipulation by unscrupulous promoters. Religious monopolies similarly argue that protectionist measures, including registration requirements for foreign religions and anti-proselytism legislation, protect citizens from fraudulent cults. Third, defenders argue that state protection should continue in industries which provide services, such as

---

176 Gross, *supra* note 128, at 720; Cava, *supra* note 9, at 535 (noting that the Orthodox Church is financially unable to compete with well-funded foreign churches). In Poland, Orthodox Church leaders have also argued for "tighter control of the [non-Orthodox] sects". John Anderson, *Catholicism and Democratic Consolidation in Spain and Poland, in* CHURCH AND STATE 147 (noting that in some "rural areas [in Poland problems arise] where clerical influences sometimes lead to expressions of hostility towards minority groups").

177 *See, e.g.*, Sergei Kazovsky, *Strangers Among Our Own*, RUSSKII KURIER, Aug. 2, 2004, http://www.stetson.edu/~psteeves/relnews/0408a.html (describing a local campaign to label Mormon members as American spies); *Russian Jesuits Struggle for Rights*, MIR RELIGII, May 12, 2001, http://www.stetson.edu/~psteeves/relnews/0105b.html (describing the Russian "popular tradition" of labeling Jesuits as Vatican spies); Pavel Zaiakin, *International Report from the Lutheran Mission of Khakasia*, September 25, 1998, http://www.stetson.edu/~psteeves/relnews/9809c.html (quoting local government official as stating that all Lutherans are American spies).

178 *Report on the Russian Federation*, *supra* note 160.

179 Michael S. Serrill, *What the Pope Will Find: John Paul II Returns to a Region where Catholic Marxism is out of Favor: The Big Threat: Evangelicals*, 147 TIME INT'L 7, Feb. 12, 1996, 1996 WL 88224716 at *3.

180 Edward L. Cleary, *infra* note 266, at 22.

181 Vashkevich, *supra* note 150, at 708 (noting the "tightening control over the invitation of foreign clergy" in Belarus and noting that the nationalist nature of this legislation is demonstrated when the limits are most severely imposed on foreign religions). Commentators have asserted that the late nineteenth century US legislation, the Alien Contract Labor Act, "intentionally [rather than inadvertently] prohibited foreign clergy from coming to the United States to work" by not making an exception for clergy. John F. Manning, *The Absurdity Doctrine*, 116 HARV. L. REV. 2387, 2424–25 (2003). A federal prosecutor asserted that:

> in no department of service has competition been more active than in clerical work. Our choicest and most desirable metropolitan pulpits are invaded by the foreign product. Eight of the best-paying and best-attended churches in New York are at the present time served by imported … clergymen. *Parsons Need Protection*, *supra* note 34, at 9.

182 Alwall, *supra* note 139, at 196 (pointing out the interrelation between Sweden's strongly assimilationist immigration policy and religious climate).

farming, that are fundamental to the culture and well-being of the citizenry. States also insist that fundamental traditions, such as a dominant religion, must be preserved for the benefit of citizens.

Consumer access, availability, and service

Defenders often claim that without state protection, their service would no longer be available to the general public since competition would raise prices. Industry commentators who opposed pro-competitive legislation, like the Telecommunications Act of 1980, often used arguments about the effects on citizens.[183] In defending AT&T against competition, Chairman DeButts also contended that the "inevitable result of competition would be an increase in the rates which existing carriers would have to charge for residential service".[184] He insisted that the result would be increased costs on the "local ratepayer".[185] In opposition to the Telecommunications Act of 1980 which aimed to deregulate AT&T, a commentator argued that it would result in an "increase in local service charges" of over "$20 per month for each residential and small business customer".[186] Rather than focusing on the harms to the companies, industry defenders often focus on harm to vulnerable consumers. Some defenders simply believe that some state protection serves "the public interest".[187]

Industries claim that state protected industries make vital services available to the general citizenry.[188] AT&T Chairman deButts explained that AT&T felt "an unusual obligation to see to it that the service shall at all times be adequate, dependable and satisfactory".[189] AT&T also claimed that "the goal of the Bell System was service, subject only to the requirement that it earn a reasonable profit".[190] He further claimed that threats to break up AT&T contradicted "the basic aim of the United States telecommunications policy ... that is the widest availability of

183 H.R. 6121, *Hearings Before the Subcommittee on Monopolies and Commercial Law of the Committee on the Judiciary*, 96th Cong. 302 (Sept. 9 and 16, 1980) [hereinafter *Hearings on Monopolies*] (letter of John E. Bryson, President California Public Utilities Commission).

184 Merrill Brown, *Ex-ATT Head: I Tried to be Competitive; Ex-ATT Chief: We Worried About Network, Competition*, WASH. POST, Aug. 28, 1981, D10 (internal quotations omitted).

185 Temin and Galambos, *supra* note 83, at 98.

186 *Hearings on Monopolies, supra* note 183, at 302–03 (noting that if the "legislation were to be enacted in its present form, small telephone customers would suffer extremely burdensome increases in basic rates in the future").

187 Michael Isikoff, *Sprint Suit Against ATT Dismissed*, WASH. POST, June 27, 1984, at C6. In the suit brought by Southern Pacific Communications Corp. against AT&T alleging monopolization of the long-distance telephone market, a lower court judge, Charles R. Richey, was accused by the Court of Appeals of expressing "his personal policy view that an AT&T monopoly, and not competition, is in the public interest". *Id.*

188 *See, e.g.*, Temin and Galambos, *supra* note 83, at 11 (Congress passed the Communications Act to "make available, so far as possible, to all the people of the United States a rapid, efficient, nationwide, and worldwide wire and radio communication services wth adequate facilities at reasonable charges") (internal quotations omitted).

189 Temin and Galambos, *supra* note 83, at 97 (Chairman deButts claimed that "AT&T also had an obligation ... to oppose competition and favor regulation"). He also claimed that "universal service" was the key to the Bell's "grand system". *Hearings on Communications, supra* note 79, at 19 (statement of Chairman deButts). Chairman deButts also testified before Congress that he "grew up in the Bell System believing in the company's obligation to serve all the people and to maintain the ability to provide that service". Brown, *supra* note 184, at D10 (internal quotations omitted).

190 Temin and Galambos, *supra* note 83, at 98 (Gifford and deButts both made this assertion).

high-quality telecommunications service at the lowest cost to the entire public".[191] DeButts also warned Congress that "[b]y fragmenting responsibility for service, they jeopardize its quality ... [and] [b]y forcing rates for basic service up, they restrict its availability to the average American".[192]

AT&T provides a good example of an industry player who insisted that without state protection, it could not make its services available to the general public at an affordable price.

Protection from fraud of unscrupulous promoters

States justify protection of both industries and religions through claiming that citizens need state protection respectively from the fraud of unscrupulous promoters and dangerous cults. In the industrial arena, states may justify protection through a legitimate interest in protecting its consumers from fraud. States also insist on limiting the access of foreign religions to citizens, through foreign registration or anti-proselytism laws. States also closely investigate foreign religions and refuse to grant unfavourable religions advantages received by favoured religions.

Industry

States often insist that protection of an industry is vital to protecting consumers from fraud. States have traditionally regulated many areas where they uphold "a legitimate interest in the protection of ... [their] people against fraud and deception".[193] While simple state regulation would suffice to protect consumers, states may insist that additional protectionist measures are necessary to protect consumers.

Religious analogues

States claim that through protection of religious monopolies they are protecting citizens from fraud of so-called dangerous cults.[194] States may pass registration requirements to make it difficult to establish a foreign religion or pass anti-proselytism legislation to stop foreign religions from taking advantage of their citizens.[195] For example, in Greece, the government defends criminal prohibitions

191 *Hearings on Communications, supra* note 79, at 10 (statement of Chairman deButts).

192 *Hearings on Communications, supra* note 79, at 10, 11 (statement of Chairman deButts) (claiming also that he was just in Congress to "protect the interest of our customers" and support the goal of making "telephone service as widely affordable as possible"). Chairman deButts also warned Congressmen that AT&T had "faced competition before and it was nearly destroyed by it". *Id.* at 12. He explained that after "Bell's patents [expired] in the 1890s, rival telephone companies battled for the same territory ... [resulting in] price-cutting [which] produced wretched service and customers [having to] subscribe to two or more companies to reach all the people in the community in which they lived". *Id.*

193 *Florida Lime and Avocado Growers, Inc. v Paul*, 373 US 132, 144 (1963) (noting that states have traditionally had the right to regulate the "sale of food products at retail markets within their borders") (internal quotations omitted).

194 Tad Stahnke, *The Right to Engage in Religious Persuasion, in* Facilitating Freedom, *supra* note 36, at 583, 604–05 (discussing protection of consumers in the religious marketplace by governments allegedly protecting against fraud and misrepresentation).

195 *Id.* at 586–87.

against proselytism through claiming that the government retains a right to "protect a person's religious beliefs and dignity".[196] The Greek government considers proselytizing by minority religions an attempt to influence citizens "by immoral and deceitful means".[197] In addition, proselytism has been referred to as an attempt to "brainwash" and "violate individual [citizens'] consciences".[198] The European Court of Human Rights has limited Greek attempts to prevent proselytizing in *Kokkinakis*,[199] but even facially neutral bars to proselytizing may be used discriminatorily against minority religions.[200] In *Kokkinakis*, for example, the applicant claimed that under the Greek law, "it would surpass 'even the wildest academic hypothesis' to imagine, for example, the possibility of a complaint being made by a Catholic priest or by a Protestant clergyman against an Orthodox Christian who had attempted to entice one of his flock away from him. It was even less likely that an Orthodox Christian would be prosecuted for proselytizing on behalf of the 'dominant religion.' "[201]

Another increasingly common method of "protecting" citizens against the supposed harms of new and minority religions is the formation of "cult" or "sect" observatories and the creation of lists of so-called "cults" or "sects". Belgium has formed a Centre for Information and Advice on Harmful Sectarian Movements[202] and the Belarussian government formed a government committee to "concentrate its efforts on stopping the activity of neomystical, destructive sects".[203] This committee categorized Orthodox, Roman Catholic, Jewish and Islamic faiths as "traditional" faiths and other faiths, including Protestantism, as "non-traditional".[204] Numerous Western European countries and organizations, including Germany, the Netherlands, Sweden, France, Belgium, the Council of Europe, and the European Parliament have had study commissions and have issued reports addressing alleged dangers of new religious movements.[205] The French and Belgian reports concluded with lists of over a hundred so-called "sects".[206]

196 *Kokkinakis v Greece*, App. No. 14307/88, 17 Eur. H.R. Rep. 397, at para. 42 (1994).

197 *Kokkinakis*, at para. 42. *See also Larissis and Others v Greece*, App. Nos. 23372/94, 26377/94, 26378/94, 27 Eur. H.R. Rep. 329, para. 27 (1998). The Greek anti-proselytism law proscribes that "proselytism . . . is . . . any direct or indirect attempt to intrude on the religious beliefs of a person of a different religious persuasion (*eterodoxos*), with the aim of undermining those beliefs, either by any kind of *inducement* or promise of an inducement or moral support or material assistance, or by *fraudulent means* or by taking advantage of the other person's inexperience, trust, need, low intellect or naivety") (emphasis added). *Id.*

198 *Larissis*, 27 Eur. H.R. Rep. 329 (Valticos, J. dissenting) (noting that proselytism is "incompatible with freedom of opinion, which is a fundamental human right").

199 *Kokkinakis*, 17 Eur. H.R. Rep. 397.

200 Stahnke, *supra* note 194, at 586–87.

201 *Kokkinakis*, 17 Eur. H.R. Rep. 397, at para. 29.

202 *See supra* note 93.

203 Vashkevich, *supra* note 150, at 700 (the Committee was called the Belarus State Committee of Religious and National Affairs (SCRNA) and was directed by the Council of Ministers). In June 1997, the Council of Ministers also prohibited "organization of summer camps for children and teenagers by unregistered religious organizations". *Id.* In addition, only religious associations have the right "to establish their own mass media, invite foreign citizens to conduct religious activities, create religious schools for training priests, divines, and church staff, and establish cloisters and monastic communities". *Id.* at 705.

204 *Id.* The SCRNA also considers Asian faiths as nontraditional.

205 Barker, *Why the Cults?*, *supra* note 123, at 584–85.

206 *Rapport fait au nom de la commission d'enquête sur les sectes* [France], *supra* note 93; Duquesne and Luc Williams, *Enquête parliamentaire visant à élabore une politique en vue de lutte contre les pratiques illégale des sectes et le danger qu'elles représentent pour le société et pour les personnes particulièrement les mineurs d'âge* (1997) [Belgium].

To protect its citizens from the fraud of "psycho cults", the German government also instituted government investigations of some foreign religious activities. The German government, through "constitutional protection agencies", "track[s] and sometimes infiltrate[s] movements suspected of working against Germany's ... constitution".[207] The German ruling party claims that its "constitution is ... under attack from the religious minorities and so-called psycho cults that are gaining strength at the expense of the established Lutheran and Catholic state churches".[208]

Dominant churches have also initiated anti-cult media campaigns. One tactic of the Russian Orthodox Church in deterring its members from joining new foreign religions is through "using the media to introduce into Russian society ... characteristically anti-cult concepts, language and images".[209] Although not part of an official anti-cult campaign, in Guatemala, a Catholic Archbishop, resentful of Protestant success in attracting converts, claimed that "evangelical teachings are the opium of the masses".[210]

Registration laws are also often used to "protect" against minority religions and limit their access to legal entity status. Registration is required as a prerequisite to any religious activity in much of Central Asia and in China.[211] Registration laws also may limit registration of religious organizations to dominant groups through facially neutral requirements such as excessively high numbers of members or the requirement of an extended period of existence in the country.[212] The Belarus government denied some non-traditional faiths permission to "legally register at the national level",[213] "endanger[ing]" the "existence" of many faiths.[214] Russia has

207 Davis, *supra* note 98, at 110 (noting also that Germany's constitution "states that the freedom of belief and conscience and the freedom to possess religious and philosophical beliefs are inviolable").

208 Davis, *supra* note 98, at 110 (emphasis added). The German "Commission of Inquiry" has been formed to investigate state threats from "sects and psycho-cults". *Id.* at 122. Many also describe a "climate of intolerance [in Germany] toward religious minorities". *Id.*

209 Shterin and Richardson, *supra* note 98, at 157. The anti-cult language includes "brainwashing, mind control, destructive cult, totalitarian sect". *Id.* (internal quotations omitted). Images include "zombies, broken families, [and] crime". *Id.* The local media (located in the provinces as opposed to the "central media" located in the largest cities) has especially incited horror about "foreign religions". *Id.* at 159.

210 Serrill, *supra* note 179, at *3.

211 W. Cole Durham, Jr., *supra* note 36, at 321 (describing how religious registration laws are often used as methods of control of minority religions); *Central Asia: Islam and the State, infra* note 249; *Roadblock, infra* note 278, at 2 (statement of Hon. Christopher H. Smith, Co-Chairman of the Commission on Security and Cooperation in Europe) (noting that he has observed "over the past decade ... a troubling drift away from a robust and vibrant protection of religious freedom in a growing number of Organization for Security and Cooperation in Europe (OSCE) states"). He also noted that "some OSCE countries [including Western European countries like Austria] have developed new laws and regulations that serve as a roadblock to the free exercise of religious belief". *Id.* at 2.

212 W. Cole Durham, Jr., *supra* note 36, at 321 (giving examples such as Slovakia's requirement of 20,000 members and Russia's requirement of 15 years' presence in the country to establish a centralized religious organization); W. Cole Durham et al., *A Comparative Analysis of Religious Association Laws in Post-Communist Europe, in* Laws on Religion and the State in Post-Communist Europe 330 (2004) (giving other examples).

213 *Id.* The SCNRA regulations have had an impact on limiting the activities of nontraditional religions as Full Gospel Pentecostal churches are "regularly refused registration". *Id.* at 702. Members of the Krishna Church have been evicted from their homes because they have been using private property to worship without "special permission from the local authorities". *Id.* at 702–03.

214 *Id.* at 704. The "Union of Evangelical Christian Baptists, the Union of Evangelical Faith Christians, the Association of Communities of Full Gospel Christians, and the Conference of Christian Adventists condemned the bill saying it would favor some religious organizations and limit opportunities for worship". *Id.* Other limitations include "requiring permission to conduct religious processions outside temples". *Id.* at 708.

also passed legislation requiring foreign religious organizations to register with the government, supporting a widely held belief that "foreign religious organizations and new religious movements defraud the spiritually feeble [and] brainwash vulnerable youth".[215]

Fundamental nature of product or service

Both religious and industrial monopolies rely on the fundamental nature of the industry or religion of a country to justify protectionism. Just as states insist that protection of key industries, such as steel, automobiles and airlines, are fundamental to the functioning of their state, states justify protection of religion by claiming that their traditional church-state relationship relies on state protection. The closest analogy to religion in the industrial sector is farming, which like religion has been considered vital to citizens' traditions and "moral character".

Industry

State-controlled industries have been justified because of the fundamental nature of certain industrial products and services. In the United States, it was common for states in the 1950s, 1960s and 1970s to own industries of "industrial and service enterprises in key sectors, such as steel, telecommunications, fertilizers, automobiles, petrochemicals, hotels, airlines and banking".[216] Often in these areas governments officially created public monopolies to justify state protection.[217] The US government also supported cartelization in "transportation, natural resource industries, and retail trade", as a means of protection.[218]

States often consider agriculture as one of the most fundamental products because of its importance for sustenance but also because of the moral importance of farming to a society. The US government subsidized exports in agriculture and developed "marketing quotas and special penalty taxes" for products such as "tobacco, cotton and potatoes".[219] The government justified protectionist policies because it claimed that since agriculture was "the fundamental economic activity upon which all others rested", the "balance of market power between agriculture and industry" could not be maintained until agriculture was regulated.[220] Along

---

215 Gross, *supra* note 128, at 720. Protectionist measures are often a result of public outcry for legislation to protect them from "dangerous" "sects and cults". *Id.* at 718.

216 White, *supra* note 40, at 20.

217 *See, e.g.*, Merrill Sheils and William J. Cook, Newsweek, *A Giant Eyes New Vistas*, Feb. 25, 1980 (describing the implications of the break-up of the public monopoly, AT&T).

218 Hawley, *supra* note 27, at 15 (also pointing out that in the mid-1930s there were "oligopolistic understandings" or "cartel agreements" which "eliminated price competition" in industries such as "automobiles, chemicals, motion pictures, farm implements, aluminium, cigarettes, newsprint, anthracite coal, glass containers, optics, lead, sulphur and tin plate").

219 *Id.* at 192 (internal quotations omitted).

220 *Id.*

with the "fundamental" nature of farming to the US economy, it was also fundamental to the American moral character.[221] Protectionists relied on the fact that "political symbols of the family farm and the yeoman farmer, the sturdy, honest, independent, morally upright individual" constituted "the very foundation of America's individualistic and democratic ideals".[222] Farming as an occupation was deemed to be "somehow purer, cleaner, and morally better than other occupations" and "[t]o many people, farmers and non-farmers alike, it justified the salvation of farming as a way of life".[223] The moral argument to protect farming also spread to "food-processing industries".[224] Even in recent years, various nations still believe that fundamental products or services are best provided to the public through "strong government involvement".[225]

Religious analogues

Some countries justify granting advantages to a religious monopoly by relying on the fundamental nature of a religion to citizens. Often states rely on the historical importance of a religion to citizens' tradition and culture to justify protection.[226] Orthodoxy, in particular, has drawn on a theological tradition of a "territorial understanding of faith", which would exclude other Christian religions from proselytizing in their lands.[227] In 2002, a Belarussian law recognized "the defining role of the Orthodox Church in the historical formation and development of spiritual, cultural, and state traditions *of the Belarussian people*".[228] Establishment of the fundamental nature of the Orthodox Church in Belarus, justifies state protectionist policies.[229] Russian traditional thinking perceives "the church body, society, and the state as a single whole", in which church-nation takes priority over

221 *Id.* (internal quotations omitted).

222 *Id.*

223 *Id.* (noting also that this support of the moral and fundamental nature of farming "explained in part why agriculture was able to dodge most of the anti-monopoly agitation and find ways of using government powers to fix prices, plan production, and regularize markets"). *See also id.* at 482 (noting that "[t]he country, so it was said, could not be prosperous unless its farmers were prosperous").

224 *Id.* at 482 ("Monopolistic arrangements in certain food-processing industries could be camouflaged as an essential part of the farm program").

225 Lando, *supra* note 42, at 2185 (citing France as an example because "the government pioneered the Minitel to provide a two-way-link in three million homes") and noting that "France Telecom retains a strong monopoly in many areas, and has made only minimal allowances of open competition despite a 1991 public law which privatized it. Germany has also relied heavily on government-owned monopoly providers for telecommunications services" and still allows voice telephony monopoly in telecommuni cations services. *Id.* at 2191, 2192. In general, up until 1994 "state owned monopolies still control[ed] the majority of EC [European Community] telephone services and each EC member state (except for Britain) still offer[ed] 'exclusive rights' to a single telecommunications company". *Id.* at 2196–97.

226 *See supra* p 15–Religious analogues.

227 Elliott and Corrado, *infra* note 267, at 120; *see also* Guroian, *infra* note 263, at 240 (describing the "corporate and organic concepts of church and peoplehood embraced by Orthodox theology").

228 Vashkevich, *supra* note 150, at 704 (emphasis added). The law also recognized the "spiritual, cultural, and historical role of the Roman Catholic Church in the territory of Belarus" as well as the "inseparability from the general history of the Belarussian people of the Lutheran Church, Judaism, and Islam". *Id.* (internal citations omitted).

229 *See supra* notes 183 and 269 and accompanying text for discussion of Belarussian protectionist legislation.

individuals.[230] Some religions, such as the Church of Sweden, have simply claimed that their traditional church systems are "incompatible with religious liberty".[231] Often, religion has been seen as a vital cultural carrier, and thus preserving a national religion is associated with retaining a sense of culture, nation, and community. Makau Mutua has described how "religion is often the first point of attack in the process of acculturation" and the destruction of communities, particularly in African history.[232]

HARMS OF PROTECTIONISM FOR INDUSTRIAL MONOPOLIES AND RELIGIOUS MONOPOLIES, STATE AND SOCIETY, AND CITIZENS

This section demonstrates not only how the arguments for protection made by religious and industrial monopolies are unconvincing, but that protectionism actually harms the three constituents it attempts to benefit.

Harms of protectionist measures for industrial monopolies

While industrial and religious monopolies argue and agitate for their own protection and importance, lessons from industry suggest that protection rarely creates the advantages sought. The asserted advantages often do not transpire and protection of religion and industry may actually lead to less efficient industries, less church autonomy and possibly oppressive dominant religions.

Less efficient industry

Industrial protection including state control and regulation, quotas, and non-tariff barriers may actually create *less* efficient industries. In passing the Sherman and Clayton Acts, Congress recognized that monopolies create inefficiency and attempted to avoid this through antitrust laws.[233] The current economic consensus also contends that state ownership, control and regulation of industries is "less

---

230 Chaplin, *supra* note 157, at 286–87.

231 Goran Gustafsson, *Church-State Separation Swedish-Style, in* Church and State 56 (describing a proposal by four members of the Riksdag in 1956 about the relationship between the Church of Sweden and the state). In 1972 a government-established committee suggested that Sweden should treat "all religious associations" equally and stop "preferential treatment of any denomination, including the Church of Sweden". Stegeby, *supra* note 9, at 722. However, the government faced with an "impending election" declared in 1973 that "it did not intend to recommend any substantial changes to the existing church-state relationship". *Id.*

232 Makau Mutua, *Proselytism and Cultural Integrity, in* Facilitating Freedom, *supra* note 36, at 651, 666 ("Unless groups are given protection against invasion and control by others, their cultural and ethnic identities could be quashed by more powerful cultures and political systems. The violent advocacy of proselytizing religions in Africa could be seen as a negation of this right particularly because religion is often the first point of attack in the process of acculturation"); *see also* Proselytization and Communal Self-Determination in Africa (Abdullahi Ahmed An-Na'im ed., 1999).

233 Kenneth G. Elzinga, *The Goals of Antitrust: Other than Competition and Efficiency, What Else Counts?* 125 U. Pa. L. Rev. 1191, 1191–92, 1213 (1977) (pointing out that Congress recognized efficiency as a "central goal" of antitrust but concluding that equity is another goal of antitrust).

efficient than privately held commercial entities".[234] This has been confirmed by the success of newly privatized state-operated industries in France, Italy and Spain.[235] The result of state protection is often "little or no funding for research and development to improve efficiencies or services" as well as "over employment and low productivity".[236] Protectionism also "prevents the shielded industry from developing the sophistication required to compete in a global market".[237] Further, exclusion of foreign products and quotas "limit the vigor of existing competitors".[238] In addition, the countries with the most successful privatization in Eastern Europe are the countries without any protections from foreign investors.[239] Even in revealing the harm to US industries caused by foreign protection, rather than urging policy makers to weaken antitrust laws, industry specialists and congresspersons argued that the answer was increased enforcement of US antitrust laws internationally.[240] Industry experts insisted that free competition was best for American business. [241]

A comparison between the United States airline industry and the European airline industry demonstrates the potential harms of state protection. Since the 1920s,

---

234 White, *supra* note 40, at 20 (noting that "state-owned enterprises" "are protected from competition through government regulations that grant them monopoly power in key sectors" and that World Bank studies of the "performance changes for a combined sample of two hundred eleven companies, from fifty industries [from both developing and industrialized countries] over a period of more than twenty years" report "substantial increases in sales, profitability, capital investments and operating efficiency in the privatized companies and industries" as well as a "slight increase, on average, in number of employees after privatization"). In addition, White points out a New York University study of "one hundred twenty-eight privatized firms and ninety state-owned industries" in the Czech Republic, Hungary and Poland where researchers found "immediate increases in revenues and productivity following privatization". *Id.* at 20. He further points out other benefits to privatization which include: more capital for technology and training and investment, management free of political constraints, fiscal stability, capital market development, more social programs by governments who no longer use state resources to support industry, and increased attraction of foreign investment. *Id.* at 20–21.

In the mid-1930s planners posited that "the antitrust approach of breaking down and destroying concentrated economic power was outmoded, impractical, and undesirable" and would "impair efficiency and lower the standard of living". Hawley, *supra* note 27, at 175.

235 White, *supra* note 40, at 20 (pointing out that in "1997 proceeds from selling state-owned enterprises worldwide hit a record $162 billion. France, Italy and Spain all launched huge, popular and very successful public share issue privatizations. Telecom Italia's $15 billion offering in November 1997 was the largest in European history.... [and] France Telecom and the multiple Spanish offerings from Telefonica and Argentaria likewise transformed share ownership patterns in their countries"). In the Czech Republic, "twenty thousand small businesses" were sold in public auctions. *Id.* at 23.

236 White, *supra* note 40, at 20.

237 Michael J. Chapman and Paul J. Tauber, *Liberalizing International Trade in Legal Services: A Proposal for an Annex on Legal Services Under the General Agreement on Trade in Services*, 16 MICH. J. INT'L L. 941, 953 (1995).

238 Marc Crane, *The Future Direction of Antitrust*, 56 ANTITRUST L. J. 3, 6–7 (1987) (adding also that "[d]umping decrees exclude low-price products"). Economically, one harm of state protection is "public-sector deficits and foreign-debt burdens" resulting from government subsidization. White, *supra* note 40, at 20 (adding also that "governments in these circumstances borrow heavily or print money to cover these costs, which leads to high inflation, the discouragement of further investment and resultant capital flight" and this may eventually lead to an inability to "compete in the international marketplace").

239 White, *supra* note 40, at 25 (noting that "[s]ome of the most successful privatizations in Eastern Europe strongly encouraged foreign investors").

240 *Hearings on Antitrust, supra* note 49, at 1 (statement of Senator Metzenbaum) ("For too long, we in the United States have tolerated unfair foreign competition which attacks our industries, robs America of jobs, and undermines our global competitiveness."). The Act would not allow industries to "take advantage of weak or nonexistent competition law enforcement in their home markets to compete unfairly in markets that do have strong competition laws and effective enforcement". *Id.* at 136 (Appendix).

241 Industry specialists insisted that American businesses were "most responsive when ... under the heat of competition, including foreign competition". *Hearings on Antitrust, supra* note 49, at 105 (statement of Eleanor Fox).

the United States airline industry existed as "government-organized cartels".[242] The United States government stopped protection of the US airline industry throughout the 1980s. Commentators point out that the growth of the industry has been stunted by state regulation.[243] By 1990, after privatization of the airline industry, "the number of passenger-miles" in the US domestic airline industry had increased by 95%" and "[f]ares had fallen about 20% in real terms".[244] Throughout the 1990s, European airlines faced trouble competing with deregulated American airlines with the surge in international travel since European airlines were "still bloated and inefficient government-owned companies".[245] When European airlines finally privatized throughout the 1990s, many were better able to compete internationally. Lufthansa President Juergen Weber commented in 1993 that "[h]ad Europe been deregulated 15 years ago, we would have been [more competitive]".[246]

While some commentators still tout the benefits of some form of state protectionism, most do not encourage "monopolistic protectionism".[247] Many countries have recognized that "excessive protection from foreign competition", and state subsidies are "outdated attitudes" that need to be eliminated to achieve "economic modernization".[248]

Lack of church autonomy and religious oppression

Two potential harms resulting from state protection of religious monopolies include lack of church autonomy and religious oppression from the dominant religion. First, when a state grants extra protections for a religion, the church becomes increasingly dependent on the state and church autonomy is often sacrificed. A church may "lose its identity . . . and become merely an agency of the state".[249]

---

242 *Don't Coddle or Curb Them; The Pain in the World's Airline Industry can be Eased by more American-Style Deregulation, Not Less*, THE ECONOMIST 18, 1991 WL 4960745 (Feb. 23, 1991).

243 *Id.* at 18.

244 *Id.* at 18 (also noting that "[p]assengers had saved more than $100 billion on their tickets and enjoyed far more choice" but also pointing out that American officials failed to enforce antitrust rules in the airline industry allowing, by 1991, "90% of America's domestic passenger traffic[to be] carried by the eight largest airlines").

245 Richard M. Weintraub, *Flying High Over Europe: US Airlines Gain Ground as Deregulation Strains International Treaties*, WASH. POST, Aug. 1, 1993, at H01 (stating that American airlines were deregulated in the 1980s).

246 *Id.* at H01 (however he also noted that "even then it wouldn't be the same [since] half of all the passengers who fly take off and land in the United States", giving US airlines an advantage).

247 *See, e.g.*, Batra, *supra* note 9, at 61 (arguing against free trade and for "competitive protectionism" which allows domestic monopolies to be broken up while still allowing them to be protected from foreign competition as opposed to "monopolistic protectionism" which protects a domestic firm from foreign and domestic competition).

248 Gabriel Garcia, Comment, *Economic Development and the Course of Intellectual Property Protection in Mexico*, 27 TEX. INT'L L.J. 701, 723 n.81 (1992) (quoting Mexican President Salinas' goals in modernizing Mexican economic policies which include easing restrictions on foreign investment in Mexico). *Id.* at 728. Despite the importance of protecting jobs and maintaining strategic industries for defence purposes, many commentators insist that state protectionist actions harm the economy. Crane, *supra* note 238, at 7, 19.

249 Goran Gustafsson, *Church-State Separation Swedish-Style*, *in* STATE AND CHURCH, *supra* note 2 at 54 (documenting a 1929 proposal by bishops that "the church, while retaining its position as an established state-church, should become less dependent on the state"); International Crisis Group, *Central Asia: Islam and the State*, Report No. 59, July 10, 2003, http://www.crisisweb.org/home/index.cfm?id=1442andl=1 (describing how Central Asian governments "use Islam as a conduit to promote their own ideologies and campaigns, and in general as a tool of the state").

In established or dominant churches, governments are often involved in the appointment of religious leaders.[250] Greece and Bulgaria, for example, have tried to intervene in the selection of the Muslim leadership in their countries, but these attempts have been rejected by the European Court of Human Rights.[251] Increased financial support for dominant religions often corresponds to increasing regulation and government interference in religious autonomy.[252] The state may also exert pressure on religious leaders and withhold funds or allow protectionist legislation to coerce the church to do its will.[253] The church may lose its ability to guide its members according to independent inspiration but instead be guided by the coercive influence of the state. In the process of disestablishing the Church of Sweden, proponents argued that the vibrancy of a religion is undermined by government control, even if designed for beneficial reasons.[254] Control by the state lessens the authenticity of the religious voice and ultimately reduces the effectiveness of both the religious message and the religion's work as a governmental tool: "the more government controls it, the less authority the religious hierarchy has with believers and the less impact it has on carrying government ideology to the population".[255]

Second, a religious monopoly may become oppressive and with state aid stifle minority religions.[256] Religious persecution may be the final result of a state sanctioned protection of a dominant religion. In Germany, commentators document a cycle of religious persecution beginning with state protection.[257] The first stage includes identifying "unacceptable religions ... through granting of exclusive

250 Roland Minnerath, *Church Autonomy in Europe*, in CHURCH AUTONOMY 381, 391 (Gerhard Robbers ed., 2001) (citing Greece, England, and pre-Vatican II Catholic countries); Cornelius D. de Jong, THE FREEDOM OF THOUGHT, CONSCIENCE AND RELIGION OR BELIEF IN THE UNITED NATIONS (1946–1992) 445–48 (2000) (citing Tunisia, Greece); Felix Corley, *Turkmenistan: Religious Freedom Survey 2004*, Forum 18 News Service, April 7, 2004, *available at* http://www.forum18.org/Archive.php? article_id=296 (describing the removal of the Chief Mufti by President Niyazov in January 2003).

251 *Serif v Greece*, App. No. 38178/97, Eur. Ct. H.R. (1999); *Hasan and Chaush v Bulgaria*, App. No. 30985/96, Eur. Ct. H.R. (2000).

252 See, *e.g.*, Rik Torfs, *Church Autonomy in Belgium*, in CHURCH AUTONOMY, *supra* note 250, at 607, 621–23 (describing the "important impact" state financial support has on "the organising and financing of church activities", recognizing that "ignoring that financial support has a link with church autonomy would be . . . naïve").

253 *E.g.*, current regulation in Turkmenistan which requires "imam-hatybs to place the Turkmen flag above mosque entrances, to begin every sermon by praising 'Turkmenbashi', 'Father of the Turkmens', as President Saparmurat Niyazov insists on being called. Also, a copy of Niyazov's book, the Ruhnama (Book of the Soul), must be placed at the entrance to every mosque and Muslims must touch it as if it were a sacred object." Igar Rotar, *Turkmenistan: State Interference with Islamic Religious Life in the North-East*, Forum 18 News Service (4 March 2004), available on-line at <http://www.forum18.org/>. In Algeria, the state appoints imams and removes those who oppose government policies. FREEDOM OF RELIGION AND BELIEF: A WORLD REPORT 23 (Kevin Boyle and Juliet Sheen eds., 1997).

254 *See* E. Kenneth Stegeby, *An Analysis of the Impending Disestablishment of the Church of Sweden*, 1999 BYU L. REV. 703.

255 *Central Asia: Islam and the State*, *supra* note 249.

256 Derek H. Davis, *Religious Persecution in Today's Germany: Old Habits Renewed, in* RELIGIOUS LIBERTY IN NORTHERN EUROPE IN THE TWENTY-FIRST CENTURY 112 (Derek H. Davis, ed. 2000).

257 This cycle has been documented several times throughout German history, with the most obvious example of Hitler during World War II. *Id.* at 112, 123. Davis quotes Pierre van Paassen who insisted that "Hitler could never have perpetrated the Holocaust" without Germans' "unfriendly attitude toward the Jews . . . and by the anti-Semitic teaching in our churches and schools". *Id.* at 123.

license to the official religion or religions".[258] Second, a state establishes a "unified position" among "political leaders, clergy, and intellectuals . . . against minority groups".[259] Third, minority religions are categorized as "rival societies rather than religions"[260] and presented as a threat to the state. Fourth, the government legally restricts minority religions members' "movement, commerce, or the right to bear arms".[261] Finally, the dominant religion may participate in the "forced removal" of the minority group in the most extreme cases.[262]

The stifling of minority religions not only has an impact on the minority religions affected, but also has negative consequences for the majority religions in a society. New religious movements often act as an indicator of what some members of society feel is missing in their lives, and can challenge and invigorate more traditional religions to better meet the needs of their members.[263] Christopher Eberle and Christian Smith argue that religious pluralism vivifies religion and thus "politically active religious citizens, and even those willing to support their favoured coercive laws on the basis of the parochial religious commitments, have a vested interest in refusing coercively to impose their favored religious orthodoxy on a diverse population".[264] Citing numerous other scholars, they note a "convergence of voices, then in support of the claim that religious communities benefit from pluralism and thus from a political regime that protects the religious freedom from which pluralism ensues".[265] An example of why this works in practice can be seen in the following anecdote: when Bolivian Roman Catholic bishops complained to the Pope during his visit to Bolivia about the growth of minority religions, he is reported to have responded that "these other religious groups were nourishing the people . . . if the Pentecostals are gaining adherents, it is because the bishops and Bolivian Catholics are not doing their job".[266] In addition, when a majority church becomes a persecutor of other religions, even if accomplished together with the state, this may itself over time also undermine the powerful religious claims and the purity and power of a religious mission of a group.[267]

258 *Id.* at 112 (internal quotations omitted).

259 *Id.* at 112.

260 *Id.* at 112.

261 *Id.* at 112.

262 *Id.* at 112.

263 Eileen Barker, *NRMs: Their Incidence and Significance, in* New Religious Movements: Challenge and Response 26–28 (Bryan Wilson and Jamie Creswell eds., 1999); *see* Vigen Guroian, *Evangelism and Mission in the Orthodox Tradition, in* Sharing the Book: Religious Perspectives on the Rights and Wrongs of Proselytism 231, 243–44 (John Witte, Jr. and Richard C. Martin eds., 1999) (suggesting that the Orthodox respond to the challenge of proselytism by reinvigorating itself and focusing on its mission).

264 Christopher J. Eberle, Religious Conviction in Liberal Politics 26–27, 44–45 (2002).

265 *Id.* at 45 (citing Roger Finke, Rodney Stark, Joes Casanova, and others).

266 Edward L. Cleary, *The Catholic Church, in* Religious Freedom and Evangelization in Latin America 11, 25 (Paul E. Sigmund ed., 1999).

267 *See, e.g.*, Mark Elliott and Sharyl Corrado, *The 1997 Russian Law on Religion: The Impact on Protestants*, 27 Religion, State and Soc. 109, 122 (1999) (quoting the leader of the Orthodox Church in America as arguing that suppressive policies towards other religions in Russia would "in the long run . . . have a negative impact also on the mission of the Russian Orthodox Church").

Harms of protectionist measures for state and society

Decrease in democracy

Historically as well as today, US and international[268] commentators reject protection of industry because it decreases democracy through concentrating power in a few corporate hands. Early American colonists opposed state protection and monopolies[269] because they were associated with the British monarchy rather than a new American democracy.[270] In passing the Sherman Act, a major goal of Congress was to avoid concentration of power,[271] which caused anti-democratic harms.[272] Similarly, when enacting section 7 of the Clayton Act in 1950, Congress worried that an economy "dominated by a few corporate giants could . . . facilitate overthrow of democratic institutions and the installation of a totalitarian regime".[273] In fact, after

---

268 Internationally, experts agree that "an economic system based on private enterprise and free-market competition best serves human goals" and that "[g]overnment intervention—whether by government participation in the market or by direct or indirect regulation—should occur exceptionally and only to the minimum extent necessary to remedy serious market failure". *Hearings on Antitrust, supra* note 49, at 128 (statement of Abott B. Lipsky, Jr. who served as a member of the Special Committee on International Antitrust of the American Bar Association, Section of Antitrust Law).

269 Thorelli, *supra* note 74, at 36. Monopoly was opposed even before the Sherman Act in America due to experiences with monopolistic privilege in England. "Several colonial statutes are said to have prohibited" monopolistic practices because of "popular antagonism to monopoly". *Id.* at 36–37.

270 Colonists felt that "monopoly was the antithesis of the very spirit of individualistic pioneering characteristic of life on the new continent" and had been one of the main reasons emigrants had left Great Britain in the first place. Thorelli, *supra* note 74, at 37. Although opposition to monopoly existed even before the Sherman Act, when the Sherman Act was first enacted it was not enforced against "tight combinations as holding companies and mergers". Hawley, *supra* note 27, at 6 (noting that "[i]t was not until the progressive era in the early twentieth century that major changes in the political and ideological climate began to take place" when people began to be "increasingly dubious . . . about the doctrines of laissez faire and Social Darwinism"). For this reason, many colonists rejected England's practice of granting "chartered trade monopolies". Thorelli, *supra* note 74, at 37.

271 One major argument against monopoly from the advent of the Sherman Act and also the consensus for "almost a century" has been the "hostility to the concentration in private hands of power". *United States v Columbia Steel Co.*, 334 US 495, 536 (1948) (noting that "[p]ower that controls the economy should be in the hands of elected representatives of the people, not in the hands of an industrial oligarchy"). *See also United States v Aluminum Co. of Amer. et al.*, 148 F.2d 416, 428, n.1 (2d Cir. 1945) (noting that "great industrial consolidations are inherently undesirable, regardless of their economic costs"); Robert Pitofsky, *The Political Content of Antitrust* 127 U. Pa. L. Rev. 1051, 1051–52 (1979) (noting that "excessive concentration of economic power will breed antidemocratic political pressures"); Harlan M. Blake and William K. Jones, *In Defense of Antitrust*, 65 Colum. L. Rev. 377, 383 (1965) (pointing out that "antitrust operates to forestall concentrations of economic power, which, if allowed to develop unhindered, would call for much more intrusive government supervision of the economy"); Harlan M. Blake, *Conglomerate Mergers and the Antitrust Laws*, 73 Colum. L. Rev. 555, 575 (the Sherman Act was concerned with the "threat to opportunities of individuals and smaller businessmen to compete on an equal basis in a competitive system" with heavy concentration of economic power); Fredrick M. Rowe, *The Decline of Antitrust and the Delusions of Models: The Faustian Pact of Law and Economics*, 72 Georg. L.J. 1511, 1541 (1984) ("antitrust sought to stem a tide of concentration"). Some cases have linked a concentration of power over a product to make "a prima facie case of intent and purpose to exercise illegal restraints and to monopolize". *See also Kobe, Inc. v Dempsey Pump Co.*, 198 F.3d 416, 423 (10th Cir. 1952).

272 *Columbia Steel Co.*, 334 US at 536 (stating that "Industrial power should be decentralized . . . [and] should be scattered into many hands so that the fortunes of the people will not be dependent on the whim or caprice, the political prejudices, the emotional stability of a few self-appointed men"). The Sherman Act also aimed to "improve the free market system" to avoid other solutions such as Marxism or heavy government regulation. Pitofsky, *supra* note 271, at 1057.

273 Pitofsky, *supra* note 271, at 1054, 1055 (pointing out that "it is remarkable that historical and contemporaneous democracies are almost invariably associated with market systems, while totalitarian regimes (fascist and communist) almost always are not"). In addition during congressional debate over section 7 of the Clayton Act representatives pointed out that Nazi Germany "built up a great series of industrial monopolies in steel, rubber, coal and other materials. The monopolies soon got control of Germany,

World War II to reconstruct the former totalitarian German and Japanese economies, the United States rooted out state controlled and protected industries and "create[d] alternative centers of power that could not readily be marshaled behind authoritarian regimes".[274] Politicians feared not only that citizens would lose power to influence change with increased concentration of power but that there would be a decrease in "local initiative and civic responsibility" and ultimately a loss of democratic values.[275]

In addition, concentration of wealth through state protection decreases democracy since governments may not be able to control industries once they gain too much power. While proponents of protection insist that larger companies provide better service, governments have also come to realize that the larger the size of the company, the more difficult it becomes for the government to "monitor resources to keep the giant in line"[276] and deregulate it when necessary.[277]

Social reform and hostility

Religious protectionist practices may harm society through decreasing social reform through minority religions and through creating hostility and violence. First, state protectionism may stifle minority religions thereby decreasing social reform

brought Hitler to power and forced virtually the whole world into war. . . . A high degree of concentration throughout industry fosters the formation of cartels and readily enables a war-minded government to mobilize for hostilities . . . as the history of war preparations in Germany [demonstrates during] both World War I and World War II." 95 CONG. REC. 11, 486 (1949 (statement of Rep. Celler). *See also Brown Shoe Co. v United States*, 370 US 294, 315 (1961) ("[t]he dominant theme pervading congressional consideration of the 1950 amendments [to the Clayton Act] was a fear of what was considered to be a rising tide of economic concentration in the American economy"). Even in recent cases the rejection of concentrations of power is emphasized. *United States v Syufy Enter.*, 903 F.2d 659, 663 (9th Cir. 1990) (pointing out that competition is important in avoiding "permanent concentrations of power").

In passing the Clayton Act senators also worried that monopoly leads to citizens "losing power to direct their own economic welfare . . . [and in turn the] means to direct their political future". 96 CONG. REC. 16,452 (1950) (statement of Senator Kefauver). *See also* Derek C. Bok, *Section 7 of the Clayton Act and the Merging of Law and Economics* 74 HARV. L. REV. 226, 234–37 (1960) (stating that Congressmen worried that powerful industries would increase "government control" which would "corrode" freedom).

274 Louis B. Schwartz, *"Justice" and Other Non-Economic Goals of Antitrust* 127 U. PA. L. REV. 1076, 1078 (1979) (decartelization and imposing antitrust laws to root out monopolies was one way that the United States reconstructed the German and Japanese economies after World War II).

275 Bok, *supra* note 273, at 236; Pitofsky, *supra* note 271, at 1071. Several cases have relied partly on the desire not to concentrate power into too few hands. *See United States v Phillipsburg Nat'l Bank and Trust Co.*, 399 US 350, 370–71 (1970) (defendants arguing that allowing the merger would increase competition for nationally influential banks and would actually increase competition nationally); *United States v Phila. Nat'l Bank*, 374 US 321 (1963).

276 *Id.* (discussing the Justice Department's antitrust suit against AT&T and noting that "smaller companies worry about AT&T's sheer size" and noting that the government is "turning loose something with billions of dollars that can do anything it wants . . . [a]nd the FCC won't be able to do anything about it until the landscape is littered with corpses of former competitors") (quoting Herbert N. Jasper, Executive Vice President of an industry group fighting the Telecommunications Act of 1980, which was backed by AT&T) (internal quotations omitted). In 1980, commentators did not believe that the Telecommunications Act of 1980 would pass during that year but "almost all observers predict[ed] that when a new law is finally passed, it [would] be one that AT&T approves". *Id.* AT&T was held liable for "restraining trade and using monopoly power in one market to limit competition in another market, and combin[ing] or conspir[ing] among its units to monopolize the field". Merrill Brown, *ATT Loses $105 Million Scrap Wire Antitrust Suit*, WASH. POST, March 9, 1984, at C1.

277 However, as many governments who allow monopolies find out, the larger the company and the more government protection, the bigger the fight the company will put up when threatened with deregulation. *See* Merrill Sheils and William J. Cook, *A Giant Eyes New Vistas*, NEWSWEEK, Feb. 25, 1980.

movements.[278] In the United States, religious communities were the driving force behind the Civil Rights Movement which "provide[d] legal protections" to African Americans.[279] If "strict religious registration laws" existed during this time, the government could have deterred many in this movement under the "pretext of state security".[280] Since historically religious movements have been beneficial, limiting the existence of religious groups may decrease democratic social reform.[281] A large body of scholarship has been devoted to the role that religions can play as mediating structures in promoting civil society and social reform.[282] This role is not limited to dominant religious groups. Indeed, the development of minority religions is often itself an attempt to change society. A major scholar of new religious movements, Eileen Barker, has argued that new religious movements "may occasionally function as a barometer of what at least some members of a society feel they need but is not being supplied by other means", allowing new religious movements "a significant role to play as a dissenting force in society".[283]

Ultimately, protectionist arguments for religion, like those for industry, lead to a weakening of democracy itself. The European Court of Human Rights has articulated this concept, explaining that the "social tension" that might arise from allowing religious splinter groups is an unavoidable effect of pluralism, which is inseparable from democracy.[284] Robert Audi explains that governmental preferences for a particular religion undermine liberal democracy in three ways. First, preferences based on religion violate the libertarian principle. Government preferences of religion undermine freedom in the choice of a religion by applying direct or indirect pressure on its citizens to adopt the favoured religion.[285] Second, religious protectionism violates equality principles, particularly significant in liberal democracy, with its emphasis on freedom as well as basic political equality.[286] "Even if the existence of certain disproportionate powers does not necessarily (or at least does not directly) restrict anyone's liberty, concentration of power in a religious group as such easily impairs democracy in which citizens should have equal

278 *Roadblock to Religious Liberty: Religious Registration, Commission on Security and Cooperation in Europe*, Oct. 11, 2001, 107th Cong. 3 [hereinafter *Roadblock*] (statement of Hon. Christopher H. Smith, Co-Chairman of the Commission on Security and Cooperation in Europe).

279 *Roadblock, supra* note 278, at 3 (statement of Hon. Christopher H. Smith, Co-Chairman of the Commission on Security and Cooperation in Europe); John T. Noonan, Jr. and Edward McGlynn Gaffney, Jr., Religious Freedom: History, Cases, and Other Materials on the Interaction of Religion and Government 891–93 (2001) (pointing out that the Southern Christian Leadership Conference "was the force that developed the infrastructure of the civil rights movement" and was the "moral, material, and organizational support to local protesters, otherwise isolated and at a disadvantage with the white power structure").

280 *Roadblock, supra* note 278, at 3 (statement of Hon. Christopher H. Smith, Co-Chairman of the Commission on Security and Cooperation in Europe).

281 *Id.* (noting that restrictions on religious groups "removes from society forces that operate for the general welfare").

282 *See, e.g.*, Richard John Neuhaus, The Naked Public Square: Religion and Democracy in America (1984); Stephen L. Carter, the Culture of Disbelief (1993); Martin E. Marty with Jonathan Moore, Politics, Religion and the Public Good (2000); J. Philip Wogaman, *The Church as Mediating Institution: Theological and Philosophical Perspective, in* Democracy and Mediating Structures: A Theological Inquiry (Michael Novak ed., 1980); Paul J. Weithman, Religion and the Obligations of Citizenship (2002); Robert Audi, Religious Commitment and Secular Reason (2000).

283 Barker, *NRMs: their Incidence and Significance, supra* note 263, at 26–27.

284 *Serif v Greece*, App. No. 38178/97, Eur. Ct. H.R., (Dec. 14, 1999).

285 Robert Audi, Religious Commitment and Secular Reason 33–35 (2000).

286 *Id.* at 36–37.

opportunities to exercise political power on a fair basis."[287] Recognizing that many traditional democracies have some form of religious protectionism, he notes that in such a case, even if necessary safeguards against abuses are in place, such a system implies that "the ideal of liberal democracy has not been fully reached, that protections of liberty and basic political equality must be maintained in relation to the established church, and that a rationale is needed to justify its continuance insofar as a liberal democracy is the nation's political ideal".[288] Audi also argues that religious preferences undermine the liberal democratic ideal of neutrality. Neutrality can apply to both liberty concerns—equal freedom to accept or reject all religious views—and to equality concerns—government preference towards a religion may well create a creation of a dominant bloc of voters or polarize government along religious lines, which undermines equalitarian participation in government.[289] Neutrality in belief can also be undermined by government grants of special benefits upon particular qualifications, which qualifications themselves may shape the action of religious groups.[290]

Finally, state protection of a religious monopoly may result in "hostility toward minority religious groups which can serve as a catalyst for violence".[291] Progressive polarization of the state and a minority religion, which may happen with increasing government protections for a dominant religion, has been identified as an important step in leading to violent conflict between a government and a minority religion.[292] Governments can escalate the polarization by "cultural opponents of NRMs [new religious movements]".[293] Although the state action is not necessarily required to provoke violence, "it should be of considerable concern when cultural opponents are successful in recruiting government agents in campaigns to assail apocalyptic religious movements. With the state's monopoly on the legitimate use of force and its expansive power to regulate social life, minority religions are often at the mercy of the state's social control agents. An overwhelming show of force, or a threat of force, can induce acts of violence in apocalyptic groups."[294] One commentator demonstrates that in a state with a virtual religious monopoly, restriction of minority religious rights leads to violence.[295] In Israel, for example, "separate religious courts for every religious community" and substantive laws that rely solely on Jewish principles draw attention to the differences in the community and create inequity between the Jews and Muslims in the country.[296] One scholar has

287 *Id.* at 36.

288 *Id.* at 37

289 Id. at 37–39.

290 *Id.* at 39–40.

291 *Id.* (citing the "violence against Jehovah's Witnesses and other evangelical groups in Georgia" as an example); *see also* Malcolm D. Evans, *Historical Analysis of Freedom of Religion or Belief as a Technique for Resolving Religious Conflict, in* FACILITATING FREEDOM, *supra* note 36, at 1; Mark Juergensmeyer, TERROR IN THE MIND OF GOD: THE GLOBAL RISE OF RELIGIOUS VIOLENCE (3d ed., 2003).

292 David G. Bromley, *Dramatic Denouements, in* CULTS, VIOLENCE AND RELIGION 11, 26–27 (David G. Bromley and J. Gordon Melton eds., 2002).

293 Stuart A. Wright, *Public Agency Involvement in Government-Religious Movement Confrontations, in* CULTS, VIOLENCE AND RELIGION, *supra* note 292, at 102, 108–110.

294 *Id.* at 110–11.

295 S.I. Strong, *Law and Religion in Israel and Iran: How the Integration of Secular and Spiritual Laws Affects Human Rights and the Potential for Violence,* 19 MICH. J. INT'L L. 109, 110–13 (1997) (using Iran and Israel as the prime examples of religious states).

296 Strong, *supra* note 295, at 214–215.

suggested that these structural inequities lead to religious minorities "perceiv[ing that] violence [is] the only way to effectuate change in society".[297] In Iran as well, the violent 1979 Islamic Revolution was partly justified by a religious minority whose rights of worship were constrained under the secular rule of Shah Pahlavi.[298] Not only can state protection of dominant religions lead to violence by minority religions but it may accompany violence against minority groups. In Russia, the anti-extremism legislation adopted to allow liquidation of some non-traditional religions, was instituted "shortly after the widespread appearance of booby-trapped anti-Semitic signs".[299] The anti-extremism legislation was spurred by "increasing ranks of nationalist, fascist, and other intolerant groups that attribute Russia's present economic and social ills to ethnic and national minorities".[300]

Harms of protectionist measures for citizens

Decreased individual liberty

Among industries and religions, harms to citizens result from lack of individual choice due to limits on foreign and domestic competition. Anti-monopoly legislation and bans of other protectionist measures are intended to encourage "individual liberty" for a consumer.[301] They also encourage diversity of individual choices.[302] Likewise, state protection of religion lessens individual liberty, human rights, and liberal democracy.[303] In many international and US laws, religious freedom has been declared as a "fundamental right of every individual".[304] International norms also protect against state discrimination in the protection of fundamental rights,

297 Strong, *supra* note 295, at 215 (concluding that "[i]f the goal is to create more peaceful and rights-oriented societies, one group cannot have total control over the definition of culture and the amount of religio-legal integration in the State; to do so will inspire permanent division in society and perpetuate violent power struggles between groups as repressed minorities attempt to find a way to gain the respect they need and deserve"). The religious minorities may feel that they are justified to use violence to obtain rights "already established under international law", like "nondiscrimination on the basis of religion". *Id.* at 203 (also pointing out that violent religious minorities may claim that they "are pursuing rights that are not currently recognized in law or theory but are a logical extension thereof and that violence is necessary to force the State to recognize these new types of rights").

298 *Id.*

299 Gross, *supra* note 128, at 718. The legislation "gained additional momentum following the June 2002 soccer riots . . . that ended in . . . vandalism of cars and Japanese restaurants, and racial violence, including assaults on five Japanese students". *Id.* at 719.

300 *Id.* at 718–19.

301 Blake and Jones, *supra* note 271, at 383–84 (pointing out that an "individual who wants to be an entrepreneur rather than an employee ought not to have his opportunities restricted by unnecessary barriers to entry, or by trade practices designed specifically to eliminate him from the field").

302 *United States v Syufy Enterprises*, 903 F.2d 659, 663 (9th Cir. 1990) ("competition . . . promotes diversity, giving consumers choices to fit a wide array of personal preferences").

303 For a fuller discussion of the relation between protection of dominant religions and a weakening of liberal democracy, see *supra* text accompanying notes 232–38.

304 Annual Report 2003, *supra* note 99, at 1; International Religious Freedom Act of 1998, Pub. L. No. 105–92, 22 U.S.C. § 6402 (2000). In addition, Article 18 of the Universal Declaration of Human Rights holds that "[e]veryone has the right to freedom of thought, conscience and religion; this right includes freedom to change his religion or belief, and freedom, either alone or in community with others and in public or private, to manifest his religion or belief in teaching, practice, worship and observance", which is reiterated in Article 18 of the International Covenant on Civil and Political Rights and Article 9 of the European Convention for the Protection of Human Rights and Fundamental Freedoms (hereinafter "European Convention"). Stahnke also provides a thorough discussion of how limitations on the right to proselytize violate international human rights law. Stahnke, *supra* note 194, at 588–99.

such as freedom of religion,[305] which protection extends against governmental discrimination in "any field regulated and protected by public authorities".[306] Not only does state protection violate the fundamental right to freedom of religion, but prohibitions on religious competition may also constrain citizens' freedom of association or freedom of speech rights.[307]

Availability and service

State protection of industrial monopolies may actually decrease availability of services for citizens. Today, although pressure to "impose protectionist measures" may be intense,[308] most industrialized countries agree that "open competition is the best way to achieve greater enhanced services".[309] Most policymakers no longer contend that state-controlled public monopolies benefit consumers.[310]

Less developed countries still claim that they are entitled to some state protection to provide "basic service" to their residents.[311] Some commentators agree that developing countries are entitled to protectionist measures such as import barriers and subsidies to be able to compete with industrialized countries.[312] However, often this same argument is made with countries protecting struggling *religions* arguing that the state should protect former dominant religions that are now struggling. Particularly in post-Communist Europe, leaders of dominant religions argue that their denomination is "in a weakened condition and needed time to regain its strength after seventy years of Soviet rule".[313]

---

305 International Covenant on Civil and Political Rights, Article 2(1), 26; European Convention, Article 14.

306 *S.W.M. Broeks v The Netherlands*, U.N. GAOR, Hum. Rts. Comm., Comm. No. 172/1984, ¶12.3 (April 9, 1987); U.N. GAOR, Hum. Rts. Comm., General Comment No. 22(48) on Article 18, ¶ 12 (July 20, 1993).

307 Case of *Metropolitan Church of Bessarabia and Others v Moldova*, App. No. 45701/99, Eur. Ct. H.R. (2001), *at* http://www.ehcr.coe.int/eng (finding overlapping rights to freedom of association and freedom of religion in the establishment of a legal entity); *Roadblock, supra* note 278, at 3 (statement of Hon. Christopher H. Smith, Co-Chairman of the Commission on Security and Cooperation in Europe); *see also Sidiropoulos v Greece*, App. No. 57/1997/841/1047, Eur. Ct. H.R., at para. 40 (1998), *at* http://www.ehcr.coe.int/eng ("That citizens should be able to form a legal entity in order to act collectively in a field of mutual interest is one of the most important aspects of the right to freedom of association, without which that right would be deprived of any meaning").

308 Jeanne Asherman, *The International Monetary Fund: A History of Compromise*, 16 N.Y.U. J. Int'l L. Pol. 235, 304 (1984).

309 Lando, *supra* note 42, at 2185.

310 *Id.* at 2197 (noting that "monopolistic control by PTTs [Postal Telegraph and Telecommunications Administrations] does not benefit telecommunications users").

311 *Id.* at 2185 (less developed countries often still insist that a public monopoly is the best way of providing "basic service" to their residents). These countries fear that open competition will result in companies "enhancing service on the existing hard-wire lines" and "neglecting the less profitable laying of more lines . . . leaving some residents with no service at all". *Id.* at 2185. Some commentators have supported developing countries employing protectionist measures for infant industries, but not for dying industries in developed countries. Asherman, *supra* note 308, at 304 n.353.

312 Gregory Shaffer, *WTO Blue-Green Blues: The Impact of US Domestic Politics on Trade-Labor, Trade-Environment Linkages for the WTO's Future*, 24 Fordham Int'l L.J. 608, 624–27 (2000) (arguing that developing countries should "retain more discretion to promote infant industries and other policies through subsidies and import barriers than under WTO rules"); General Agreement on Tariffs and Trade, opened for signature Oct. 30, 1947, 61 Stat. pts. 5, 6, T.I.A.S. 1700, 55 U.N.T.S. 187, Art. XVIII (legitimizing the infant industry argument); Kevin C. Kennedy, *A Review of Globalization and its Discontents*, 35 Geo. Wash. Int'l L. Rev. 251 (2003) (noting that developing countries have used GATT Art XVIII to justify protectionist measures).

313 Guroian, *supra* note 263, at 231 (citing Armenian Orthodox leaders).

Even if commentators justify industrial protection for less developed countries, commentators cannot similarly justify protection of religion. Protection of religion cannot be justified in the same sense because religious freedom is not a matter of economic policy that states can differ on, but a human right recognized (at least in name) by most countries and by internationally recognized agreements.[314] Although commentators may be able to justify state protectionism of industry with less developed countries, allowing state protection of religion is less defensible.

The similarities between the arguments made by industrial and religious monopolies for state protection are remarkable. Although many arguments are similar, dominant religions also express several unique arguments in favor of state protection. The next section explores the acute interests made in the case of religious protection.

MORE ACUTE INTERESTS IN CASE OF RELIGION

Religious monopolies often justify state protection with acute interests in protecting citizens. Religions claim that state protection is necessary to allow citizens to be inculcated with moral values, retain a sense of community and place, and recognize proper social roles.

Inculcation of moral values

States take interest in increasing morality where religion has been absent from public life and in states with dominant religions. A reason for state protection of a dominant religion in some Eastern European countries may be to fill a "spiritual vacuum" in a society and in general to raise the "moral level" of the citizenry.[315] In Greece, the Orthodox Church's role in society is to "preserve the faith . . . of its people".[316] In Denmark religion is such a vital part of the culture that educators rely on religious teachings of the Danish National Church to familiarize students with "fundamental values in Danish culture".[317] Other state churches are legally obligated to teach morals of the dominant religion in state schools.[318] Norway used

314 Although some commentators might argue that religious "protection" may be in the eye of the beholder. They may point out that European, Eastern, and Eastern Christian religions focus more on "group rights" than individual rights. Payne, *supra* note 87, at 263. Therefore, instead of considering "the right of religious freedom . . . [as] the right of the individual to believe as he or she desires, rather it is the freedom of the church to exist". This is why proselytism by minority churches is often outlawed by these countries. *Id.* at 263 (noting Greece as an example of this phenomenon with its anti-proselytism legislation). Regardless of whether a country claims to be protecting "group rights", granting advantages to certain religions still violates principles established by international agreements. There are also several international agreements recognizing the importance of freedom of religion.

315 Schlafly, *supra* note 33, at 110 (citing studies showing that in Russia, "although 75 percent of Russians are baptized and 50 percent consider themselves Orthodox, only 5 percent go to church more than once a month and only 10 percent confess and communicate at least once a year". *Id.* at 135.

316 Payne, *supra* note at 87, at 266. *See* note 5 *supra* and accompanying text for discussion of how the Greek Orthodox Church is the dominant religion in Greece.

317 Dubeck, *supra* note 87, at 48. *See* note 122 *supra* and accompanying text for discussion of how the Danish National Church is the national church of Denmark.

318 Canas, *supra* note 64, at 272 (pointing out that in Portugal state churches must allow "Catholic morals and religion" to be taught "by the church in some state schools" because it is the "major church").

to require the teaching of the doctrine of the Church of Norway to improve the morals of the students, but eventually determined that this could be done without a more inclusive religious message.[319]

Community and place

Many dominant churches identify a community of followers over which they have fellowship, which may include citizens who are non-believers. In many countries, the centre of community and culture has been and remains the dominant church.[320] Dominant churches may insist on identifying their members to the public in an effort to solidify a community of followers.[321] Through creating a united community of worshippers a dominant church justifies its place as the "prevailing religion in the land".[322] Leaders of dominant religions, in Spain for example, reject state legislation and constitutional referendums that fail to promote Catholic religious values and fail to mention "God or Catholic values" because of perceived harms to their community. The Catholic Church in Spain rejects all states documents that are "an attempt to foist an agnostic constitution on a nation of the baptized".[323] Part of maintaining the "dignity and personality" of a community of followers may include actively opposing proselytism by minority religions.[324] Russian Orthodox leaders consider the Orthodox Church a community "to which even its unchurched sons and daughters rightfully belong".[325] Protecting religion is often seen as a means of protecting cultural integrity, particularly in African communities that were subject to proselytizing as part of colonization.[326]

Social roles

Religious monopolies claim they benefit society by promoting appropriate social roles through preserving the faith of the citizens. Some states, like Ireland, recognize the dominant church as a "guardian of the Faith professed by the great majority of

319 Inge Eidsvåg et al., *The Emergence of Interfaith Dialogue: The Norwegian Experience, in* FACILITATING FREEDOM, *supra* note 36, at 777.

320 *Id.* at 271 (claiming that "[f]or centuries the Catholic Church has been one of the most important cent[ers] of culture (and until the last century probably the only one)").

321 Mavrogordatos, *supra* note 5, at 122 ("Until recently, birth certificates, compulsory identity cards, and other official records in Greece routinely included religious affiliation: Christian Orthodox for almost 97 per cent [sic] of Greek citizens") (internal quotations omitted).

322 *Id.* at 122 (internal quotations omitted). This practice was outlawed in May 2000 and the Greek Orthodox church "apparently perceived this move as a first step in the gradual erosion of its institutional monopoly, and refused to accept it". *Id.*

323 Anderson, *supra* note 5, at 141 (describing comments of Cardinal Martin of the Catholic Church in response to constitutional clauses that "left the door open for the introduction of divorce legislation").

324 *Kokkinakis*, 17 Eur. H.R. Rep. 397, at para. 34 (citing the Greek government which forbids proselytism and "attache[s] a criminal penalty to this prohibition" in Article 13 of the 1975 Constitution). *See, e.g.*, John Warwick Montgomery, THE REPRESSION OF EVANGELISM IN GREECE: EUROPEAN LITIGATION VIS-À-VIS A CLOSED RELIGIOUS ESTABLISHMENT 24, 655, 99, 135 (2001) (discussing the "Athens 3" case where charges of proselytism led to a fine of 50,000 drachmas "as pecuniary satisfaction for moral damage which she suffered") and (noting that the "main aim of the [anti-proselytism] legislation, as applied in practice, is to protect the dominant religion" "to the detriment of all other faiths").

325 Schlafly, *supra* note 33, at 137.

326 Mutua, *supra* note 232.

the citizens".[327] This recognition is not just in name and has been relied on in an Irish Supreme Court decision granting custody over a child to the mother "because she was a Catholic rather than to the father, who was a Protestant".[328] To be raised to fulfil his proper social roles, the Court reasoned that he required a Catholic upbringing. In addition, the dominant church in Greece, the Orthodox Church, is viewed as the "protector of the collective tradition and the way of life of the nation".[329] In addition, dominant religions place emphasis on educating children in the tenets of the dominant religion in schools.[330]

The similarities between the arguments made by industries and religion relying on state protection are remarkable, despite a few acute interests expressed only by religious monopolies.

CONCLUSION: COMMODIFICATION OF RELIGION

Religious monopolies receive protectionist legislation through asserting benefits to religion, state and society, and citizens. Industries and religious groups claim benefits including better service, preserving social stability and national security for state and society, and protection of citizens from fraud. The remarkable similarity between the arguments for protection of industry and religion demonstrates that protectionist arguments in the religion context treat religion like a garden variety market commodity. Even if it is inappropriate to treat religion in the same way as industry, the asserted benefits of state protection of industry have been broadly discredited in other contexts, therefore demonstrating that the same arguments should fail in the religious context.

While some state protection of religious monopolies may not officially violate religious freedom under international law,[331] this paper explains how the arguments

---

327 Kissane, *supra* note 5, at 77 (describing Ireland's Article 44.1.2 referring to the "Holy Catholic Apostolic and Roman Church").

328 *Id.* at 77.

329 Payne, *supra* note 87, at 269.

330 In Greece, the religious instruction is only in the Orthodox faith. Mavrogordatos, *supra* note 5, at 121. The Council of State (the Greek Supreme Court) "ruled unconstitutional a reduction in the hours of religious instruction in the schools". *Id.*

331 See the discussion of this point in W. Cole Durham, Jr., *Freedom of Religion or Belief: Laws Affecting the Structuring of Religious Communities* (Warsaw: OSCE/ODIHR, 1999), available on-line at http://www.osce.org/odihr/documents/background/religion/. Violations under the International Religious Freedom Act of 1998 (US law based on international treaties and agreements), 22 U.S.C. § 6402 (2000) include:

(A) arbitrary prohibitions on, restrictions of, or punishment for—
  i. assembling for peaceful religious activities such as worship, preaching and prayer, including arbitrary registration requirements;
  ii. speaking freely about one's religious beliefs
  ii. changing one's religious beliefs and affiliation;
  iv. possession and distribution of religious literature, including Bibles; or
  v. raising one's children in the religious teachings and practices of one's choice

  OR

(B) any of the following acts if committed on account of an individual's religious belief or practice: detention, interrogation, imposition of an onerous financial penalty, forced labor, forced mass resettlement, imprisonment, forced religious conversion, beating, torture, mutilation, rape, enslavement, murder, and execution.

Id. § 6402(13)(A)–(B). See also Bahiyyih G. Tahzib, FREEDOM OF RELIGION OR BELIEF: ENSURING EFFECTIVE INTERNATIONAL LEGAL PROTECTION (1996), for a thorough discussion of international norms protecting freedom of religion and belief.

for protection made by religious and industrial monopolies are unconvincing.[332] In fact not only are they unconvincing, but state protection may actually harm the three constituents they aim to benefit. Protection of industry and religion may lead to a weaker industry or religion, a decrease in democracy, and limits on individual freedom. State protection of religion, which is more harmful than protection of industry, may degrade the liberty of citizens, undermine the autonomy and vibrancy of all religions, and allow oppression by dominant religions. Democracy and liberty are two of the key values that underlie the arguments against economic protectionism, and are also the values most threatened by religious attempts at protectionism. Since the "manner in which a society" protects freedom of religion is the true "litmus test of its commitment to human rights",[333] perhaps it is time that a more critical eye be focused upon the arguments made in the case of religious protectionism.

332 For further discussion *see* p 9–*Domestic and International Unfair Competition*, p 17–*National Security* and p 29–*Protection from Fraud of Unscrupulous Promoters*.

333 Arzt, *supra* note 63, at 378; *see* Barker, *NRMs*, *supra* note 263, at 28 ("If one had to select one criterion that might indicate the extent to which a society was 'open' or 'closed,' the legal position of NRMs [new religious movements] would be a not altogether ridiculous choice. For somewhat finer tuning, the second criterion could well be the legal treatment of NRMs").

INTERNATIONAL TRADE LAW AND COMMON MISTAKE: HAS THERE REALLY BEEN A SATISFACTORY CLARIFICATION OF WHAT FUNDAMENTAL LEGAL PRINCIPLES APPLY?

*Des Taylor**

INTRODUCTION

Law students learn at an early stage in their legal studies that a person cannot easily avoid contractual arrangements merely by subsequently alleging that they made a "mistake" at the time when they entered into such arrangements. It is only in certain specific circumstances that the courts will hold that a contractual obligation is void or voidable because of "mistake"—and there are various fundamental legal principles which enable lawyers to establish what those specific circumstances are. Many of these "fundamental legal principles" were laid down by the courts many years ago[1] and most lawyers, in their everyday business lives, usually proceed confidently in the belief that, provided they know the fundamental legal principles and apply them precisely to the problem at hand, they will be advising their client correctly as to the legal position. However, from time to time, the courts hand down a further judgment which then raises the possibility that either the relevant law is in fact not what most lawyers have assumed it to be (from the earlier judgment or judgments) *or* that the enunciation of the applicable "fundamental legal principles" given in the earlier judgment lacked clarity, requiring yet further clarification of the fundamental legal principles from the court.

This article examines a judgment handed down in the area of international trade law, regarding common mistake—and endeavours to determine whether such judgment has really been a satisfactory clarification of what fundamental legal principles apply. The relevant judgment is that of the English Court of Appeal in *Great Peace Shipping Ltd v Tsavliris Salvage (International) Ltd*[2] (the "*Great Peace* decision").

Since Australian law has its origins in English law, this article considers some international trade law aspects associated with the *Great Peace* decision by outlining the English and Australian law concerning common mistake prior to the English Court of Appeal's *Great Peace* decision. The nature and significance of the *Great Peace* decision and its effect on English and Australian jurisprudence are fully discussed

---

* Des Taylor LLM(Advanced)(UQ), SJD(UTS), PhD(UQ), Lecturer in Law, University of Southern Queensland (Toowoomba, Australia). I am genuinely grateful to Professor Gabriel Moens of Murdoch University (Murdoch, Australia) for his encouragement and advice regarding the researching and writing of this article. Any errors are of course my own.

1 The two leading English cases dealing with common mistake are *Bell v Lever Brothers Ltd.* [1932] AC 161 and *Solle v Butcher* [1950] 1 KB 671. In Australia, cases such as *Taylor v Johnson* (1983) 151 CLR 422, *McRae v Commonwealth Disposals Commission* (1951) 84 CLR 377 and *Svanosio v McNamara* (1956) 96 CLR 186 have adopted and followed (at least to some extent) the principles laid down by English courts.

2 [2002] EWCA Civ 1407.

with conclusions given as to whether *there really has been a satisfactory clarification of what fundamental legal principles apply.*

THE INTERNATIONAL TRADE LAW ASPECTS

The (English) Court of Appeal's *Great Peace* decision arose out of an international trade law contractual arrangement.

Often the relevance of landmark decisions which arise in the context of international trade law is confined to the arena of international trade law.[3] However, it is interesting and heartening for international trade lawyers that the *Great Peace* decision has wider relevance beyond just the international trade law arena. The *Great Peace* decision lays out (supposedly)[4] the fundamental legal principles that apply for an important area of the law generally, namely that relating to common mistake. Nevertheless, even apart from its landmark importance in the law generally (concerning common mistake), the *Great Peace* decision is also important, at a lower level, in the general area of international trade law. If a similar situation were again to arise in international shipping, the parties (and their legal advisers) would know that, as a result of the *Great Peace* decision, a salvage company like Tsavliris would not be able to avoid liability for hire charges in respect of a vessel which it had called on to go to the assistance of another vessel merely because, at the time the contractual arrangements had been made, the hired vessel was, because of mistaken information given by a third party, not in the location that the parties believed it to be. In fact, this is the reason Tsavliris took the matter on appeal to the (English) Court of Appeal even though a comparatively small amount of money was involved, namely the outcome would be a precedent when similar situations subsequently arose. As indicated by Tsavliris's lawyers:

> Tsavliris is the premier worldwide emergency salvage response company. The majority of its work is undertaken on the basis of Lloyd's Open Form Salvage Agreements on a "No Cure No Pay" basis. It commonly exposes itself to considerable financial risk in undertaking salvage operations, especially where it is necessary to charter in tugs, vessels or equipment to assist in a particular operation ... For Tsavliris, although the outcome was disappointing, this adds to a series of important legal cases in which it has been involved, and in which decisions of substantial importance to the salvage industry have been made including Choko Star, Pa Mar, Herdentor, Tesaba and Toisa Puma.[5]

---

3 See e.g. *Pyrene Co. Ltd. v Scindia Navigation Co. Ltd.* [1954] 2 QB 402, *Kwei Tek Chao v British Traders & Shippers* [1954] 2 QB 459 and *United City Merchants (Investments) Ltd. v Royal Bank of Canada* [1982] 2 WLR 1039.

4 The purpose of this article is, inter alia, to make a determination as to whether or not the *Great Peace* decision has, in reality, satisfactorily clarified what fundamental legal principles apply when the issue of 'common mistake' is raised.

5 See the letter from Roland Jackson of Shaw and Croft, Solicitors, London entitled *Why the Great Shipping case incurred 69 pages of judgment* in Lloyd's List International of 23 October 2003.

THE ENGLISH AND AUSTRALIAN POSITIONS REGARDING COMMON MISTAKE—PRIOR TO THE "GREAT PEACE" DECISION

English position

Australian case law on common mistake is based on English judicial interpretative approaches. This paper considers two aspects:

a. common mistake at common law; and
b. common mistake in equity.

Common mistake at common law

In very limited circumstances, the common law will grant relief to a mistaken party. The common law does recognize three types of mistake. These are *common mistakes, mutual mistakes* and *unilateral mistakes*. A common mistake occurs when each party makes exactly the same mistake; a mutual mistake occurs when the parties misunderstand each other and are, therefore, at cross-purposes; a unilateral mistake occurs when one party is mistaken and the other party knows or ought to be aware of the mistake made. This article focuses only on the law concerning the first type of mistake recognised by the courts, namely common mistake.

Common mistake can be put into three categories:

a. common mistake as to the existence of the subject matter;
b. common mistake as to title; and/or
c. common mistake as to the quality of the subject matter.

At common law, in order to have the courts declare a contract void because of common mistake, more is required than just establishing the making of *any* sort of common mistake. Khoury and Yamouni, when speaking of common mistake at common law, summarize the position in the following terms:

> The courts will not render a contract void on the ground of common mistake *unless* the common mistake involves a matter which is *so fundamental* to the contract that both parties regard it as a condition precedent to the existence of a binding contract. Whether a common mistake is of that nature will, of course, depend upon the facts of the case. However, the decided cases suggest that to be fundamental, the common mistake must either relate to the very existence of the subject matter of the contract or involve the sale of property to a person who already owns it. By way of contrast, a common mistake as to the quality, nature or value of the subject matter is not sufficient.[6]

A case which is often quoted to illustrate the first "res extincta" situation (i.e. a common mistake as to the very existence of the subject matter of the contract) is *Scott v Coulson*.[7] In that case, Scott entered into a contract to assign a life insurance policy to Coulson. However, unknown to both the assignor and the assignee of the policy, the assured had already died. It was held by the English Court of Appeal that the

6 D. Khoury and Y.S. Yamouni, *Understanding Contract Law* (6th edition. Chatswood, Australia: LexisNexis Butterworths, 2003) at 268. Emphasis added.

7 [1903] 2 Ch 249.

contract of assignment was void for common mistake.[8] The second "res sua" situation (i.e. a common mistake involving the "sale"[9] of property to a person who already owns it) can be seen in such cases as *Cooper v Phibbs*.[10] In that case, when his uncle died, the nephew contracted with his cousins (the uncle's daughters) to lease a fishery, which all parties believed had been the uncle's property and which had passed to the cousins on his death. However, in actual fact, the nephew was already the true owner of the fishery. The House of Lords held that the mistake made the contract liable to be set aside—and it was so set aside. As regards the third situation (which is normally *not* sufficient for the courts at common law to intervene, i.e. a common mistake as to the quality, nature or value of the subject matter), a case which is often mentioned by way of illustration is *Leaf v International Galleries*.[11] In that case, Leaf purchased a painting entitled "Salisbury Cathedral" from International Galleries which both parties honestly believed was painted by Constable. When it was later revealed that the painting was not by Constable, Leaf sought to have the contract declared void for common mistake. The English Court of Appeal held that there was no operative common mistake (i.e. it was not one that allows any resulting contract to be set aside). Denning LJ in his judgment stated the legal position in the following terms:

> This was a contract for the sale of goods. There was a mistake about the *quality* of the subject-matter, because both parties believed the picture to be a Constable; and that mistake was in one sense essential or fundamental. But such a mistake does not avoid the contract: there was no mistake at all about the *subject-matter* of the sale. It was a specific picture, "Salisbury Cathedral". The parties were agreed in the same terms on the same subject-matter, and that is sufficient to make a contract . . .[12]

The leading case (in English law) regarding common mistake at common law—especially common mistake as to the quality of the subject matter—is *Bell v Lever Brothers Ltd*.[13] The facts of that case were as follows. Bell (along with Snelling) had been appointed managing director of a Lever Brothers subsidiary in Africa. He was employed for a five-year period at a salary of £8,000 per annum. After serving three years of that term, Bell was made redundant and his employer agreed to pay him £30,000 for the premature termination of his contract. Soon after the payment had been made, Lever Brothers became aware that during his period as managing director, Bell had breached his duty to the company by trading on his own account. It was also advised that such a breach would render Bell liable to dismissal without any compensation. Consequently, Lever Brothers brought an action to recover the £30,000. It alleged that the termination contract was void for common mistake—namely, that the contract was negotiated on the basis that both parties believed that some payment was obligatory. However, it was held by the House of Lords that the mistake was not such as to render the contract void. The majority of the judges took the view that, irrespective of what the parties thought about the need for payment,

8 Another case is *Couturier v Hastie* (1852) 8 Ex 40; 155 ER 1250 (where specific goods had ceased to exist in a commercial sense before the time of the contract). That legal position has been given statutory force in the various Sale of Goods Acts, e.g. Section 11 of the Sale of Goods Act 1923 (NSW).

9 For present purposes, 'sale' can be regarded as also covering 'leasing'.

10 (1867) LR 2 HL 149.

11 [1950] 2 KB 86.

12 *Id.* 89. Emphasis added.

13 [1932] AC 161. Hereinafter this case will generally be referred to as *Bell v Lever Brothers*.

the subject matter of the contract was the same—the termination of Bell's employment. It was immaterial that the same result could have been achieved by other means. Atkin LJ, in dismissing the claim, indicated the reluctance of the courts to grant relief on the ground of mistake.[14] He also laid down, in the following passage, the fundamental principle the court would use when considering whether a contract is void for common mistake (as to the quality of the subject matter):

> Mistake as to quality of the thing contracted for raises more difficult questions. *In such a case a mistake will not affect assent unless it is the mistake of both parties, and is to the existence of some quality which makes the thing without the quality essentially different from the thing as it was believed to be.*[15]

This test for common mistake is very narrow[16] and extremely difficult to satisfy.[17] It has subsequently been interpreted to mean that "the mistake must render the subject matter of the contract essentially and radically different from the subject matter which the parties believed to exist" at the time the contract was made.[18]

Common mistake in equity

Since equity follows the common law, contracts which are at common law regarded as being void for common mistake in the first and second abovementioned situations (i.e. where there is common mistake as to the existence of the subject matter[19] or where there is common mistake involving an owner purchasing his or her own property[20]) will likewise be considered by equity as being void.[21] However—at least until the time of the handing down of the *Great Peace* decision[22]—it has been considered that equity can intervene in two situations involving common mistake. Firstly, it can order the rectification of an agreement which has been inaccurately expressed in written form. Secondly, it may—in certain circumstances—set aside a contract concluded on the basis of a common mistake even though that common mistake does not relate to a "res extincta" situation[23] or to a "res sua" situation.[24] The first situation ("rectification") is relatively straightforward. As Graw indicates, if the parties to a contract reach agreement and then draw up a written document which,

14 *Id.* 224. There are normally two reasons given for the reluctance of the courts to grant relief for mistake, namely (a) there is the fear that a liberal attitude by the courts (to the allowing of contracts to be set aside for mistake) would encourage persons to resort to fraudulent claims of mistake in order to avoid their contractual obligations and (b) the setting aside of contracts on the ground of mistake could have unjust effects on innocent third parties.

15 *Id.* 218. Emphasis added.

16 In this regard, see e.g. the comment of Lord Phillips in *Great Peace Shipping Limited v Tsavliris (International) Limited* [2002] EWCA Civ 1407 at para 86.

17 Hence it is often considered that the only instances, at common law, where a contract will be held to be void for common mistake are where the common mistake is as to the existence of the subject matter or where the common mistake is as to title.

18 *Associated Japanese Bank (International) Ltd. v Credit Du Nord S.A.* [1989] 1 WLR 255 at 268.

19 i.e. a 'res extincta' situation.

20 i.e. a 'res sua' situation.

21 Equity will thus refuse to grant specific performance of such contracts.

22 *Great Peace Shipping Limited v Tsavliris Salvage (International) Ltd.* [2002] EWCA Civ 1407.

23 i.e. a common mistake as to the very existence of the subject matter of the contract.

24 i.e. a common mistake involving the sale of property to a person who already owns same.

by mistake, fails to record that agreement accurately, the court may rectify the document by ordering that the mistaken portion be struck out and replaced with the words that do reflect what they actually agreed.[25] It is considered that this is still the position, i.e. the capability of the court to do this has not been affected by the *Great Peace* decision—and it is not proposed to examine this first situation further. The second situation is, however, directly relevant to the focus of this article.

It was mentioned earlier that a common mistake merely as to the *quality* of the subject matter is not sufficient to enable the *common law* to set aside a contract unless *"it is the mistake of both parties, and is to the existence of some quality which makes the thing without the quality essentially different from the thing as it was believed to be."*[26] As indicated above, this very narrow test laid down by Atkin LJ in *Bell v Lever Brothers* is extremely difficult to satisfy. However, despite this common law position, it has also (for many years) been the general belief that, in some of the scenarios where the common law would not allow common mistake to make a contract *void*, a court—exercising its *equitable jurisdiction*—could nevertheless hold the contract to be *voidable* and, if appropriate, set it aside on such terms as the court thinks fit. The basis for this belief is the English Court of Appeal's decision in *Solle v Butcher*.[27]

The facts in *Solle v Butcher* were as follows. Butcher leased a flat to Solle for seven years at a fixed annual rental of £250 per annum. After occupying the flat for two years, it was discovered that the maximum rent payable for the flat under the rent restrictions legislation in force at the time was £140 per annum. The only way Butcher could have increased that amount was if he had served a notice of increase prior to Solle's signing the lease. He did not serve such a notice because both he and Solle believed that, due to certain structural alterations carried out on the flat, the flat was not subject to the legislation. In fact, Solle, who was also Butcher's letting agent for other flats that he owned, had obtained legal opinion to that effect. He also advised Butcher that £250 per annum was a reasonable rent for the flat. Notwithstanding that advice, Solle brought an action against Butcher claiming the excess paid over the previous two years and a declaration that he could remain in the flat for the remainder of the lease for £140 per annum. Butcher counterclaimed, seeking a declaration that the lease was void for common mistake.

Early in his judgment in *Solle v Butcher*, Lord Denning stated:

> [It] is necessary to remember that mistake is of two kinds: first, mistake which renders the contract *void*, that is, a nullity from the beginning, which is the kind of mistake that was dealt with by the courts of common law; and, secondly, mistake which renders the contract not void, but *voidable*, that is, liable to be set aside on such terms as the court thinks fit, which is the type of mistake which was dealt with by the courts of equity. Much of the difficulty which has attended this subject has arisen because, before the fusion of law and equity, the courts at common law, in order to do justice in the case in hand, extended this doctrine of mistake beyond its proper limits and held contracts to be void which were really only voidable, a process which was capable of being attended with much injustice to third persons who had bought goods or otherwise committed

25 Stephen Graw, *An Introduction to the Law of Contract* (4th edition. Sydney: LBC Information Services, 2002) at 255.

26 *Bell v Lever Brothers Ltd* [1932] 1 AC 161 at 218. Emphasis added.

27 [1950] 1 KB 671.

> themselves on the faith that there was a contract . . . Since the fusion of law and equity, there is no reason to continue this process . . .[28]

After indicating that *Bell v Lever Brothers* is the starting point for any consideration of the law concerning common mistake, Lord Denning said:

> The correct interpretation of that case, to my mind, is that, once a contract has been made, that is to say, once the parties, whatever their inmost states of mind, have to all outward appearances agreed with sufficient certainty in the same terms on the same subject matter, then the contract is good unless and until it is set aside for failure of some condition on which the existence of the contract depends, or for fraud, or on some equitable ground.[29]

According to Lord Denning, the contract in *Solle v Butcher* was not void at *common law* for common mistake. In this regard, he commented:

> [I]t is clear that here there was a contract. The parties agreed in the same terms on the same subject matter. It is true that the landlord was under a mistake which was to him fundamental: he would not for one moment have considered letting the flat for seven years if it meant that he could only charge £140 a year for it. He made the fundamental mistake of believing that the rent he could charge was not tied down to a controlled rent; but, whether it was his own mistake or a mistake common to both him and the tenant, it is not a ground for saying that the lease was from the beginning a nullity.[30]

Lord Denning then went on to consider mistakes which render a contact *voidable* (i.e. liable to be set aside on some *equitable* ground). As to when *equity* will intervene to set aside a contract if the parties were under a common mistake, Lord Denning said:

> Whilst presupposing that a contract was good at law, or at any rate not void, the court of equity would often relieve a party from the consequences of his own mistake, so long as it could do so without injustice to third parties. . . . *A contract is also liable in equity to be set aside if the parties were under a common misapprehension either as to facts or as to their relative and respective rights, provided that the misapprehension was fundamental and that the party seeking to set it aside was not himself at fault.*[31]

The last sentence is Lord Denning's formulation of the test as to when equity will intervene to set aside a contract for common mistake. According to such test, equity will intervene to set aside a contract for common mistake *if* the following conditions are met:

a. there is a common misapprehension;
b. that misapprehension is of a "fundamental" nature; or
c. the party seeking to have the contract set aside is not at fault.

In *Solle v Butcher*, the (English) Court of Appeal—exercising its *equitable* jurisdiction and on the basis that the conditions required by the aforementioned test had been satisfied—was prepared to set aside the contract (and did) upon terms which it considered just to both parties. Basically, those terms gave the tenant the right to choose either to stay on for what he agreed was a fair rent (£250) or to vacate the premises.

---

28 *Id*. 690–691. Emphasis added.
29 *Id*. 691.
30 *Id*. 692.
31 *Id*. 692–693. Emphasis added.

To this point—i.e. up to and just prior to the *Great Peace* decision—the position concerning common mistake in English law has been considered to be as follows:

a. a common mistake would normally only render a contract *void* if it related to the actual existence of the subject matter of the contract[32] or if the object of a purported sale already belonged to the buyer;[33] and
b. in all other cases, the contract would stand as is, unless the court—exercising its *equitable jurisdiction* (after being satisfied as to the fulfilment of the conditions laid down by Lord Denning in his abovementioned test in *Solle v Butcher*)—set the contract aside on whatever terms it considered fair in the circumstances.

However, despite this seemingly straightforward position, the courts and lawyers generally over the last 50 years have experienced substantial difficulties in trying to reconcile *Solle v Butcher* with *Bell v Lever Brothers*. It has been very difficult for them to identify, with precision, exactly what compatible principles regarding common mistake such cases have laid down.[34]

Australian position

An examination of the Australian case law shows that the Australian courts have (to the time of the *Great Peace* decision) followed at least to some extent the English case law (of *Bell v Lever Brothers* and *Solle v Butcher*) regarding common mistake at common law and in equity.

As regards common mistake at common law in Australia, Carter and Harland state:[35]

> In *Taylor v Johnson*,[36] the High Court of Australia recognized the authority of Lord Atkin's speech[37] in *Bell v Lever Brothers*, for the proposition that the *formation* of contracts is to be determined objectively, with the consequence that, until the objective approach is displaced, there is a contract which remains binding unless and until it is set aside for fraud, failure of an agreed condition precedent or on some equitable ground. The theme of the Australian cases, beginning with *McRae v Commonwealth Disposals Commission*,[38] is that although the speech of Lord Atkin in *Bell v Lever Brothers* is a correct statement of the law, the test is so rarely satisfied as to be of marginal significance.

And later (as regards common mistake in equity in Australia),

> The equitable doctrine of common mistake, broadly as formulated by Denning LJ . . . has also received some measure of support in Australia.[39]

32 i.e. a 'res extincta' situation.

33 i.e. a 'res sua' situation.

34 See e.g. J.C. Smith, *Contracts – Mistake, Frustration and Implied Terms* (1994) 110 LQR 400, John Cartwright, *Solle v Butcher and the Doctrine of Mistake in Contract* (1987) 103 LQR 594 and C.J. Slade, *The Myth of Mistake in the English Law of Contract* (1954) 70 LQR 385.

35 J.W. Carter and D.J. Harland, *Contract Law in Australia* (4th edition. Butterworths: Sydney, 2002) at [1224] and [1229].

36 (1983) 151 CLR 422.

37 [1932] AC 161 at 217–27.

38 (1951) 84 CLR 377.

39 The footnote reference here in the original wording is a direction to other commentary (elsewhere in the same book) concerning the Australian case of *Taylor v Johnson* (1983) 151 CLR 422.

The High Court of Australia decisions in which *Solle v Butcher* has been cited with approval (or at least passages of Lord Denning's judgment therein) include *McRae v Commonwealth Disposals Commission,*[40] *Svanosio v McNamara*[41] and *Taylor v Johnson.*[42]

THE "GREAT PEACE" DECISION

The Court of Appeal's decision in *Great Peace Shipping Limited v Tsavliris (International) Limited* was handed down on 14 October 2002 in the form of a single judgment.[43] Its particular importance lies in the fact that it is a recent statement on the part of the (English) Court of Appeal as to the current state of the (English) law of common mistake. In its judgment, the Court of Appeal commenced by mentioning that:

a. In the judgment of the House of Lords in 1932 in *Bell v Lever Brothers,*[44] Lord Atkin made a speech which has been treated as the definitive exposition of the rules of law governing the effect of mistake on contract;
b. In 1950, in *Solle v Butcher,*[45] Denning LJ (in the Court of Appeal) identified an equitable jurisdiction which permits the court to intervene where the parties have concluded an agreement that was binding in law under a common misapprehension of a fundamental nature as to the material facts or their respective rights; and
c. Over the last 50 years, judges and jurists have wrestled with the problem of reconciling these two decisions and identifying with precision the principles that they lay down.[46]

The facts

In September 1999, the "Cape Providence" was on its way from Brazil to China with a cargo of iron ore when it suffered serious structural damage in the South Indian Ocean. Tsavliris (the defendant) learned that the vessel was in difficulties and offered its salvage services (which were accepted). To find a tug, Tsavliris approached a firm of London brokers, Marint. A tug was found, but it was going to take five or six days for the tug to reach the "Cape Providence" from Singapore. As there was serious concern that in the meantime the vessel might go down with the loss of her crew, Marint was asked by Tsavliris to try to find a merchant vessel in the vicinity of the "Cape Providence" which would be willing to assist, if necessary, with the evacuation of the crew. Marint contacted Ocean Routes (a respected organisation which provides weather forecasting services to the shipping industry and

40 (1951) 84 CLR 377 at 402, 407.
41 (1956) 96 CLR 186 at 195–6.
42 (1983) 151 CLR 422 at 429–431.
43 [2002] EWCA Civ No. 1407.
44 [1932] AC 161.
45 [1950] 1 KB 671.
46 *Great Peace Shipping Limited v Tsavliris (International) Limited* [2002] EWCA Civ No. 1407 at para 1.

receives reports about vessels at sea). Ocean Routes advised Marint that the "Great Peace" (a vessel owned by the plaintiffs, Great Peace Shipping Limited) was the nearest to the "Cape Providence" and should be close to a rendezvous position within about twelve hours. A contract was duly entered into between the Great Peace Shipping Limited and Tsavliris. The hire was to be for a minimum of five days and the purpose of the charter was to escort and stand-by the "Cape Providence" for the purpose of saving life. After the contract had been concluded, the parties discovered that the information supplied by Ocean Routes was wrong and the vessels were in fact 410 miles away from each other. If the information previously given to Marint by Ocean Routes had been accurate, the vessels should have been only about 35 miles apart when the contract was concluded. In the meantime, the "Cape Providence" was passed by a vessel called the "Nordfarer". Tsavliris thereupon contracted with the owners of the "Nordfarer" directly and at the same time instructed Marint to cancel the "Great Peace" contract (which was done). The plaintiff (Great Peace Shipping Limited) claimed US$82,500 as being the minimum five days' hire due under the contract entered into by it with Tsavliris (or, alternatively, the same sum as damages for the defendants' alleged wrongful repudiation of the charter). However, the defendant (Tsavliris) was not prepared to pay any monies to Great Peace Shipping Limited. The defence of Tsavliris to the plaintiff's claim was that:

a. the charter contract had been rendered *void* by a *common mistake at common law* since, unknown to both parties, the vessels were not in close proximity to each other (and this turned the contract into something essentially different from that for which the parties bargained); or alternatively
b. the charter contract was *voidable* for *common mistake in equity* (since the parties had entered into the contract under a common mistake as to a matter "fundamental" to the agreement in question) and they were therefore entitled to rescind the contract.

The "common mistake at common law" defence

In the *Great Peace* case the parties were agreed as to the express terms of the contract (i.e. that the "Cape Providence" would deviate towards the "Great Peace" and, on reaching her, escort her so as to be on hand to save the lives of her crew, should she founder). The common mistake relied upon by the defendant (Tsavliris)—as being the basis for its non-liability to make payment to the plaintiff (Great Peace Shipping Limited)—was as to an assumption that it claimed underlay the agreed contract. This assumption was that the "Cape Providence" was within a few hours sailing of the "Great Peace". Tsavliris argued that performance of the contract, in the circumstances as they turned out to be, would have been fundamentally different from the performance contemplated by the parties, so much so that the effect of the mistake was to deprive the agreement of the consideration underlying it and, under common law, the effect of such a mistake was to render the contract void. The foundation for this submission was *Bell v Lever Brothers* and the test for common mistake at common law laid down therein by Lord Atkin.[47]

47 *Bell v Lever Brothers Ltd.* [1932] AC 161 at 218.

The Court of Appeal (in *Great Peace*) said that it was unquestionably a common assumption of both parties when the contract was concluded that the two vessels were in sufficiently close proximity to enable the "Great Peace" to carry out the service that it was engaged to perform. The Court of Appeal then asked the question: *Was the distance between the two vessels so great as to confound that assumption and to render the contractual adventure impossible of performance?*[48] In the lower court, Toulson J had addressed this issue in the following paragraph of his judgment:

> Was the "Great Peace" so far away from the "Cape Providence" at the time of the contract as to defeat the contractual purpose—or in other words to turn it into something essentially different from that for which the parties bargained? This is a question of fact and degree, but in my view the answer is no . . . A telling point is the reaction of the defendants on learning the true positions of the vessels. They did not want to cancel the agreement until they knew if they could find a nearer vessel to assist. Evidently the defendants did not regard the contract as devoid of purpose, or they would have cancelled at once.[49]

and the Court of Appeal agreed with such conclusion.[50] The Court of Appeal felt that it was legitimate for Toulson J to have regard to the fact that the appellants did not want to cancel the agreement with the "Great Peace" until they knew whether they could get a nearer vessel to assist. In the view of the Court of Appeal, this reaction was a telling indication that the fact that the vessels were considerably further apart than the appellants had believed did not mean that the services that the "Great Peace" was in a position to provide were essentially different from those which the parties had envisaged when the contract was concluded. The "Great Peace" would arrive in time to provide several days of escort service. The appellants would have wished the contract to be performed but for the adventitious arrival on the scene of a vessel prepared to perform the same services. The fact that the vessels were further apart than both parties had appreciated did not mean that it was impossible to perform the contractual adventure. The parties entered into a binding contract for the hire of the "Great Peace". That contract gave the appellants an express right to cancel the contract subject to the obligation to pay the "cancellation fee" of five days' hire. When they engaged the "Nordfarer" they cancelled the "Great Peace". According to the Court of Appeal, they thus became liable, in consequence, to pay the cancellation fee and there was no injustice in that result.[51] Thus the defence of common mistake at common law failed.

The "common mistake in equity" defence

Tsavliris argued in the alternative that the facts gave rise to a right of rescission in equity, such a right arising whenever the parties contracted under a common mistake as to a matter that could be described as fundamental or material to the agreement in question. The foundation for that submission was *Solle v Butcher*.[52]

48 *Great Peace Shipping Limited v Tsavliris (International) Limited* [2002] EWCA Civ No. 1407 at para 162. Emphasis added.

49 *Great Peace Shipping Ltd v Tsavliris Salvage (International) Ltd* (2001) 151 NLJ Law Reports 1696 at para 56.

50 *Great Peace Shipping Limited v Tsavliris (International) Limited* [2002] EWCA Civ No. 1407 at para 162. Emphasis added.

51 *Id.* paras 165–166.

52 *Id.* para 34.

According to the (English) Court of Appeal, a small number of cases in the last 50 years have purported to follow *Solle v Butcher*, yet none of them have defined the test of mistake that gives rise to the equitable jurisdiction to rescind in a manner that distinguishes this from the test of a mistake that renders a contract void in law, as identified in *Bell v Lever Brothers*.[53] Nor, over 50 years, has it proved possible to define satisfactorily two different qualities of mistake, one operating in law and one in equity.[54] The Court of Appeal said that, in *Solle v Butcher*, Denning LJ identified the requirement of a common misapprehension that was "fundamental", and that adjective has been used to describe the mistake in those cases which have followed *Solle v Butcher*—but the Court of Appeal did not find it possible to distinguish, by a process of definition, a mistake which is "fundamental" from Lord Atkin's mistake as to quality which "makes the thing contracted for essentially different from the thing that it was believed to be".[55] The Court stated that it was only concerned with the question whether relief might be given for common mistake in circumstances wider than those stipulated in *Bell v Lever Brothers*. But that, according to the Court of Appeal, is a question as to where the common law should draw the line; not whether, given the common law rule, it needs to be mitigated by application of some other doctrine.[56] The common law has drawn the line in *Bell v Lever Brothers*.[57] The effect of *Solle v Butcher* is not to supplement or mitigate the common law; it is to say that *Bell v Lever Brothers* was wrongly decided.[58] The Court of Appeal's conclusion was that it is impossible to reconcile *Solle v Butcher* with *Bell v Lever Brothers*.[59] In his judgment,[60] Toulson J had demonstrated the extent of the confusion in this area of the law and the Court of Appeal concluded that, if coherence is to be restored to this area of the law, it can only be by declaring that there is no jurisdiction to grant rescission of a contract on the ground of common mistake where that contract is valid and enforceable on ordinary principles of contract law.[61] That was the conclusion of Toulson J in the lower court and that conclusion was now endorsed by the Court of Appeal.

The Court of Appeal towards the end of its judgment stated that, in *Great Peace*, the Court of Appeal had been provided with the first opportunity for a full and mature consideration of the relation between *Bell v Lever Brothers* and *Solle v Butcher* and, in the light of that consideration, the Court of Appeal could see no way that *Solle v Butcher* can stand with *Bell v Lever Brothers*.[62] Accordingly the defence on the ground of common mistake in equity was also dismissed because—as stated by Lord Phillips in his judgment (which was unanimously accepted by the entire Court of Appeal)—"there is no jurisdiction to grant rescission of a contract on the ground

53 *Id.* para 153.

54 *Ibid.*

55 *Id.* para 154.

56 *Id.* para 156.

57 *Ibid.*

58 *Ibid.*

59 *Id.* para 157.

60 *Great Peace Shipping Ltd v Tsavliris Salvage (International) Ltd* (2001) 151 NLJ 1696 at paras 110 to 121 inclusive.

61 *Great Peace Shipping Limited v Tsavliris (International) Limited* [2002] EWCA Civ No. 1407 at para 157.

62 *Id.* para 160.

of common mistake where the contract is valid and enforceable on ordinary principles of contract law".[63]

THE ENGLISH AND AUSTRALIAN POSITIONS REGARDING COMMON MISTAKE SINCE THE "GREAT PEACE" DECISION

English position

At the present time, pursuant to the (English) Court of Appeal's judgment in *Great Peace Shipping* and the House of Lords' earlier decision in *Bell v Lever Brothers*, the English position regarding common mistake is as follows.

The issue of common mistake will only arise where the contract itself does not deal with the question of which party should bear the risk of a particular set of circumstances occurring or does not deal with sufficient certainty with the situation that has arisen. The fundamental principle concerning common mistake (and test for same) is that laid down in *Bell v Lever Brothers*. That fundamental principle is that a mistake will not affect assent unless it is the mistake of both parties and is as to the existence of some quality which makes the thing without the quality essentially different from the thing as it was believed to be.[64] Lord Atkin's test has subsequently been interpreted to mean that "the mistake must render the subject matter of the contract essentially and radically different from the subject matter which the parties believed to exist" at the time the contract was made.[65] In *Great Peace*, the Court of Appeal has also indicated that the following five elements must be present if common mistake is to avoid a contract:

1. there must be a common assumption as to the existence of a state of affairs;
2. there must be no warranty by either party that that state of affairs exists;
3. the non-existence of the state of affairs must not be attributable to the fault of either party;
4. the non-existence of the state of affairs must render performance of the contract impossible; and
5. the state of affairs may be the existence, or a vital attribute, of the consideration to be provided or circumstances which must subsist if performance of the contractual adventure is to be possible.[66]

Because the *Bell v Lever Brothers* test for common mistake is so narrow and difficult to satisfy, it seems that, almost always, the only situations where the court will intervene to declare the contract void for common mistake will be where there was a common mistake as to the existence of the subject matter ("res extincta") or where there was a common mistake involving an owner purchasing his or her own property ("res sua"). There is no jurisdiction in equity to grant rescission of a contract on the ground of common mistake where the contract is valid and enforceable on

63 *Id.* para 157.

64 *Bell v Lever Brothers Ltd* [1932] 1 AC 161 at 218.

65 *Associated Japanese Bank (International) Ltd. v Credit Du Nord S.A.* [1989] 1 WLR 255 at 268.

66 *Great Peace Shipping Limited v Tsavliris (International) Limited* [2002] EWCA Civ No. 1407 at para 76.

ordinary principles of common law. The Court of Appeal's judgment in *Solle v Butcher* is inconsistent with the House of Lord's decision in *Bell v Lever Brothers* and hence (in view of the *Great Peace* decision) is no longer good authority.

To date, there has been no indication that the *Great Peace* case will be taken on appeal to the House of Lords. Obviously a decision by the House of Lords confirming the Court of Appeal's decision in *Great Peace* would put beyond doubt any questioning of the Court of Appeal decision. However, in *Great Peace*, the Court of Appeal, after coming to the conclusion that it was impossible to reconcile *Solle v Butcher* with *Bell v Lever Brothers*, did then turn its attention to the question as to what, according to the principles of case precedent, is the correct approach where the Court of Appeal concludes that a decision of the Court of Appeal cannot stand with an earlier decision of the House of Lords. First of all, it noted that there was *Noble v Southern Railway Company*[67] where the Court of Appeal held itself bound to follow a previous decision of the Court of Appeal that was on all fours—*Clarke's case*[68]—notwithstanding that this was in conflict with an earlier decision of the House of Lords—*McFerrin's case*.[69] However, as the Court of Appeal pointed out, in *Noble* Lord Wright had made the following comment on this situation:

> I can understand the difficulty in which both the county court judge and the Court of Appeal were placed in the present case. What a court should do when faced with a decision of the Court of Appeal manifestly inconsistent with the decisions of this House is a problem of some difficulty in the doctrine of precedent. I incline to think it should apply the law laid down by the House and refuse to follow the erroneous decision.[70]

The Court of Appeal in *Great Peace* also noted that Lord Lane CJ, when delivering the judgment of the Court of Appeal, invoked this statement of opinion in *Holden & Co v Crown Prosecution Service*.[71] At issue there was the scope of the jurisdiction of the court to order a solicitor to pay personally costs thrown away in criminal proceedings. The court was faced with reasoning on the point in a previous decision of the Court of Appeal which was at odds with an earlier decision of the House of Lords. Lord Lane, having referred to the opinion of Lord Wright, went on to hold that the court regarded itself as free to disregard the previous decision of the Court of Appeal.

Then, after also mentioning that whilst:

a. it was in some doubt as to whether this line of authority goes far enough to permit it to hold that *Solle v Butcher* is not good law;
b. it was very conscious that it was not only scrutinising the reasoning of Lord Denning in *Solle v Butcher* and in *Magee v Pennine Insurance*,[72] but it was also faced with a number of later decisions in which Lord Denning's approach has been approved and followed; and
c. a Division of the Court of Appeal had recently made it clear in *West Sussex Properties Ltd v Chichester DC* that they felt bound by *Solle's case*,

67 [1940] AC 583.

68 (20) BWCC 309.

69 [1926] AC 377.

70 *Noble v Southern Railway Company* [1940] AC 583 at 598.

71 [1990] 2 QB 261.

72 [1969] 2 QB 507.

the Court of Appeal went on to state that, in this case (*Great Peace*), it had heard full argument, which had provided what it believed to have been the first opportunity in the Court of Appeal for a full and mature consideration of the relation between *Bell v Lever Brothers* and *Solle v Butcher*. In the light of that consideration, the Court of Appeal could see no way that *Solle v Butcher* could stand with *Bell v Lever Brothers* and, accordingly, in these circumstances, it would so hold. Thus, it is submitted, the Court of Appeal's action in over-ruling *Solle v Butcher* does have a valid basis.

To date, there have been at least two English cases where the (English) Court of Appeal's decision in *Great Peace* has been mentioned and followed. These cases are:

a. *Huyton S.A. v Distribuidora Internacional De Productos Agricolas S.A.*[73]
b. *Beximco Pharmaceuticals Ltd & Ors v Shamil Bank of Bahrain E.C.*[74]

The first is a decision of the (English) High Court and the second is a decision of the (English) Court of Appeal.

Australian position

At the time of the writing of this article, the *Great Peace* decision has been mentioned in at least two Australian cases, namely *Donkin v Official Trustee in Bankruptcy*[75] and *Harris v Digital Pulse Pty. Ltd.*[76] In *Donkin v Official Trustee in Bankruptcy* (which was a decision of the Queensland Supreme Court on 26 November 2003), the *Great Peace* decision was applied by Chesterman J in the following terms:

> A recent decision of the Court of Appeal, *Great Peace Shipping Ltd v Tsavliris Salvage (International) Ltd* [2002] 3 WLR 1617 appears to have reinstated the law concerning common mistake and concluded that where parties contract on the basis of a common mistake as to the subject matter of their contract the contract is void. The mistake must be shared by both parties and must relate to facts as they existed at the time the contract was made. If the mistake renders the subject matter of the contract essentially and radically different from the subject matter which the parties believed to exist the contract will be void.[77]

In *Harris v Digital Pulse Pty. Ltd.* (which was a decision of the New South Wales Court of Appeal on 7 February 2003), the *Great Peace Shipping* decision was merely cited in paragraph 455 (as having overruled *Solle v Butcher*).

Apart from this "applying" in one instance and "citing" in another of the *Great Peace* decision, there appears to be no reported Australian case—since the *Great Peace* decision—where *Solle v Butcher* has been applied or followed.

Obviously, until there is a ruling by the High Court of Australia, it cannot definitely be said that *Solle v Butcher* is no longer good law in Australia. However, as Carter has stated, "Australian approval of *Solle* has always been somewhat guarded".[78] Thus it may be that eventually the (Australian) High Court will decide

73 [2002] EWHC 2088 (Comm) (25 October 2002).
74 [2004] EWCA Civ 19 (28 January 2004).
75 [2003] QSC 401.
76 [2003] NSWCA 10.
77 *Donkin v Official Trustee in Bankruptcy* [2003] QSC 401 at para 52.
78 *Carter on Contract* at para [22–260] in LexisNexis Butterworths Online at http:www.lexinexis.com.au/aus/default.asp (28 April 2004).

that Australian law concerning common mistake should go the same way as it has in the United Kingdom (following the *Great Peace* decision). In the meantime, there is already available as a precedent at least one judgment of the Queensland Supreme Court[79] applying the *Great Peace* decision. There is also the Australian case precedent situation that, whilst the Australian courts are no longer bound by decisions of the English courts, decisions of such English courts as the Court of Appeal can be highly persuasive authority in those areas of Australian law where the law is to some extent unclear.

REFLECTIONS ON THE QUESTION POSED

The question posed in the title of this article is: *Has there really been a satisfactory clarification (by the Court of Appeal's Great Peace decision) of what fundamental legal principles apply (when an issue of common mistake is raised)?* It is proposed to examine this question in two segments—firstly, has there been "a clarification" of what fundamental legal principles apply and, secondly (provided of course there is a positive answer to the first question), has this clarification been "satisfactory". This examination is conducted in the context of the law concerning common mistake as it now is in the United Kingdom.

Has there been 'a clarification'?

The answer is clearly yes. The *Great Peace* decision has brought clarity to an area of the law that has been debated for over 50 years. Because of the (English) Court of Appeal's decision in *Great Peace,* there is a now solely a doctrine of common mistake at common law (which is quite narrow and which is based on the House of Lords' decision in *Bell v Lever Brothers*). This new clarity of the law is assisted by the Court of Appeal's enunciation of a new five-stage test for common mistake, details of which have been given above.[80] There is no longer any separate doctrine of common mistake in equity, the Court of Appeal's earlier decision in *Solle v Butcher*—which has caused so much anguish for courts and lawyers over the last 50 years in trying to reconcile same with the House of Lords' decision in *Bell v Lever Brothers*—has been over-ruled. No longer is there the very difficult problem of trying to distinguish Lord Denning's 'fundamental' common mistake from Lord Atkin's common mistake as to quality which makes the thing contracted for essentially different from the thing that it was believed to be.

Henceforth, when common mistake is raised as an issue, the courts will, firstly, examine the express and implied terms of the contract in order to see if the parties can be regarded as having allocated the risk of the pre-contractual mistake. Where the contract is silent—expressly or impliedly—on the aspect of risk allocation, the court will then apply the doctrine of common mistake at common law (as laid down in *Bell v Lever Brothers*). Apart from those situations where there has been a common

79 *Donkin v Official Trustee in Bankruptcy* [2003] QSC 401.

80 See also s 5.1 above as well as *Great Peace Shipping Limited v Tsavliris (International) Limited* [2002] EWCA Civ No. 1407 at para 76.

mistake as to the existence of the subject matter ("res extincta") or a common mistake involving an owner purchasing his or her own property ("res sua"), a party alleging common mistake will only succeed if he or she can satisfy the very narrow and restrictive test for common mistake adopted by the House of Lords in *Bell v Lever Brothers* which is that a common mistake merely as to the *quality* of the subject matter is not sufficient to enable the *common law* to set aside a contract unless '*it is the mistake of both parties, and is to the existence of some quality which makes the thing without the quality essentially different from the thing as it was believed to be.*'[81] As indicated above, Lord Atkin's very narrow test laid down in *Bell v Lever Brothers* is extremely difficult to satisfy.

There has indeed been a 'clarification' of what fundamental legal principles apply when an issue of common mistake is raised.

Has the clarification been 'satisfactory'?

Since the overriding approach of the courts will now be generally to uphold the sanctity of contracts (especially commercial contracts) and to imply an assumption of risk (by a particular party) from the circumstances, it is reasonable to assume that there will in future be even less scope for the application of the common law doctrine of common mistake and hence even less likelihood of contracts being held to be void. All this is very good for legal certainty. However it is acknowledged that the complete removal of the remedial flexibility previously enjoyed by the courts (such flexibility having arisen as a result of *Solle v Butcher*) may cause difficulties in that the court no longer has the discretion, in deserving individual cases, to impose a just and equitable solution in lieu of the strict legal position that applies at common law.

Lord Phillips was not unaware of this aspect and did address it in his judgment in the following terms:

> We can understand why the decision in *Bell v Lever Brothers Ltd* did not find favour with Lord Denning. An equitable jurisdiction to grant rescission on terms where a common fundamental mistake has induced a contract gives greater flexibility than a doctrine of common law which holds the contract void in such circumstances. Just as the Law Reform (Frustrated Contracts) Act 1943 was needed to temper the effect of the common law doctrine of frustration, so there is scope for legislation to give greater flexibility to our law of mistake than the common law allows.[82]

Whilst it cannot be denied that the 'flexibility' which accompanies the court's equitable jurisdiction has enabled justice to be done in some deserving individual cases in the past, the proper way to allow a court to again have an element of discretion and flexibility for such deserving individual cases is (as indicated by Lord Phillips in the above passage) by way of legislation, not by some legally untenable extension of the law of equity as was done in *Solle v Butcher*. Such legislation could, for example, be in the form of a codified doctrine of common mistake which allows for an appropriate element of discretion on the part of the court when determining the terms of an order in a matter in which common mistake has been raised as an

81 *Bell v Lever Brothers Ltd* [1932] 1 AC 161 at 218. Emphasis added.
82 *Great Peace Shipping Limited v Tsavliris (International) Limited* [2002] EWCA Civ No. 1407 at para 161.

issue. Such code could also provide some sort of protection for innocent third parties.

The 'clarification' of what fundamental legal principles apply when an issue of common mistake is raised has indeed been 'satisfactory'. Thus, the overall answer to the question posed in the title of this article—*Has there really been a satisfactory clarification (by the Court of Appeal's Great Peace decision) of what fundamental legal principles apply (when an issue of common mistake is raised)?*—is yes.

CONCLUSION

The significance of the *Great Peace* decision is that it has provided a much-needed and satisfactory clarification of the law concerning common mistake. A decision of the (English) Court of Appeal that was inconsistent with a House of Lord's decision (and which accordingly has caused legal uncertainty for over 50 years) has been overruled by the Court of Appeal itself. In the English court hierarchy, the House of Lords is the final court of appeal for both criminal and civil cases and hence superior (in the court hierarchy) to the Court of Appeal. Legal certainty has been maintained in that not only is it now easier to know what fundamental legal principles apply when an issue of common mistake is raised but also henceforth the approach of the House of Lords to common mistake—as laid down in *Bell v Lever Brothers*—will apply even to cases brought in the Court of Appeal.

Obviously, if a similar situation again arose, Tsavliris (or a party in a similar situation) would protect itself by insisting that, in its hire contract with the other party, there be an express 'condition' that the ship to render assistance is in fact at the location understood by the contracting parties, otherwise Tsavliris has the right to rescind the contract without penalty. Unfortunately, in the *Great Peace* scenario, this was not done and the reason why (namely that the contractual arrangements were made by non-lawyers with insufficient time available to cover all bases) is indicated by the lawyers for Tsavliris in the following comment:

> It was, of course, fairly unusual for a salvor to be contracting in a merchant vessel to provide stand-by services, and it was also unfortunate, to say the least, that the negotiations between the broker and the manager of Great Peace took place on the assumption that the Great Peace was in fact in close proximity to the Cape Providence and her true position was not established before the contract was concluded. While from the legal perspective it is very useful to have such a comprehensive and thorough review of the law of mistake undertaken by the Court of Appeal, it is very doubtful if any of the active participants involved in Greece, London and Hong Kong during the night of September 24/25 1999 would have thought that three years later the Court of Appeal, led by the Master of the Rolls, would deliver a 69-page judgment analysing the consequences of their actions.[83]

Nevertheless, one consolation for parties seeking redress as a result of some contractual situation is that the *Great Peace* decision only concerns 'common mistake'. Just as 'common mistake' was only one of the issues in *Bell v Lever Brothers*,[84] so

83 See the letter from Roland Jackson of Shaw and Croft, Solicitors, London entitled *Why the Great Shipping case incurred 69 pages of judgment* in Lloyd's List International of 23 October 2003.

84 See e.g. Catharine MacMillan, *How temptation led to mistake: an explanation of Bell v Lever Brothers, Ltd* (2003) 19 LQR 625.

might parties in other situations similarly find that, even though in their particular scenario common mistake is an issue but which cannot be established, nevertheless they might still be able to obtain relief from the courts because there are some other grounds (such as frustration, misrepresentation or unconscionability) that can be established.

Whilst the House of Lords' decision in *Bell v Lever Brothers* and the Court of Appeal's decision in *Solle v Butcher* are arguably the most significant 'common mistake' cases of the twentieth century, the (English) Court of Appeal's decision in *Great Peace* is now (at least to date) arguably the most significant 'common mistake' case of the twenty-first century—and it has arisen out of an international trade law situation.

POSTSCRIPT

Since the preparation of this article, there has been an important Australian judgment concerning common mistake, following the English Court of Appeal's judgment in *Great Peace Shipping Ltd v Tsavliris Salvage (International) Ltd*.[85] This has been the judgment of the Queensland Court of Appeal in *Australia Estates Pty Ltd v Cairns City Council*.[86] This judgment was handed down on 2 September 2005, with:

a. *Great Peace Shipping Ltd v Tsavliris Salvage (International) Ltd*[87] being followed and applied;
b. *Bell v Lever Brothers Ltd*[88] being cited;
c. *Solle v Butcher*[89] not being followed.

85 [2002] EWCA Civ 1407.
86 [2005] QCA 328.
87 [2002] EWCA Civ 1407.
88 [1932] AC 161.
89 [1950] 1 KB 671.

WHOSE LIFE IS IT ANYWAY? A COMMENT ON THE TERRI SCHIAVO CASE

*Meredith Blake**

ABSTRACT

The plight of the American woman Terri Schiavo provides the contextual background for this discussion which looks at the particular challenge to the law posed by patients in a persistent vegetative state (PVS). This paper begins with an analysis of this condition, aiming to indicate that its characteristics are such that the issue of decision-making in relation to patients in a PVS is one of such ethical sensitivity that the law in this area should respond carefully and thoroughly to these concerns. The discussion then focuses upon the legal approach to the management of such patients as it has developed within existing US case law, looking to the rationale behind the existing legal framework. Following from this, the paper takes a comparative approach to the issue, exploring the English and Australian judicial attitudes to decision making with respect to the adult incompetent patient, having particular regard to relevant developments in human rights jurisprudence. The discussion ultimately concludes with a comparison between the concepts of substituted judgment and best interests, and concludes that the former concept, whilst evidentially problematic, is not, like the latter, fundamentally flawed.

INTRODUCTION

A rare opportunity to explore the ethical and legal dilemmas associated with the management of the permanently comatose patient surfaced in March last year when the case of American woman Terri Schiavo attracted international attention. By that stage the case had an "extensive legal history",[1] dating back to February 2000 when a Florida trial court decided that Schiavo was in a PVS and that her feeding tube should be removed.[2] Schiavo's plight subsequently became the subject of a series of appeals by her parents seeking reversal of this finding. A second extensive hearing in October 2003 confirmed the original ruling[3] and ordered that the hospice managing Schiavo must cease supplying nutrition and hydration through her feeding tube. At that point the legislature made the first of two interventions into the legal fray. The first of these involved the Florida legislature enacting new laws

* Senior Lecturer, School of Law, University of Notre Dame Australia.

1 Per Altenbernd J in Case No. 2D05–968 (Second District Court of Appeal, March 16, 2005).

2 *Re Guardianship of Schiavo* 780 So 2d 176 (Fla 2d DCA 2001). The court followed decisions of the Florida Supreme Court which had decided that the express right of privacy in art 1, s 23 of the Florida Constitution gave both competent and incompetent persons the right to forgo life-prolonging procedures (*John F. Kennedy Mem'l Hosp v Bludworth*, 452 So. 2d 921 (Fla 1984)).

3 *Re Guardianship of Schiavo* 851 So 2d 182 (Fla. 2d DCA 2003).

allowing the Governor to stay the withdrawal.[4] The Supreme Court subsequently found that this legislation was unconstitutional as a violation of the separation of powers under the Florida Constitution.[5] In March 2005, in a final attempt to prevent the withdrawal of their daughter's feeding tube, Schiavo's parents filed a motion for a declaration that the trial court's judgment of February 2000 was void.[6] In denying this motion the District Court for the Middle District of Florida[7] considered whether a second piece of legislation introduced by Congress mandated that injunctive relief be granted to the plaintiffs to enable them to have a full trial on the merits of their claims.[8] The court decided against granting this relief.

In the Court of Appeals for the Eleventh Circuit,[9] the question whether the District Court had erred in not granting the injunction was answered in the negative.[10] At a later hearing it considered the terms of the legislation and concluded that it was unconstitutional, as it sought to force the District Court to engage in a "de novo" review of Schiavo's claims. In so doing the Circuit Court (by majority) found that the provisions constituted "legislative dictation of how a federal court should exercise its judicial functions" and therefore "invades the province of the judiciary and violates the separation of powers principle".[11]

The focus of this paper is not upon the constitutional issue of separation of powers, determinative though this was of the legislative and legal attempts to reinsert Schiavo's feeding tube. The concern is instead upon the law which permitted the court to take the decision to withdraw the tube,[12] an issue which both the majority and minority members of the Circuit Court of Appeals considered. It is this aspect of the case which is most relevant to this discussion, which explores the legal issues arising from the management of patients in a persistent vegetative state. Whilst the family feuding[13] and the political intervention guaranteed public exposure of Terri Schiavo's plight, the moral debate which accompanied the

4 Chapter 2003–418.

5 *Bush v Schiavo* 885 So.2d 321 (Fla 2004). The court decided that the legislation was not a valid general law according to *Dept. of Legal Affairs v Sanford-Orlando Kennel Club*.

6 On the basis that the trial court, and not a guardian, made the decision as to what Schiavo would elect to do in light of her PVS, and on the basis that their daughter was denied a full and fair opportunity to defend her rights.

7 2005 U.S. Dist. LEXIS 4265 (March 22, 2005).

8 Pub.L.109–3.

9 *Schiavo v Schiavo* No. 05–11556 (March 23, 2005).

10 The plaintiffs also added a number of further grounds to the appeal based around the Due Process clause of the constitution. One of these was that the procedural aspect of the Due Process clause requires that decision to remove hydration and nutrition from an incapacitated person must be supported by clear and convincing evidence and that there was not enough evidence in that case to meet the standard. This argument was rejected.

11 *T Schiavo (incap), ex rel R Schindler v M Schiavo*, US Court of Appeals Eleventh Circuit, March 30, 2005, No 05–11628 at p9. The two dissenting members of that Court found that the legislation in question did not raise a separation of powers problem; rather it was a situation where "Congress has prescribed a particular approach to a particular problem in the general domain of federal jurisdiction, without presuming to dictate—in any respect—our performance of a court's essential function: 'to say what the law is'."

12 According to *Re Guardianship of Browning*, 568 So.2d 4 (Fla. 1990) there must be "clear and convincing evidence of what her wishes would have been if she could have envisioned her situation whilst still able to make her wishes known"

13 In which her parents were pitted against her former husband, firstly on the matter of the withdrawal of her treatment, and secondly on the custody of her body—see *The Australian*, March 25, 2005. The 11th Circuit Court of Appeals referred to the "passionate inter-family struggle" (per Birch J).

publicity is ultimately most relevant to the law's efforts to deal with medical intervention associated with PVS patients.

A LIFE WORTH LIVING?

If nothing else, the debate provoked by Terri Schiavo's situation serves as a reminder that the difference between a human life not worth saving, and one that is, depends on opinion rather than fact. Terri Schiavo was 26 when in February 1990 she suffered a heart attack which deprived her brain of oxygen for approximately five minutes. Although comatose, her chances for some sort of recovery were initially thought to be quite good, and she was given intensive therapy in the hope of bringing her out of her coma. Schiavo's parents maintained till the end that she was capable of some recovery and that she had, in fact, communicated with them on several occasions. Images distributed on the world wide web of Schiavo apparently smiling in response to her mother were utilised by the pro-life lobby as evidence that she was, in fact, conscious.

Most of the medical opinion,[14] however, indicated that she was in a persistent vegetative state.[15] The distinguishing features of this condition involve an irregular but cyclic state of sleeping and waking unaccompanied by any evidence of attention or inattention or learned responses.[16] It is a condition of permanent unconsciousness, and as such raises the critical issue of the difference between human life and human personhood, consciousness (and particularly the capacity to be self-conscious) being regarded by many as essential to the latter.[17] For many utilitarian ethicists personhood is the primary determinant in the construction of the morality regime applicable to the medical treatment of human beings.[18]

The condition also raises the issue of what is meant by "permanent"[19]—this is a presumption rather than a certainty, and there remain lingering doubts as to how acceptable that presumption is.[20] The prospect of recovery, however unlikely,

---

14 See *Re Guardianship of Schiavo* So 2d, 2005 (Fla. 2d DCA) and the reference to the "highly qualified physicians" who testified as to Schiavo's condition. Also note the conclusion of Dr Jay Wolfson, appointed a special guardian ad litem for Mrs Schiavo: he was unable to independently observe any "consistent, repetitive, intentional, reproducible interactive and aware activities"—see *Re Guardianship of Schiavo* So 2d, 2005 (Fla. 2d DCA).

15 First identified by B Jennett and F Plum—"Persistent Vegetative State after Brain Damage" (1972) 1 Lancet 734.

16 Such patients, although lacking consciousness, are capable of movement and retain both cranial nerve and spinal reflexes. There are therefore degrees of vegetativeness—see Mason and McCall Smith *Law and Medical Ethics* at p394.

17 See R E Cranford and D R Smith—"Consciousness: The Most Critical Moral (Constitutional) Standard for Human Personhood" (1987) 13 Am J Law Med 233—"Consciousness is the most critical moral, legal and constitutional standard, not for human life itself, but for human personhood".

18 See, e.g., Peter Singer *Practical Ethics*, 2nd ed., Cambridge University Press (1993) and Jonathan Glover, *Causing Death and Saving Lives*, Penguin (1977).

19 Note that the original use of the term "persistent" contemplated recovery from that state. Some academics have argued that any discussion of the management of the condition with a view to the ending of life should not be based on the term "persistent" as originally understood, but instead the term "permanent"—see, e.g., Mason and McCall Smith, ibid, at p395.

20 The Multi-society Task Force in America defined the persistent vegetative state as a vegetative state present one month after acute traumatic or non-traumatic brain injury; it concluded that a permanent state can be assumed if the patient has been vegetative for one year—see Multi-society Task Force on PVS "Medical Aspects of the Persistent Vegetative State" (1994) 330 New Engl J Med 1499.

exercises a constant influence on the perception of what is the appropriate way to manage such patients. Indeed patients in a persistent vegetative state may have a life expectancy of many years if they are given hydration and nutrition and remain free from potentially fatal infection. They are therefore not "terminally ill" on most people's understanding of that term.

There are therefore several reasons why the Terri Schiavo, and PVS cases generally, represent a troubling ethical and legal dilemma. Three essential characteristics are particularly relevant in this respect:

Medical treatment or the basic necessities of life?

Terri Schiavo, like many PVS patients, required no assistance other than the provision of intravenously supplied hydration and nutrition.[21] Food and water do not naturally fall within the concept of "medical treatment". It is arguable that everyone has a basic right to food and water and to refuse to supply this to a person is inhumane. Put this way, the provision of sustenance seems a more fundamental humanitarian obligation than the provision of medical treatment. In *Airedale NHS Trust v Bland*,[22] the House of Lords accepted that the provision of hydration and nutrition did represent medical treatment,[23] a view essential to their conclusion that it was lawful to withdraw treatment in that case.[24]

The US case law indicates a similar approach to the issue,[25] as does Australian law.[26] However it is a view rejected by Catholic doctrine which only permits withdrawal of *extraordinary* treatment, which the provision of food and water is not.[27]

Reflexive versus directed reactions

Many PVS patients are able to breathe independently, a consequence of the fact that, whilst the upper cortex of the brain is dead, the brain stem is functioning. Human beings in such a condition have been described as:

21 On occasions she had required antibiotics.

22 [1993] 1 All ER 821.

23 Rejecting the Official Solicitor's argument that artificial hydration and nutrition were of a different order from medical treatment.

24 Because the legality of the withdrawal was discussed in the context of the doctor's duty. A doctor has a duty to act in the best interests of the patient.

25 See *Cruzan v Director, Missouri Dept of Health* (1990) 110 S Ct (US Sup Ct) per Justices O'Connor ("Whether or not the techniques used to pass food and water into the patient's alimentary tract are termed 'medical treatment' it is clear that they all involve some degree of intrusion and restraint") and Brennan ("No material distinction can be drawn between the treatment to which Nancy Cruzan continues to be subject—artificial nutrition and hydration—and any other medical treatment"). See also Council on Ethical and Judicial Affairs of the American Medical Association", *Current Opinions*, Opinion 2.20 (1989)—"Life-prolonging medical treatment includes medication and artificially or technologically supplied respiration, hydration or nutrition". But see John Keown, "Restoring Moral and Intellectual Shape to the Law after Bland" (1997) 113 LQR 481 who doubts Lord Goff's analogy between tube-feeding and mechanical ventilation. He is of the view that even if the patient has lost the ability to swallow, the tube is not treating anything. Also note *Re Conroy* in which the New Jersey Supreme Court held that there was a difference between artificial feeding and spoon-feeding.

26 See Gardner; *Re BWV* [2003] VSC 173 at [78].

27 See R Gillon in "Editorial" (1981) 7 J of ME 56.

> the ultimate tragedy in human life—a human being who is alive in the cardiovascular sense in that he or she can breathe and maintain a heart beat, and who is, equally, not brain stem dead, but who, at the same time, has no contact with the outside world and will never have such contact again.[28]

However, the fact that many such patients exhibit reflexive reactions to certain stimuli can suggest that they *are* engaging with the outside world.

Incapacity to feel pain

Whilst PVS patients are capable of limited reflexive movement they are incapable of feeling pain. Their treatment regime is therefore unaccompanied by ordinary medical measures directed toward the relief of suffering. As a consequence, the doctrine of double effect, whereby death may be legally brought about as a result of pain relief, is not applicable.[29]

Taken together these characteristics point towards the central concern raised by the medical treatment of PVS patients. This is the fear that the withdrawal of treatment constitutes a form of euthanasia. This is a term as infamous for its emotional resonance as its uncertainty, but it essentially involves the intentional bringing about of death for beneficent reasons.[30] For current purposes, a useful definition is provided by Jonathan Glover, who claims that it means:

> killing someone, on account of his [or her] distressing physical or mental state, where this is thought to be in his [or her] best interests.[31]

In practical application, the term can be used to describe a wide range of situations, including the withdrawal of life-sustaining treatment, assisted suicide and mercy killing.[32] Any specification commonly resides in the use of either or both of the terms "active/passive" and "voluntary/involuntary".[33] The former term has been applied to distinguish between active intervention in hastening death, and that of withdrawal of treatment. The latter refers to the distinction between requested assistance

28 Mason and McCall Smith at p395.

29 See *R v Adams* [1957] Crim LR 365 and *Airedale National Health Service Trust v Bland* [1993] 1 All ER 821. Also see P Foot, "Morality as a System of Hypothetical Imperatives", *Philosophical Review* (1972).

30 Mason and McCall Smith (at p414) refer to *Stedman's Medical Dictionary* which contains two definitions—a quiet, painless death and the intentional putting to death by artificial means of persons with incurable or painful disease. They state that the former is etymologically correct but the latter more closely mirrors the public view. They also point out that "To hide behind semantics is obfuscatory. Any useful discussion of euthanasia must accept the, admittedly unpalatable, fact that it involves some form of killing."

31 See J Glover, *Causing Death and Saving Lives* (Penguin Books, 1977) at p182. Note that the literature indicates a number of definitions, some of which use emotive terminology, avoided by Glover in his definition.

32 In *Airedale National Health Trust v Bland* [1993] 1 All ER, Lord Goff specifically excludes the first two situations from the ambit of euthanasia, but in *DPP v Pretty* it was clear that the House of Lords felt that assisted suicide raised the spectre of euthanasia. Mercy killing is defined by Kennedy and Grubb in *Medical Law* as "a deliberate act done by a doctor to bring about the death of a patient at the patient's request", and is distinguished from physician-assisted suicide on the basis of the degree of assistance proferred by the doctor. In their view, therefore, mercy killing would not include the killing of another in their best interests.

33 See G Zdenkowski, "The International Covenant on Civil and Political Rights and Euthanasia", 1997 UNSW Law Journal 170 at 171 for five different situations which might be regarded as representing euthanasia.

in death,[34] and assistance taken without an expression of preference by the individual.[35]

We are here concerned with the possible death, ostensibly for his or her own good, of someone who cannot express any views on the matter and who must therefore use a proxy[36] to express any view that his or her life be ended through the termination of life-sustaining treatment. Although on some views the withdrawal of treatment does not represent euthanasia,[37] it is very difficult to maintain an argument that in such circumstances death is not brought about intentionally for the good of the patient.[38] It could quite feasibly be argued that the withdrawal of treatment from such patients does constitute a form of passive, non-voluntary euthanasia.

There are therefore good reasons to be cautious in the legal approach to the management of PVS patients. Society has long shown itself to be reluctant to confront issues arising from the management of the brain damaged adult. This can be contrasted with the apparent acceptance of the selective non-treatment of newborns.[39] Legal authority indicates that the very poor quality of the infant's life is a consistent factor in this acceptance.[40] The circumstances of the PVS adult patient are similarly indicative of a poor quality of life. One reason for the differing approach to the neonate cases might be accounted for by the argument from suffering—the newborns in question are inevitably facing pain and suffering through the intrusive treatment required to keep them alive,[41] whilst the PVS patient is unable to feel pain. Another alludes to an intuitive response based on the difference between a life not really begun and one which might have been in full flower when the brain damage occurs. Ronald Dworkin[42] refers to the critical interests (beliefs as to the value of life) and experiential interests (such as hobbies) which formerly competent persons have developed; interests which a neonate has had no opportunity to develop.[43]

The management of the PVS patient is therefore attended by emotional responses and intuitive moral uncertainty. Thus, despite the fact that hundreds of cases concerning life-sustaining medical treatment are heard every year by the

34 Thus engaging the issue of a valid consent. Consent obtains its force from the value of autonomy (see below): a valid consent in law requires the patient to understand the treatment, to voluntarily exercise consent and to know the basic nature and purpose of the treatment—see *Re C (adult: refusal of treatment)* [1994] 1 All ER 819.

35 Usually because the patient is incompetent to make that decision. See Glover, *Causing Death and Saving Lives*: non-voluntary euthanasia is "killing someone . . . where he is either not in a position to express any views on whether he wants to be killed". Involuntary euthanasia refers to killing someone against their express wishes, a practice widely condemned and not able to utilize many of the moral and legal arguments supporting voluntary euthanasia.

36 Such as a family member or member of the attending medical team.

37 This is the deontological approach adopted in *Airedale National Health Service Trust v Bland* [1993], largely dependent upon ethical views such as those espoused by Phillippa Foot.

38 Although see Lord Goff in *Airedale NHS Trust v Bland* in which he rejects the idea that a doctor in withdrawing treatment in such circumstances intends death. The doctor is, in his view, only allowing "nature to take its course".

39 See Mason and McCall Smith at p393 and Kennedy and Grubb at p2157.

40 A quality of life test in relation to neonates was first broached in *Re B (a minor) (wardship:medical treatment)* [1981] 1 WLR 1421, and refined in *Re J* [1990] 3 All ER 821.

41 See, e.g., *Re C (a minor) (medical treatment)* [1998] Lloyd's Rep Med 1.

42 *Life's Dominion, An Argument about Abortion and Euthanasia*, Harper Collins (1993).

43 Such interests are associated with autonomous beings. Dworkin argues that critical interests survive incompetency.

American judiciary,[44] the ethical and legal issues raised by the PVS patient are not yet resolved. Of particular significance in this context is the issue of who can make the decision as to whether to withdraw treatment, and the basis upon which that decision is made.

SUBJECTIVITY AND SUBSTITUTED JUDGMENT

Given the particular characteristics and prognosis of the PVS patient, particular scrutiny should be directed to the role of the decision-maker, and the justification for any decision to withdraw treatment. The condition raises fundamental questions about the value and purpose of life. This fact creates implications for the decision-making process; the most obvious being whether the decision-maker is able to separate his or her own perceptions about what is a worthwhile life in dealing with the question of whether to withdraw treatment from another person. The law in most western jurisdictions has sought to develop "objective" and "patient subjective" approaches to the issue; treatment can be withdrawn either on the basis that it is in the "best interests" of the patient, or that the patient had expressed a wish that treatment be withdrawn in such circumstances, through a common law or legislative "living will". This essentially reflects the current position in England, although the position in several Australian jurisdictions is less clear.[45]

A series of US cases have sought to expand upon this two-tiered approach, relying on the human rights jurisprudence of the US Constitution, in particular the due process clause of the 14th amendment. That clause has been interpreted to protect certain liberty interests of the individual, including a right to privacy protecting bodily integrity.[46] These cases have utilised this protection as a basis for a subjective approach to decision-making in relation to the permanently incompetent adult, specifically through the mechanism of "substituted judgment".

It was *Re Quinlan*[47] where this concept was first broached in this context. The subject of the action before the New Jersey Supreme Court was a young woman described as being in a chronic vegetative state[48] and dependent upon ventilator support. The Court unanimously found that, were she competent, Quinlan's right to privacy[49] would have allowed her to refuse ventilation,[50] and that this right endured when incompetent. The finding indicates a preference for subjective

44 Between 1975 and 1989, between 2,900 and 7,000 life-sustaining medical treatment cases were heard and some 50 to 75 went to appeal. See T L Hafemeister et al, "The Judicial Role in Life-Sustaining Medical Treatment Decisions" (1991) 7 Issues in L & M 53.

45 See pp 80–5 of this chapter.

46 In *Roe v Wade* 410 US 113 (1973), the right of privacy was firmly established under the due process clause. It was utilised in that case in the sense of protecting an individual's personal autonomy.

47 (1976) 429 US 922.

48 At that point the term "persistent vegetative state" and knowledge of its pathology had yet to be established within the international medical community.

49 Under the New Jersey State constitution.

50 It is therefore regarded as establishing the now clearly accepted proposition that there is a right under certain circumstances to refuse life-sustaining medical treatment. It also endorsed drawing a distinction between suicide and the passive withdrawal of life support.

decision-making in such situations.[51] To this end, the court cited the importance of evidence from her friends as to what her wishes would be.[52] The basic tenet of proxy decision-making was thereby endorsed.

These two features of the *Quinlan* decision were further explored in *In the Matter of Claire Conroy*.[53] This case concerned an elderly woman who, although not in a persistent vegetative state, was:

> . . . severely demented, was unable to respond to verbal stimuli, and . . . had no higher functioning or consciousness.[54]

In this respect the specific facts of the case can be distinguished from the situation of the PVS patient; the court specifically stated that the issue in question was "the circumstances under which life-sustaining treatment may be withheld or withdrawn from incompetent, institutionalised, elderly patients with severe and permanent mental and physical impairments and a limited life expectancy".[55] The case remains relevant to the present discussion, however, because in dealing with this specific issue the court put in place a generic framework for decision-making in relation to adult incompetent patients.

Once again the underlying aim behind that framework was, as much as possible, to respect both aspects of the patient's right to bodily integrity—the right to consent to medical intervention and the right to refuse it. It therefore sought to determine and effectuate, insofar as possible, the decision that the patient would have made if competent. It is worth comparing the position of the Jehovah's Witness patient who has clearly indicated, prior to his or her incompetency, a desire to refuse life-saving blood transfusions. Absent any strict instructions, knowledge that a patient is a devout Jehovah's Witness may necessarily require a substituted decision to that effect. The rationale of the decision-making process can therefore be contrasted with the traditional doctrine of parens patriae by which the court has powers to act in the best interests of an individual. The essential difference is between subjectivist and objectivist models of decision-making.

The court's preference for a subjective approach in *Re Quinlan* ultimately informed the hierarchical structure of decision-making which it introduced. Under this structure life-sustaining treatment may be withheld or withdrawn from an incompetent patient when it is *clear* that the particular patient would have refused the treatment under the circumstances involved. This mandate reflects the essence of the "subjective" test, where there are clear instructions from the patient, given either through a living will document or through an oral directive to a family member, friend or health care provider.[56] Given the absence of clear instructions from Claire Conroy, this test was not satisfied on the facts. The court therefore held that life-sustaining treatment could be withheld or withdrawn from a patient in her situation

---

51 The case also stands as an example of court advocation of shared decision-making in such circumstances; although her father was appointed her guardian and given authority to withdraw treatment, this was subject to the agreement of her doctors and the hospital ethics committee.

52 Although the court concluded that this evidence was insufficiently conclusive, it was accepted 10 years later.

53 (1985) 486 A 2d 1209 (NJ Supreme Court).

54 Per Schrieber J.

55 At p1220.

56 Exercised either via a durable power of attorney or appointment of a proxy authorising a particular person to make the decisions on the patient's behalf.

if either of two "best interests" tests—a "limited objective" or a "pure objective" test—was satisfied. The former applied where there was no formal statement of intent from the patient but where there was some trustworthy evidence that the patient would have refused the treatment[57] and the decision-maker (a proxy) is satisfied that it is clear that the burdens of the patient's continued life with the treatment outweigh the benefits of that life for him.[58] In the absence of trustworthy evidence, or any evidence at all, that the patient would have declined the treatment, life-sustaining treatment could still be withdrawn on the basis of the "pure objective" test,[59] where the net burdens of the patient's life with the treatment clearly and markedly outweighed the benefits that the patient was deriving from life.[60] On the facts the court determined that the evidence did not satisfy any of these three tests.

The "limited objective" test was subsequently subjected to criticism; the label appeared to undermine the commitment of the court to give effect wherever possible to the views and values of the patient. It was re-termed "substituted judgment" to reflect this preferred subjective interpretation.[61] The new term was intended to indicate that, properly understood, the test requires that the decision-maker should take account of the views and values of the now incompetent person as a guide in determining what the now incompetent person would have chosen for himself. The sort of evidence required to establish those views and values, and the standard of proof to be applied to such evidence, remained, however, uncertain.

A much anticipated opportunity to clarify the substituted judgment test arose in *Cruzan v Missouri*,[62] a decision which went on appeal to the US Supreme Court. Nancy Cruzan had been in a PVS for three years when her parents requested that feeding and hydration be discontinued.[63] The Missouri Supreme Court decision rejected their application, holding that under the common law of Missouri for there to be a withdrawal of treatment, there had to be "clear and convincing evidence" to the effect that the patient would not wish, under the circumstances which obtain, to be treated. They found that this evidence was not present on the facts. The court

57 Discerned from general statements and reactions of the patient.

58 Further the recurring, unavoidable and severe pain of the patient's life should be such that the effect of administering life-sustaining treatment would be inhumane. This requirement of the presence of pain (as opposed to other factors such as continuing and indefinite loss of dignity) has been critically discussed by academics—see E Keyserlinck, *Sanctity of Life or Quality of Life* (1979).

59 Comprises the situation where the patient may never have considered the issue of life-sustaining treatment. In such cases, a surrogate decision-maker cannot presume that treatment decision made by a third party on the patient's behalf will further the patient's right to self-determination. The State has parens patriae powers over the incompetent person and therefore the courts can allow a decision to be made for an incompetent that serve the incompetent's best interests. This authority permits the state to authorise guardians to withhold or withdraw life-sustaining treatment from an incompetent patient if it is manifest that such action would further the patient's best interests in a narrow sense of the phrase, even though the subjective test may not be satisfied. The test as explained in *Conroy* has been criticised for limiting the assessment of "burden" to the experience of pain by the patient. Later cases and academic writings have referred to the significance of the diminished value of dignity in such circumstances, even in the absence of pain—see, eg, Kennedy and Grubb, op. cit. at p2104, and Keyserlinck.

60 The court took the view that more wide-ranging powers to make decisions about other people's lives would create an intolerable risk for socially isolated and defenceless people suffering from physical or mental handicaps.

61 See *Re Jobes* (1987) which also concerned a PVS patient. Although there was no evidence that she had made a prior decision concerning her treatment, the NJ Supreme Court permitted her family members to decide what treatment she should receive on the basis of the substituted judgment test.

62 (1990) 497 US 261.

63 Unlike Karen Quinlan, Nancy Cruzan did not require the assistance of a ventilator.

further held that under the State Constitution, a citizen's right to liberty and equal protection[64] did not confer a right to privacy.[65] As a consequence there was no right to have nutrition and hydration terminated.

The decision did not appear to support the notion of "substituted judgment". The question then became whether the Supreme Court would find that this was unconstitutional given the due process clause of the 14th amendment. As a starting point the majority (per Rehnquist CJ) assumed for the purposes of the case that a competent person has a constitutionally protected right to refuse lifesaving hydration and nutrition as a part of the 14th Amendment "liberty interest". Additionally they found an incompetent patient's "liberty" interest under the 14th Amendment to the US Constitution required the application of a substituted judgment test. However the Supreme Court went on to affirm (by a 5/4 margin) that the Missouri law requiring "clear and convincing evidence" of the patient's wishes was consistent with this constitutional guarantee. Rehnquist CJ referred to the evidence adduced which "consisted primarily of Nancy Cruzan's statements made to a house mate about a year before her car accident that she would not want to live should she face life as a 'vegetable', and other observations to the same effect. The observations did not deal in terms with withdrawal of medical treatment or of hydration and nutrition." He went on to state:

> We do not think the Due Process Clause requires the State to repose judgment on these matters with anyone but the patient herself . . . there is not automatic assurance that the view of close family members will necessarily be the same as the patient's would have been had she been confronted with the prospect of her situation while competent.[66]

Cruzan therefore did not deliver the clarification required in connection with the substance and working of the substituted judgment test. Whilst holding that the due process clause of the 14th amendment of the Constitution mandated such a test, a simultaneous finding that the evidence required to satisfy such a test should be placed at the highest level of "clear and convincing", suggests that the only room left for subjective decision-making in connection with the incompetent patient is where there is an anticipated refusal of such treatment, or a living will.[67]

Subsequently, the Supreme Court of Pennsylvania dealt with the case of *Re Fiori*,[68] concerning a man who had been in a PVS for 15 years and was tube-fed. The case merits consideration in light of its clear endorsement of the "substituted judgment" test, and its recognition that a prior express statement is not a prerequisite to the application of this test. The Court stated that the surrogate decision maker can consider the "patient's personal value system for guidance" where there was no expressed view as to the use of life support. This is clearly significant where the patient in question is in a persistent vegetative state, and is one who has never clearly expressed a preference for termination of treatment. The view taken was that the patient's interests are sufficiently protected by the surrogate or proxy consent of a close family member, reinforced by the written approval of two physicians.

---

64 Under Art 1 and ss 2 and 10 of the Missouri State Constitution.

65 The state court found that the right to privacy did not apply to require the treatment to be withdrawn. This right had been developed under the US constitution by the Supreme Court to protect the right to contraception within marriage and the right to abortion.

66 This approach was subsequently rejected by all states other than Missouri and New York.

67 See Kennedy and Grubb, ibid. at p2146.

68 (1995) 652 A 2d 1350.

That view was challenged by the circumstances of the *Schiavo* litigation. When the question of whether Terri Schiavo's nutrition tube should be withdrawn first came to trial, the clear disagreement between her guardian (her husband) and her parents prompted the court to take the decision of whether Schiavo would have elected to forgo further use of the tube.[69] It decided that there was clear and convincing evidence to that effect. That conclusion was challenged by Schiavo's parents right to the end of the lengthy litigation.[70] Their appeals served to isolate two as yet unresolved questions arising from the concept of substituted judgment.

Firstly, it remains unsettled as to what evidence is required to satisfy the "substituted judgment" test.[71] *Cruzan* only went so far as to state that the requirement of "clear and convincing evidence" of what the patient would have wanted given his or her situation, is consistent with the US constitution. There is therefore no requirement for states to incorporate this standard of proof in relation to substitute decision-making. Florida, the jurisdiction in which Schiavo's case arose, has adopted such a standard—the law requires "clear and convincing evidence of what her wishes would have been if she could have envisioned her situation while still physically able to make her wishes known".[72] Thus Schiavo's parents' claim[73] that the guarantee of due process requires such a standard was rendered irrelevant. Even given this high standard, the issue of what sort of evidence will provide "clear and convincing" proof of the patient's wishes persists. The majority of the Circuit Court of Appeals refused to revisit the evidence produced in the District Court that was found to be satisfactory. In their view:

> ... there was abundant testimony before the state trial court to prove by that evidentiary standard that Mrs Shiavo would have wanted nutrition and hydration to be withdrawn under these circumstances ... While there was some conflict in the evidence, credibility determinations are within the province of the fact finder ... it is not the role of an appellate court to second-guess credibility determinations.

The court went on to find that even if the sufficiency of the evidence was a proper question for consideration by an appeal court:

> ... there is no substantial question in this case about whether a rational fact finder could have found, as the Florida court did, that there was clear and convincing evidence that Mrs Schiavo would not have wanted nutrition and hydration continued in these circumstances. Given the credibility determinations that the state trial court was authorised to and did make, the evidence clearly was sufficient to meet the clear and convincing evidence standard.

---

69 Under the Florida Constitution the court retains the power to take the decision of whether artificial life support should be terminated when family members cannot agree or when a guardian believes that it would be more appropriate for a neutral judge to make the decision—see, e.g., *Browning*, 543 So. 2d at 269.

70 One of their arguments was that the initial judgment was void because the trial court and not a guardian made the decision as to what Schiavo would elect to do in light of her vegetative state, claiming that this provided insufficient due process and was a violation of her privacy.

71 What constitutes an "expression of intention" for the subjective test? And what evidence can the surrogate use to predict what the patient would have wanted? See *DeGrella v Elston* (1993) 858 SW 2d (Ky Supreme Court).

72 The requirement as set out in *Re Guardianship of Browning*, 568 So. 2d 4 (Fla. 1990)

73 See *Schiavo 1*, 780 So.2d at 178.

The position of the majority, therefore, was that the evidence did satisfy the "clear and convincing" standard, although no specific reason was given for that conclusion.

In finding that the applicants had made out a basis for a rehearing, the dissenting judges disagreed both on the constitutional and the evidential point. In relation to the latter, Tjoflat and Wilson JJ firstly found that there was a "plausible claim" that the Due Process Clause *requires* clear and convincing evidence of an individual's wishes before withdrawal of life-sustaining treatment can be made. They made it clear that "plausible" did not mean that it was a claim certain of success. But they took the view that caution was required given that it was a life-and-death issue. Their finding would therefore have opened the possibility for establishing that standard of proof as a requirement under the constitution, not merely an option.

But it is the second point, that which relates to the substance of the evidence, which is most worthy of attention. The dissenters went on to find that:

> If such a right exists, it is not enough to simply say that the state statute does, in fact, require clear and convincing evidence . . . while it is clear that the state court purported to use the clear and convincing evidence standard, the plaintiffs argue that there is simply insufficient evidence to support its findings under that standard. The relevant question here is whether a rational fact finder could have found by clear and convincing evidence that Mrs Schiavo would have wanted nutrition and hydration to be withdrawn under these circumstances.

By way of a footnote, the judges made the salient point that "To give the plaintiffs the reasoned attention they deserve, and to *develop the certainty the law demands*,[74] we should rehear this case en banc".

The lack of certainty as to what can constitute clear and convincing evidence is the real point of contention here. That the opportunity was not taken in the *Schiavo* case to clarify the issue is therefore unfortunate. There is much to be said for the argument that when evidence of a person's wishes or physical or mental condition is equivocal it is best to err, if at all, in favour of preserving life.

IS THE BEST INTERESTS TEST BETTER?

Given the lingering question of what constitutes sufficient evidence for the purposes of substituted judgment, it is relevant to consider the approach adopted in England and Australia towards the issue of decision-making in relation to the PVS patient. The clear embracing (at least in name) of subjectivism as a basis for decision-making in relation to the incompetent patient, and specifically the PVS patient, in the USA, raises an interesting contrast with the position in these jurisdictions. In England, the issue of the management of PVS patients first arose in the case of *Airedale NHS Trust v Bland*[75] in which the House of Lords decided that it was lawful to withdraw artificial feeding and hydration from a young man in a persistent vegetative state.

---

74 My emphasis.
75 [1993] 1 All ER 821.

Two factors were central to the decision. Firstly the withdrawal of the tube was an omission not a positive act.[76] Secondly, the withdrawal of the treatment was consistent with the doctors' duty—the duty to act only continued insofar as any action was in a patient's best interests; being in a persistent vegetative state, it was no longer in Tony Bland's best interests to be kept alive.[77] Moreover the decision was regarded as one for the treating doctors to take—a subsequent suggestion that relatives had a role to play in the decision[78] has been criticised.[79] The case set a precedent for the clinical management of such patients. Moreover, as a result of the various obiter dicta statements of the law lords on the boundaries between lawful and unlawful assisted deaths, it has remained determinative of English law's approach to euthanasia.

Arguably, the case would not have attracted such judicial attention had Tony Bland exercised an anticipatory refusal of treatment. That he was only seventeen years of age at the time of the accident is no doubt of significance here. Had he indicated his wishes, the treatment might have been withdrawn on the basis of the common law as explained in *Re T* (1992). In that case the Court of Appeal indicated the right of a competent person to exercise their autonomy by refusing, in advance of incompetence, specific treatment in specific circumstances. In *Bland* itself Lord Keith stated that a patient's right to refuse treatment "extends to the situation where the person, in anticipation of his . . . entering into a condition such as PVS, gives clear instructions that in such event he is not to be given medical care, including artificial feeding, designed to keep him alive."[80]

The idea of the anticipatory refusal reflects the "subjective" approach as explained in *Conroy*. Whilst *Conroy* itself prompted many US states to introduce statutory living wills, this has only just happened in England.[81] Any withdrawal of treatment in that jurisdiction has until very recently been on the basis of the common law, which clearly does not allow for the idea of substituted judgment. The recently enacted Mental Capacity Act in that country requires that advance decisions about the withdrawal of "life-sustaining treatment" must be in writing.[82] It also enables a competent person ("the donor"), to appoint an attorney ("the donee") under a lasting power of attorney to make decisions about his or her health care, including the withdrawal of life-sustaining treatment. However the Act makes it

76 Although in *Airedale National Health Trust v Bland* [1993], Lords Mustill, Browne-Wilkinson and Bridge all expressed their dissatisfaction with reliance upon this difference. See Lord Browne-Wilkinson at 885, where he states that distinguishing between acts and omissions may "appear to some to be irrational", and Lord Mustill at 887 where he stated that acts and omissions are "for all relevant purposes indistinguishable" and to adopt the distinction is "only to emphasise a legal structure which is already morally and intellectually misshapen". See J M Finnis, "*Bland*: Crossing the Rubicon" (1993) 109 LQR 329 for a revealing analysis of the *Bland* decision.

77 Cf Lord Mustill in *Airedale National Health Trust v Bland*—he was of the view that such patients have no interests.

78 See Sir Stephen Brown P in *Re G* [1995] 2 FCR 46.

79 See Kennedy and Grubb, *Medical Law* at p2141.

80 *Bland* at 860. Also see Lord Goff at 865. A specific advance decision to die was considered in *Re AK* [2001] 1 FLR 129 (patient suffering from motor neurone disease). See now the Mental Capacity Act 2005 (UK) which gives statutory effect to the common law.

81 See the Mental Capacity Act 2005 (UK).

82 Mental Capacity Act 2005 (UK).

clear that any decision made by the donee must be made in the best interests of the donor[83].

The best interests test therefore remains the basis for discontinuing life-sustaining treatment in relation to PVS patients under English law. This is so whether a person has appointed a donee, or not (in which case the *Bland* best interests test would apply[84]). Given this situation, it is worth considering the compatibility of the best interests approach with the Human Rights Act 1998 (UK). Could it be argued, for example, that the Act requires the introduction of substituted judgment, much as the US Supreme Court has ruled that the due process clause of the 14th amendment requires this (albeit with an uncertain evidentiary standard)?

Such a question requires consideration of the central protections of Articles 2, 3 and 8 of the European Convention on Human Rights, which is the basis of the substantive content of the Human Rights Act. These provisions in turn protect the right to life, to freedom from inhuman and degrading treatment and to respect for private and home life. Jurisprudence of the European Court has established that Article 3 is synonymous with the right to dignity, and Article 8 with the right to autonomy or self-determination[85]. It has been established in both philosophical literature and the case law[86] that these three rights are central matters to be considered in the ending of life in the clinical setting[87].

The compatibility of the law in *Bland* with the Human Rights Act arose for consideration in 2000. Dame Elizabeth Butler-Sloss in the Family Court found that the withdrawal of artificial hydration and nutrition from patients in a persistent vegetative state was not in violation of Article 2.[88] In her view the omission to provide treatment by the medical team would only be incompatible with Article 2 and the right to life where the circumstances were such as to impose a positive obligation on the public authority to take steps to prolong the person's life. There would only be such an obligation if it were in the best interests of the patient to continue to provide such treatment.[89] The President observed that there was no continuing obligation to maintain life in such circumstances in many parts of the

83 Section 4 of the Act lists a number of criteria which must be taken into account by the donor including the donor's past and present wishes and feelings. Any decision is subject to any advance directive made after the lasting power if attorney was exercised.

84 The Court of Protection created by the Act does not have the power to refuse consent to the carrying out or continuation of life-sustaining treatment in relation to an incompetent person.

85 In protecting the right to respect for private, family and home life, Art 8 covers a variety of rights in a wide field of individual activities and has been interpreted as enshrining the general principle of self-determination or autonomy. The Court and Commission have not attempted to comprehensively elucidate on what interests are covered but it is clear that "privacy" includes matters outside what might conventionally be thought to fall within that term and is about more than personal space and confidentiality:

> "In the opinion of the Commission, however, the right to respect for privacy . . . comprises also, to a certain degree, the right to establish and develop relationships with other human beings, especially in the emotional field for the development and fulfilment of one's own personality."

86 See, eg, *Airedale NHS Trust v Bland* [1995] per Lord Goff at 840.

87 See, eg, Kennedy and Grubb, *Medical Law* and John Harris, *The Value of Life: An Introduction to Medical Ethics* (Routledge, 1985).

88 In *NHS Trust A v M* and *NHS Trust B v H* (2000).

89 In English law, the *Bland* decision stands as a precedent for the position that patients in a persistent vegetative state are better off dead than alive, and the cases which have followed that decision have indicated the potential for such a judgment to be made with respect to persons whose physical conditions do not involve the complete sensory deprivation which is definitive of the persistent vegetative state.

world, and therefore this position was consistent with democratic values. Whilst compatibility with Article 2 has been accepted for the present, it is less certain whether the failure of English law to embrace substituted judgment is consistent with Article 8. That latter article is inherently grounded in the principle of self determination and doubts remain as to whether the best interests test is reconcilable with such a principle.[90]

In Australia, there is a relative dearth of authority on the issue of the ending of life in the clinical setting. In most jurisdictions there is guardianship legislation which permits the appointment of guardians in relation to adult incompetent persons. It is clear that in some Australian jurisdictions such guardians have the power to consent to the withdrawal of treatment from PVS patients.[91] However it is not clear whether this power is exercised on the basis of substituted judgment or the best interests of the patient. Given that the guardian in such circumstances is likely to be a person unknown to the patient, it would be a reasonable presumption that the best interests test is the basis for decision making. However in 2003 the Victorian Supreme Court proceeded on the basis that the power exercised by the Public Advocate in that case was on the basis of what the patient would have decided were she competent.[92] In other jurisdictions it is not apparent whether the relevant legislation extends to the withdrawal of life-sustaining treatment.[93] In those jurisdictions it has generally been assumed that the law as set out in *Bland* applies.[94]

In several Australian jurisdictions legislation has been introduced which provides an additional means of surrogate decision-making in relation to incompetent adults.[95] These statutory provisions enable persons, whilst competent, to appoint an attorney or guardian under an enduring power of attorney to make health care decisions, including the withdrawal of life-sustaining treatment.[96] Whilst the legislation in some jurisdictions expressly indicates that the decision as to withdrawal of life-sustaining treatment is to be made on the basis of substituted judgment,[97] the position is less clear in other jurisdictions.[98]

The clear refusal of English law to accept the concept of substituted judgment and the lack of clarity in several Australian jurisdictions on the legal basis for surrogate decision making in relation to incompetent adults have particular ramifications for the PVS patient. This is because the condition is one brought about by trauma to the brain or respiratory system, and usually unassociated with any previous illness

90 See, eg, *Dept. of Health and Community Services (NT) v JWB and SMB* (1992) 175 CLR 218 per Justice Brennan.

91 See the Medical Treatment Act 1988 (Vic.), the Guardianship and Administration Act 2000 (Queensland).

92 *Re BWV (Gardner)* [2003] VSC 173.

93 In particular see the Guardianship and Administration Act (WA), 1990 and "Medical Treatment for the Dying" (Department of Health WA), Discussion Paper, May 2005. Also see the Guardianship Act 1987 (NSW).

94 That is, a court could make a declaration as to whether the withdrawal of treatment was lawful on the basis of the best interests test.

95 The legislation also gives statutory effect to the common law concept of anticipatory refusals through living will provisions. See the Medical Treatment Act (ACT) 1994, the Powers of Attorney Act 1998 (Qu), and the Consent to Medical Treatment and Palliative Care Act 1995 (SA).

96 The Medical Treatment Act 1994 (ACT), the Powers of Attorney Act 1998 (Queensland), the Consent to Medical Treatment and Palliative Care Act 1995 (SA).

97 See, eg, Medical Treatment Act 1994 (ACT).

98 See, eg, Powers of Attorney Act 1998 (Qu).

or condition. Add to this the statistical reality that such patients are likely to be young or middle-aged, and the consequence is that they may not have laid out specific instructions sufficient to satisfy the requirements, whether at common law or under legislation, of the "living will". It may be argued, therefore, that in relation to such patients[99] it is appropriate to introduce a "half-way" house which can accommodate the situation where a decision can be taken on the basis of the proxy's knowledge of that person's values or beliefs. Indeed, as suggested, this might be required as part of the right to respect for privacy under the Human Rights Act 1998 (UK).

This suggestion can be countered by an argument that the best interests test is objective, and therefore not tainted with the risk of abuse as is a test dependent upon a third party's interpretation of the patient's wishes. Certainly, critics of the substituted judgment test have pointed to this risk. Professor Ronald Dworkin, for example, has stated:

> It is a controversial concept, not the least because of the inherent difficulties of attempting to assess what an incompetent patient would have decided were he competent, whether that assessment should be subjective or objective, how it can really differ from a "best interests" approach.[100]

But this criticism is not aimed at the subjectivist approach per se. It is pointing to the evidential difficulties associated with the concept. These are not insignificant, as is evident from the US case law where there is a noticeable absence of authority as to the necessary standard of proof, and what can satisfy that standard. The point is not a trite one, for, as has been pointed out, as much as a subjectivist approach is about respecting an incompetent person's rights, it also runs the risk of robbing that person of rights. To that end it has been argued that in the absence of adequate proof of the patient's wishes, it is naïve to pretend that the right to self-determination serves as the basis for substituted judgment.[101] Indeed it is arguable that in this situation there is an interference with the patient's right to privacy.[102]

However, notwithstanding this valid concern, there is no escaping the reality that the best interests test is not, and never can be, an objective one. In the application of the best interests test to the PVS patient this paternalism is most keenly felt. It is an assessment which inherently involves a quality of life judgment. The reluctance of the US courts to fully embrace an approach which requires them to find that the life of a patient in a PVS is not worth living may be partially due to the influence of the religious right in that country. However discomfort with the concept is also apparent from academic literature and case law.[103] This criticism indicates that the test is both generally and intrinsically flawed. The principal objection is that it is not founded in any clear principle: the concept of "best interests" does not tell us anything in itself, and is arguably a conclusive term susceptible to judicial

---

99 And also in relation to those suffering from AIDS or motor neurone disease—see *The Living Will* (Working Party Report, Age Concern and Centre of Medical Law and Ethics, King's College) (1988).

100 Dworkin, "Law and Medical Experimentation" (1987) 13 MONASH University Law Rev 189 at 200.

101 See *Re Storar* 52 NY 2d 363 at 376–77.

102 See Smith "*In Re Quinlan*: Defining the Basis for Terminating Life Support Under the Right of Privacy" 12 Tulsa LJ (1976).

103 See I Kennedy, *Treat Me Right* (OUP, 1988) and Brennan J in *Dept. of Health and Community Services (NT) v JWB and SMB* (1992) 175 CLR 218.

manipulation dependent upon the circumstances.[104] Further concern has arisen over the paternalistic nature of the test.[105]

In the circumstances under discussion, these criticisms of the best interests approach are particularly resonant. Whilst the evidential problems associated with substituted judgment are significant, they do not critically damage the more persuasive rights-based arguments in favour of a more subjective approach.[106]

CONCLUSION

This paper has sought to analyse some of the legal concerns arising from the *Schiavo* case, and, in so doing, indicate that ethical arguments continue to wage their influence in the public's perception of what is appropriate in the clinical ending of life. However, it is concluded that ultimately the question of who can make decisions in such situations, and on what basis, is a legal question. The subjectivist approach favoured by the USA is purportedly based on fundamental guarantees of self-determination found in the Constitution. In England, a limited subjective approach prevails, one which rejects the doctrine of substituted judgment in favour of a purportedly more objective approach in the form of the best interests test, whilst in Australia there remains uncertainty in several jurisdictions as to whether the doctrine is accepted. The human rights jurisprudence on this point appears to support the compatibility of this test with the right to life guarantee, although it is less evident that it is compatible with the right to respect for private life. Whilst there are clear deficiencies in both approaches in terms of protecting the incompetent person's rights, it is suggested that the best interests test is inherently flawed, whilst the substituted judgment approach is conceptually sound. However, judicial and legislative caution is advised in relation to the evidence needed to satisfy the test—the line between promotion of and interference with human rights is a fine one.

104 The best interests approach has been criticised in connection with sterilisation cases in particular—see *JWB* case.

105 See, in particular, Brennan J in *Dept. of Health and Community Services (NT) v JWB and SMB* (1992) 175 CLR 218, in the context of the sterilisation of incompetent individuals.

106 Support for such an approach can be garnered from the seminal writings of Ronald Dworkin. He draws a distinction between experiential interests (require capacity to have these) and critical interests (survive the loss of capacity). He argues that how and in what circumstances we die is capable of being one of a person's critical interests. Andrew Grubb utilises this idea of critical interests to argue that, notwithstanding the English law's refusal to accept substituted judgment, a person's religious or other moral beliefs could be taken into account in determining whether treatment continues. See Andrew Grubb, "The Persistent Vegetative State: A Duty (Not) To Treat and Conscientious Objection" (1997) 4 EJHL 157.

THE UNITED STATES-AUSTRALIA FREE TRADE AGREEMENT

Jasmine Morris

ABSTRACT

This paper argues that the current treaty-making process in Australia is inadequate to deal with treaties such as Free Trade Agreements (FTAs). The Australia-United States Free Trade Agreement 2004 (Australia-United States FTA) will be used as a device to illustrate the validity of this argument.

The power to enter into treaties that bind Australia is now clearly one that is held exclusively by the Commonwealth Executive. It is a power that is largely unfettered and may even be exercised without the approval of the Cabinet. The necessary formalities are minimal, however the repercussions of entering into a FTA are extensive.

INTRODUCTION

Since 2003 Australia has entered into the Australia-Singapore Free Trade Agreement 2003, Australia-Thailand Free Trade Agreement 2004 and Australia-United States FTA.[1] The increase in the number and scope of FTAs, and their growing influence on domestic activities has led to increasing concern about the treaty-making power. Previously Constitutional commissions and Senate committees exclusively called for reforms, but now it is a popular issue and is generating interest from community and business groups.

Proposals for reform include further consultation and information on proposed FTAs and greater involvement of Parliament in the entering into of FTAs. As FTAs continue to play a significant role in the lives of Australians, it seems that the Executive's power to enter into them should be reformed in a manner that requires greater scrutiny and accountability.

THEORETICAL BACKGROUND—TREATIES

"Treaty" is a term used broadly to define international agreements,[2] which are intended to be binding under international law as defined in Art 2 (1) of the *Vienna*

---

1 Department of Foreign Affairs and Trade, *Free Trade Agreements—Australia's Approach* (2004) <http://www.dfat.gov.au/trade/negotiations/australias_approach.html> at 22 September 2004.

2 A treaty may also be called a "convention", "protocol", "covenant" or "exchange of letters". Department of Foreign Affairs and Trade, *Treaties and Treaty Making* (2004) <http://www.dfat.gov.au/treaties/making/making1.html> at 23 August 2004.

Convention on the Law of Treaties 1969.[3] Treaties are necessary where a matter cannot be adequately addressed by one country alone, for example an agreement in regards to international trade needs to be agreed upon by the two trading countries. The need to act cooperatively at an international level is essential in regards to trade arrangements.

It has been held by the Department of Foreign Affairs and Trade that there are two types of treaty. They are defined in terms of categories.[4] Category A treaties comprise approximately two-thirds of Australia's treaty action, and for the most part are "... uncontroversial in nature and relatively routine in form".[5] They are to be considered by the Joint Standing Committee on Treaties within fifteen sitting days of Parliament, before Australia commits to the treaty.[6] Category B treaties are generally more controversial and can be of "... major political, economic or social significance".[7] As the Government believes that it is important that Category B treaties should be scrutinised, the tabling period is extended to 20 days.[8]

An FTA is a form of treaty, which relates specifically to trade and may be multilateral (agreed by many countries) or bilateral (agreed between two countries only).[9] The *Australia-United States FTA* is a bilateral treaty, which promotes free trade between Australia and the United States. It sets out a preferential agreement, aimed at securing maximum access to each other's markets by lifting trade barriers and removing or lowering import taxes (tariffs) and quotas.[10] In turn, the FTA facilitates the trade of goods and services between countries and boosts their economy.[11] An FTA also encompasses "hidden" trade barriers (which are not essentially linked to import taxes) such as quarantine laws, production and export subsidies and domestic monopolies.[12]

An FTA is classified as a Category B treaty, as its effects are extensive and, in the case of the Australia-United States FTA, require that a large amount of legislation be amended. FTAs must abide by international bodies that not only govern treaty law, but also international trade law set out by the World Trade Organisation.[13] For these reasons, this paper argues that the current treaty-making process is inadequate and requires greater scrutiny from Parliament and input from State and Territory governments.

---

3 K Ryan (ed), *International Law in Australia* (2nd ed, Sydney: The Law Book Company Limited, 1984) 86 and M Dixon, *Textbook on International Law* (4th ed, London: Blackstone Press Limited, 2000) 56.

4 Department of Foreign Affairs and Trade, *Category A and Category B treaties* (2004) <http://www.dfat.gov.au/treaties/making/category.html> at 23 August 2004.

5 Department of Foreign Affairs and Trade, *Category A and Category B treaties*, above n 4.

6 Department of Foreign Affairs and Trade, *Category A and Category B treaties*, above n 4.

7 Department of Foreign Affairs and Trade, *Category A and Category B treaties*, above n 4.

8 Department of Foreign Affairs and Trade, *Category A and Category B treaties*, above n 4.

9 Department of Foreign Affairs and Trade, *Free Trade Agreements* (2004), <http://www.dfat.gov.au/trade/negotiations/wto_agreements.html> at 15 March 2004.

10 However, each individual country maintains its own tariff policy against non-parties to the agreement. Department of Foreign Affairs and Trade, *Free Trade Agreements*, above n 9.

11 Department of Foreign Affairs and Trade, *Free Trade Agreements*, above n 9.

12 Senate Select Committee on the Australia-United States Free Trade Agreement, *Select Committee on the Free Trade Agreement between Australia and the United States of America Final Report* 2004 (Canberra: Senate Select Committee, 2004) 1.

13 Senate Select Committee on the Australia-United States Free Trade Agreement, *Select Committee on the Free Trade Agreement between Australia and the United States of America Final Report*, above n 12, 1.

The term "treaty" and "FTA" may be used interchangeably throughout this paper.

THE AUSTRALIA-UNITED STATES FREE TRADE AGREEMENT

The Australia-United States FTA was first talked about publicly in a speech to the American Australian Association in New York by Michael Thawley,[14] Australia's Ambassador to the United States in December 2000.[15] By mid-2001, the Centre for International Economics and Asia-Pacific Economic Cooperation had released reports[16] which gave support to the Australia-United States FTA, and in August 2001 Prime Minister Howard stated in Parliament that:

> We believe that it would be to the advantage of Australia if we could negotiate a free trade agreement with the Americans . . . [W]e . . . contend that we ought to make an attempt to negotiate . . .[17]

In March 2003 Australian Trade Minister Mark Vaile released Australia's formal list of objectives.[18] Stephen Deady for Australia and Ralph Ives for the United States headed the first round of talks in Canberra between 17 and 21 March 2003.[19] In May 2003, Australian Prime Minister John Howard and United States President George W. Bush confirmed in Crawford, Texas that they wished to pursue the Australia-United States FTA with a target date for the conclusion of negotiations being December 2003.[20]

The Australia-United States FTA aims at ensuring that exporters achieve greater access to overseas markets.[21] The Trade Minister, Mark Vaile, stated that the

---

14 Australian Ambassador to the United States Michael Thawley, *Speech to the American Australian Association*, 13 December 2000 (New York).

15 In March 2001, Foreign Minister Downer had further talks with the United States Trade Representative, Robert Zoellick, in relation to the FTA and Trade Minister Vaile made an official proposal in Washington in April 2001. Mid 2001, Prime Minister Howard pursued the Australia-United Stated FTA idea by making a visit to Washington to celebrate the 50th Anniversary of the ANZUS Treaty. By mid-2002 the United States legislature had passed the necessary Trade Promotion Authority to deal with the FTA. The Bush administration was also given "fast track" authority by Congress to negotiate the trade agreement with Australia. In November 2002, Howard and Zoellick commenced negotiations and public submissions were called for. Senate Select Committee on the Australia-United States Free Trade Agreement, *Select Committee on the Free Trade Agreement between Australia and the United States of America Final Report*, above n 12, 2.

16 Centre for International Economics, *Economic impacts of an Australian-United States Free Trade Area* 2001 (Canberra and Sydney: Centre for International Economics, 2001) and Asia Pacific Economic Cooperation Study Centre, *An Australia-USA Free Trade Agreement—Issues and Implications* 2001 (Melbourne: The Australian APEC Study Centre, Monash University, 2001)

17 House of Representatives Hansard, *Prime Minister Honourable J Howard MP*, No. 13, 30 August 2001 30679.

18 Senate Select Committee on the Australia-United States Free Trade Agreement, *Select Committee on the Free Trade Agreement between Australia and the United States of America Final Report*, above n 12, 2.

19 Senate Select Committee on the Australia-United States Free Trade Agreement, *Select Committee on the Free Trade Agreement between Australia and the United States of America Final Report*, above n 12, 2.

20 Senate Select Committee on the Australia-United States Free Trade Agreement, *Select Committee on the Free Trade Agreement between Australia and the United States of America Final Report*, above n 12, 2.

21 Department of Foreign Affairs and Trade, *Australia-United States Free Trade Agreement—Free Trade Agreements and Multilateral Negotiations* (2004) <http://www.dfat.gov.au/trade/negotiations/us_fta/outcomes/22_multi_negs.html> at 20 April 2004.

Australia-United States FTA "... offers enormous opportunities to all Australian companies interested in profiting in the world's largest and most dynamic economy".[22]

The Department of Foreign Affairs and Trade has commissioned two studies both on the economic and wider implications of the Australia-United States FTA.[23] These studies showed that the Australia-United States FTA may:[24]

(a) produce large net welfare gains for both countries;

(b) increase Australia's imports and exports;

(c) increase United States investment into Australia, particularly in the agricultural and mining sectors; and

(d) boost Australia's gross domestic product.[25]

The final agreement provides for:

(a) Australian exporters having essentially free and open access to manufactured goods and services in the United States market;

(b) over 97 per cent of Australia's manufacturing exports to the United States having duty-free access (United States exports were worth $5.84 billion in 2003);

(c) substantially improved access for Australia's agricultural sector, including for our beef and dairy producers, with more than 66 per cent of agricultural tariffs being removed;

(d) full access for Australian goods and services to the $270 billion market for federal government procurement in the United States; and

(e) enhanced legal protection that guarantees market access and non-discriminatory treatment for Australian service providers in the United States market.[26]

Specifically, the Australia-United States FTA includes provisions on matters including:

(a) trade of goods;

(b) rules of origin (manufactured products must be "substantially transformed" in either Australia or United States before they can benefit from the agreement);

(c) technical standards and regulations (requirement for food and manufactured goods, such as labelling to conform to United States requirements);

(d) trade remedies (such as anti-dumping and safeguard measures);

---

22 The Hon. Mark Vaile—MP Minister for Trade Australia, *Media Release—Free Trade Agreement with the United States* (2004) <http://www.trademinister.gov.au/releases/2004/mvt008_04.html> at 4 April 2004.

23 Centre for International Economics, *Economic impacts of an Australian-United States Free Trade Area* 2001 (Canberra and Sydney: Centre for International Economics, 2001) and Asia Pacific Economic Cooperation Study Centre, *An Australia-USA Free Trade Agreement—Issues and Implications* 2001 (Melbourne: The Australian APEC Study Centre, Monash University, 2001).

24 Freehills, *Australia-United States free trade talks face final hurdles* (2003) <www.freehills.com> at 20 February 2004.

25 Department of Foreign Affairs and Trade, *Background Paper* (2003) <http://www.dfat.gov.au/trade/negotiations/United States_bkg.html> at 20 February 2004.

26 The Hon. Mark Vaile—MP Minister for Trade Australia, *Media Release—Free Trade Agreement with the United States*, above n 22.

(e) agriculture trade (two-thirds of agricultural tariffs will be eliminated and a further 9 per cent will be removed in the next four years);
(f) health (the Pharmaceutical Benefit Scheme will be maintained);
(g) automotive (customs duties are to be removed on almost all automotive products);
(h) manufacturing (almost all Australia's exports to the United States will be duty-free);
(i) customs procedures;
(j) government procurement ($200 billion market in United States government purchases of goods and services will be open to Australia);
(k) services (access to the United States markets will be enhanced for Australian suppliers);
(l) investment (promotion of two-way investing between Australia and the United States);
(m) telecommunications (pro-competitive regulatory framework for Australian and United States telecommunication companies);
(n) intellectual property rights (Australia's intellectual property laws will be amended to be in line with the United States intellectual property market); and
(o) electronic commerce (no barriers to trade conducted electronically).[27]

The Australia-United States FTA has been controversial however. In a media release from the Democrats, Senator Aden Ridgeway commented, "the potential gains from the Australia US Free Trade Agreement have been grossly overstated by the Government . . .".[28] The release advocated the "importance of careful and thorough scrutiny . . .",[29] which will be developed in this paper.

STRUCTURE OF PAPER

This paper is divided into three chapters, along with an Introduction and Conclusion. Chapter 1 addresses the treaty-making process in Australia, including the power to enter into FTAs under the *Commonwealth Constitution*[30] and an outline of the domestic steps in order for a FTA to be entered into.

Chapter 2 identifies the inadequacies of the domestic treaty-making process and explores the possibility of international law provisions assisting the inadequate domestic treaty process in Australia, but evaluates that this option is not ideal.

27 Department of Foreign Affairs and Trade, *Background Paper*, above n 25 and Department of Foreign Affairs and Trade, *Key Outcomes* (2003) <http://www.dfat.gov.au/trade/negotiations/us_fta/outcomes/02_key_outcomes.html> at 5 May 2004.

28 Parliament of Australia, *Democrats Media Senator Aden Ridgeway—Senate Inquiry Shows Major Flaws in FTA* (2004) <http://parlinfoweb.aph.gov.au/piweb/Repository/Media/pressrel/MMTC60.pdf> at 5 September 2004.

29 Parliament of Australia, *Democrats Media Senator Aden Ridgeway—Senate Inquiry Shows Major Flaws in FTA*, above n 28.

30 *Commonwealth Constitution* 1900 (Cth) ss 51(i), 51(ix), 51(xviii), 51(xxix), 61.

Chapter 3 suggests ways that the current treaty-making process in Australia could be amended to strengthen the international position of Australia and uphold the federal system internally.

The paper concludes by reinforcing the central argument that the current treaty-making process is inadequate in dealing with category B treaties and that the introduction of reforms proposed would facilitate a more efficient and accountable process.

CHAPTER 1: AUSTRALIA'S TREATY-MAKING PROCESS AND THE AUSTRALIA-UNITED STATES FREE TRADE AGREEMENT

Introduction

In Australia it is the role of the Executive government to negotiate international treaties.[31] The Federal Parliament's role is confined to passing the legislation, which is necessary domestically to give effect to the provisions of the Australia-United States FTA.[32] The steps necessary to implement treaties will be the focus of this chapter.

The Constitution and the treaty-making process

Under the Australian Commonwealth Constitution,[33] there are two powers specifically relevant to the treaty-making process. The power to enter into treaties is an executive power conferred by s 61.[34] The power to implement treaties however is a legislative power, contained in s 51(xxix).[35]

Section 61 of the *Commonwealth Constitution*[36] states:

> The executive power of the Commonwealth is vested in the Queen and is exercisable by the Governor-General as the Queen's Representative, and extends to the execution and maintenance of . . . [the] constitution, and of the laws of the Commonwealth.[37]

Case law reveals that s 61 grants "royal prerogative" power to the Executive.[38] Royal prerogative power includes the power to enter into international treaties.[39] Therefore the power to enter into treaties is a Federal Executive power, through the Governor-General, within s 61 of the Commonwealth Constitution.[40] The power is exercised on

31 Commonwealth Constitution 1900 (Cth) s 61.

32 Commonwealth Constitution 1900 (Cth) ss 51(i), 51(ix), 51(xviii), 51(xxix).

33 Commonwealth Constitution 1900 (Cth).

34 Commonwealth Constitution 1900 (Cth) s 61.

35 Commonwealth Constitution 1900 (Cth) s 51(xxix).

36 Commonwealth Constitution 1900 (Cth) s 61.

37 Commonwealth Constitution 1900 (Cth) s 61.

38 *Davis v Commonwealth* (1988) 166 CLR 79 at 93; 82 ALR 633.

39 *Simsek v Macphee* (1982) 148 CLR 636 at 641–2; 40 ALR 61.

40 Commonwealth Constitution 1900 (Cth).

the advice of the Executive government and in the case of the Australia-United States FTA, is administered by the Australian Trade Minister, Mark Vaile.[41]

Although it is within executive power to negotiate and execute the Australia-United States FTA,[42] the Australia-United States FTA is not self-executing and requires incorporation by legislation into domestic law.[43] The legislative power to implement treaties in domestic law is granted in s 51(xxix) of the Commonwealth Constitution[44] and is known as the "external affairs" power.[45] Section 51 of the Commonwealth Constitution[46] states:

> The Parliament shall, subject to this Constitution, have power to make laws for the peace, order, and good government of the Commonwealth with respect to:- . . . (xxix) External affairs.[47]

High Court cases have confirmed that the "external affairs" power includes the power to implement treaties, which have been entered into pursuant to the Executive's power under s 61 of the Commonwealth Constitution.[48]

Current scope of the external affairs power

The latest High Court cases have shown that the Commonwealth has a broad power to legislate over matters with respect to "external affairs",[49] under

41 Michael Pryles, Jeff Waincymer and Martin Davies, *International Trade Law Commentary and Materials* (NSW: LBC Information Services, 1996).

42 *Simsek v MacPhee* (1982) 148 CLR 636 at 641–2; 40 ALR 241.

43 *Bradley v Commonwealth* (1973) 128 CLR 557; 1 ALR 241.

44 Commonwealth Constitution 1900 (Cth) s 51(xxix).

45 Austlii, *Australia and International Treaty Making Information Kit* (2002) <http://www.austlii.edu.au/au/other/dfat/infokit.html> at 31 March 2004.

46 Commonwealth Constitution 1900 (Cth).

47 Commonwealth Constitution 1900 (Cth) s 51(xxix).

48 *R v Burgess; ex parte Henry* (1936) 55 CLR 608 at 643–4 Latham CJ interpreted s 61 of the *Commonwealth Constitution* as including the "negotiation and making of treaties with foreign countries"; *Richardson v Forestry Commission* (1988) 164 CLR 261 (*Lemonthyme Forests case)*; and *Victoria v Commonwealth* (1996) 187 CLR 416 (*Industrial Relations Act case*).

49 A timeline and summary of the development of this power may be necessary to understand the scope of the "External Affairs" power under s 51(xxix) of the Commonwealth Constitution 1900 (Cth), which is as follows: *R v Burgess; ex parte Henry* (1936) 55 CLR 608 The High Court held that the Commonwealth can use s 51(xxix) to implement treaties but the subject must be "indisputably international in character" (Dixon J 55 CLR at 669). The treaty cannot be a mere device to obtain a state power (55 CLR at 687), the law must implement the treaty significantly (55 CLR at 658) and s 51(xxix) cannot contravene any other section of the Commonwealth Constitution (55 CLR at 642); *Airlines of New South Wales Pty Ltd v New South Wales (No 2)* (1965) 113 CLR 54 Took the same narrow view as *R v Burgess; ex parte Henry* (1936); *Koowarta v Bjelke-Petersen* (1982) 153 CLR 168 The winning judgment, Stephen J held that under s 51(xxix), the Commonwealth can legislate over a State power so long it is a "matter of international rather than merely domestic concern" (153 CLR at 216). However this case is no longer good law, see the *Tasmanian Dam case* (1996); *Commonwealth v Tasmania (Tasmanian Dam case)* (1983) 158 CLR 1 The outcome in this case was that s 51(xxix) gives the Commonwealth power to implement treaties of "international concern", but if treaty imposes an "obligation", it is automatically a law of international concern, therefore in this case the Commonwealth law was valid (Brennan J 158 CLR at 219). However this case is no longer good law—see the *Lemonthyme Forest case* (1988); *Lemonthyme Forest case* (1988) 164 CLR 261 The High Court held that s 51 (xxix) extended to the Commonwealth having power to legislate where there were "reasonably apprehended obligations" (164 CLR at 295) imposed by a possible treaty; *Industrial Relations Act case* (1996) 187 CLR 416 The High Court held that following the *Tasmanian Dam case* there is no need for the law to be of an "international concern". The fact that the treaty was entered into was enough to attract a law on this matter. However to be a law, with respect to external affairs, it

s 51(xxix).[50] Basically, the Commonwealth Executive can enter into whatever treaty it likes without any parliamentary scrutiny, and without any consultation with States and Territories.

Despite the breadth of the external affairs power, there are still some restrictions.[51] One restriction is that s 51(xxix)[52] has been interpreted by the High Court as requiring a treaty to be bona fide,[53] and not merely an attempt to gain legislative power.[54] The Australia-United States FTA seems quite clearly to be bona fide, as there are many reports supporting its implementation and an ulterior motive is not legally in issue.

Another restriction identified is that, for a law to be implemented under the "external affairs" power, it must be "reasonably capable of being considered appropriate and adapted to implementing the treaty".[55] For this there must be "reasonable proportionality"[56] between the purpose of the treaty and the means adopted by Parliament to achieve that purpose.[57] Therefore the treaty must impose an obligation and not a mere recommendation that legislation be implemented to give effect to the treaty.[58] The Australia-United States FTA imposes specific obligations, therefore based on this decision the Commonwealth could validly legislate in regards to any of these obligations, albeit a State power.[59]

It is relevant to note that the Commonwealth is yet to have a significant loss before the High Court in relation to the "external affairs" power. However in a speech Justice Dawson gave in 1994, he commented that:

> It is probably too early to speak with confidence, but there are signs that the Court is searching for some means of curbing the use of the external affairs power for purposes plainly inconsistent with the federal compact.[60]

must be "reasonably capable of being considered appropriate and adapted to implementing the treaty" (187 CLR at 487) and for this there must be "reasonable proportionality" (187 CLR at 487) between the purpose of the treaty and the means adopted by parliament to achieve that purpose. Therefore the treaty must impose an obligation, not be a mere recommendation. In the case of the Australia-United States FTA the Commonwealth could validly legislate over the State powers as the FTA imposes specific obligations.

50 Commonwealth Constitution 1900 (Cth) s 51(xxix).

51 Brian R Opeskin and Donald R Rothwell (eds), *International Law and Australian Federalism* (Melbourne: Melbourne University Press, 1997) 79.

52 Commonwealth Constitution 1900 (Cth) s 51(xxix).

53 Bona fide means in good faith or with an honest intention. Peter Butt and Peter Nygh (eds), *Butterworths Concise Australian Legal Dictionary* (2nd ed, Sydney: Butterworths, 1998) 55.

54 *R v Burgess; ex parte Henry* (1936) 55 CLR 608, at 642, 674–5, and 687; *Airlines of New South Wales Pty Ltd v New South Wales [No1]* (1964) 113 CLR 1, at 50–1; *Koowarta v Bjelke-Petersen* (1982) 153 CLR 168, at 200, 217, 231, and 260; *Tasmanian Dam case* (1983) 158 CLR 1, at 122, 219 and 259; *Horta v Commonwealth* (1994) 181 CLR 183, at 195.

55 *Industrial Relations Act case* (1996) 187 CLR 416, at 487.

56 *Industrial Relations Act case* (1996) 187 CLR 416, at 487.

57 *Industrial Relations Act case* (1996) 187 CLR 416, at 487.

58 *Industrial Relations Act case* (1996) 187 CLR 416, at 487.

59 For example States powers include employment (*Industrial Relations Act case* (1996) 187 CLR 416) and the environment (*Lemonthyme Forest case* (1988) 164 CLR 261).

60 Justice Dawson, "*Do Judges Make Laws? Too Much?*" 22 August 1994 (University of Adelaide) 25. However since that speech the High Court has confirmed again the wide breadth of the external affairs power in *Industrial Relations Act case* (1996) 187 CLR 416. In that case, Dawson J reiterated this idea of the external affairs power being limited but accepted the decision of the majority as discussed above at n 49.

Other Commonwealth powers

The Commonwealth does not solely rely on the "external affairs" power to implement the Australia-United States FTA, it has other powers it can rely upon such as trade,[61] quarantine[62] and copyrights and patents.[63]

The trade and commerce power under s 51(i)[64] provides the power to legislate in regards to all commercial transactions, dealings and exchanges between people encompassing either tangible or intangible goods and services,[65] including their transport.[66] However this power can only be in regards to interstate and overseas trade, not intrastate[67] and it does not extend to production and manufacture[68] other than incidentally.[69]

The Commonwealth also has the power to legislate in regards to quarantine[70] under s 51(ix),[71] the essence of quarantine being to restrict or prohibit the movement of persons or things.[72]

The copyright power is also held by the Commonwealth under s 51(xviii)[73] and provides for the Commonwealth to make laws with respect to copyrights, patents of inventions and designs and trade marks, which are necessary under the Australia-United States FTA.[74]

Domestic treaty-making process[75]

Negotiation

As a bilateral treaty, Australia and the United States government negotiated the Australia-United States FTA by correspondence and meetings.[76] Chief Negotiator

61 Commonwealth Constitution 1900 (Cth) s 51(i).

62 Commonwealth Constitution 1900 (Cth) s 51(ix).

63 Commonwealth Constitution 1900 (Cth) s 51(xviii).

64 Commonwealth Constitution 1900 (Cth).

65 *Bank of New South Wales v Commonwealth* (1948) 76 CLR 1 at 381–2.

66 *W & A McArthur Ltd v Queensland* (1920) 28 CLR 530 at 546–7.

67 *W & A McArthur Ltd v Queensland* (1920) 28 CLR 530 at 548.

68 *Grannall v Marrickville Margarine Pty Ltd* (1955) 93 CLR 55.

69 *Redfern v Dunlop Rubber Australia* (1964) 110 CLR 194.

70 The Commonwealth and States benefit from concurrent powers of quarantine under Commonwealth Constitution ss 51(ix), 107, 108 and shown by legislation at a Commonwealth level, the Quarantine Act 1908 (Cth) and state level, such as the Health Act 1911 (WA).

71 Commonwealth Constitution 1900 (Cth).

72 *McCarter v Brodie* (1950) 80 CLR 432.

73 Commonwealth Constitution 1900 (Cth), s 51(xviii).

74 Commonwealth Constitution 1900 (Cth), s 51(xviii).

75 In recognition of the need for improvement of the treaty-making process, the Australian Government reviewed its treaty process in 1996 and reforms were put in place in July 1998. These reforms included: (a) A fifteen day minimum tabling period of treaties in Parliament (now extended to 20 days for category B treaties); (b) A Joint Standing Committee to review treaties; (c) A National Interest Analysis to be performed on all treaties; (d) A Regulation Impact Statement to be compiled for prospective treaties; (e) A Senate Select Committee to review treaties; (f) An Australian Treaties Library to table treaties; and (g) Implementing legislation to be completed before the treaty enters into force. Austlii, *Australia and International Treaty-making Information Kit* (2002) <http://www.austlii.edu.au/au/other/dfat/infokit.html> at 31 March 2004.

76 Michael Pryles, Jeff Waincymer and Martin Davies, above n 41, 902.

Steve Deady (from the Department of Foreign Affairs and Trade), Mark Vaile (the Australian Trade Minister), and Michael Thawley (Australia's Ambassador to the United States) led the Australian negotiations.[77]

The Trade Minister, Mark Vaile and his United States counterpart, Trade Representative Ambassador Robert Zoellick concluded negotiations for the Australia-United States FTA on 8 February.[78]

Signature

Under s 61[79] the "external affairs" power is ". . . vested in the Queen and is exercisable by the Governor-General as the Queen's Representative",[80] therefore any treaty action must have the approval of the Queen or the Governor-General before a treaty is signed.[81] For this to occur, the Governor-General is given advice from the Federal Executive Council[82] in relation to the treaty[83] and then gives a document of authority known as "Full Powers" to the Minister to prove that he/she has the power to sign the treaty on behalf of Australia.[84] This act of giving Full Powers to Mark Vaile, the Trade Minister, authorised him to sign the draft text of the Australia-United States FTA on behalf of Australia. Mark Vaile, and United States Trade Representative, Ambassador Robert Zoellick, signed the final text of the Australia-United States FTA on 18 May 2004 in Washington.[85]

The signing of the FTA by both Australia and the United States may be perceived as binding both countries to the Australia-United States FTA.[86] However, the Department of Foreign Affairs and Trade has specified that the signature does not mean Australia becomes bound at international law to the terms of AUSFTA, as Art 23.4.1 of Chapter Twenty Three of the Australia-United States FTA states that the FTA:

> . . . shall enter into force 60 days after the date on which the Parties exchange written notifications certifying that they have completed respective necessary internal requirements, or on such other date as the Parties may agree.[87]

---

77 Australian Trade Minister Mark Vaile, *Second Reading Speech on the Introduction of the United States Free Trade Agreement* 2004 (Australian Parliament).

78 Department of Foreign Affairs and Trade, *Domestic Approval Processes for an Australia-United States Free Trade Agreement (AUSFTA)* (2004) <http://www.dfat.gov.au/trade/negotiations/us_fta/outcomes/21_domestic_approval.html> at 23 May 2004.

79 Commonwealth Constitution 1900 (Cth) s 61.

80 Commonwealth Constitution 1900 (Cth) s 61.

81 Michael Pryles, Jeff Waincymer and Martin Davies, above n 41, 902.

82 The Federal Executive Council consists of the Prime Minister and other Ministers, which advise the Governor-General and give legal advice to cabinet decisions. Parliament of Australia, *Glossary—Federal Executive Council* (2003) <http://www.aph.gov.au/find/glossary.htm_f> at 20 September 2004.

83 Michael Pryles, Jeff Waincymer and Martin Davies, above n 41, 902.

84 Michael Pryles, Jeff Waincymer and Martin Davies, above n 41, 902.

85 Department of Foreign Affairs and Trade, *Domestic Approval Processes for an Australia-United States Free Trade Agreement (AUSFTA)* above n 78.

86 Vienna Convention on the Law of Treaties, Art 11. Sets out the different ways in which an FTA may be formed. It states. "The consent of a State to be bound by a treaty (FTA) may be expressed by signature, exchange of instruments constituting a treaty, ratification, acceptance, approval or accession, or by any other means if so agreed."

87 Australia-United States Free Trade Agreement 2004, Art 23.4.1, Chapter Twenty Three.

The Australia-United States FTA therefore becomes legally binding by way of subsequent ratification,[88] via exchange of diplomatic notes.[89] However, the signature does have the effect of indicating that Australia and the United States intend to be bound by *an* FTA. In the case of *Minister for Immigration and Ethnic Affairs v Teoh* (1995)[90] it was stated by Mason CJ and Deane J that the fact that a treaty is not incorporated into domestic law by legislation does not have the consequence that the treaty has no significance whatsoever for Australian law.[91] Article 18 of the Vienna Convention on the Law of Treaties 1969 states that the signing of a treaty establishes an obligation to refrain from acts which would defeat the object and purpose of the treaty.[92] The Senate Select Committee also noted that, "once signed, trade agreements effectively bind future governments and are difficult to change."[93] This should be taken into account when considering the other steps in the treaty-making process in Australia and whether they are worthwhile.

Twenty-day minimum tabling period

The current treaty-making process requires that all Category B treaty actions proposed by the government be tabled in Parliament at least 20 sitting days

88 Vienna Convention on the Law of Treaties, Art 14. Art 14 specifically states: "1. The consent of a State to be bound by a treaty is expressed by ratification when: (a) the treaty provides for such consent to be expressed by means of ratification; (b) it is otherwise established that the negotiating States were agreed that ratification should be required; (c) the representative of the State has signed the treaty subject to ratification; or (d) the intention of the State to sign the treaty subject to ratification appears from the full powers of its representative or was expressed during the negotiation. 2. The consent of a State to be bound by a treaty is expressed by acceptance or approval under conditions similar to those which apply to ratification." This essentially provides for consent to be bound by a treaty by ratification, acceptance or approval. Ratification in terms of foreign relations is the process by which a signatory state to a treaty confirms that it intends to be bound by that treaty. The sovereign, head of state, foreign minister or parliament in accordance with the constitution of Australia and the United States perform ratification (by exchange of diplomatic notes). Martin Dixon and Robert McCorquodale, *Cases and Materials on International Law* (3rd ed, London: Blackstone Press Limited, 2000) 66–67.

89 Exchange of diplomatic notes in terms of foreign relations means that notes are given by one party to the other, which allows Australia and the United States to recognise the obligations that exist between them. Once the exchange of diplomatic notes has occurred, both Australia and the United States will have indicated that they intend to be bound by the particular terms set out in the FTA. The exchange of diplomatic notes, and thus the formation of the agreement, is also known at international law as ratification. Peter Butt and Peter Nygh (eds), above n 53, 161.

90 *Minister for Immigration and Ethnic Affairs v Teoh* (1995) 183 CLR 273; 128 ALR 353.

91 *Minister for Immigration and Ethnic Affairs v Teoh* (1995) 183 CLR 273 at 287. This case concerned a treaty that had been ratified, but not implemented by way of legislation, therefore it is unable to be used as a specific illustration of the issue regarding signature in this paper. It was held by the majority in this case however, that while ratification of a treaty by Australia does not incorporate that treaty into Australian law, it creates a "legitimate expectation" that the Commonwealth administrative decision-makers will act according to its terms. Gabriel A Moens and John Trone, "International treaties in Australian law: legitimate expectations and the Teoh case" (1995) 25 *Australia and World Affairs* 57. It should be noted that the effect of treaties on administrative decision-making is beyond the scope of this paper.

92 Vienna Convention on the Law of Treaties 1969 Art 18 "A State is obliged to refrain from acts, which would defeat the object and purpose of a treaty when: (a) it has signed the treaty or has exchanged instruments constituting the treaty subject to ratification, acceptance or approval, until it shall have made its intention clear not to become a party to the treaty; or (b) it has expressed its consent to be bound by the treaty, pending the entry into force of the treaty and provided that such entry into force is not unduly delayed." Therefore Australia and the United States have an obligation not to defeat the object and purpose of the Australia-United States FTA, after they signed the agreement on 18 May 2004, and prior to its entry into force.

93 Senate Select Committee on the Australia-United States Free Trade Agreement, *Select Committee on the Free Trade Agreement between Australia and the United States of America Final Report*, above n 12, 30.

before action is taken to bind Australia at international law to the terms of the treaty.[94]

The draft text of the Australia-United States FTA was tabled in both Houses of Parliament on 4 March 2004 and signed on 18 May 2004.[95] This early publication was a departure from Australia's normal practice, which has been to release the text of a treaty *after* signature.[96] However it was necessary in this case because the United States requires the draft text of a treaty to be published at least 90 days before signature.[97]

The purpose of tabling the FTA in Parliament for 20 days is so that parliamentary committees can consider and comment on the text, before ratification binds Australia to obligations at international law.[98] This is imperative because certain considerations may need to be taken into account so that all international obligations are complied with, because if they are not it may lead to penalties or possibly even the termination of the treaty. The effectiveness of the 20-day period is arguable because it is generally done after signature. As signature indicates that Australia will not defeat the object and purpose of the treaty, it is unlikely that the treaty will be changed.[99] Any findings during the 20 days therefore are in reality a waste of time. (This will be discussed later in this paper in regards to necessary reforms in relation to the treaty-making process and FTAs.)

National interest analysis

When a treaty is tabled in Parliament, the text of the proposed treaty action must be accompanied by a National Interest Analysis (NIA), which explains why the Government considers that the treaty is in Australia's national interest. The NIA describes the FTAs obligations and outlines the costs and benefits for Australia.[100]

An NIA includes information regarding:

(a) the economic, environmental, social and cultural effects of the proposed treaty;

(b) the obligations imposed by the treaty;

(c) how the treaty will be implemented domestically;

94 A Category A treaty has a minimum tabling period of 15 days, however as this paper is concerned with FTAs, which are Category B treaties, I will specify the treaty-making process in regards to them. Department of Foreign Affairs and Trade, *Category A and Category B treaties*, above n 4.

95 Department of Foreign Affairs and Trade, *Domestic Approval Processes for an Australia-United States Free Trade Agreement (AUSFTA)*, above n 78.

96 Department of Foreign Affairs and Trade, *Domestic Approval Processes for an Australia-United States Free Trade Agreement (AUSFTA)*, above n 78.

97 Department of Foreign Affairs and Trade, *Domestic Approval Processes for an Australia-United States Free Trade Agreement (AUSFTA)*, above n 78.

98 Note that the general practice in Australia is to table the agreement after signature but before ratification; however the Senate Select Committee have commented that the fact that signature does effectively bind future governments makes the treaty difficult to change. Senate Select Committee on the Australia-United States Free Trade Agreement, *Select Committee on the Free Trade Agreement between Australia and the United States of America Final Report*, above n 12, 30.

99 Vienna Convention on the Law of Treaties 1969, Art 18.

100 Department of Foreign Affairs and Trade, *Domestic Approval Processes for an Australia-United States Free Trade Agreement (AUSFTA)* above n 78.

(d) the financial costs associated with implementing and complying with the terms of the treaty; and
(e) the consultation that has occurred with State and Territory governments, industry and community groups and other interest groups.[101]

The NIA for the Australia-United States FTA was delivered to the Joint Standing Committee on Treaties on 24 March 2004 and tabled in Parliament on 30 March 2004.[102] This means that the Federal Parliament considered it before Australia was due to sign the FTA on 18 May 2004.[103] However, this was only the case because of the requirement of the United States to do so.[104] Generally the NIA would not be tabled until *after* signature,[105] and in that case any negative findings established in the NIA would be of no use, because the Federal Parliament is obligated to fulfil the treaty's object and purpose by this point.[106]

Regulation Impact Statement

A Regulation Impact Statement (RIS) is a report on how a treaty could affect the regulation of business or restrict competition.[107]

The RIS for the Australia-United States FTA identifies and discusses:

(a) issues;
(b) objectives;
(c) options;
(d) impact analysis, including macroeconomic, business, consumer and business impacts;
(e) consultations; and
(f) implementation and review.[108]

The RIS attached to the NIA was delivered to the Joint Standing Committee on Treaties on 24 March and tabled in Parliament on 30 March 2004.[109] Thus it was also considered by Parliament before Australia was due to sign the FTA on 18 May 2004,

101 Parliament of Australia, *National Interest Analysis—Australia United States of America Free Trade Agreement*, 2004 (Canberra: Joint Standing Committee, 2004).

102 Parliament of Australia, *National Interest Analysis—Australia United States of America Free Trade Agreement*, 2004 (Canberra: Joint Standing Committee, 2004).

103 Department of Foreign Affairs and Trade, *Domestic Approval Processes for an Australia-United States Free Trade Agreement (AUSFTA)*, above n 78.

104 Department of Foreign Affairs and Trade, *Domestic Approval Processes for an Australia-United States Free Trade Agreement (AUSFTA)*, above n 78.

105 Department of Foreign Affairs and Trade, *Domestic Approval Processes for an Australia-United States Free Trade Agreement (AUSFTA)*, above n 78.

106 Vienna Convention on the Law of Treaties 1969, Art 18.

107 Department of Foreign Affairs and Trade, *Domestic Approval Processes for an Australia-United States Free Trade Agreement (AUSFTA)* above n 78.

108 Parliament of Australia, *Regulation Impact Statement—Australia-United States of America Free Trade Agreement*, 2004 (Canberra: Joint Standing Committee, 2004).

109 Parliament of Australia, *Regulation Impact Statement—Australia-United States of America Free Trade Agreement*, 2004 (Canberra: Joint Standing Committee, 2004).

but only because the United States stipulated this requirement.[110] In Australia the normal practice is to table the RIS *after* signature,[111] so any detrimental conclusions made in the RIS would be ineffective, because Parliament can not say no to the agreement at this point, ". . . only to certain bits of the enabling legislation required for parts of the Agreement".[112] All implementing legislation must be passed after signature anyway, because Australia has an obligation not to defeat the object and purpose of the treaty.[113]

Joint Standing Committee on Treaties

The Joint Standing Committee on Treaties (JSCOT) is a Parliamentary committee established by the Government in 1996 as part of a package of reforms "to improve the openness and transparency of the treaty-making process in Australia".[114] Its role is to review and report on all treaty actions proposed by the Government before action is taken which will bind Australia to the terms of the treaty.[115] After the draft text of the Australia-United States FTA was tabled in both Houses of Parliament on 4 March 2004, it was then referred to the JSCOT, along with a NIA and a RIS.[116]

The JSCOT has the power to inquire and report on:

(a) matters arising from treaties and related National Interest Analysis and proposed treaty actions presented or deemed to be presented to Parliament;

(b) any question relating to a treaty which is referred to the committee from either the House of Representatives or a Minister; and

(c) such other matters as may be referred to the committee by the . . . Minister for Foreign Affairs and on such conditions as the Minister prescribes.[117]

The JSCOT has become the key medium for wide consultation on the Australia-United States FTA and its objective is to enhance the community's awareness of particular treaties.[118] The JSCOT report on the Australia-United States FTA was provided to the Federal Parliament to be considered before legislative amendments

110 Department of Foreign Affairs and Trade, *Domestic Approval Processes for an Australia-United States Free Trade Agreement (AUSFTA)*, above n 78.

111 Department of Foreign Affairs and Trade, *Domestic Approval Processes for an Australia-United States Free Trade Agreement (AUSFTA)*, above n 78.

112 Parliament of Australia, *Democrats Media Senator Aden Ridgeway—FTA signed but not sealed and still won't deliver* (2004) <http://parlinfoweb.aph.gov.au/piweb/Repository/Media/pressrel/G1KC60.pdf> at 20 September 2004.

113 Vienna Convention on the Law of Treaties 1969, Art 18.

114 Parliament of Australia, *Joint Standing Committee on Treaties—Committee establishment, role and history* (2002) <http://www.aph.gov.au/house/committee/jsct/ppgrole.htm> at 1 September 2004.

115 Parliament of Australia, *Joint Standing Committee on Treaties—Committee establishment, role and history*, above n 114.

116 Department of Foreign Affairs and Trade, *Domestic Approval Processes for an Australia-United States Free Trade Agreement (AUSFTA)* above n 78.

117 Department of Foreign Affairs and Trade, *Domestic Approval Processes for an Australia-United States Free Trade Agreement (AUSFTA)* above n 78.

118 JSCOT issued a number of "media alerts" requesting the public to "comment on the US Free Trade Agreement" including 11 March 2004, 17 March 2004, 13 April 2004, 23 June 2004. Parliament of Australia, *Joint Committee on Treaties Committee activities (inquiries and reports)—Media Releases* (2004) <http://www.aph.gov.au/house/committee/jsct/usafta/media.htm> at 28 July 2004.

were introduced to implement the FTA in August 2004.[119] However the Australia-United States FTA was already signed on 18 May 2004,[120] therefore the effectiveness of JSCOT's report is questionable. By the time the report was considered, Australia was already obligated under international law, by signature, not to defeat the object and purpose of the FTA.[121] The Senate Select Committee in their report in August 2004 commented that:

> [t]he crucial point for trade agreements is "prior to signature", because once a treaty has been signed it would be extremely unlikely for the government to refuse to ratify a treaty on the basis of, say, any JSCOT recommendations or indeed for any other reasons.[122]

Senate Select Committee

The Senate has also established the Senate Select Committee to review treaties including FTAs. This committee made a final report on 5 August 2004 in relation to the Australia-United States FTA.[123] This report included a discussion of:

(a) the outcomes;
(b) trade policies;
(c) intellectual property;
(d) pharmaceuticals and health;
(e) sanitary and phytosanitary measures;
(f) local media content;
(g) manufacturing;
(h) investment;
(i) trade in services;
(j) agriculture; and
(k) political recommendations and remarks.[124]

The report by the Senate Select Committee was considered by Parliament ahead of the tabling of legislative amendments necessary for Australia to implement the FTA in August 2004.[125] However, the Executive signed the Australia-United States FTA on the 18 May 2004,[126] prior to the publication of the Senate Select Committee Report

119 Department of Foreign Affairs and Trade, *Domestic Approval Processes for an Australia-United States Free Trade Agreement (AUSFTA)* above n 78.

120 Department of Foreign Affairs and Trade, *Domestic Approval Processes for an Australia-United States Free Trade Agreement (AUSFTA)* above n 78.

121 The signature of a treaty establishes an obligation to refrain from acts which would defeat the object and purpose of the Australia-United States FTA. *Vienna Convention on the Law of Treaties* 1969, Art 18.

122 Senate Select Committee on the Australia-United States Free Trade Agreement, *Select Committee on the Free Trade Agreement between Australia and the United States of America Final Report*, above n 12, 38.

123 Senate Select Committee on the Australia-United States Free Trade Agreement, *Select Committee on the Free Trade Agreement between Australia and the United States of America Final Report*, above n 12.

124 Senate Select Committee on the Australia-United States Free Trade Agreement, *Select Committee on the Free Trade Agreement between Australia and the United States of America Final Report*, above n 12.

125 Department of Foreign Affairs and Trade, *Domestic Approval Processes for an Australia-United States Free Trade Agreement (AUSFTA)* above n 78.

126 Department of Foreign Affairs and Trade, *Domestic Approval Processes for an Australia-United States Free Trade Agreement (AUSFTA)* above n 78.

in August 2004.[127] The usefulness of this report therefore is dubious, as Australia already has obligations not to defeat the object and purpose of the treaty before the Parliament has a chance to consider the findings of the report.[128]

Parliamentary involvement

There is no constitutional requirement for parliamentary involvement in the treaty-making process.[129] However if domestic law needs to be changed in order to implement the treaty, as is the case with the Australia-United States FTA, then this must be done by legislation enacted by the Federal Parliament and/or the State and Territory parliaments.[130] "[T]he assumption cannot be made that Parliament, Federal or State, will necessarily pass implementing legislation after that consent is given."[131]

The Australia-United States FTA was signed before legislation had been implemented. It is therefore arguable whether the treaty-making process in Australia is actually giving Parliament a choice to implement the FTA, as if it does not, the signature could give rise to penalties being imposed under international trade law[132] or even give the United States the opportunity to terminate the agreement[133] for defeating the object and purpose of the FTA.[134]

The Federal Parliament passed legislation enabling Australia to fulfil its commitments under the Australia-United States FTA on 13 August 2004.[135] This

---

127 Senate Select Committee on the Australia-United States Free Trade Agreement, *Select Committee on the Free Trade Agreement between Australia and the United States of America Final Report*, above n 12.

128 *Vienna Convention on the Law of Treaties* 1969, Art 18.

129 Brian R Opeskin and Donald R Rothwell (eds), above n 51, 84.

130 Brian R Opeskin and Donald R Rothwell (eds), above n 51, 84.

131 Department of Foreign Affairs and Trade, *The Negotiation, Conclusion and Implementation of International Treaties and Arrangements* 1994 (Canberra: Australian Government Publishing Service, 1994) paragraph 56.

132 The World Trade Organisation can impose penalties for serious breaches. Senate Select Committee on the Australia-United States Free Trade Agreement, *Select Committee on the Free Trade Agreement between Australia and the United States of America Final Report*, above n 12, 30.

133 Vienna Convention on the Law of Treaties 1969, Art 60.

134 Vienna Convention on the Law of Treaties 1969, Art 18.

135 For the Australia-United States FTA to be implemented, these Commonwealth Bills require approval by the House of Representatives and the Senate, as well as assent by the Governor-General. Public servants in the Department of Foreign Affairs and Trade draft the Bills, with help from lawyers at the Office of Parliamentary Counsel. The Trade Minister Mark Vaile introduced both of these Bills into Parliament. In the House of Representatives the first reading was on 23 June 2004. The Bills were given to all members to read, and became public. In the second reading, members of the Government and Opposition debated the Bills in general. The Opposition opposed the Bills on certain points, namely to do with the Pharmaceutical component of the Australia-United States FTA. The House of Representatives however also had to refer the Bills to the various committees handling the Australia-United States FTA for extra consideration. Members have to examine each part of the Bills in detail. The third reading is a brief formality, where a vote is taken on the Bill (which was not opposed). The Government passed the Bills in the House of Representatives on 24 June 2004, primarily because it has the majority of members. In the Senate, the Trade Minister Mark Vaile explained the ideas of the Bill. The Bills were amended in the Senate because the Government does not have a majority in that Chamber and the Opposition opposed certain parts of the Bills. As the Bills were amended in the Senate, the amendments had to be agreed to by the House of Representatives. The Governor-General signs the Bill into law once the House of Representatives pass the amendments. This occurred on 13 August 2004. The provisions of the Bills will commence on 1 January 2005 or the day on which the Australia-United States FTA comes into force, whichever is the later. The Bills will not commence if the FTA does not come into force. Parliamentary Education Office, *Facts about Parliament—Making Laws* (2004) <http://www.peo.gov.au/resources/facts.htm_laws> at 15 July 2004.

would mean the FTA could be implemented as early as 1 January 2005.[136] It should be taken into consideration, however, that there may be some situations when Parliament will not pass the legislation necessary to implement a FTA. There is a very real chance of this happening, as "in the case of the current AUSFTA, where cultural protection, intellectual property and the Pharmaceutical Benefits Scheme have been contentious issues . . ."[137] it was observed that "the Senate [could have] . . . vote[d] down some of the relevant domestic legislative instruments."[138]

Entry into force

Article 24 of the Vienna Convention on the Law of Treaties 1969 stipulates the method by which a treaty can enter into force at international law. It states that a ". . . treaty enters into force in such a manner and upon such date as it may provide or as the negotiating states may agree".[139]

Australia and the United States will agree on a date for entry into force, which will occur via exchange of diplomatic notes as set out in Art 23.4 of Chapter Twenty Three of the Australia-United States FTA. It states that the ". . . Agreement shall enter into force 60 days after the date on which the Parties exchange written notifications certifying that they have completed respective necessary internal requirements, or on such other date as the Parties may agree."[140] Both governments were working towards entry into force on 1 January 2005, requiring an exchange of notes on or before 2 November 2004.[141]

Registration

Australia and the United States are both members of the United Nations[142] therefore the Australia-United States FTA must be registered with the United Nations under Art 102 of the United Nations Charter 1945.[143]

Publication

After the Australia-United States FTA is registered with the United Nations, the text is published in the United Nations Treaty Series.[144] The texts of all treaties to which

136 Department of Foreign Affairs and Trade, *Background Paper,* above n 25.

137 Senate Select Committee on the Australia-United States Free Trade Agreement, *Select Committee on the Free Trade Agreement between Australia and the United States of America Final Report*, above n 12, 40.

138 Senate Select Committee on the Australia-United States Free Trade Agreement, *Select Committee on the Free Trade Agreement between Australia and the United States of America Final Report*, above n 12, 40.

139 Vienna Convention on the Law of Treaties 1969, Art 24.

140 *Australia United-States Free Trade Agreement* 2004, Chapter Twenty-Three, Art 23.4.1.

141 Parliament of Australia, *National Interest Analysis—Australia United States of America Free Trade Agreement*, 2004 (Canberra: Joint Standing Committee, 2004).

142 Department of Foreign Affairs and Trade, *Australia and the United Nations* (2004) <http://www.dfat.gov.au/un/aus_un3.html> at 20 August 2004.

143 Michael Pryles, Jeff Waincymer and Martin Davies, above n 41, 904.

144 Michael Pryles, Jeff Waincymer and Martin Davies, above n 41, 904.

Australia is a party since 1948 have been published in the Australian Treaty Series, which is now available through the Department of Foreign Affairs and Trade.[145]

Important thematic points

By looking at Australia's treaty-making process in a step-by-step approach, it is revealed that a lot of the "mechanisms" in place to provide a so-called check and balance of the Executive government's power to enter into treaties are ineffective. This is illustrated by the fact that these mechanisms, such as publication of a NIA and RIS, and reports by JSCOT and the Senate Select Committee take place after Australia has already signed the treaty.

The Government may assert that signature does not mean Australia is bound by the particular and exact terms of the treaty as this only occurs once the agreement enters into force.[146] However it has been established that signature obligates Australia to refrain from acts which would defeat the object and purpose of the treaty.[147]

CHAPTER 2: THE INADEQUACIES OF AUSTRALIA'S TREATY-MAKING PROCESS WITH REGARD TO THE AUSTRALIA-UNITED STATES FREE TRADE AGREEMENT

Introduction

It is necessary for the purposes of this paper to identify the inadequacies of Australia's treaty-making process in relation to the implementation of FTAs. It is submitted that there are three main reasons why the treaty-making process is inadequate, as identified from analysing the implementation of the Australia-United States FTA. These include the fact that there are no mechanisms to ensure that implementing legislation will be passed, no mechanisms to make sure that obligations at an international law level will be satisfied and only minimal consultations to ensure that interests of States and Territories are protected.

This chapter will also take into consideration provisions at international law that may provide for dealing with these inadequacies, but evaluates that this is not an ideal solution.

No mechanisms to ensure that implementing legislation will be passed

In order to implement the Australia-United States FTA, legislation is necessary to put in place the changes.[148] The NIA and RIS assess the legislative impact of the FTA,

---

145 Michael Pryles, Jeff Waincymer and Martin Davies, above n 41, 904.

146 Department of Foreign Affairs and Trade, *Domestic Approval Processes for an Australia-United States Free Trade Agreement (AUSFTA)* above n 78.

147 Vienna Convention on the Law of Treaties 1969, Art 18.

148 Senate Select Committee on the Australia-United States Free Trade Agreement, *Select Committee on the Free Trade Agreement between Australia and the United States of America Final Report—Additional Information* 2004 (Canberra: Senate Select Committee, 2004), Chapter 4.

and determine what legislation needs to be amended.[149] The Office of Parliamentary Counsel handles all necessary legislative amendments.[150]

The starting point for the legislative changes necessary to implement the Australia-United States FTA was in the form of two Bills,[151] the US Free Trade Agreement Implementation Bill 2004[152] and the US Free Trade Agreement Implementation (Customs Tariff) Bill 2004.[153] These Bills were introduced to Parliament on 23 June and were passed on 13 August 2004 (receiving Royal Assent on 16 August 2004).[154]

In relation to the US Free Trade Agreement Implementation Act 2004 (Cth), Trade Minister, Mark Vaile, in his Second Reading Speech on the Introduction of the United States Free Trade Agreement,[155] stated that:

> The US Free Trade Agreement Implementation Bill 2004 consists of 9 schedules amending relevant Australian legislation to fulfil our obligations under the FTA. Passage of this legislation is the primary process in our domestic implementation—prompt passage will allow us to meet the target date of 1 January 2005 we have agreed with the United States for entry into force.[156]

The large amount of legislation necessary to be amended and implemented to give effect to Category B treaties, such as the Australia-United States FTA, shows that it may be necessary for the normal 20-day tabling period to take place prior to signature. Particularly because:

---

149 Senate Select Committee on the Australia-United States Free Trade Agreement, *Select Committee on the Free Trade Agreement between Australia and the United States of America Final Report—Additional Information*, above n 148, chapter 4.

150 Senate Select Committee on the Australia-United States Free Trade Agreement, *Select Committee on the Free Trade Agreement between Australia and the United States of America Final Report—Additional Information*, above n 148, chapter 4.

151 A Bill is a legislative document in the form of a proposed Act of Parliament that has not yet been passed by Parliament and received Royal Assent. Peter Butt and Peter Nygh (eds), above n 53, 51.

152 The US Free Trade Agreement Implementation Act 2004 (Cth) includes an extra schedule relating to broadcasting. The ten schedules amend legislation, as follows:

> Schedule One: Amends the Customs Act 1901 (Cth); Schedule Two: Amends the Agricultural and Veterinary Chemicals Code Act 1994 (Cth); Schedule Three: Amends the Australian Wine and Brandy Corporation Act 1980 (Cth); Schedule Four: Amends the Life Insurance Act 1995 (Cth); Schedule Five: Amends the Foreign Acquisitions and Takeovers Act 1975 (Cth); Schedule Six: Amends the Commonwealth Authorities and Companies Act 1997 (Cth); Schedule Seven: Amends the Therapeutic Goods Act 1989 (Cth); Schedule Eight: Amends the Patents Act 1990 (Cth); Schedule Nine: Amends the Copyright Act 1968 (Cth); and Schedule Ten: Amends the Broadcasting Services Act 1992 (Cth). Scaleplus Law Resource, *US Free Trade Agreement Implementation Bill 2004—First Reading* (2004) <http://www.scaleplus.law.gov.au/html/bills/0/2004/0/2004062412.htm> at 1 September 2004 and Scaleplus Law Resource, *US Free Trade Agreement Implementation Bill 2004—Explanatory Memorandum* (2004) <http://www.scaleplus.law.gov.au/html/ems/0/2004/0/2004062410.htm> at 1 September 2004.

153 Amending this Act implements the Australia-United States FTA in terms of the duty-free access for certain goods and the preferential rates of customs duty for other goods. The purpose of the US Free Trade Agreement Implementation (Customs Tariff) Act 2004 (Cth) is to amend the Customs Tariff Act 1995 (Cth).

154 US Free Trade Agreement Implementation Act 2004 (Cth); US Free Trade Agreement Implementation (Customs Tariff) Act 2004 (Cth); Scaleplus Law Resource, US Free Trade Agreement Implementation Bill 2004—First Reading (2004) <http://www.scaleplus.law.gov.au/html/bills/0/2004/0/2004062412.htm> at 1 September 2004 and Scaleplus Law Resource, US Free Trade Agreement Implementation Bill 2004—Explanatory Memorandum (2004) <http://www.scaleplus.law.gov.au/html/ems/0/2004/0/2004062410.htm> at 1 September 2004.

155 Australian Trade Minister Mark Vaile, above n 77.

156 Australian Trade Minister Mark Vaile, above n 77.

> . . . it was not until the implementing legislation was introduced to parliament that the Select Committee was in a position to examine whether, or to what extent, that legislation might address many of the concerns that had been raised by witnesses in the course of its inquiry.[157]

Also the NIA and RIS, which are completed *after* signature,[158] play an important role in analysing what legislation specifically needs to be amended or implemented.[159]

> Under the existing state of affairs, the government can sign off on an agreement, but find itself confronted with, say, amendments by the Senate of some elements of the domestic legislation necessary to implement the agreement. If the prospect of such amendments was known in advance, the trade negotiators could take them into account.[160]

This makes it clear that it would be beneficial for Australia's treaty-making process to be changed, so that the minimum 20-day tabling period for the RIS, NIA and committee reports was *before* signature. Additionally, a requirement that the Federal Parliament approve the legislation amendments prior to the signing of the agreement would ensure that implementing legislation would be passed. The fact that a FTA has so many obligations to fulfil under international law makes it imperative that Australia is able to pass all necessary legislation. This proposal for reform will be discussed further in Chapter 3.

No mechanisms to ensure international law will be satisfied

The Australia-United States FTA must abide by the World Trade Organisation and the International Law Commission (which compiled the Vienna Convention on the Law of Treaties 1969) at international law. If Australia does not satisfy its obligations under international law, it may face penalties or have to deal with the other party terminating the treaty.

World Trade Organisation

The World Trade Organisation[161] (WTO) is the only international organisation that deals with the rules governing trade between countries.[162] It allows member

157 Senate Select Committee on the Australia-United States Free Trade Agreement, *Select Committee on the Free Trade Agreement between Australia and the United States of America Final Report*, above n 12, 39.

158 Department of Foreign Affairs and Trade, *Domestic Approval Processes for an Australia-United States Free Trade Agreement (AUSFTA)* above n 78.

159 Senate Select Committee on the Australia-United States Free Trade Agreement, *Select Committee on the Free Trade Agreement between Australia and the United States of America Final Report*, above n 12, 39.

160 Senate Select Committee on the Australia-United States Free Trade Agreement, *Select Committee on the Free Trade Agreement between Australia and the United States of America Final Report*, above n 12, 39.

161 The WTO was established as a result of the Uruguay Round of the General Agreement on Tariffs and Trade (GATT) negotiations (1986–93). GATT was a forum for trade negotiations through which members reached consensus and agreements on improvements to GATT. On 15 April 1994, 124 countries and the European Union approved the WTO agreement at a Ministerial Meeting held in Marrakesh, Morocco. The Marrakesh Protocol of 15 April 1994 afforded political backing to the Agreement, which established the WTO to come into force on 1 January 1995 (the WTO was previously known as the General Agreement on Tariffs and Trade from 1947). John Mo, *International Commercial Law* (3rd ed, NSW: Butterworths, 2003) 578–9.

162 Both Australia and the United States are members of the World Trade Organisation—World Trade Organization, *The World Trade Organization* (1997) <http://www.ip-law.co.il/DomainNames/treat8.htm> at 22 April 2004.

countries to decide on trade rules and has set up a process to resolve trade disputes.[163]

The guiding principles of the WTO are set out in the WTO preamble and include:[164]

(a) raising standards of living, particularly for developing countries;
(b) ensuring full employment;
(c) maintaining the volume of production and trade of goods and services;
(d) utilising world resources while upholding sustainable development principles;
(e) protecting, managing and preserving the environment;
(f) participating in non-discriminatory free trade; and
(g) establishing a viable multilateral trading system.[165]

The Australia-United States FTA had adopted some of these values by incorporating them into Art 22.1 of Chapter Twenty Two. It means both the Australian and United States governments are:

> Free to enact laws, regulations or policies considered necessary to, for example:
>
> (a) protect public morals or maintain public order;
> (b) protect human, animal or plant life or health;
> (c) protect national treasures of artistic, historic or archaeological value; and
> (d) conserve exhaustible natural resources.[166]

Article 22.2 of Chapter Twenty Two of the Australia-United States FTA also provides for Australia and the United States to legislate freely in relation to protecting their security interests.[167]

It is contended that if the Commonwealth does not consult sufficiently with the Federal Parliament, States and Territories in relation to the FTA, they could legislate inconsistently with WTO principles[168] or could block the passing of legislation to uphold these principles in the Senate. Therefore it is imperative that the Executive maintains an extensive communication channel with the Federal Parliament and the States and Territories, or seek their formal approval before signing the FTA (further discussion on the alternatives for improving this inadequacy will be discussed in Chapter 3).

163 Department of Foreign Affairs and Trade, *Australia and the World Trade Organization* (2004) <http://www.dfat.gov.au/trade/fs_australia_and_the_wto.html> at 15 March 2004.

164 M Rafiqul Islam, *International Trade Law* (NSW:LBC Information Services, 1999) 45–46.

165 M Rafiqul Islam, above n 164, 46.

166 Department of Foreign Affairs and Trade, *Australia-United States Free Trade Agreement—Guide to the Agreement* (2004) <http://www.dfat.gov.au/trade/negotiations/us_fta/guide/1_22_23_Legal_Institutional.html> at 15 March 2004.

167 Department of Foreign Affairs and Trade, *Australia-United States Free Trade Agreement—Guide to the Agreement*, above n 166.

168 Note that if a State law is inconsistent with a law of the Commonwealth, the State law is deemed invalid (though not void) to the extent of the inconsistency. Commonwealth Constitution 1900 (Cth) s 109.

Consequences of breaching World Trade Organisation principles

If Australia does not take careful consideration of WTO principles when implementing FTAs then it may have to contend with a penalty imposed. "[T]rade agreements impose binding justiciable constraints on governments regarding the conduct of fiscal, monetary, trade and investment policies"[169] and the WTO "... impose penalties for serious breaches."[170]

That is why it is imperative that the treaty-making process for category B treaties such as FTAs is mindful of the wide-ranging effects and obligations it must fulfil.

> Unlike labour, human rights and environmental agreements, trade treaties incorporate ... binding enforcement mechanisms, including sanctions and compensation, making them more analogous to private law or contract law than traditional human rights treaties.[171]

Legislative drafters need more time to scrutinise the text of FTAs and the legislation already in place to ensure restrictions imposed by international law are upheld by implementing legislation. The minimum 20-day tabling period appears to be too late to cope with such an extensive treaty action that is already binding[172] once tabled (as treaties are generally tabled after signature),[173] particularly for future FTAs, which will not have the benefit of the extended 90-day tabling period prior to signature as fixed by the United States.[174]

International Law Commission

At an international law level, the Australia-United States FTA may be affected by the disciplinary codes set out by the International Law Commission,[175] such as the Vienna Convention on the Law of Treaties 1969.[176]

Vienna Convention on the Law of Treaties

The Vienna Convention on the Law of Treaties 1969 is the principal piece of work undertaken by the International Law Commission.[177] The Convention was adopted

169 Senate Select Committee on the Australia-United States Free Trade Agreement, *Select Committee on the Free Trade Agreement between Australia and the United States of America Final Report*, above n 12, 30.

170 Senate Select Committee on the Australia-United States Free Trade Agreement, *Select Committee on the Free Trade Agreement between Australia and the United States of America Final Report*, above n 12, 30.

171 Senate Select Committee on the Australia-United States Free Trade Agreement, *Select Committee on the Free Trade Agreement between Australia and the United States of America Final Report*, above n 12, 30.

172 Vienna Convention on the Law of Treaties 1969, Art 18.

173 Senate Select Committee on the Australia-United States Free Trade Agreement, *Select Committee on the Free Trade Agreement between Australia and the United States of America Final Report*, above n 12, 30.

174 Department of Foreign Affairs and Trade, *Domestic Approval Processes for an Australia-United States Free Trade Agreement (AUSFTA)*, above n 78.

175 Resolution 174 (II) of the General Assembly (the main policy-making body of the United Nations Organisation) established the International Law Commission in 1947 to promote the progressive development of international law and its codification. Martin Dixon and Robert McCorquodale, above n 88, 68.

176 Martin Dixon and Robert McCorquodale, above n 88, 68.

177 Martin Dixon and Robert McCorquodale, above n 88, 68.

by the Vienna Conference in 1969 but did not enter into force until 1980.[178] The Convention only applies to treaties concluded after its entry into force.[179] Australia is bound to the Convention, therefore the Australia-United States FTA must comply with the provisions it sets out.[180] The United States however is only a signatory[181] but the rules the Convention sets out are enforceable by the United States as "the Vienna Convention . . . is a restatement of customary rules, binding States regardless of whether they are parties to the Convention . . . by the International Court of Justice."[182]

The Vienna Convention on the Law of Treaties 1969 sets out many principles, which must be abided by Australia, in order to fulfil its obligations under the Convention. Two of these that will be discussed include the principle, "pacta sunt servanda" and the notion of having implementing legislation in place prior to treaties entering into force.

"Pacta sunt servanda"[183]

An essential rule set out by the Report of the International Law Commission to the General Assembly[184] is "pacta sunt servanda". Article 26 of the Vienna Convention on the Law of Treaties 1969 adopted this rule.[185] It means that every treaty in force is binding on the parties to it and must be performed by them in good faith.[186] This rule in practical terms will mean that if the United States complies with its obligations in relation to the FTA then Australia will also be obligated to do so. For legal regulation of the international community, the principle of "pacta sunt servanda" is imperative.

Implementing legislation must be in place prior to a treaty entering into force

Article 27 of the Vienna Convention on the Law of Treaties 1969 specifies that implementing legislation must be passed before the Australia-United States FTA will come into effect.[187] It states that, "[a] party may not invoke the provisions of its internal law as justification for its failure to perform a treaty."[188] Thus if Australia does not pass legislation necessary to implement the Australia-United States FTA, Australia will contravene Art 27 and may face a penalty under international law.

---

178 Martin Dixon, above n 3, 56.

179 Sam Blay, Ryszard Piotrowicz and B Martin Tsamenyi (eds), *Public International Law an Australian Perspective* (Melbourne: Oxford University Press, 1997) 95.

180 Sam Blay, Ryszard Piotrowicz and B Martin Tsamenyi (eds), above n 179, 95.

181 The United States is not a party to the Vienna Convention on the Law of Treaties, as consent for ratification has been pending before the United States Senate since 1972. Maria Frankowska, "The Vienna Convention on the Law of Treaties Before United States Courts" (1988) 28 *Virginia Journal of International Law*, 281, 286.

182 Maria Frankowska, above 181, 286.

183 Latin for "pacts must be respected". Wikipedia Encyclopedia, *Pacta sunt servanda* (2004) <http://en.wikipedia.org/wiki/Pacta_sunt_servanda> at 25 September 2004.

184 Report of the International Law Commission to the General Assembly *Yearbook of the International Law Commission*, 1966, vol. II, 172, 211.

185 Martin Dixon and Robert McCorquodale, above n 88, 68.

186 Martin Dixon and Robert McCorquodale, above n 88, 68.

187 Vienna Convention on the Law of Treaties 1969, Art 27.

188 Vienna Convention on the Law of Treaties 1969, Art 27.

It should be noted however that a "federal clause" may be included in the treaty, which has the effect of allowing Australia to have laws that may be inconsistent with the Australia-United States FTA.[189] Federal clauses are permissible under Art 46 of the Vienna Convention on the Law of Treaties 1969, as it expresses:

1. A State may not invoke ... its consent to be bound by a treaty ... [because] of its internal law ... unless that violation was manifest and concerned a rule of its internal law of fundamental importance.
2. A violation is manifest if it would be objectively evident to any State conducting itself in the matter in accordance with normal practice and in good faith.[190]

The Australia-United States FTA, however, does not contain a "federal clause", therefore must abide by the stringent obligation under Art 27 of the Vienna Convention of the Law of Treaties 1969 to uphold the principles agreed upon under the FTA, despite any internal legislating incompetencies. If the States and Territories or the Senate do not pass implementing legislation of the Australia-United States FTA then Australia could face a penalty under international law for breaching Art 27.[191]

Consequences of breaching the Vienna Convention on the Law of Treaties

The penalty for not complying with treaty obligations entered into under the Vienna Convention on the Law of Treaties 1969 is that the party adversely affected by the breach will be entitled to terminate the FTA.[192] This is something that Australia would wish to avoid, as the benefits achievable under the FTA would be lost. It would also suggest to the international community that Australia's treaty-making capacity is not reliable.[193]

Minimal consultations do not ensure that States' and Territories' interests are protected

Australia has a federal system of government,[194] seen in the allocation of legislative responsibilities between the Commonwealth and the States.[195] Australia's federal system of government poses some problems for the Commonwealth being able to legislate over State powers, in order to implement the Australia-United States FTA.[196] Section 51 of the Commonwealth Constitution[197] divides legislative powers between the Commonwealth and States to uphold the federal system of government. Legislative powers not expressly specified in s 51 of the Commonwealth

189 Vienna Convention on the Law of Treaties 1969, Art 46.

190 Vienna Convention on the Law of Treaties 1969, Art 46.

191 Vienna Convention on the Law of Treaties 1969, Art 27.

192 Vienna Convention on the Law of Treaties 1969, Art 60.

193 Note: a party may waive its right to terminate under the Vienna Convention on the Law of Treaties 1969, Art 45.

194 This is a system of national government where legislative, executive and judicial powers are divided between a central government and the states (this concept is known as "division of powers"). Peter Butt and Peter Nygh (eds), above n 53, 173.

195 Peter Butt and Peter Nygh (eds), above n 53, 173.

196 Such as the area of employment (*Industrial Relations Act case* (1996) 187 CLR 416) and the environment (*Lemonthyme Forest case* (1988) 164 CLR 261), which are State powers.

197 Commonwealth Constitution 1900 (Cth).

Constitution,[198] or those powers not given or made exclusive to the Commonwealth are referred to as residual powers,[199] over which the States have jurisdiction.[200] If the Commonwealth legislates in regard to a State power, the legislation could be held to be unconstitutional, unless the States approve it.[201]

In the "Request for additional information on States views of the Australia-United States Free Trade Agreement",[202] Queensland and Victoria both commented that the FTA might trigger State legislative changes.[203] The Queensland State government stated that although it does "not have to amend or enact any legislation prior to the AUSFTA entering into force",[204] some amendments will need to be made in relation to its Purchasing Policy and Local Industry Policy to comply with the provisions in the government procurement chapter.[205] The Victorian State government expressed that it:

> ... does not consider that the AUSFTA would create a head of power for the Commonwealth to legislate on matters of State authority; nor would it extend the authority of the Commonwealth in any other way [however] ... there is a need to review existing arrangement(s) for Commonwealth-State consultation(s) on treaties ...[206]

otherwise the Commonwealth may at some stage use its extensive "external affairs" power to encroach State powers.

A statement by the Western Australian Executive Director of the Office of Federal Affairs, Petrice Judge,[207] at the "Joint Standing Committee on Treaties: Australia-United States FTA Discussion"[208] made it clear that the consultations with States were inadequate for the purposes of entering into the *Australia-United States FTA* which has "... wide ranging consequences ... across areas of state responsibility".[209] She recommended that:

---

198 Commonwealth Constitution 1900 (Cth).

199 For example States power includes employment (*Industrial Relations Act case* (1996) 187 CLR 416) and the environment (*Lemonthyme Forest case* (1988) 164 CLR 261).

200 The Commonwealth has responsibility over explicit topics and the States have power over wide and unspecified powers subject to a few exclusions and the paramountcy of Commonwealth laws. Peter Butt and Peter Nygh (eds), above n 53, 173.

201 Under s 51(xxxvii) of the Commonwealth Constitution 1900 (Cth) a State or States can refer state matters to the Commonwealth, so that the Commonwealth can legislate in regards to that matter.

202 Senate Select Committee on the Australia-United States Free Trade Agreement, *Select Committee on the Free Trade Agreement between Australia and the United States of America Final Report—Additional Information,* above n 148, Chapter 4.

203 Senate Select Committee on the Australia-United States Free Trade Agreement, *Select Committee on the Free Trade Agreement between Australia and the United States of America Final Report—Additional* Information, above n 148, Chapter 4, 3.

204 Senate Select Committee on the Australia-United States Free Trade Agreement, *Select Committee on the Free Trade Agreement between Australia and the United States of America Final Report—Additional Information,* above n 148, Chapter 4, 9.

205 Senate Select Committee on the Australia-United States Free Trade Agreement, *Select Committee on the Free Trade Agreement between Australia and the United States of America Final Report—Additional Information,* above n 148, Chapter 4, 9.

206 Senate Select Committee on the Australia-United States Free Trade Agreement, *Select Committee on the Free Trade Agreement between Australia and the United States of America Final Report—Additional Information,* above n 148, Chapter 4, 4.

207 Joint Standing Committee on Treaties Hansard, *Executive Director Office Federal Affairs Department of the Premier and Cabinet Western Australia, P Judge,* Australia-United States Free Trade Agreement, 23 April 2004.

208 Joint Standing Committee on Treaties Hansard, above n 207.

209 Joint Standing Committee on Treaties Hansard, above n 207, TR2.

> ... in future negotiations it be made clear to the other party at the outset that Australia will have at least one representative of the states and territories on the Australian negotiating team.[210]

The effect that the Commonwealth's dominant role has on particular states makes it evident that there is a need for reform to limit the Executive's power, or at least scrutinise the implementation of Category B treaties more thoroughly.[211] In a letter from the Department of the Premier and Cabinet of Western Australia to the Senate Select Committee on the Free Trade Agreement between Australia and the United States, the Western Australia government identified and addressed some key inadequacies of the "formal mechanism(s) to protect the interests of the States and Territories".[212] It was identified that currently " ... the States and Territories have to rely on the precedence of the High Court and the goodwill of the Commonwealth."[213] This is obviously not a formal system that the States and Territories can rely upon with certainty. It was conveyed that

> ... [w]hile it is acknowledged that the Commonwealth Government is vested with the power to enter into an international treaty, the States and Territories must have proper opportunity to provide comment, particularly on issues that ultimately impact on State and Territory legislation and/or economies.[214]

International law provisions that may be able to help Australia's inadequate treaty-making process

The Vienna Convention on the Law of Treaties 1969 sets out a range of procedures that may be able to deal with the inadequacies of Australia's treaty-making process. These mechanisms include making reservations, amending and terminating.[215]

Making reservations

Reservations are the means by which Australia and the United States can expressly state that there are some provisions of the FTA which they do not accept.[216] This would be in situations where a party realises it needs to preserve its own particular

---

210 Joint Standing Committee on Treaties Hansard, above n 207, TR2.

211 Western Australia, Queensland and Victoria are the only States discussed in this paper, as they were the only States that published comments regarding the effect of the Australia-United States FTA on their powers. Senate Select Committee on the Australia-United States Free Trade Agreement, *Select Committee on the Free Trade Agreement between Australia and the United States of America Final Report—Additional Information*, above n 148, Chapter 4.

212 Senate Select Committee on the Australia-United States Free Trade Agreement, *Select Committee on the Free Trade Agreement between Australia and the United States of America Final Report—Additional Information*, above n 148, Chapter 4, 1.

213 Senate Select Committee on the Australia-United States Free Trade Agreement, *Select Committee on the Free Trade Agreement between Australia and the United States of America Final Report—Additional Information*, above n 148, Chapter 4, 1.

214 Senate Select Committee on the Australia-United States Free Trade Agreement, *Select Committee on the Free Trade Agreement between Australia and the United States of America Final Report—Additional Information*, above n 148, Chapter 4, 3.

215 Department of Foreign Affairs and Trade, *Australia-United States Free Trade Agreement—Guide to the Agreement*, above n 166.

216 Vienna Convention on the Law of Treaties 1969, Art 2.

interest. Reservations can have the effect of excluding the legal effect of a particular provision altogether or modifying or qualifying the extent of a provision.[217]

Reservations may be made at various stages of the formation of a treaty. This includes when the parties are signing, ratifying, accepting, approving or acceding to the treaty.[218] Therefore it is important that during the formation stage of the treaty, there is enough time to scrutinise the provisions of the treaty.

Making, accepting or objecting to a reservation must be in writing and communicated to the other party.[219] For example, in the case of the Australia-United States FTA, if Australia wished to make a reservation regarding audiovisual services, it would have to express the reservation in writing and submit it to the United States. Reservations can also be withdrawn at any time unless the treaty states otherwise[220] and an objection to a reservation may also be withdrawn at any time unless the treaty states otherwise.[221] It has been held by case law that a State who makes a reservation may still be regarded as bound by the rest of the FTA.[222] Thus if Australia were to make a reservation in regards to a term of the Australia-United States FTA, Australia would still be bound by the rest of the provisions in the FTA.

Australia and the United States have already specified particular reservations in Annex II of the Australia-United States FTA. The reservations are specified as "Non-Conforming Measures."[223] In Australia's schedule, the sectors covered by a reservation include:

(a) social services;
(b) broadcasting and audiovisual services;
(c) distribution services;
(d) education services;
(e) maritime; and
(f) transport.[224]

In the United States' schedule, the sectors covered by a reservation include:

(a) communications;
(b) social services;
(c) minority affairs; and
(d) transportation.[225]

---

217 Vienna Convention on the Law of Treaties 1969, Art 21.

218 Vienna Convention on the Law of Treaties 1969, Art 19. There are certain circumstances where a reservation is prohibited including if the treaty expressly forbids the reservation, if the reservation is not one specifically allowed for under the treaty; or if the reservation is incompatible with the object and purpose of the treaty.

219 Vienna Convention on the Law of Treaties 1969, Art 23.

220 Vienna Convention on the Law of Treaties 1969, Art 22 (1).

221 Vienna Convention on the Law of Treaties 1969, Art 22 (2).

222 International Court of Justice *Reservations to the Convention on the Prevention and Punishment of the Crime of Genocide* ICJ Rep 1951, 15.

223 Australia-United States Free Trade Agreement 2004, Annex II-1.

224 Australia-United States Free Trade Agreement 2004, Annex II-Australia–1.

225 Australia-United States Free Trade Agreement 2004, Annex II-United States-1.

These reservations were the outcome of each country's own domestic analysis of what is in the countries' best interest. The allowance for reservations may assist the inadequacy of Australia's process to ensure that all provisions under the signed draft FTA are implemented by legislation. If the legislation is not passed to give effect to a certain provision in the FTA, Australia may submit a reservation up until ratification.[226] This is not ideal however, because the United States could object to the reservation.

Amending

A treaty can be amended by agreement between the parties under Art 30 of the Vienna Convention on the Law of Treaties 1969,[227] though a separate treaty known as a "protocol" is usually the method for changing the provisions of a treaty.[228]

The Australia-United States FTA has specifically set out provisions for the amendment of the FTA. Article 23.3 of Chapter Twenty Three of the Australia-United States FTA states that:

> 1. The Parties may agree, in writing, to amend this Agreement. An amendment shall enter into force after the Parties complete any necessary internal requirements and on such date as the Parties may agree.[229]

The idea of making amendments in order to deal with problems that become evident with FTAs entered into by Australia, due to a lack of scrutiny at the negotiation stage ". . . could involve long lead times, loss of trade access or payment of compensation".[230] Therefore relying on the amendment provision under Art 39 of the Vienna Convention on the Law of Treaties 1969 and Art 23.3 of the Australia-United States FTA is not ideal.

> . . . [I]t is essential that parliament is fully aware of the content of trade agreements and has the opportunity to debate such agreements, prior to Australia being bound to comply with the agreement in question,[231]

so that amendment is not necessary.

Terminating

Article 54 of the Vienna Convention on the Law of Treaties 1969 allows for a party to terminate or withdraw from a treaty, by conforming with termination and withdrawal provision(s) set out in the treaty. Termination and withdrawal provisions are set out in Art 23.4.2 of Chapter Twenty Three of the Australia-United States FTA. It states that either party may terminate the FTA by giving the other party six

226 Vienna Convention on the Law of Treaties 1969, Art 19.

227 Vienna Convention on the Law of Treaties 1969, Art 39.

228 Martin Dixon and Robert McCorquodale, above n 88, 68.

229 Australia-United States Free Trade Agreement 2004, Art 23.3, Chapter Twenty Three.

230 Senate Select Committee on the Australia-United States Free Trade Agreement, *Select Committee on the Free Trade Agreement between Australia and the United States of America Final Report*, above n 12, 30.

231 Senate Select Committee on the Australia-United States Free Trade Agreement, *Select Committee on the Free Trade Agreement between Australia and the United States of America Final Report*, above n 12, 30.

months notice in writing.[232] Article 23.4.3 of Chapter Twenty Three of the Australia-United States FTA also provides for an extension of another six months (therefore 12 months) for the party to give notice before termination.[233]

The Vienna Convention on the Law of Treaties 1969 sets out provisions in regards to when a party may be entitled to terminate the treaty. For example, if a party to the FTA breaches its obligation(s) under the treaty, the party affected by the breach will be entitled to terminate.[234] Article 60[235] states that:

> 1. A material breach of a bilateral treaty by one of the parties entitles the other to invoke the breach as a ground for terminating the treaty or suspending its operation in whole or in part.
>
> . . .
>
> 3. A material breach of a treaty, for the purposes of this article consists of:
>
> a repudiation of the treaty not sanctioned by the present Convention; or
>
> the violation of a provision essential to the accomplishment of the object or purpose of the treaty.[236]

Article 45 of the Vienna Convention on the Law of Treaties 1969, however, states that a party may also waive its right to terminate.[237]

The consequences of terminating a treaty are set out in Art 70,[238] which states that unless otherwise provided in the treaty or agreed between the parties, the termination of a treaty:

(a) releases the parties from any obligations to further perform the treaty; and

(b) does not affect any right, obligation or legal situation of the parties created through the execution of the treaty prior to its termination.[239]

Australia would not want a treaty terminated due to an inability to fulfil its obligations if implementing legislation is not passed. Termination of an FTA could possibly tarnish Australia's international trading reputation and means that Australia misses out on the potential benefits of the FTA.

Important thematic points

This chapter has identified the inadequacies of Australia's treaty-making process, including the lack of mechanisms to ensure that implementing legislation is passed, that international law can be fulfilled and that States' and Territories' interests are protected. It is important to ensure that Australia's inadequate treaty-making process is improved, because Australia cannot rely on international law provisions

232 If the Australia-United States Free Trade Agreement (2004) did not specifically have termination or withdrawal provisions, the party terminating or withdrawing would have to give 12 months notice of its intention to terminate or withdraw under Art 56 of the Vienna Convention on the Law of Treaties 1969.

233 Australia-United States Free Trade Agreement 2004, Art 23.4.3, Chapter Twenty Three.

234 Martin Dixon and Robert McCorquodale, above n 88, 101.

235 Vienna Convention on the Law of Treaties 1969.

236 Vienna Convention on the Law of Treaties 1969, Art 60.

237 Vienna Convention on the Law of Treaties 1969, Art 45.

238 Vienna Convention on the Law of Treaties 1969.

239 Vienna Convention on the Law of Treaties 1969, Art 70.

such as reservations, amendments or termination. Relying on these provisions could damage Australia's international reputation and involve Australia losing the benefits it could have maintained if the problems relating to the treaty were identified and resolved prior to signature. The vast impact that FTAs have on an international level and on shaping Australia's federal system of government indicates that there is significant justification for the Federal Parliament to scrutinise these agreements.

CHAPTER 3: PROPOSALS FOR REFORMING AUSTRALIA'S TREATY-MAKING PROCESS FOR IMPLEMENTING FREE TRADE AGREEMENTS

Introduction

There have been a number of proposals to reform the treaty-making process in Australia. They indicate a growing concern that the treaty-making process does not involve adequate consultation with the States and Territories and that it is not sufficiently accountable. Recommendations are aimed at improving the scrutiny of treaties by the Federal Parliament and furthering consultations between the Executive and States and Territories.

Such reforms include parliamentary scrutiny, legislative reform for parliamentary approval of treaties prior to signature, a Treaties Council, communication between the different levels of government, emulating the United States treaty-making process and implementing the Senate Select Committee's proposal for reform. It is anticipated that if these reforms were in place, Australia's treaty-making process would be adequate because it would ensure Australia would be able to fulfil its obligations under international law and would endorse Australia's federal system of government.

Parliamentary scrutiny

FTAs are entered into for Australia's national interest.[240] The Federal Parliament and the Federal government both share this interest. With treaties increasingly affecting both the distribution of legislative powers within Australia and the position of individuals, there is a case for greater parliamentary involvement in the treaty-making process. There has been criticism of the

> sense of inevitability and haste in the manner in which Australia has joined treaties . . . [and the] absence of openness and inadequate parliamentary and community involvement in the treaty process.[241]

The scrutiny of the Federal Parliament has to some extent been put into practice by the 1996 reforms, which involve the tabling of treaties for at least 20 sitting days before ratification (for Category B treaties, which include FTAs, and 15 sitting

240 Senate Select Committee on the Australia-United States Free Trade Agreement, *Select Committee on the Free Trade Agreement between Australia and the United States of America Final Report*, above n 12, 40.

241 Brian R Opeskin and Donald R Rothwell (eds), above n 51, 336.

days for Category A treaties), together with a NIA and RIS.[242] It has been stated however that the " . . . tabling of treaties is not intended to be an exercise in ascertaining Parliament's views about whether or not Australia should become a party".[243] This is also illustrated by the general practice to sign the treaties prior to tabling in the Federal Parliament.[244]

In addition the JSCOT and Senate Select Committee have been established, however it has been commented that these bodies "may in time suffer from the defects of the parliamentary committee system generally [such as] . . . desultory attendance and performance, [and] the lack of real power to effect change".[245]

In any event, by the time a report is considered, the treaty is usually already signed.[246]

> The crucial point for trade agreements is "prior to signature", because once a treaty has been signed it would be extremely unlikely for the government to refuse to ratify a treaty . . .[247]

In relation to the Australia-United States FTA, the United States stipulated that the Agreement be tabled prior to signature,[248] however the treaty-making process still proved to be somewhat ineffective. This was because when Parliament had the opportunity to debate the implementing legislation the Trade Minister, Mark Vaile, in his Second Reading Speech on the Introduction of the United States Free Trade Implementation Bill[249] put pressure on the Government to hasten the implementation by stating:

> Delay or dismissal of this legislation will not simply defer the benefits of the Agreement. There appears to be a naive view among some opposite that delaying passage of this legislation, or consideration of the Agreement as a whole, would afford an opportunity to review at leisure the provisions of this Agreement, and even to renegotiate aspects of it. This is a dangerous delusion that ignores the reality of the negotiating process for a treaty with any sovereign government . . . [T]he idea that we could re-open the text of the Agreement . . . to secure a different outcome, is completely out of touch with reality. To delay or reject passage of this legislation would be seen by the United States Government and Congress as rejection of the only FTA text that was acceptable to the United States.[250]

This type of pressure questions the capacity of the Federal Parliament to have any real participation in the implementation of treaties. It appears that a more formal approach to the Federal Parliament having a role in the treaty-making process, such as an Act giving it certain powers, may be necessary rather than the current administrative authority that has been shown to be inadequate.

---

242 Brian R Opeskin and Donald R Rothwell (eds), above n 51, 140.

243 Brian R Opeskin and Donald R Rothwell (eds), above n 51, 88.

244 Once a treaty has been signed, Australia then has an obligation not to defeat the object and purpose of the treaty. Vienna Convention on the Law of Treaties 1969, Art 18.

245 Brian R Opeskin and Donald R Rothwell (eds), above n 51, 88.

246 Department of Foreign Affairs and Trade, *Domestic Approval Processes for an Australia-United States Free Trade Agreement (AUSFTA)* above n 78.

247 Senate Select Committee on the Australia-United States Free Trade Agreement, *Select Committee on the Free Trade Agreement between Australia and the United States of America Final Report*, above n 12, 38.

248 Department of Foreign Affairs and Trade, *Domestic Approval Processes for an Australia-United States Free Trade Agreement (AUSFTA)* above n 78.

249 Australian Trade Minister Mark Vaile, above n 77.

250 Australian Trade Minister Mark Vaile, above n 77.

The changes to the treaty-making process in 1996 are to some extent useful, as they do require a greater level of formal consultation and communication with the Federal Parliament and State and Territory governments than pre-1996.[251] On the other hand they do not go very far as they have been implemented solely by way of changes to administrative practice and without legislative backing (which was recommended by the Senate Committee in 1995).[252]

Legislative reform

In 1984 Senator Peter Durack introduced a private member's Bill into the Senate proposing to amend the Commonwealth Constitution[253] so as to confine the "external affairs" power[254] to matters with a substantial relationship to other countries or matters outside the Commonwealth. The constitutional amendment was not supported so Senator Durack subsequently advocated modification of the power by political convention.[255]

Senator Vicki Bourne, of the Australian Democrats, introduced the Parliamentary Approval of Treaties Bill 1995 (Cth) to Parliament.[256] This sought to effect what Senator Bourne claimed was a:

> ... fundamental democratic principle ... that an executive government must seek parliamentary approval before making a treaty binding upon Australia. Treaty-making has historically been an executive prerogative, but the growth in the number and scope of international agreements has meant that the status quo can no longer be justified.[257]

The Bill was to apply to "any agreement or proposed agreement in writing between two or more countries"[258] and provided that "[a]ction by which a treaty would enter into force in respect of Australia must not be taken before the treaty is approved in accordance with this Act".[259]

Under the Parliamentary Approval of Treaties Bill 1995 (Cth), Ministers would be required to publish a declaration in the gazette to propose that Australia enter into a particular treaty.[260] In addition, the treaty would then have to be tabled in each House of Parliament within 15 sitting days of gazettal,[261] together with a "treaty

---

251 From the 1960s to mid 1990 treaties were tabled in bulk approximately every six months, including treaties that were already signed and ratified. For example, on 30 November 1994, of the eleven bilateral treaties tabled, seven had already come into force. Accordingly, Australia was already obliged by international law to comply with them, denying any meaningful Federal Parliamentary scrutiny. Brian R Opeskin and Donald R Rothwell (eds), above n 51, 87.

252 Senate Select Committee, *Trick or Treaty? Commonwealth Power to Make and Implement Treaties* 1995 (Canberra: Senate Select Committee, 1995) Chapter 14.

253 Commonwealth Constitution 1900 (Cth).

254 Commonwealth Constitution 1900 (Cth) s 51(xxix).

255 Cranwell G, "The Case for Parliamentary Approval of Treaties in Australia" (2001) 8 *Murdoch University Electronic Journal of Law*.

256 Initially the Bill was introduced on 29 June 1994.

257 Senate Hansard, Parliamentary Approval of Treaties Bill 1995: Second Reading, *Senator V Bourne*, 31 May 1995, 661.

258 Parliamentary Approval of Treaties Bill 1995 (Cth) clause 3.

259 Parliamentary Approval of Treaties Bill 1995 (Cth) clause 4.

260 Parliamentary Approval of Treaties Bill 1995 (Cth) clause 5 (1).

261 Parliamentary Approval of Treaties Bill 1995 (Cth) clause 5 (2).

impact statement"[262] and "a statement setting out the consultations which have occurred between the Commonwealth, the states and the territories in respect of the treaty".[263] The members of each House would then have 15 sitting days to give a notice of motion requesting that that House consider the treaty. The treaty would be deemed to have been approved if no notice of motion was given within the 15 sitting days.[264] If a notice of motion was given, no action could be taken by the Executive to bring the treaty into effect until the relevant House of Parliament approved the treaty.[265] If the treaty was not approved, then the Executive would not have the power to enter into the treaty.[266]

The Parliamentary Approval of Treaties Bill 1995 (Cth) was not approved in 1995 largely due to the calling of an election in 1996.[267] However the fact that the Bill was not comprehensive enough to deal with additional issues, such as sensitive treaties, urgent treaties or reservations, meant it was not strongly supported.[268] It is submitted that with the prospect of further FTAs being implemented including an Australia-New Zealand FTA, Australia-Malaysia FTA and Australia-Egypt Trade FTA in 2005–2006,[269] it may be necessary to implement a legislative mechanism, such as the Parliamentary Approval of Treaties Bill 1995 (Cth) to ensure Australia's federal system of government is upheld and international obligations can be fulfilled with certainty.[270]

If a new Bill of this kind was to be confined further to just regulate Category B treaties, which includes FTAs, this would improve and be of benefit to the Australian treaty-making process.

Treaties Council

In 1996, the Council of Australian Governments[271] and the Senate Select Committee[272] reviewed the treaty-making process of the day. The suggested outcome from this review was to implement a Treaties Council.[273]

262 Parliamentary Approval of Treaties Bill 1995 (Cth) clause 5 (3) (a).

263 Parliamentary Approval of Treaties Bill 1995 (Cth) clause 5 (3) (b).

264 Parliamentary Approval of Treaties Bill 1995 (Cth) clause 6.

265 Parliamentary Approval of Treaties Bill 1995 (Cth) clause 6.

266 Senate Select Committee, *Trick or Treaty? Commonwealth Power to Make and Implement Treaties*, above n 252.

267 Brian R Opeskin and Donald R Rothwell (eds), above n 51, 89.

268 G Cranwell, "The Case for Parliamentary Approval of Treaties in Australia" (2001) 8 *Murdoch University Electronic Journal of Law*.

269 Department of Foreign Affairs and Trade, *Free Trade Agreements—Australia's Approach*, above n 1.

270 Note that there may be an issue in regards to the Separation of Powers doctrine between the Executive and Legislature. The doctrine of Separation of Powers is embodied in the Commonwealth Constitution and upholds that the three arms of government (Executive, Legislative, and Judicial) are separate and that their respective functions are mutually exclusive. *Attorney-General (Cth) v R., Ex parte Boilermakers' Society of Australia* (1957) 95 CLR 529. However the separation of legislative and executive power is not strictly adhered to; *Victorian Stevedoring and General Contracting Co Pty Ltd v Dignan* (1931) 46 CLR 73. The discussion of this doctrine is beyond the scope of this paper.

271 Council of Australian Governments, *Principles and Procedures for Commonwealth-State Consultation on Treaties* 1996 (Canberra: Council of Australian Governments, 1996).

272 Senate Select Committee, *Trick or Treaty? Commonwealth Power to Make and Implement Treaties*, above n 252.

273 Senate Select Committee on the Australia-United States Free Trade Agreement, *Select Committee on the Free Trade Agreement between Australia and the United States of America Final Report* above n 12, 33.

The Treaties Council was to consist of the Prime Minister, Premiers and Chief Ministers and was to have an advisory function.[274] The role of the Treaties Council was to consider treaties of particular sensitivity and importance to the States and Territories.[275] It was to meet at least once a year,[276] however since the implementation of this recommendation in 1996 the Treaties Council has only met once, in 1997,[277] and has not met to consider the Australia-United States FTA,[278] even though the Victorian State government requested it in July 2003.[279]

In a letter from the Department of the Premier and Cabinet of Western Australia to the Senate Select Committee on the Free Trade Agreement between Australia and the United States, Western Australia commented that:

> [a] Treaties Council could be an effective mechanism, as it can provide the opportunity for consultation with Heads of Government on significant treaties such as the AUSFTA. Western Australia recommends that the Treaties Council be called upon to meet and function in line with the agreed principles and procedures ... The Treaties Council, if used as it was intended when established, has the capacity to be the best mechanism for the Commonwealth-State consultation on treaty matters, including all trade treaties.[280]

It is suggested in this paper that a Treaties Council may help overcome some of the inadequacies identified in Australia's current treaty-making process, in particular in regards to facilitating communication between Federal and State and Territory governments. This in turn would contribute to each treaty being scrutinised further and give rise to the Federal government being more accountable for its treaty actions.

More extensive communication between the Federal, State and Territory governments during negotiations

The Commonwealth Government has attempted to ensure that States and Territories are less likely to pursue a Constitutional challenge, which could defeat the object and purpose of the Australia-United States FTA if successful. According to the Department of Foreign Affairs and Trade (DFAT), the Commonwealth Government consulted State and Territory governments in

274 Senate Select Committee on the Australia-United States Free Trade Agreement, *Select Committee on the Free Trade Agreement between Australia and the United States of America Final Report* above n 12, 33.

275 Senate Select Committee on the Australia-United States Free Trade Agreement, *Select Committee on the Free Trade Agreement between Australia and the United States of America Final Report* above n 12, 33.

276 Senate Select Committee on the Australia-United States Free Trade Agreement, *Select Committee on the Free Trade Agreement between Australia and the United States of America Final Report* above n 12, 34.

277 Senate Select Committee on the Australia-United States Free Trade Agreement, *Select Committee on the Free Trade Agreement between Australia and the United States of America Final Report* above n 12, 34.

278 Senate Select Committee on the Australia-United States Free Trade Agreement, *Select Committee on the Free Trade Agreement between Australia and the United States of America Final Report—Additional Information*, above n 148, Chapter 4, 3.

279 Senate Select Committee on the Australia-United States Free Trade Agreement, *Select Committee on the Free Trade Agreement between Australia and the United States of America Final Report—Additional Information*, above n 148, Chapter 4, 3.

280 Senate Select Committee on the Australia-United States Free Trade Agreement, *Select Committee on the Free Trade Agreement between Australia and the United States of America Final Report—Additional Information*, above n 148, Chapter 4, 3.

> developing and negotiating the Australia-United States FTA.[281] The DFAT has a website that acts as a medium for the States and Territories to access media transcripts, background papers and answers to frequently asked questions and the department issued a newsletter to Federal and State Members of Parliament.[282]

The negotiating team of the DFAT had meetings with State government departments, and State and Territory governments were briefed before and after each negotiating round.[283] The Trade Minister, Mark Vaile, discussed the Australia-United States FTA with his Trade Policy Advisory Committee, the WTO Advisory and the Agricultural Trade Consultative Groups.[284] Mr Vaile, De-Anne Kelly (Mr Vaile's Parliamentary Secretary), the FTA negotiating team, government departments, Austrade and Invest Australia also conducted sessions with State and Territory governments.[285]

The JSCOT has examined the Australia-United States FTA and reported to the Parliament on the effects that the implementation of the FTA will have on State and Territory governments. The National Interest Analysis states that:

> The States and Territories were consulted before, during and after the negotiations through meetings in capitals, joint meetings in Canberra and through other forums, such as the National Trade Consultations and Commonwealth State/Territory Standing Committee on Treaties processes. The States and Territories were able to send a representative to the final negotiating rounds and participated closely in framing out negotiating objectives for the Government Procurement Chapter, and in ensuring the appropriate framing of reservations to the Cross-Border Trade in Services and Investment Chapters.[286]

However the Western Australian government commented that:

> It was disappointing [that] they were not kept informed of the results of the negotiation ... [c]onsequently, Western Australia was unaware ... [of final provisions] until the draft text was made public.[287]

The Department of the Premier and Cabinet of Western Australia also mentioned ideas to facilitate State and Territory involvement in relation to FTAs; these include:

(a) to assemble a negotiating team prior to the commencement of the FTA negotiations, that includes at least one representative from each of the states and territories; and

281 Department of Foreign Affairs and Trade, *Australia-United States Free Trade Agreement—Public Consultation* (2004) <http://www.dfat.gov.au/trade/negotiations/us_fta/outcomes/20_public_consultation.html> at 27 July 2004.

282 Department of Foreign Affairs and Trade, *Australia-United States Free Trade Agreement—Public Consultation*, above n 281.

283 Department of Foreign Affairs and Trade, *Australia-United States Free Trade Agreement—Public Consultation*, above n 281.

284 Department of Foreign Affairs and Trade, *Australia-United States Free Trade Agreement—Public Consultation*, above n 281.

285 Department of Foreign Affairs and Trade, *Australia-United States Free Trade Agreement—Public Consultation*, above n 281.

286 Parliament of Australia, *National Interest Analysis—Australia United States of America Free Trade Agreement*, 2004 (Canberra: Joint Standing Committee, 2004), paragraph 16.

287 Senate Select Committee on the Australia-United States Free Trade Agreement, *Select Committee on the Free Trade Agreement between Australia and the United States of America Final Report—Additional Information*, above n 148, Chapter 4, 7.

(b) that states and territories be kept informed of developments during the final negotiations as soon as is practicable, particularly on areas that affect them.[288]

The current commitment to the extent of communication between the Federal government and the States and Territories is disputable. The amount of communication necessary between the two levels of government is questionable as each treaty has a different level of controversy and impact on States and Territories. It is suggested, however, that certain rules be set in place for dealing with FTAs because they are so extensive in scope and generally do affect the States and Territories. It is submitted that if the Federal government were to commit to extensive negotiations with States and Territories, this would assist the treaty-making process. This would enable the States and Territories to discuss their concerns prior to any international obligations becoming binding and would ensure that the Executive was seen to be making an attempt to protect the States' and Territories' interests, thus preserving the Federal system of government.

Improving Australia's treaty-making process by emulating the process in the United States

Federations deal with treaty-making in different ways. Most federations confine treaty-making to the federal sphere, such as Australia where the Commonwealth has the power to enter and implement treaties.[289]

A large number of countries have a system for parliamentary approval of treaties before they become parties to them. These countries are able to subject treaties to a formal system of scrutiny. This currently does not happen in Australia.[290]

The treaty-making process in the United States facilitates a level of congressional (parliamentary) scrutiny that is worth emulating in Australia. It provides for the Executive to negotiate FTAs, while also allowing Congress to monitor and approve.[291] This is done through legislation providing for a Trade Promotion Authority (TPA),[292] which is an agreement between the Congress and the President about how trade negotiations will be handled. "It is an attempt to achieve cooperation and coordination between the executive and legislative branches of government."[293] Under the TPA, Congress indicates specific negotiations and objectives that it would like to see achieved.[294] Congress also outlines how the Executive will

288 Senate Select Committee on the Australia-United States Free Trade Agreement, *Select Committee on the Free Trade Agreement between Australia and the United States of America Final Report—Additional Information*, above n 148, Chapter 4, 7.

289 Senate Select Committee, *Trick or Treaty? Commonwealth Power to Make and Implement Treaties*, above n 252.

290 Senate Select Committee, *Trick or Treaty? Commonwealth Power to Make and Implement Treaties*, above n 252.

291 Senate Select Committee on the Australia-United States Free Trade Agreement, *Select Committee on the Free Trade Agreement between Australia and the United States of America Final Report*, above n 12, 38.

292 *Trade Act* 2002 (United States of America) HR 3009.

293 Senate Select Committee on the Australia-United States Free Trade Agreement, *Select Committee on the Free Trade Agreement between Australia and the United States of America Final Report*, above n 12, 39.

294 Senate Select Committee on the Australia-United States Free Trade Agreement, *Select Committee on the Free Trade Agreement between Australia and the United States of America Final Report*, above n 12, 39.

inform them of developments in trade negotiations.[295] In return for the Congress having an influence on the treaty negotiations, the TPA includes an agreement from Congress that once a trade negotiation is finished, the House and the Senate will pass the implementing legislation without amendments.[296] Members of Congress are given only the chance to vote the agreement up or down, but not to change it.[297] Basically, it is the case that Congress is already satisfied with the terms of the treaty because it was able to influence the terms of the treaty at the negotiation stage.

> There appears to be no formal impediment, constitutional or otherwise, to the Australian parliament adopting a similar arrangement to that operating in the US Congress. Not only will such an arrangement provide for transparency and accountability in the negotiation and execution of trade agreements, but it will also give considerable comfort to the government in terms of securing the implementation of the agreement.[298]

Senate Select Committee proposal for reform

In 2004 the Senate Select Committee made a final report on the *Australia-United States FTA*.[299] In this report they proposed a "... process for parliamentary scrutiny and endorsement of proposed trade treaties".[300] This proposal encapsulated the ideas of parliamentary scrutiny, legislative reform, and further communication as discussed above. The new process is also similar to that of the United States current system. It recommends that:

> (a) prior to ... commencing negotiations for bilateral or regional free trade agreements, the government shall table in both houses of parliament a document setting out its priorities and objectives, including comprehensive information about the economic, regional, social, cultural, regulatory and environmental impacts which are expected to arise;
>
> (b) These documents shall be referred to the Joint Standing Committee on Foreign Affairs, Defence and Trade for examination by public hearing and report to the parliament within 90 days;
>
> (c) Both houses of parliament will then consider the report of the Joint Standing Committee on Foreign Affairs, Defence and Trade, and vote on whether to endorse the government's proposal or not;
>
> (d) Once parliament has endorsed the proposal, negotiations may begin;
>
> (e) Once the negotiation process is complete, the government shall then table in parliament a package including the proposed treaty together with any legislation required to implement the treaty domestically; and

295 Senate Select Committee on the Australia-United States Free Trade Agreement, *Select Committee on the Free Trade Agreement between Australia and the United States of America Final Report*, above n 12, 39.

296 Senate Select Committee on the Australia-United States Free Trade Agreement, *Select Committee on the Free Trade Agreement between Australia and the United States of America Final Report*, above n 12, 39.

297 Senate Select Committee on the Australia-United States Free Trade Agreement, *Select Committee on the Free Trade Agreement between Australia and the United States of America Final Report*, above n 12, 39.

298 Senate Select Committee on the Australia-United States Free Trade Agreement, *Select Committee on the Free Trade Agreement between Australia and the United States of America Final Report*, above n 12, 39.

299 Senate Select Committee on the Australia-United States Free Trade Agreement, *Select Committee on the Free Trade Agreement between Australia and the United States of America Final Report*, above n 12.

300 Senate Select Committee on the Australia-United States Free Trade Agreement, *Select Committee on the Free Trade Agreement between Australia and the United States of America Final Report*, above n 12, 40.

(f) The treaty and the implementing legislation are then voted on as a package, in an "up or down" vote, that is, on the basis that the package is either accepted or rejected in its entirety.[301]

Also:

> This process should be set out in legislation . . . [which] should specify the form which the government should present the proposal to parliament and require the proposal to set out clearly the objectives of the treaty and the proposed timeline for negotiations.[302]

This proposal is suitable to deal with the inadequacies of Australia's treaty-making process, identified in this paper, as it covers parliamentary scrutiny prior to signature ((a)–(f)) and communication with States and Territories ((b)).

Administration, timeliness and other considerations for implementing reforms

Administration

The administrative requirements necessary to implement the reforms discussed above would be meetings and other communication between the Executive, Federal Parliament and State and Territory governments. If legislative reforms were put in place, Parliament would absorb most of the administrative burden. There is a certain amount of administration being carried out by the current treaty-making process, by JSCOT and the Senate Select Committee, but as they do not have any real power it may be appropriate to delegate the treaty-making process to a more appropriate body such as Parliament. It would also be necessary to change the time at which reports are to be submitted, to before the signature of the FTA. After signature, any administrative matters carried out are ineffective because Australia is already bound not to defeat the object and purpose of the treaty.[303]

Timeliness

Any of the reforms suggested in this paper would slow down the making and implementation of treaties by Australia, which will lead to more detailed legislation to implement treaties and ultimately to better the treaty-making process.

> [G]iven the potential impact of trade agreements such as the [Australia-United States FTA] on all areas of Australian society, and the binding effects of these agreements on future parliaments, any possible delays are more than justified by the benefits . . .[304]

The "scare" tactics shown by Trade Minister Mark Vaile's comments earlier in this chapter[305] demonstrate that the current rapid treaty implementation is due to a sense of apprehension by the government that the implementing legislation will not

301 Senate Select Committee on the Australia-United States Free Trade Agreement, *Select Committee on the Free Trade Agreement between Australia and the United States of America Final Report*, above n 12, 41.

302 Senate Select Committee on the Australia-United States Free Trade Agreement, *Select Committee on the Free Trade Agreement between Australia and the United States of America Final Report*, above n 12, 41.

303 Vienna Convention on the Law of Treaties 1969, Art 18.

304 Senate Select Committee on the Australia-United States Free Trade Agreement, *Select Committee on the Free Trade Agreement between Australia and the United States of America Final Report*, above n 12, 41.

305 See discussion under Parliamentary Scrutiny section of this Chapter.

be passed. This should not be an issue when entering into treaties, particularly Category B treaties such as FTAs, which have such considerable effects on Australia.

Urgent and sensitive treaties

It is recognised that there will occasionally be a need to "fast track"[306] a proposed treaty for security or other reasons, as the proposed reforms may mean that the negotiating process takes longer. Certain provisions could be put in place to handle these situations.

Important thematic points

Once implemented, the reforms discussed above should satisfy the demands for greater openness, scrutiny and accountability in treaty-making and should considerably increase the opportunities for State and Territory government participation in the treaty-making process.

The Senate Select Committee have commented that:

> With a formal parliamentary arrangement in place the trade agreement would progress on the basis of "no surprises". This can only benefit all parties to the agreement and will ensure that Australia is able to negotiate with authority internationally.[307]

CONCLUSION

The goal of this paper has been to identify the inadequacies of the current treaty-making process in respect to FTAs and explore ways of improving the effectiveness and accountability of the system.

Chapter 1 of this paper discussed the Executive's power to enter into treaties under s 61 of the Commonwealth Constitution,[308] the Commonwealth's "external affairs" power under s 51(xxix) of the Commonwealth Constitution[309] and outlined the steps involved in Australia's treaty-making process.

The inadequacies of this process were identified in Chapter 2, including the insufficient mechanisms to ensure implementing legislation is passed, or international law can be fulfilled and the minimal consultations with States and Territories to protect their interests. Chapter 2 also identified the repercussions if the treaty-making process is not amended. These could include the Senate blocking implementing legislation, international obligations not being fulfilled exposing Australia to penalties at international law, Australia having its international trade reputation tarnished, and as seen in previous years, State and Territory governments pursuing constitutional challenges against the Commonwealth for its use of s 51(xxix).

306 Senate Select Committee on the Australia-United States Free Trade Agreement, *Select Committee on the Free Trade Agreement between Australia and the United States of America Final Report*, above n 12, 41.

307 Senate Select Committee on the Australia-United States Free Trade Agreement, *Select Committee on the Free Trade Agreement between Australia and the United States of America Final Report*, above n 12, 40.

308 Commonwealth Constitution 1900 (Cth), s 61.

309 Commonwealth Constitution 1900 (Cth), s 51(xxix).

Finally Chapter 3 suggests reforms for improving the treaty-making process in Australia, such as parliamentary scrutiny prior to signature, legislative reform, a Treaties Council, extensive communication between Federal, State and Territory governments, emulating the treaty-making process in the United States and implementing a proposal from the Senate Select Committee. Factors such as the administration and time of implementing these reforms were also taken into account in Chapter 3.

The Australian Government is currently pursuing a number of other FTAs anticipated to be entered into in 2005–2006. These include an Australia-New Zealand FTA, Australia-Malaysia FTA, Australia-China FTA, Australia-Japan FTA and Australia-Egypt FTA.[310] It is submitted that the reforms suggested in this paper would facilitate a more efficient and accountable treaty-making process and should be implemented before we enter into any more FTAs.

TABLES

Table of cases

Airlines of New South Wales Pty Ltd v New South Wales (No 1) (1964) 113 CLR 1.

Airlines of New South Wales Pty Ltd v New South Wales (No 2) (1965) 113 CLR 54.

Attorney-General (Cth) v R. Ex parte Boilermakers' Society of Australia (1957) 95 CLR 529.

Bank of New South Wales v Commonwealth (1948) 76 CLR 1.

Bradley v Commonwealth (1973) 128 CLR 557; 1 ALR 241.

Commonwealth v Tasmania (1983) 158 CLR 1 ("*Tasmanian Dam case*").

Davis v Commonwealth (1988) 166 CLR 79; 82 ALR 633.

Grannall v Marrickville Margarine Pty Ltd (1955) 93 CLR 55.

Horta v Commonwealth (1994) 181 CLR 183.

Koowarta v Bjelke-Petersen (1982) 153 CLR 168.

McCarter v Brodie (1950) 80 CLR 432.

R. v Burgess, ex parte Henry (1936) 55 CLR 608.

Redfern v Dunlop Rubber Australia (1964) 110 CLR 194.

Richardson v Forestry Commission (1988) 164 CLR 261 ("*Lemonthyme Forest case*").

Simsek v Macphee (1982) 148 CLR 636; 40 ALR 61.

Minister for Immigration and Ethnic Affairs v Teoh (1995) 183 CLR 273; 128 ALR 353.

Victoria v Commonwealth (1996) 187 CLR 416 ("*Industrial Relations Act case*").

Victorian Stevedoring and General Contracting Co Pty Ltd v Dignan (1931) 46 CLR 73.

W & A McArthur Ltd v Queensland (1920) 28 CLR 530.

Reservations to the Convention on the Prevention and Punishment of the Crime of Genocide ICJ Rep 1951 15.

310 Department of Foreign Affairs and Trade, above n 1.

Table of statutes

Agricultural and Veterinary Chemicals Code Act 1994 (Cth).
Australian Wine and Brandy Corporation Act 1980 (Cth).
Broadcasting Services Act 1992 (Cth).
Commonwealth Authorities and Companies Act 1997 (Cth).
Commonwealth Constitution 1900 (Cth).
Copyright Act 1968 (Cth).
Customs Act 1901 (Cth).
Foreign Acquisitions and Takeovers Act 1975 (Cth).
Health Act 1911 (WA).
Health Act 1958 (Vic).
Life Insurance Act 1995 (Cth).
Patents Act 1990 (Cth).
Quarantine Act 1908 (Cth).
Therapeutic Goods Act 1989 (Cth).
Trade Act 2002 (United States of America) HR 3009.
US Free Trade Agreement Implementation Act 2004 (Cth).
US Free Trade Agreement Implementation (Customs Tariff) Act 2004 (Cth).

Table of Bills

Administrative Decisions (Effect of International Instruments) Bill 1997 (Cth).
Parliamentary Approval of Treaties Bill 1995 (Cth).
US Free Trade Agreement Implementation Bill 2004 (Cth).
US Free Trade Agreement Implementation (Customs Tariff) Bill 2004 (Cth).

BIBLIOGRAPHY

Textbooks

Ademuni-Odeke, *The Law of International Trade* (London: Blackstone Press Limited, 1999).

Blay S, Piotrowicz R and Tsamenyi B, *Public International Law an Australian Perspective* (Melbourne: Oxford University Press, 1997).

Brownlie I, *Principles of Public International Law* (3rd ed, Oxford: Clarendon Press, 1985).

Butt P and Nygh P (eds), *Butterworths Concise Australian Legal Dictionary* (2nd ed, Sydney: Butterworths, 1998).

Chuah J, *Law of International Trade* (London: Sweet and Maxwell, 1998).

Dixon M, *Textbook on International Law* (4th ed, London: Blackstone Press Limited, 2000).

Dixon M and McCorquodale R, *Cases and Materials on International Law* (3rd ed, London: Blackstone Press Limited, 2000).

Hanks P and Cass D, *Australian Constitutional Law Materials and Commentary* (6th ed, Sydney: Butterworths, 2001).

Harris B, *Essential Constitutional Law* (Sydney: Cavendish Publishing (Australia) Pty Ltd, 2000).

Islam M, *International Trade Law* (Sydney: LBC Information Services, 1999).

Lumb R and Moens G, *The constitution of the Commonwealth of Australia annotated* (Sydney: Butterworths, 1995).

Mo J, *International Commercial Law* (3rd ed, NSW: Butterworths, 2003).

Moens G and Gillies P, *International Trade and Business Law, Policy and Ethics* (Sydney: Cavendish Publishing (Australia) Pty Ltd, 1998).

Omar I, *Butterworths Questions and Answers—Constitutional Law* (Sydney: Butterworths, 1998).

Omar I, *Butterworths Questions and Answers—Constitutional Law* (2nd ed, Sydney: Butterworths, 2003).

Opeskin R and Rothwell D, *International Law and Australian Federalism* (Melbourne: Melbourne University Press, 1997).

Pryles M, Waincymer J and Davies M, *International Trade Law Commentary and Materials* (NSW: LBC Information Services, 1996).

Reicher H (ed), *Australian International Law Cases and Materials* (Sydney: Law Book Company, 1995).

Ryan K (ed), *International Law in Australia* (2nd ed, Sydney: The Law Book Company Limited, 1984).

Journal articles

Cranwell G, "The Case for Parliamentary Approval of Treaties in Australia" (2001) 8 *Murdoch University Electronic Journal of Law*.

Crock M, "Federalism and the external affairs power" (1983) 14 *Melbourne University Law Review* 238.

Frankowska M, "The Vienna Convention on the Law of Treaties Before United States Courts" (1988) 28 *Virginia Journal of International Law* 281.

Mitchell R, "The effect of the external affairs power upon the balance of power between Commonwealth and states" (1995) 2 *Canberra Law Review* 103.

Moens G A and Trone J, "International treaties in Australian law: legitimate expectations and the *Teoh* case" (1995) 25 *Australia and World Affairs* 57.

Rothwell D, "The High Court and the external affairs power: a consideration of its outer and inner limits" (1993) 15 *Adelaide Law Review* 209.

Online materials

Austlii, *Australia and International Treaty Making Information Kit* (2002) <http://www.austlii.edu.au/au/other/dfat/infokit.html> at 31 March 2004.

Department of Foreign Affairs and Trade, *Australia and the World Trade Organization* (2004) <http://www.dfat.gov.au/trade/fs_australia_and_the_wto.html> at 15 March 2004.

Department of Foreign Affairs and Trade, *Australian Treaties* Database (2004) <http://www.info.dfat.gov.au/treaties> at 5 April 2004.

Department of Foreign Affairs and Trade, *Australia-United States Free Trade Agreement—Guide to the Agreement* (2004) <http://www.dfat.gov.au/trade/negotiations/us_fta/guide/1_22_23_Legal_Institutional.html> at 15 March 2004.

Department of Foreign Affairs and Trade, *Free Trade Agreements* (2004), <http://www.dfat.gov.au/trade/negotiations/wto_agreements.html> at 15 March 2004.

Department of Foreign Affairs and Trade, *Background Paper* (2003) <http://www.dfat.gov.au/trade/negotiations/us_bkg.html>> at 20 February 2004.

Department of Foreign Affairs and Trade, *Category A and Category B treaties* (2004) <http://www.dfat.gov.au/treaties/making/category.html> at 23 August 2004.

Department of Foreign Affairs and Trade, *Treaties and Treaty Making* (2004) <http://www.dfat.gov.au/treaties/making /making1.html> at 23 August 2004.

Department of Foreign Affairs and Trade, *Key Outcomes* (2003) <http://www.dfat.gov.au/trade/negotiations/us_fta/outcomes/02_key_outcomes.html> at 5 May 2004.

Department of Foreign Affairs and Trade, *Overview* (2004) <http://www.dfat.gov.au/trade/negotiations/us_fta/outcomes/01_overview.html> at 5 May 2004.

Department of Foreign Affairs and Trade, *Domestic Approval Processes for an Australia-United States Free Trade Agreement (AUSFTA)* (2004) <http://www.dfat.gov.au/trade/negotiations/us_fta/outcomes/21_domestic_approval.html> at 23 May 2004.

Department of Foreign Affairs and Trade, *Australia-United States Free Trade Agreement—Free Trade Agreements and Multilateral Negotiations* (2004) <http://www.dfat.gov.au/trade/negotiations/us_fta/outcomes/22_multi_negs.html> at 20 April 2004.

Department of Foreign Affairs and Trade, *Australia-United States Free Trade Agreement* (2004) <http://www.dfat.gov.au/trade/negotiations/us.html> at 27 May 2004.

Department of Foreign Affairs and Trade, *Australia and the United Nations* (2004) <http://www.dfat.gov.au/un/aus_un3.html> at 20 August 2004.

Department of Foreign Affairs and Trade, *Australia-United States Free Trade Agreement—Public Consultation* (2004) <http://www.dfat.gov.au/trade/negotiations/us_fta/outcomes/20_public_consultation.html> at 27 July 2004.

Department of Foreign Affairs and Trade, *Free Trade Agreements—Australia's Approach* (2004) <http://www.dfat.gov.au/trade/negotiations/australias_approach.html> at 22 September 2004.

Freehills, *Australia-United States free trade talks face final hurdles* (2003) <www.freehills.com> at 20 February 2004.

Parliament of Australia, *Democrats Media Senator Aden Ridgeway—Senate Inquiry Shows Major Flaws in FTA* (2004) <http://parlinfoweb.aph.gov.au/piweb/Repository1/Media/pressrel/MMTC60.pdf> at 5 September 2004.

Parliament of Australia, *Democrats Media Senator Aden Ridgeway—FTA signed but not sealed and still won't deliver* (2004) <http://parlinfoweb.aph.gov.au/piweb/Repository1/Media/pressrel/G1KC60.pdf> at 20 September 2004.

Parliament of Australia, *Glossary—Federal Executive Council* (2003) <http://www.aph.gov.au/find/glossary.htm_f> at 20 September 2004.

Parliament of Australia, *Joint Standing Committee* (2002) <http://www.aph.gov.au/house/committee/jsct/index.htm> at 31 March 2004.

Parliament of Australia, *Joint Standing Committee on Treaties—Committee establishment, role and history* (2002) <http://www.aph.gov.au/house/committee/jsct/ppgrole.htm> at 1 September 2004.

Parliament of Australia, *Joint Committee on Treaties Committee activities (inquiries and reports)—Media Releases* (2004) <http://www.aph.gov.au/house/committee/jsct/usafta/media.htm> at 28 July 2004.

Parliamentary Education Office, *Facts about Parliament—Making Laws* (2004) <http://www.peo.gov.au/resources/facts.htm_laws> at 15 July 2004.

Scaleplus Law Resource, *US Free Trade Agreement Implementation Bill 2004—First Reading* (2004) <http://www.scaleplus.law.gov.au/html/bills/0/2004/0/2004062412.htm> at 1 September 2004.

Scaleplus Law Resource, *US Free Trade Agreement Implementation Bill 2004—Explanatory Memorandum* (2004) <http://www.scaleplus.law.gov.au/html/ems/0/2004/0/2004062410.htm> at 1 September 2004.

Scaleplus Law Resource, *US Free Trade Agreement Implementation (Customs Tariff) Bill 2004—Explanatory Memorandum* (2004) <http://www.scaleplus.law.gov.au/html/ems/0/2004/0/2004062411.htm> at 1 September 2004.

The Hon. Mark Vaile—MP Minister for Trade Australia, *Media Release—Free Trade Agreement with the United States* (2004) <http://www.trademinister.gov.au/releases/2004/mvt008_04.html> at 4 April 2004.

Vienna Convention on the Law of Treaties 1969, *The International Law of Treaties* (2003) <http://www.public-international-law.net/> at 21 April 2004.

World Trade Organization, *The World Trade Organization* (1997) <http://www.ip-law.co.il/DomainNames/treat8.htm> at 22 April 2004.

Wikipedia Encyclopedia, *Pacta sunt servanda* (2004) <http://en.wikipedia.org/wiki/Pacta_sunt_servanda> at 25 September 2004.

Treaties/charters/conventions

Australia United-States Free Trade Agreement (draft) 2004
General Agreement on Tariffs and Trade 1947
General Agreement on Tariffs and Trade 1994
United Nations Charter 1945
Vienna Convention on the Law of Treaties 1969
World Trade Organisation Agreement 1994

Parliamentary Reports/Discussion Papers

Asia Pacific Economic Cooperation Study Centre, *An Australia-USA Free Trade Agreement—Issues and Implications* 2001 (Melbourne: The Australian APEC Study Centre, Monash University, 2001).

Centre for International Economics, *Economic impacts of an Australian-United States Free Trade Area* 2001 (Canberra and Sydney: Centre for International Economics, 2001).

Council of Australian Governments, *Principles and Procedures for Commonwealth-State Consultation on Treaties* 1996 (Canberra: Council of Australian Governments, 1996).

Department of Foreign Affairs and Trade, *Estimates Committee* 1994 (Canberra: Australian Senate, 1994).

Department of Foreign Affairs and Trade, *The Negotiation, Conclusion and Implementation of International Treaties and Arrangements* 1994 (Canberra: Australian Government Publishing Service, 1994).

Federal-States Relations Committee, *International Treaty Making and the Role of the States* 1997 (Victoria: Parliament of Victoria, 1997).
Parliament of Australia, *National Interest Analysis—Australia United States of America Free Trade Agreement*, 2004 (Canberra: Joint Standing Committee, 2004).
Parliament of Australia, *Regulation Impact Statement—Australia United States of America Free Trade Agreement*, 2004 (Canberra: Joint Standing Committee, 2004).
Senate, *Official Record of the Debates of the Australasian Federal Convention* 1891 (Sydney: Australasian Federal Convention, 1891).
Senate Select Committee on the Australia-United States Free Trade Agreement, *Select Committee on the Free Trade Agreement between Australia and the United States of America Final Report* 2004 (Canberra: Senate Select Committee, 2004).
Senate Select Committee on the Australia-US Free Trade Agreement, *Select Committee on the Free Trade Agreement between Australia and the United States of America Final Report—Additional Information* 2004 (Canberra: Senate Select Committee, 2004).
Senate Select Committee, *Trick or Treaty? Commonwealth Power to Make and Implement Treaties* 1995 (Canberra: Senate Select Committee, 1995).
Report of the International Law Commission to the General Assembly *Yearbook of the International Law Commission*, 1966, vol. II, 172.

Hansard

House of Representatives Hansard, *Prime Minister Honourable J Howard MP*, No. 13, 30 August 2001.
Joint Standing Committee on Treaties Hansard, *Executive Director, Office Federal Affairs, Department of the Premier and Cabinet, Western Australia P Judge*, Australia-United States Free Trade Agreement, 23 April 2004.
Senate Hansard, Parliamentary Approval of Treaties Bill 1995: Second Reading, *Senator V Bourne*, 31 May 1995, 661.

Speeches

Australian Ambassador to the United States Michael Thawley, Speech to the American Australian Association, 13 December 2000 (New York).
Australian Trade Minister Mark Vaile, Second Reading Speech on the Introduction of the United States Free Trade Agreement 2004 (Australian Parliament).
Justice Dawson, "Do Judges Make Laws? Too Much?" 22 August 1994 (University of Adelaide).

MILITARY OCCUPATION AND THE RULE OF LAW: THE LEGAL OBLIGATIONS OF OCCUPYING FORCES IN IRAQ

Ben Clarke[1]

ABSTRACT

This paper provides a contemporary analysis of the law of belligerent occupation with particular reference to the rights and duties of occupying forces. Relevant sources of international law are examined, and tensions between relevant treaty law and state practice in occupied Iraq are considered. In assessing the nature and scope of certain duties under the law of occupation, difficult questions are posed. Are occupying powers required to deploy sufficient troops and resources during the invasion phase of military operations to ensure that from the moment that territory is occupied they are able to guarantee the protection of the civilian population, prevent looting, safeguard infrastructure and maintain public order? To what extent may the laws and institutions of an occupied state be altered by the occupier? Finally, existing mechanisms for ensuring the accountability of occupying powers for non-compliance with their obligations under the law of occupation are considered. Specific measures to achieve this objective (including the further codification of the law of occupation and greater oversight of the actions of occupiers by the Security Council) are considered.

INTRODUCTION

The international law of occupation and contemporary Iraq

The invasion and occupation of Iraq has attracted significant juridical interest. A year after Coalition forces invaded Iraq, debate over the legality of that use of force shows no sign of abating.[2] By contrast, the question of the legality of the *occupation* is less contentious. While the first few months of Coalition occupation were not sanctioned by the international community, the occupation was officially endorsed on

---

1 Senior Lecturer in Law, College of Law, University of Notre Dame Australia; bclarke@nd.edu.au. PhD candidate (Melb) Thesis topic: *The Rule of Law and Military Operations: Accountability of Coalition Forces in Occupied Iraq*. Special thanks to Bruce "Ossie" Oswald, Brit Conidi (PhD Candidates University of Melbourne), Chris Chapman (Juris Doctor Candidate UNDA), Professor Gabriel Moens and three anonymous referees for their useful comments on earlier drafts of this paper. All remaining errors are the property of the author and "may not be reproduced without permission".

2 At the time of writing there are growing concerns in the UK that legal advice given by Attorney-General Lord Goldsmith to Prime Minister Tony Blair may have been "revised" to satisfy the Chief of Defence Staff: War Chief Reveals Legal Crisis by Anthony Barnett and Martin Bright *Observer* March 7, 2004 http://www.globalpolicy.org/security/issues/iraq/attack/law/2004/0307warchief.htm date accessed 11 March 2004. For an analysis of arguments for and against the legality of the war see: Charlotte Ku, "When Can Nations Go To War? Politics And Change In The UN Security System"

23 May 2003 when the Security Council passed Resolution 1483.[3] By this time, Coalition forces faced intense scrutiny over their obligations as occupying powers. This paper provides a contemporary analysis of the powers and duties of occupiers under international law. The nature and scope of these norms of occupation are assessed by reference to relevant sources of international law including (i) the classic treaties on occupation, (ii) customary law, (iii) applicable UN resolutions and (iv) relevant domestic law.

In assessing the fundamental obligations of the occupying forces in Iraq, the following questions require analysis:

1. What are the powers and obligations of occupying forces under contemporary international law?
2. Do the occupied retain sovereignty over their state during a belligerent occupation? If so, how if at all may they exercise these rights?
3. What mechanisms (if any) exist to ensure compliance by occupying forces with their obligations?
4. Do the occupying powers have a legal mandate to fulfil a reformist agenda in Iraq that includes the reshaping of national institutions?
5. Is it realistic to expect Coalition forces to meet all of their obligations under the law of occupation in a complex and dangerous environment of competing interests and needs?
6. Do occupying powers have a duty to ensure that sufficient troops and resources are deployed to protect the civilian population, prevent looting, guard infrastructure and maintain public order in the "post conflict" phase?

Tensions between the law of occupation, Security Council Resolution 1483, and Coalition practice in Iraq are also highlighted. In addition, existing mechanisms for ensuring the accountability of occupying powers for non-compliance with their obligations under the law of occupation are assessed. The paper concludes by asking whether the international law of occupation offers an adequate legal framework for regulation of belligerent occupations in the 21st century.

Invasion, occupation and the status of occupied territory

The invasion and conquest of sovereign states is illegal under contemporary inter-

24 Mich. J. Int'l L. 1077. It has been suggested that eight out of ten international lawyers have concluded that the invasion of Iraq was unlawful: Professor Mary Ellen O'Connell "The Occupation Of Iraq: What International Law Requires Now" http://jurist.law.pitt.edu/forum/forumnew107.php date accessed 30 June 2003. See also: "Howard Must Not Involve Us in an Illegal War" *The Age Newspaper* 26 February 2003. (This statement was signed by 43 international law experts and warned that an invasion of Iraq and the initiation of a war would be illegal.) Clarke, B. "Can the Gulf War (2) be justified under International Law?" (2003) http://www.findlaw.com.au/directory/archive.asp?id=321 accessed on 13 June 2003; Bill Campbell and Chris Moraitis; George Williams and Devika Hovell; Grant Niemann "Advice on the Use of Force against Iraq" MJIL Vol 4 Issue 1 2003 177; William H. Taft and Todd F. Buchwald "Preemption Iraq and International Law" 97 AJIL 557 at 557. (Taft and Buchwald assert that Operation Iraqi Freedom was permissible use of force on the basis of existing Security Council resolutions and by reference to the doctrine of pre-emptive strike.)

3 Benvenisti asserts that "the resolution refutes claims that occupation as such is illegal". "Water Conflicts during the occupation of Iraq" 97 AJIL (2003) 860 at 860.

national law.[4] Nevertheless, the occupation of territory without UN approval has been a regular occurrence throughout the history of the UN. The occupation of Palestine (by Israel), northern Cyprus (by Turkey), Panama and Afghanistan (by the US) are prominent examples.[5] Other examples include Cambodia (by Vietnam), East Pakistan (by India) and the Falkland Islands (by Argentina). What distinguishes Iraq from other instances of foreign occupation is that the occupation of Iraq represents the first instance since the inception of the UN that (1) a belligerent occupying force has fully acknowledged its status and obligations as an occupying power following a military invasion, and (2) the Security Council has endorsed the occupation.

Occupying powers do not acquire legal title to occupied territory. Instead they assume obligations as administrator of the territory during the period of occupation. Consequently, sovereignty over occupied territory does not pass to the occupying power. This fundamental norm of international law is reaffirmed by the Security Council in the preamble to Resolution 1483, where specific mention is made of "the sovereignty and territorial integrity of Iraq" and "the right of the Iraqi people freely to determine their own political future and control their own natural resources".[6]

What is the law of belligerent occupation?

Belligerent occupation is the exercise of authority over territory by military rule without the consent of the deposed regime. The Coalition's administration of Iraq is a classic example of belligerent occupation. By contrast, non-belligerent occupation is the military administration of foreign territory with the consent of the government of a state, or the various parties exercising control over its territory. The international law of occupation is a body of rules designed to regulate the way in which an occupying power governs occupied territory.[7] Its ambitious objective is to provide a legal framework for occupying powers to meet the often conflicting interests of the occupant, the displaced sovereign and the population of the occupied territory.[8] The key provisions of this body of law are found within Chapter 3 of both the Hague Regulations concerning the Laws and Customs of War on Land (hereinafter the "Hague Regulations"), and the 4th Geneva Convention Relative To The Protection Of Civilian Persons During Times Of War (1949) ("the 4th Geneva Convention") and also Arts 3 and 4 of Protocol 1 Additional to the Geneva Conventions of

4 Art 2(4) Charter of the United Nations imposes a prohibition on the use of force. The right of self-defence under Art 51 can only be exercised by states in the limited circumstances defined by the Charter or customary law. The exact parameters of the right are highly contentious. In the author's view, the invasion and occupation of a state on the pretext that the state may pose a threat to the state launching the invasion does not fall within the scope of Art 51.

5 For a detailed discussion of the occupations of Cyprus, Panama and Afghanistan see: Benvenisti, Eyal *The International Law of Occupation*. Princeton: Princeton University Press, 1993. The occupations of Palestinian territory by Israel and Northern Cyprus by Turkey both involve the prolonged occupation of territory. They have continued in spite of repeated Security Council resolutions calling for the withdrawal of the occupiers.

6 Security Council Resolution 1483 (2003).

7 Greenwood, C "Book Review and Note: The International Law of Occupation by Eyal Benvenisti" 90 A.J.I.L. 712 at 712.

8 Greenwood, C "Book Review and Note: The International Law of Occupation by Eyal Benvenisti" 90 A.J.I.L. 712 at 712.

12 August 1949, and relating to the Protection of Victims of International Armed Conflicts (hereinafter the "1977 Additional Protocol 1"). The international law of occupation is however not confined to treaty law. Other sources include customary law, applicable domestic law, and UN resolutions. Each of these sources is discussed in this paper.

The concept of occupation has been described as "juridically inoperative or disputed in practically all contemporary conflicts including those involving guerrilla warfare".[9] However, as noted above, the US and UK formally acknowledged their status and obligations as occupying powers in Iraq.[10] This represents a significant departure from practice in virtually all UN-era belligerent military occupations, as well as the practice of the UK and US during military occupations at the end of World War II.

When does the law of occupation apply?

The law of occupation applies when an occupying force exercises effective control over foreign territory. Article 42 of the Hague Regulations IV (1907) provides that "Territory is considered occupied when it is actually placed under the authority of the hostile army". However it further provides that occupation extends only to "the territory where such an authority has been established and can be exercised".[11] Article 1 of 1977 Additional Protocol 1 extends the scope of occupation to include all cases of alien occupation.[12]

Whether or not territory is occupied is a question of fact which in the initial stages at least is a matter for the occupying army to determine.[13] Occupation of foreign territory will usually be self-evident to all observers, although the precise extent of the occupation may be difficult to determine—particularly whether there is "creeping expansion" into foreign territory. Military occupation has legal consequences. Responsibilities attach to occupying forces from the moment they occupy and exercise effective control over enemy territory.

Who must comply with the law of occupation?

When territory is occupied by a foreign army, both the occupying forces and those living under occupation must comply with the law of occupation. The "occupied" may include civilians, and the military forces of the occupied territory, because the 4th Geneva Convention affords protection to both combatants and non-combatants, both being "persons protected by the convention".[14]

---

9 Michel Veuthey *Guerilla et droit humanitaire* (2nd edn., 1983), p355 cited in Adam Roberts "What is a Military Occupation?" BYIL Vol LV (1984) 249.

10 See Preamble to Security Council Resolution 1483. (Both the US and the UK voted in favour of this resolution which described them as occupying powers.)

11 Art 42, The Hague Regulations IV (1907).

12 See Hilaire McCoubrey *International Humanitarian Law* 2nd Edition Ashgate 1998 p199.

13 See Lauterpacht (Ed.) *Oppenheim's International Law* Vol II 7th Edition 1952 p 434. See also: Kelly, M.J. *Restoring and Maintaining Order in Complex Peace Operations: The Search for a Legal Framework* Kluwer.

14 See Art 4, 4th Geneva Convention.

The opposing military forces in any conflict are known as belligerents. Belligerents in an international armed conflict are bound by the law of armed conflict. Once territory is occupied, all belligerents must also conduct themselves in accordance with the law of occupation. Belligerents can include regular armies, irregulars, militia and voluntary corps,[15] and also those who spontaneously take up arms to resist invading troops (*levee en masse*).[16] In the context of the recent conflict in Iraq, Coalition (belligerent) military forces included Australian, Polish, British and US armed forces. Iraq's belligerent forces included the Iraqi Army, the Republican Guard, the Special Republican Guard, Fedayeen Saddam, foreign volunteers invited to fight on the side of the Ba'ath regime, and any groups of Iraqis who may have spontaneously armed themselves to defend Iraq from foreign invasion (*levee en masse*).

The rule of law dictates that no one is above the law, and that everyone—regardless of rank or allegiance—is subject to the law.[17] This doctrine remains applicable during a military occupation, although its application is somewhat skewed. While occupying forces are technically bound by the laws of the occupied territory, soldiers are more likely to be held accountable for breaches of their own military laws (subject to any Status of Forces Agreement recognising the jurisdiction of courts of the occupied state to deal with violations of municipal law by citizens of occupying powers). As occupying armies are effectively exercising martial law over occupied territory, it is extremely unlikely that they would ever permit local courts to prosecute their personnel. The Coalition Provisional Authority in Iraq ("the CPA") has asserted that occupying forces have immunity from local legal process under international law. CPA Administrator Paul Bremer has formally declared that Coalition military personnel as well as foreign liaison and contractor personnel are not subject to Iraqi laws or the jurisdiction of Iraqi courts.[18]

Those most likely to be prosecuted for violations of the law of occupation are those who engage in armed resistance to foreign occupation. While such resistance is not prohibited under international law,[19] the law of occupation permits the occupiers to put on trial persons who engage in acts of sabotage, espionage or launch attacks upon occupying forces. The rights of those detained by occupying forces for engaging in acts of violent resistance are discussed below.

---

15 Art 1 Hague Regulations IV (1907).

16 Art 2 Hague Regulations IV (1907).

17 The doctrine of the rule of law was popularised by A.V. Dicey in his book *Introduction to the study of law of the constitution* (1885).

18 CPA Public Notice Regarding the Status of Coalition, Foreign Liaison and Contractor Personnel 26 June 2003 date accessed 16 April 2004 http://www.cpa-iraq.org/regulations/20030626_20030626_CPANOTICE_Foreign_Mission_Cir.html.pdf.

19 The General Assembly has recognised the right of sovereign states to resist alien occupation in a number of resolutions. See for example: "Declaration on the Granting of Independence to Colonial Countries and Peoples" of the UN General Assembly. Resolution 1514 [XV] of 14 December 1960. However the nature and scope of this right has never been precisely defined by either the General Assembly or the Security Council. It is also important to note that any right to resist foreign occupation may be abrogated by the Security Council. The Council must however be acting pursuant to its powers under Chapter VII of the UN Charter. For example, where a military occupation has been endorsed by the Security Council, and resistance forces have been ordered to lay down their arms and/or desist from further military activity, further attacks upon occupying forces may be regarded as a violation of international law.

SOURCES OF THE LAW OF OCCUPATION

The principal sources of the international law of occupation are the treaties mentioned in the following paragraph. Many articles contained within these international instruments are directly applicable to military occupations. However a variety of other sources including customary law, the domestic law of the occupied and occupying states, and UN resolutions may also be applicable.

Treaty law

The principal international instruments on the law of occupation are the Hague Regulations (1907), the 4th Geneva Convention, and 1977 Additional Protocol 1.[20] These instruments collectively prescribe the rights and duties of belligerent forces (including occupying forces), as well as the rights of protected persons[21] (including civilians) who are within an occupied territory.

The Hague Regulations (1907)

The Hague Regulations (1907) were the first widely endorsed set of international rules governing conduct for occupying forces.[22] Chapter 1 is entitled "The Qualifications of Belligerents". Article 1 provides that "The laws, rights, and duties of war apply not only to armies, but also to militia and volunteer corps . . .".[23] This article covers military forces of both the occupiers and the occupied. In order to be afforded the protections of the laws of war, all belligerents (parties to the conflict) were required to ". . . carry arms openly and respect the laws and customs of war".[24] The regulations also provide a working definition of "occupation",[25] which is set out above and remains applicable to this day. They also set out a number of basic rights, duties and entitlements of both the occupier and the occupied.[26] During the drafting of these Regulations at The Hague Peace Conferences of 1899 and 1907, fundamental disagreements arose among participating states. The final document left gaps in the duties and obligations of belligerent parties.[27] During the First World War and Second World War, many of the Hague Regulations were ignored, while in other cases gaps in the laws of war were exploited.[28] Significant revision of the laws of armed conflict occurred with the promulgation of the 1949 Geneva Conventions.

---

20 For a useful discussion of the legal framework for the law of occupation arising from these Conventions see Roberts, A "What is a Military Occupation?" BYIL Vol LV (1984) 249 at pp 251–255.

21 Protected persons are defined in Art 4 of the 4th Geneva Convention as those who ". . . find themselves, in the case of a conflict or occupation, in the hands of a Party to the conflict or Occupying Power of which they are not nationals".

22 The 1907 Convention is also referred to as the "Hague Rules".

23 Art 1 Hague Regulations (1907).

24 Art 2 Hague Regulations (1907).

25 See Art 42 Hague Regulations (1907).

26 See Section III, Hague Regulations (1907) (Arts 43–56).

27 See Lester Nurick and Rodger W. Barrett "Legality of Guerrilla Forces under the Laws of War" 1946 AJIL 563 at p567.

28 For an excellent discussion of these issues see *Oppenheim's International Law*, Lauterpacht Volume II 7th Edition, Chapter XII "Occupation of Enemy Territory".

The Geneva Conventions (1949)

The Geneva Conventions of 1949[29] represented a watershed in the development of international humanitarian law in general, and the law of occupation in particular. More strident obligations were imposed on occupiers, and a number of aspects of the law of military occupation that had not been resolved during the drafting of the Hague Regulations were addressed.[30]

Each of the Geneva Conventions deals with a different area of humanitarian law. The most relevant instrument in the context of the law of occupation is the 4th Geneva Convention. Part III of this instrument sets out the general obligations of belligerents in the treatment of protected persons. Section III of Part II prescribes in detail the obligations that occupying forces owe to protected persons in occupied territory.

The law of treaties[31] provides that only state parties to agreements are bound by these instruments. While this was initially the case with respect to the Geneva Conventions, all states are now bound by these instruments under customary law.[32] Although generally designed to supplement the Hague Regulations, the Geneva Conventions have superseded certain articles of the Hague Regulations.[33]

Protocol I Additional to the 1949 Geneva Conventions (1977 Additional Protocol 1)

1977 Additional Protocol 1 was drafted by states in an attempt to adapt the laws of war to the conditions of contemporary international armed conflict (particularly the incidence of guerrilla warfare and the proliferation of national liberation movements).[34] The protocol is directly applicable to occupied territories.[35] A central focus of the protocol is the protection of civilians and victims of international armed conflict. In order to promote this objective, the obligations of occupying forces have been strengthened in a number of ways. Firstly, minimum human rights guarantees have been imported into the law of occupation. Article 75 provides that persons in the power of a party to the conflict (including occupying powers) must be afforded basic protections set out therein. Secondly, as Roberts has noted, the protocol extends the law of occupation to "territories with a controversial international status".[36]

---

29 Convention (I) for the Amelioration of the Condition of the Wounded and Sick in Armed Forces in the Field. Geneva, 12 August 1949. Convention (II) for the Amelioration of the Condition of Wounded, Sick and Shipwrecked Members of Armed Forces at Sea. Geneva, 12 August 1949. Convention (III) relative to the Treatment of Prisoners of War. Geneva, 12 August 1949. Convention (IV) relative to the Protection of Civilian Persons in Time of War. Geneva, 12 August 1949.

30 See Roberts, A "What is a Military Occupation?" BYIL Vol LV (1984) 249 at p253.

31 See Art 18, Vienna Convention on the Law of Treaties (Concluded At Vienna 23 May 1969 Entry Into Force 27 January 1980).

32 Adam Roberts & Richard Guelff, *Documents on the Laws of War*, 3rd Edition Oxford University Press 2000 at p196.

33 An example of a provision of the Hague Regulations that continues to be authoritative is Art 42. It provides the legal definition of *occupation*, a concept not defined in the Geneva Conventions.

34 Adam Roberts & Richard Guelff, *Documents on the Laws of War*, 3rd Edition Oxford University Press 2000 at 418.

35 See Art 3 1977 Additional Protocol 1.

36 Roberts, A "What is a Military Occupation?" BYIL Vol LV (1984) 249 at p 254.

However the protocol fails to address all of the outstanding deficiencies in the law of occupation. For instance, there are still no effective mechanisms for the independent enforcement of this body of law.[37] Therefore, in the event of a breach by the occupiers, accountability for such violations is a matter for the occupying powers. With no independent umpire, justice is discretionary.

Unsurprisingly, some publicists have called for revision of the law of occupation.[38] New measures that promote compliance through effective enforcement are desirable—particularly from the perspective of minimising impunity for violators. However it is questionable whether such reform will be achieved in the near future. States that are inclined to engage in foreign occupations are also likely to oppose any broadening of their international obligations. The proliferation of "Article 98" agreements entered into by the Bush Administration to shield its citizens from the jurisdiction of the International Criminal Court is illustrative of this point.[39]

Treaty obligations of European occupiers

Jurisprudence of the European Court of Human Rights confers obligations upon European member states to ensure that everyone within their jurisdiction is afforded the rights and freedoms defined in Section 1 of the European Convention on Human Rights. The UK and Spain are bound by these treaty obligations. Both have troops in Iraq, and are the effective (or delegated) occupiers of different geographical areas of Iraq. It is therefore necessary to inquire as to whether their obligations under the European Convention on Human Rights extend to the treatment of persons detained by their forces in Iraq.

In *Banković and Others v Belgium and 16 Other Contracting States* (Application No. 52207/99 [ECHR]), the Grand Chamber of the European Court of Human Rights held that extra-territorial acts would fall within its jurisdiction, when:

> the respondent state, through the effective control of the relevant territory and its inhabitants abroad as a consequence of military occupation or through the consent, invitation or acquiescence of the Government of that territory, exercised all or some of the public powers normally to be exercised by that Government.[40]

---

37 Art 90 provides for establishment of Fact Finding Commissions. The commissions are empowered to do no more than conduct enquiries into alleged grave breaches of the Geneva Conventions and Additional Protocol 1, and report findings. There is no provision for impartial tribunals to be convened to deal with crimes committed by occupying powers. Admittedly it is extremely unlikely that powerful states would ever assent to such independent scrutiny of the conduct of occupation forces.

38 See for example: Goodman, D.P. "The Need for Fundamental Change in the Law of Belligerent Occupation" 37 Stan. L. Rev. 1573 at 1608. For an excellent discussion of the deficiencies of this body of law see also Robertson, G *Crimes against Humanity*, Penguin (2002) 2nd Edition pp 193–196.

39 By September 23 2004, the US had persuaded 63 States to enter into "Article 98 Agreements" (bilateral impunity agreements) to ensure that those states do not surrender US citizens to the International Criminal Court. Press Statement 2003: "Article 98 Agreements", Richard Boucher, Washington, DC September 23, http://www.state.gov/r/pa/prs/ps/2003/24331.htm date accessed 11 March 2004.

40 "Banković and Others v. Belgium and 16 Other Contracting States Declared Inadmissible" Press release issued by the Registrar on 19.12.2001 http://www.echr.coe.int/Eng/Press/2001/Dec/Bankovicadmissibilitydecisionepress.htm date accessed 18 March 2004. The case arose out of the bombing by the North Atlantic Treaty Organisation ("NATO") of Radio-Television Serbia's headquarters in Belgrade as part of NATO's campaign of air strikes during the Kosovo conflict. Sixteen people were killed in the missile attack. The case was brought against 17 NATO states. The Court had to decide whether it had jurisdiction to determine alleged violations of the European Convention on Human Rights, where the relevant acts had occurred outside the territory of the NATO States.

1. Accordingly, EU member states with armed forces serving in occupied Iraq remain bound by the European Convention on Human Rights (ECHR) and applicable protocols where their troops are exercising "all or some of the public powers normally to be exercised by that Government". Although an attractive outcome from the perspective of human rights protection, this is a controversial decision. EU member states may be surprised that a European court has interpreted an EU Convention so broadly. Upon ratification of the treaty, many had not anticipated that the ECHR would one day find that it had jurisdiction over matters arising outside the borders of the EU. The *Banković* case is directly applicable to the activities of UK forces occupying Southern Iraq. Those detained by UK forces must be afforded the rights and protections of the ECHR. Other European forces operating in Iraq (e.g. those from Spain, Poland and Italy) are also subject to the jurisdictional requirements outlined above. They are responsible for providing security in various towns and regions of Iraq and are therefore exercising the powers of occupiers, albeit under authority delegated to them by the Security Council endorsed occupying forces.
2. The implications for these European forces operating in Iraq are significant. They must extend ECHR rights to those who they arrest, capture and detain. These rights include the right to a trial, freedom from arbitrary and prolonged detention, the right to due process (including the right to have their status determined in accordance with the 3rd Geneva Convention). Article 1 of the ECHR requires contracting parties to the Convention to undertake "to respect and to ensure respect for the present Convention in all circumstances". If those circumstances extend to the treatment of Iraqis held in UK custody, interesting legal questions arise. For instance, in the handing over of detainees by UK forces to US forces in circumstances where those persons may face the death penalty if convicted of war crimes or crimes against humanity, such a transfer may constitute a violation of the UK's obligations under the ECHR.[41] It would also appear to violate UK obligations under the 2nd Optional Protocol to the International Covenant on Civil and Political Rights (ICCPR Protocol 2).[42] Australian forces operating in Iraq are in a similar position, having also ratified ICCPR Protocol 2.

Other relevant international instruments

There are numerous UN instruments and multilateral treaties that are applicable in various ways to the military occupation of Iraq. An analysis of all such instruments is beyond the scope of this article. Two will be noted briefly. The UN Basic Principles

41 A solution to this problem is for US forces to provide guarantees that they would not expose detainees handed over by UK forces to the death penalty or to any other form of punishment or treatment that may violate the ECHR and associated protocols.

42 The 1966 International Covenant on Civil and Political Rights (ICCPR) is a comprehensive multilateral treaty for the protection of fundamental human rights. It codifies many of the rights set out in the Universal Declaration of Rights (1948). There are two Protocols to the ICCPR. The first provides a complaint mechanism for alleged breaches of the Covenant. The second is an instrument ratified by states who have given their solemn undertaking to: 1. not carry out the death penalty and 2. seek its universal abolition.

on the Use of Force and Firearms by Law Enforcement Officials[43] (Basic Principles) is instructive in the context of an occupier's duty to restore and maintain public order. It provides that law enforcement officials must exercise restraint and proportionality in the use of force to avoid unnecessary injury and loss of life.[44] Article 4 provides that "Law enforcement officials, in carrying out their duty, shall, as far as possible, apply non-violent means before resorting to the use of force and firearms. They may use force and firearms only if other means remain ineffective . . ."

While it is not suggested that this set of principles has attained customary law status, they are an important (albeit non-binding) source of "law". They constitute a set of minimal standards that should be observed by belligerent occupying forces undertaking policing functions. These UN principles could be incorporated into Status of Force agreements, or otherwise observed by states seeking to follow international best practice.

The second instrument is the International Covenant on Civil and Political Rights[45] (the ICCPR), Art 2 of which provides that "No one shall be arbitrarily deprived of his life".[46] This article should be read to preclude Coalition forces from shooting suspected looters on site (other than in self-defence). It should also be read to require restraint in the use of lethal force against persons who do not pose a physical danger to either Coalition forces or civilians.

The ICCPR is binding on Coalition forces under customary law. The Basic Principles mentioned above, although non-binding, inform the implementation of the ICCPR.[47] When considered together, these instruments are suggestive of a prohibition on the indiscriminate use of lethal force by occupying forces to quell opposition. Accordingly it can be contended that these instruments—together with the doctrines of necessity and self-defence—inform the legal framework for the use of force in occupied territory.

Customary law

The direct applicability of customary law to military occupation was recently confirmed in the *Tadic* case.[48] The Trial Chamber noted that civilians in occupied territory are entitled to be treated with the minimal standards of civilisation, so

43 Adopted by the Eighth United Nations Congress on the Prevention of Crime and the Treatment of Offenders, Havana, Cuba, 27 August to 7 September 1990. UN Document Series Symbol: ST/HR/ UN Issuing Body: Secretariat Centre for Human Rights © United Nations http://www.hri.ca/uninfo/treaties/43.shtml date accessed 26 June 2003.

44 See: Paragraph 5 (a) and (b) *UN Basic Principles on the Use of Force and Firearms by Law Enforcement Officials* http://www.hri.ca/uninfo/treaties/43.shtml date accessed 26 June 2003.

45 http://www.hri.ca/uninfo/treaties/3.shtml *UN Document Series Symbol: ST/HR/ UN Issuing Body: Secretariat Centre for Human Rights © United Nations* Date accessed 26 June 2003 Adopted and opened for signature, ratification and accession by General Assembly resolution 2200 A (XXI) of 16 December 1966.

46 Art 2, International Covenant on Civil and Political Rights.

47 The Principles on the Use of Force and Firearms by Law Enforcement Officials were adopted by consensus by the Eighth UN Congress Sept. 7, 1990. The International Covenant on Civil and Political Rights entered into force in 1976. By March 2004, it had been ratified by 148 states: http://www.un.org/Depts/Treaty/final/ts2/newfiles/part_boo/iv_boo/iv_4.html date accessed 11/7/2003.

48 The Prosecutor Of The Tribunal Against Dusko Tadic Case No. It–94–1-I Opinion and Judgment of Trial Chamber II of 17 May 1997.

long as they do not run counter to the necessities of war.[49] While the provisions of the Geneva Conventions and the Hague Regulations (1907) bind all states under customary international law,[50] not all of the Hague Regulations (1907) remain applicable to an occupation. As noted above, some of the regulations have been superseded by the 4th Geneva Convention.[51]

In addition to having entered into custom, certain norms contained in the Geneva Conventions have attained *jus cogens* status. This status is derived from the collective acceptance by states of the non-derogable nature of these norms. It renders such norms pre-eminent rules of international law. Such norms include the prohibitions on the torture of detainees. By contrast, some provisions of 1977 Additional Protocol I may not have yet attained customary law status. The US has not ratified this instrument and denies that it is bound by the protocol in its entirety.[52] Even so, many of its provisions are recognised by the US as customary, with only a few articles being contentious.[53] It is the view of this writer that non-ratifying states including the US may now be bound by the *entire* protocol. This may have occurred as a result of acquiescence (failure by states to object persistently to protocol provisions) or through a proliferation of ratifications leading to the crystallisation of all of the protocol's articles into binding customary norms. At the time of writing 161 states had ratified the protocol. An exploration of whether there is now sufficient evidence of State Practice and *opinio juris* to draw such a conclusion is a matter that goes beyond the scope of this paper.[54]

Occupying forces may also be required under their own domestic laws, rules of engagement, and military doctrine to comply with customary norms of international law. For example, US military law specifically requires its forces to comply with customary law.[55]

---

49 The Prosecutor Of The Tribunal Against Dusko Tadic Case No. It–94–1-I Opinion and Judgment of Trial Chamber II of 17 May 1997, p 202.

50 Jurisprudence of the ICTY affirms that provisions of the Geneva Conventions have customary status: see *Tadic Case*, Opinion and Judgment of Trial Chamber II of 17 May 1997, pp 192 & 199. The Trial Chamber noted in *Tadic* that it was implicit in the decision of the ICTY Appeals Chamber of 2 October 1995 that the Geneva Conventions are part of customary international law.

51 By way of example, Art 2 of The Hague Convention (1907) is now redundant. It reads: "The provisions contained in the Regulations referred to in Art 1, as well as in the present Convention, do not apply except between Contracting powers, and then only if all the belligerents are parties to the Convention". As the Hague Convention and Regulations of 1907 are now binding upon all states under customary law, Art 2 no longer has legal effect.

52 Neither 1977 Additional Protocol 1 nor 1977 Additional Protocol II have been ratified by the US. For a discussion of this issue see: Geoffrey Robertson, *Crimes against Humanity*, Penguin (2002) 2nd Edition p 196.

53 The most contentious provisions relate to the abolition of the right of reprisal and the granting ot irregulars legal status. For an overview of US concerns with 1977 Additional Protocol I see: Abraham D. Sofaer, "The U.S. Decision Not To Ratify Protocol I To The Geneva Conventions On The Protection Of War Victims (Cont'd): The Rationale For The United States Decision" 82 A.J.I.L. 784 at 785.

54 See: Theodor Meron "The Time has come for the United States to Ratify Geneva Protocol I" (1994) 88 AJIL 678. Writing in 1994, Meron asserted that "Occasional dissents from the protocol may not be . . . enough to keep the country out of the customary law regime being created by the Protocol." (682) As 161 states have now ratified 1977 Additional Protocol 1, the US may already be bound by the entire Protocol under customary law.

55 See for example US *Field Manual 27–10 on the Law of Land Warfare* (1956) paragraph 7(c) and *Field Manual 100–23 Peace Operations* (1994) Chapter 3 (I) Legal Considerations http://www.globalsecurity.org/military/library/policy/army/fm/ date accessed 19 July 2003.

Domestic law

The domestic law of the occupying power

The domestic law of occupying powers constitutes another source of legal obligations for occupying forces. Where there are a number of powers exercising control over adjoining geographical regions of occupied territory, differing domestic laws of the respective occupiers will create separate and distinct obligations for each occupier. This may have a significant impact upon the overall administration of the occupied territory by creating different norms in different zones of occupation. For example, occupying troops from different states may be operating under different rules of engagement. Rules of engagement set out the permissible methods for conducting military operations, and reflect the obligations of the relevant state under both customary and treaty law. Whilst not laws in themselves, rules of engagement enunciate the legal obligations of the respective military forces.[56] One consequence of having occupation forces operating under different rules of engagement may be that procedures for dealing with crimes allegedly committed by soldiers from different states may vary significantly depending upon the nationality of the soldier under investigation.

The domestic laws of the occupied territory itself constitute another applicable source of law. Municipal laws remain on foot during a military occupation unless suspended or repealed by the occupying powers.[57] The occupier's discretion to repeal or suspend laws of the occupied territory can only be exercised in a narrow set of circumstances. They include the removal of a local law that: (1) violates fundamental human rights,[58] (2) is inconsistent with the effective administration of justice, (3) is inconsistent with the maintenance of law and order, or (4) is an obstacle to the application of the 4th Geneva Convention itself.[59] Most domestic laws do not fall foul of the above criteria, and therefore escape repeal or suspension during a military occupation. Finite resources and the desire to maintain the status quo are factors that influence occupying powers to maintain most existing laws. Clearly, minimal disruption to civil society is promoted by non-interference with local laws, and this in turn furthers the public order and security objectives of the occupying forces.[60]

Occupying forces (like other persons present in occupied territory) are technically bound by local laws. None of the applicable treaties on occupation confer immunity on occupying forces from the jurisdiction of local courts. However

---

56 Rules of engagement documents can be drawn up for specific military operations (such as the conflict in Iraq). These documents are unusually classified. The *Rules of engagement for US Forces* (1994) reflect many of the enduring legal principles set out in the US Department of Army *Field Manual 27–10 on the Law of Land Warfare* (1956). Australian military forces operate in accordance with rules of engagement drafted in accordance with the Australian Defence Force *Doctrine on Rules of Engagement*.
See Bulman, T.P. "A Dangerous Guessing Game Disguised as Enlightened Policy: United States Law of War Obligations during Military Operations other than War" *Military Law Review* Vol 159 152 at 166.

57 Art 64, 4th Geneva Convention.

58 Kelly, M.J. *Restoring and Maintaining Order in Complex Peace Operations: The Search for a Legal Framework* Kluwer pp 188 9.

59 Art 64, 4th Geneva Convention.

60 Kelly, M.J. *Restoring and Maintaining Order in Complex Peace Operations: The Search for a Legal Framework* Kluwer p 190.

occupying powers generally consider themselves to have such immunity. This reflects the reality of military occupation and the exercise of martial law by occupying forces. Breaches of local laws by occupying troops (if they are to be dealt with at all) are punishable as breaches of the military law of the relevant occupying force. In the absence of such military justice, members of Coalition forces in Iraq who commit crimes such as rape or theft of money during searches of cars, homes and individuals, are acting with apparent impunity. This issue is discussed further below.

UN Resolutions

Resolutions of the Security Council can be a source of rights and obligations for both the occupier and the occupied,[61] and may affirm the applicability of relevant customary and treaty norms to the territory under occupation. Such resolutions may also either encourage or compel occupying forces to comply with other international norms that are not specific to the law of occupation. Resolution 1483 represents the most striking example of such a resolution. It represents a significant development in the law of occupation. Benvenisti has highlighted four unique features of Resolution 1483:[62]

1. It expressly refutes the claim that occupation as such is illegal.
2. It confirms the notion that sovereignty does not pass to the occupier on the total defeat and disintegration of the governing regime.
3. It affirms the continued applicability of international human rights law to territory in spite of foreign occupation.
4. It calls on the occupiers to pursue effective administration, importing a requirement that occupiers fulfil their duties (such as the protection of the occupied population), rather than merely being an "inactive custodian" of occupied territory.

An analysis of Resolution 1483 raises some interesting questions.

Firstly, can the obligations of the Coalition occupying powers under The Hague Regulations and the 4th Geneva Convention be reconciled with the provisions in 1483 that appear to sanction the restructuring of Iraqi society? In the event of a conflict between a treaty provision and a Security Council resolution, which prevails?

In addressing the first question it needs to be noted that Resolution 1483 provides a broader mandate for the occupying powers than that envisaged by the treaties on the law of occupation. For example, it speaks of reform to the Iraqi legal system, whereas the treaties require minimal interference with the laws and institutions of an occupied state. The abolition of the Ministry of Information by the Coalition authority appears to exceed the legitimate role of an occupying

61 General Assembly resolutions that enter into custom through implementation and recognition by states may also be a source of rights of occupying powers, while Security Council resolutions made under Chapter VII are binding on states and may therefore be a source of rights and duties.

62 Eyal Benvenisti, "Agora: Future Implications of the Iraq Conflict: Water Conflicts During the Occupation of Iraq" 97 AJIL 860 at 861–3.

power under the treaties, however it can be justified by reference to paragraph 4 of Resolution 1483.[63]

Is the Security Council empowered to extend the mandate of an occupying power beyond the limits prescribed by the treaty law of occupation? This raises the issue of whether there are limits on the power of the Security Council acting under Chapter VII. Clearly a Security Council resolution would be of doubtful validity if it called upon states to violate *jus cogens* norms of international law.[64] However if the resolution is merely inconsistent with a treaty provision, the issue is resolved by reference to the UN Charter itself. Article 103 of the Charter provides that Security Council resolutions enjoy primacy over treaty obligations when the two conflict.[65] In the *Lockerbie Bombing Case*,[66] the International Court of Justice acknowledged that pursuant to Art 103 of the UN Charter, Security Council resolution provisions can take precedence over contrary treaty obligations.[67] Accordingly, in the event of a conflict between Resolution 1483 and The Hague Regulations and/or Geneva

---

63 Paragraph 4 of Resolution 1483 calls upon the Authority "to promote the welfare of the Iraqi people through the effective administration of the territory, including in particular working towards the restoration of conditions of security and stability and the creation of conditions in which the Iraqi people may freely determine their own political future".

64 This question was addressed by Judge Lauterpacht in his separate opinion in the Bosnian Genocide Case (ICJ) 1993 (Application of the Convention on the Prevention and Punishment of the Crime of Genocide, Provisional Measures, *Bosnia v. Yugo.*, 1993 I.C.J. 3 (Apr. 8)). Ken Roberts offers a very useful analysis of the significance of Judge Lauterpacht's observations:

> Judge Lauterpacht . . . asserted that the Court does not have the right to substitute its discretion for that of the Council in determining the existence of a threat to the peace, a breach of the peace or an act of aggression. [FN126]
>
> Judge Lauterpacht also raised the issue of the Court's ability to review a Council decision which conflicts with a principle of jus cogens. [FN127] The ad hoc Court member carefully distinguished the case at hand from that of Lockerbie, in which the decision of the Council had prevailed over any treaty obligation by virtue of Article 103. The distinguishing factor in *Bosnia v. Yugoslavia* was the fact that the prohibition against genocide has long been established as a principle of jus cogens. [FN128] Because the concept of jus cogens is superior to both treaty and customary international law, the relief offered in Lockerbie by Article 103 did not apply. Insofar as Resolution 713 unwittingly supported the perpetration of genocide contrary to an established rule of jus cogens, Judge Lauterpacht suggested that the decision might become legally null and void. With regard to the elimination of the arms embargo vis-a-vis Bosnia-Herzegovina, he went as far as stating that he would be prepared to indicate the following provisional measure: "[t]hat as between the Applicant and the Respondent the continuing validity of the embargo in its bearing on the Applicant has become a matter of doubt requiring further consideration by the Security Council". [FN129]
>
> While going so far as to indicate a potential power of review for the Court, Judge Lauterpacht stopped short of any arrogation of power, structuring his suggested measure in terms which would allow the Council to do the actual reviewing. While the majority of the Court did not make any statement regarding judicial competence to review a Council decision which conflicts with a principle of jus cogens, Judge Lauterpacht's commentary may well be an indication of one direction in which the Court may increase its powers in the future.

Ken Roberts, "Second-Guessing the Security Council: The International Court of Justice and its Powers of Judicial Review" *Pace International Law Review* Spring 1995 http://www.globalpolicy.org/wldcourt/roberts.htm date accessed 14 April 2003.

65 Thomas D. Grant "How to Reconcile Conflicting Obligations of Occupation and Reform" June 2003 < http://www.asil.org/insights/insigh107a1.htm > date accessed 17 June 2003.

66 Questions of Interpretation and Application of the 1971 Montreal Convention Arising from the Aerial Incident in Lockerbie, Request for the Indication of Provisional Matters, ICJ Reports (1992) 3; see also Graefrath, B "Leave to the Court What Belongs to the Court: The Libyan Case" EJIL http://www.ejil.org/journal/Vol4/No2/art3.html date accessed 16 July 2003 last modified: Monday, 7 August 2000 12:47PM.

67 Questions of Interpretation and Application of the 1971 Montreal Convention Arising from the Aerial Incident in Lockerbie, Request for the Indication of Provisional Matters, ICJ Reports (1992) 3.

Conventions, the former will prevail. However until a Security Council resolution is in place, the treaty provisions apply.

THE OCCUPATION OF IRAQ: FROM INVADERS TO ADMINISTRATORS

The military occupation of Iraq—a truly belligerent occupation

On 19 March 2003, the US and its Coalition partners commenced a hostile conflict against Iraq. By 2 May, US forces claimed to exercise command and control over Baghdad and many other cities and towns in Iraq, while United Kingdom forces asserted control over territory in Southern Iraq, including the cities of Basra and Umm Kasr. Meanwhile, Kurdish and Coalition forces gained territory in Northern Iraq previously controlled by the Ba'athist regime. The Coalition's devastating bombing campaign precipitated the abandonment of the formal exercise of power by the Ba'athists throughout Iraq, with many senior Ba'ath party officials fleeing their posts. Although the demise of Saddam Hussein's regime was initially welcomed by many Iraqis, euphoria at liberation from a brutal dictatorship was short-lived. The power vacuum in the wake of the ousting of the Ba'ath regime was soon filled in many parts of the country by looting and lawlessness.

For Coalition forces, attempts to comply with obligations of an occupying power have been both onerous and dangerous. Formidable security, humanitarian, and rule of law challenges have persisted throughout Iraq. In many parts of the country, the experience of occupation has been characterised by the theft of national assets, lack of security, an absence of accountability for criminal conduct, the destruction or theft of private and public property (including cultural treasures), delays in the restoration of war damaged utilities, the sabotage of basic infrastructure by those opposed to Coalition occupation, revenge killings by Iraqis against Iraqis, the bombing of (1) humanitarian agencies, (2) military compounds and (3) military and aid convoys, the taking of foreign hostages, and the summary execution or assassination of foreign diplomats, foreign aid workers, captured soldiers and hostages.

Coalition preparation for military occupation

The invasion of Iraq in March 2003 was one of the most anticipated and debated military offensives in recent history.[68] International Aid Agencies, retired US military commanders, Human Rights groups, miscellaneous other NGOs, international jurists, experts on the Middle East and international relations, all clamoured to offer their advice and perspectives to Coalition forces on issues ranging from the legality of an invasion and occupation,[69] to the short and long-term

68 Others include the Korean and Vietnam Wars. The Iraq Conflict may be distinguished due to the scale of international discussion on the legality of embarking upon military conflict.

69 "THIS ILLEGAL WAR MUST BE CONDUCTED LAWFULLY" International Commission of Jurists (last modified 20 March 2003); (date accessed 20 March 2003) <http://www.icj.org/news.php3?id_article=2774&lang=en>; "ICJ DEPLORES MOVES TOWARD A WAR OF AGGRESSION ON IRAQ" (last modified 18 March 2003); (date accessed 12 June 2003) http://www.icj.org/news.php3?id_article=2770&lang=en.

humanitarian,[70] environmental,[71] social,[72] political,[73] and economic[74] consequences of conducting a war of aggression to disarm a state that was alleged to be in possession of weapons of mass destruction.

Preparations for the invasion: "Blind into Baghdad"

Journalist James Fallows' analysis of the Bush Administration's preparations for the invasion and occupation of Iraq is compelling reading. It reveals that the CIA, State Department, US Agency for International Development and the Army and Marine Corps all engaged in extensive planning.[75] His critique entirely discredits Bush Administration suggestions that the Coalition could not have envisaged—let alone planned for—the looting, lawlessness and other problems that have beset the Coalition since the collapse of the Ba'ath regime:

> Almost everything good and bad that has happened in Iraq since the fall of Saddam Hussein's regime was the subject of extensive pre-war discussion and analysis . . . The problems the United States has encountered are precisely the ones its own experts warned against.[76]

A detailed analysis of the reasons why the Bush Administration ignored pre-war warnings (and failed to implement recommendations that came from numerous governmental and independent sources) goes beyond the scope of this paper. However two reasons have immerged and warrant mention:

1. Internal fighting within the Bush Administration and distrust by the Pentagon of reports commissioned by the State Department and prepared by persons perceived to be anti-war.[77]

---

70 "International Humanitarian Law Issues In A Potential War In Iraq", Human Rights Watch Briefing Paper (last modified 20 February 2003); (date accessed 26 May 2003) <http://www.hrw.org/backgrounder/arms/iraq0202003.htm>

71 Alex Kirby "Foes urged to spare Iraq's wildlife" http://news.bbc.co.uk/1/hi/sci/tech/2761571.stm 16 February 2003, 00:17 GMT accessed 26 June 2003.

72 5 February 2003 "Experts can discuss impact of possible war" http://news.uns.purdue.edu/UNS/html3month/030205.T.Iraq.html; see also United Nations Office for the Coordination of Humanitarian Affairs, "Integrated Humanitarian Contingency Plan for Iraq and Neighbouring Countries" [Confidential Draft] (7 January 2003) http://www.casi.org.uk/info/undocs/internal.html date accessed 26 June 2003.

73 "War in Iraq: what it would mean for Asia" by Lawrence Bartlett http://origin.dailynews.lk/2003/01/22/fea05.html date accessed 26 June 2003 and Patrick Tyler "Anti-war protests a reminder of political consequences of backing US" 18 February 2003 http://www.theage.com.au/articles/2003/02/17/1045330538542.html accessed 26 June 2003.

74 Observer http://www.guardian.co.uk/Iraq/Story/0,2763,887404,00.html date accessed 26 June 2003; "The economic consequences of war" Vincent Cable.

75 "Blind Into Baghdad: The inside story of a historic failure" 2004 *The Atlantic* January/February 2004 http://www.theatlantic.com/issues/2004/01/fallows.htm date accessed 18 March 2004. The Fallows article reaffirms shortcomings expressed by the Center for Strategic and International Studies as early as July 2003. See: Anthony H. Cordesman, *Iraq and Conflict Termination: The Road to Guerilla War?* Center for Strategic and International Studies (Washington DC) revised 28 July 2003.

76 "Blind Into Baghdad: The inside story of a historic failure" 2004 *The Atlantic* January/February 2004 http://www.theatlantic.com/issues/2004/01/fallows.htm date accessed 18 March 2004.

77 "Thomas Warrick, the State Department official who directed the Future of Iraq project, was considered to be in the anti war camp": James Fallows, "Blind Into Baghdad: The inside story of a historic failure" http://www.theatlantic.com/issues/2004/01/fallows.htm date accessed 18 March 2004.

2. Fear that comprehensive planning for the occupation of Iraq would undermine the case for war—it meant facing costs and problems that were an impediment to war.[78]

One may ponder how a government planning to invade another state can justify having no plan as to how to meet its obligations as an occupier. Prior to the war, the answer that was given by US government officials at Agency for International Development meetings with NGOs was "The American troops will be liberators" (rather than occupiers), so the obligations did not apply.[79] This approach ultimately magnified the problems encountered by Coalition troops as they attempted to meet their post-invasion obligations.

The Pentagon ignores the State Department's "Future of Iraq Project"

In March 2002 the US State Department publicly announced the *Future of Iraq Project* which eventually involved 17 working groups "designed systematically to cover what would be needed to rebuild the political and economic infrastructure of the country".[80] Separate groups addressed issues including "Transitional Justice", "Water Agriculture and the Environment", "Democratic Principles" and "Procedures Public Finance" and "Oil and Energy". The final report consisted of thirteen volumes of recommendations on specific topics.

In hindsight, the report's recommendations were ignored at the Coalition's peril. Four pre-emptive warnings serve as examples of how poorly Coalition forces addressed concerns that had been raised well in advance:

1. The "fundamental importance of clean water supplies for Iraqis immediately after transition". This requirement was described as "key to Coalition/ community relations".
2. The "... importance of getting electricity grid up and running immediately—key to water systems, jobs ... Could go a long way to determining Iraqis' attitude to Coalition forces".[81]
3. "The removal of Saddam's regime will provide a power vacuum and create popular anxieties about the viability of all Iraqi institutions".
4. "The period immediately after regime change might offer those criminals the opportunity to engage in acts of killing, plunder and looting".

The Senate Foreign Relations Committee considered the case for war on 31 July 2002. During these hearings, Iraqi exile Rend Rahim France (who served on the *Future of Iraq Project*) testified that "the system of public security will break down because there will be no functioning police force, civil service, and no justice system ... there will be a vacuum of political authority and administrative authority".[82]

---

78 James Fallows, "Blind Into Baghdad: The inside story of a historic failure" *The Atlantic* January/February 2004 http://www.theatlantic.com/issues/2004/01/fallows.htm date accessed 18 March 2004.

79 Joel Charny Refugees International.

80 James Fallows, "Blind Into Baghdad: The inside story of a historic failure" *The Atlantic* January/February 2004 http://www.theatlantic.com/issues/2004/01/fallows.htm date accessed 18 March 2004.

81 James Fallows, "Blind Into Baghdad: The inside story of a historic failure" *The Atlantic* January/February 2004 http://www.theatlantic.com/issues/2004/01/fallows.htm date accessed 18 March 2004.

82 James Fallows, "Blind Into Baghdad: The inside story of a historic failure" *The Atlantic* January/February 2004 http://www.theatlantic.com/issues/2004/01/fallows.htm date accessed 18 March 2004.

Fallows' article also points to statements by senior US Army officers who were concerned that the Pentagon was ignoring professional advice on the number of troops required to occupy Iraq effectively. Warnings were issued that with too few troops, the US would be trapped in an untenable position.[83]

Phase IV: The unplanned "liberation" phase

An official army report prepared well in advance of the war also urged comprehensive planning for the occupation of Iraq.[84] The report outlines four phases of warfare: (I) deploying equipment and personnel into the region (II) preparation for battle (III) invasion and subsequent military operations, and (IV) the post-conflict phase. It stressed that planning for Phase IV had to start as early as possible. It proffered a check list of 135 tasks to be attended to immediately right after the war, and by whom.[85] Copies were circulated throughout the US Army by December 2002.[86]

The first Coalition troops to enter and occupy Baghdad were the Third Infantry Division of the US Army. Their "After Action Report"[87] reveals that there was no plan for Phase IV Operation Iraqi Freedom. The final page of the report reads:

> Issue: Plan for Phase IV operations.
>
> Discussion: Higher headquarters did not provide the 3ID (M) with a plan for Phase IV. As a result, 3ID (M) transitioned into Phase IV operations in the absence of guidance.
>
> Recommendations: Division planners should have drafted detailed plans on Phase IV operations that would have allowed it to operate independently and outside of guidance from higher headquarters. Critical requirements should have been identified prior to LD, and a plan to execute a SASO mission for at least 30 days should have been ready to execute immediately. A liaison officer (LNO) from ORHA during planning would have greatly assisted this process.[88]

The dismissal of vital material such as the *Future of Iraq Project*, the absence of any plan for Phase IV of Operation Iraqi Freedom, and the systematic failure of US troops to prevent looting and lawlessness in their spheres of occupation, demonstrate a failure by the US government to meet basic obligations under the law of occupation. The nature and source of these obligations are discussed below.

---

83 See extracts of interview with Thomas White retired general; James Fallows, "Blind Into Baghdad: The inside story of a historic failure" 2004 *The Atlantic* January/February 2004 p 22–23 http://www.theatlantic.com/issues/2004/01/fallows.htm date accessed 18 March 2004.

84 "Reconstructing Iraq: Insights Challenges And Missions For Military Forces In The Post Conflict Senario" Army War Colleges Web Site http://www.carlisle.army.mil/ssi/pubs/2003/reconirq/reconirq.htm date accessed 18 March 2004.

85 James Fallows, "Blind Into Baghdad: The inside story of a historic failure" 2004 *The Atlantic* January/February 2004 p 28 http://www.theatlantic.com/issues/2004/01/fallows.htm.

86 James Fallows, "Blind Into Baghdad: The inside story of a historic failure" 2004 *The Atlantic* January/February 2004 p 28.

87 Third Infantry Division (Mechanized) After Action Report—Operation Iraqi Freedom http://www.globalsecurity.org/military/library/report/2003/3id-aar-jul03.pdf date accessed 29 February 2004.

88 Third Infantry Division (Mechanized) After Action Report—Operation Iraqi Freedom http://www.globalsecurity.org/military/library/report/2003/3id-aar-jul03.pdf date accessed 29 February 2004.

The overall impact of pre-deployment failures by Coalition forces is something for others to quantify. However sending US forces into Iraq without: 1. basic Arabic language skills, 2. cross-cultural training, 3. awareness training on basic aspects of Islamic beliefs and practices, 4. adequate numbers of interpreters, and 5. sufficient troops to restore law and order and guarantee security until Iraqi security forces were re-established and 6. a plan for the occupation of Iraq, clearly hampered efforts to stabilise Iraq upon the collapse of the Ba'ath regime and undermined efforts by US troops to win "hearts and minds" in Iraq. These omissions are likely to have created a climate of misunderstandings and miscommunications between Iraqi citizens and US troops. This not only undermined respect for US authority, but on occasion had fatal consequences for innocent Iraqi citizens. Such tragedies appear to have fuelled militant resistance to the occupation.[89]

The legality of the war and its impact on the obligations of the occupiers

The obligations of an occupying power exist "whether or not it was lawful to use the armed force that resulted in the occupation".[90] These obligations include the provision of security,[91] basic necessities (including food and medical supplies,[92] electricity and clean water,[93]) and compliance with numerous other obligations owed to civilians under Arts 47–64 of the 4th Geneva Convention.

Beyond these obligations, Coalition forces in Iraq assumed a broader range of responsibilities including the preservation of evidence of past atrocities,[94] re-establishment of the rule of law and the justice system,[95] and coordination of the transition to responsible Iraqi government.[96] These responsibilities had to be met by the occupiers, who, simultaneously, had to respect the "sovereignty and territorial integrity of Iraq".[97] It has already been contended by others that not all of these Security Council based objectives can be reconciled with each other, or with applicable norms of occupation set out in the applicable treaties.[98] As resistance to the occupation spread throughout Iraq, balancing these obligations became a formidable challenge.

89 See for example: Human Rights Watch Report "Sidelined: Human Rights in Postwar Iraq" by Joe Stork and Fred Abrahams http://www.hrw.org/wr2k4/6.htm date accessed 14 March 2004. The Report highlights some of the consequences of the Pentagon's approach to planning for the occupation.

90 Kirgis, F "Security Council Resolution 1483 on the Rebuilding of Iraq" May 2003 AJIL <http://asil.org/insights.htm> date accessed 11 March 2004.

91 Art 43, Hague Regulations (1907).

92 Art 55, 4th Geneva Convention.

93 These obligations arise from the requirement to ensure health and hygiene [4th Geneva Convention Art 56] and also arise by implication from para 4 of Resolution 1483 (2003).

94 See also: "Principles on the Effective Prevention and Investigation of Extra-legal, Arbitrary and Summary Executions" (date accessed 16 June 2003); (last modified 2002) http://193.194.138.190/html/menu3/b/54.htm, Economic and Social Council resolution 1989/65, and United Nations Press Release HR/4667 IK/358 High Commissioner For Human Rights Concerned Over Possible Loss Of Evidence Of Past Abuses In Iraq 16 May 2003 http://www.un.org/News/Press/docs/2003/hr4667.doc.htm.

95 Art 64, 4th Geneva Convention, See also paras 3, 4 and 8 of Resolution 1483 (2003).

96 See: paras 8 and 16 Security Council Resolution 1483 (2003).

97 Preamble to Security Council Resolution 1483 (2003).

98 See for example: Thomas D. Grant "How to Reconcile Conflicting Obligations of Occupation and Reform" June 2003 <http://www.asil.org/insights/insigh107a1.htm> date accessed 17 June 2003.

Security Council Resolution 1483 and the "legality" of the occupation

Some three weeks after President Bush declared major hostilities in Iraq at an end, the UN Security Council unanimously approved Resolution 1483.[99] The text of the resolution offered no retrospective validation of the invasion of Iraq, although it does offer UN recognition of the post-invasion occupation. Even without the resolution, the occupation was already governed by The Hague Regulations and the 4th Geneva Convention. Resolution 1483 merely confirmed the applicability of these treaties. However the resolution has political significance for the Coalition forces for two reasons. Firstly it recognises the power of the occupying forces to govern Iraq pending the emergence of responsible Iraqi government, and secondly it represents a significant act by the UN's principal political body which has effectively embossed the UN's imprimatur on the military occupation of Iraq.[100] In contrast to the initial invasion, Coalition forces were able to point to Resolution 1483 as providing an unequivocal mandate for the ongoing occupation of Iraq. Secondly it has provided a platform for Coalition forces to remain in Iraq for an indefinite period,[101] and continue their search for both weapons of mass destruction and senior members of the former regime. It also demonstrates international recognition of the *fact of the occupation*, and addresses important issues including the need to safeguard the humanitarian and sovereign interests of the Iraqi people.

How does Security Council Resolution 1483 affect the duties of Coalition forces?

Resolution 1483 cements the obligations and duties of the occupying powers under international law. Its preamble acknowledges the status of the Coalition forces as occupying powers in Iraq by "... recognizing the specific authorities, responsibilities, and obligations under applicable international law of these States[102] as occupying powers under unified command (the 'Authority')".[103]

Whether this preamble is binding on the occupying powers in Iraq is a matter for conjecture. Any preliminary statements that are not contained in the operative part of the resolution are arguably no more than guiding principles.[104] An alternative approach is to view the preamble as prescribing and defining the legal framework

---

99 Resolution 1483 was passed on May 22, 2003.

100 Benvenisti has noted that Resolution 1483 marks the first time that the Security Council has "resorted to the concept of occupation to describe a situation in which foreign troops control areas through the use of force". Eyal Benvenisti, "Agora: Future Implications of the Iraq Conflict: Water Conflicts During the Occupation of Iraq" 97 AJIL 860 at 861.

101 In light of the agreement signed by the Coalition Provisional Authority and the Iraqi Governing Council in November 2003—which provides for the return of full sovereignty to Iraqis in July 2004—the legitimate occupation of Iraq as authorised in Resolution 1483 may now be said to expire on the agreed date, subject to any extension agreed by both parties.

102 It is unclear whether "these states" include Australia and Poland. The preamble to the resolution implies that only those states that signed the letter to the President of the Security Council dated 8 May 2003 are occupying powers (i.e. the United Kingdom of Great Britain and Northern Ireland and the United States of America). Australian SAS forces were involved in the ground invasion, and a small number of Australian forces remain in Iraq. It is therefore arguable that Australia has ongoing obligations under the law of occupation as an occupying power.

103 Security Council Resolution 1483 (2003).

104 See: Thomas D. Grant "How to Reconcile Conflicting Obligations of Occupation and Reform" June 2003 <http://www.asil.org/insights/insigh107a1.htm> date accessed 17 June 2003.

for the occupation. This view is reinforced by two portions of the resolution. Paragraph 5 provides that the Security Council "Acting under Chapter VII of the Charter of the United Nations . . . calls upon all concerned to comply fully with their obligations under international law including in particular the Geneva Conventions of 1949 and the Hague Regulations of 1907".[105] The second is a paragraph in the preamble which refers to a letter addressed to President of the Security Council and signed by the occupying powers. In the letter, the US and UK governments undertake to "strictly abide by their obligations under international law".[106]

Although Resolution 1483 requires the occupying forces to comply with their obligations under international law, it has been criticised for not expressly stating that the occupiers are to pay for war damage and reconstruction costs in Iraq.[107] The applicable treaty law of occupation and the law of armed conflict do not state that occupying powers must pay for war damage or compensate victims of war. However, the occupiers in Iraq could be held liable to make such reparations under principles of state responsibility if a competent tribunal was to determine that the initial invasion was illegal and unjustifiable at international law.[108]

Resolution 1483 has also been criticised for failing to require the occupying powers to:

1. safely dispose of munitions containing depleted uranium,
2. detonate or remove cluster bombs and other un-detonated munitions,
3. gather evidence of war crimes or crimes against humanity committed by the belligerent parties,
4. establish an interim Iraqi administration within a fixed period, and
5. immediately leave Iraq upon the establishment of responsible government.[109]

However, by voting in favour of Resolution 1483, US and Britain (and possibly Australia and Poland)[110] have agreed to:

---

105 Para 5 Resolution 1483. Note however that even in the absence of Resolution 1483, the Coalition forces would still have been bound by their obligations under both treaty law (the Geneva Conventions of 1949 and The Hague Regulations of 1907) and customary law.

106 Letter from the Permanent Representatives of the UK and the US to the UN addressed to the President of the Security Council S/2003/538 May 8, 2003 date accessed 23 July 2003, http://www.globalpolicy.org/security/issues/iraq/document/2003/0608usukletter.htm.

107 "The US and UK have almost complete control over the funds of the Development Fund for Iraq. At the same time, these governments are not required to pay war reparations nor are they held to their obligation as occupying powers under the Geneva Conventions to pay for the humanitarian needs caused by their illegal invasion and occupation" "Greens Oppose UN Security Council Resolution Legitimising US Invasion and Occupation of Iraq": www.gp.org/press/pr_05_29_03html dated 29 May 2003 accessed 1 July 2003.

108 As Australia participated in the initial ground invasion, it could ultimately share responsibility for these costs if liability were established.

109 While the occupying powers are not bound under international law to do any of these things, undertakings to satisfy such moral duties would assist in the promotion of fundamental norms of civilised society. The promotion of such norms is a feature of the human rights movement, the proliferation of humanitarian-minded NGOs and the accompanying expansion of principles of good governance, democracy and humanitarianism.

110 Australia and Poland have both contributed military personnel and other resources during the invasion and occupation of Iraq. Both states lobbied for a UN resolution expressly authorising the use of force in Iraq. Other states have contributed forces during the occupation phase. States such as Spain and Italy that have sent personnel to provide security in various parts of Iraq would appear to be bound by the law of occupation at least to the extent of ensuring that their forces comply with this body of law while they remain in Iraq.

i. comply with the international rule of law with respect to their role as occupying powers,
ii. a UN role in post-war Iraq,
iii. fulfil their obligations under the Geneva Conventions and Hague Regulations, and
iv. respect the sovereignty of the people of Iraq including their rights to determine their own political future and exercise control over their natural resources.

Benvenisti[111] has highlighted a number of important aspects of Resolution 1483 that impact on the powers and duties of the occupiers. The resolution calls for the occupants to pursue an "effective occupation". This requirement can be seen to strengthen both the duties *and* powers of occupying forces. Firstly it holds the Coalition to their duty to maintain law and order (without which effective administration of Iraq is impossible). At the same time, it acknowledges that without the power to implement a programme of de-Ba'athification of Iraqi society (which includes restructuring or dissolving of Iraqi ministries) it would be impossible to administer Iraq effectively or fulfil other obligations of occupiers under the 4th Geneva Convention.

The role of the UN in occupied Iraq

Resolution 1483 provides for a limited UN role in occupied Iraq. This includes involvement in coordinating humanitarian assistance and reconstruction activities and (in coordination with the Coalition Provisional Authority) assisting the people of Iraq to:[112]

> restore and establish national and local institutions for representative governance ... encouraging international efforts to contribute to basic civilian administration functions ... promoting the protection of human rights ... encouraging international efforts to rebuild the capacity of the Iraqi civilian police force ... [and] encouraging international efforts to promote legal and judicial reform.[113]

The Authority is required to work within the framework of the UN Charter "... and other relevant international law, to promote the welfare of the Iraqi people through the effective administration of the territory, including in particular working towards the restoration of conditions of security and stability and the creation of conditions in which the Iraqi people can freely determine their own political future".[114] All member states of the UN are encouraged to assist in the implementation of the resolution through the Security Council's direct appeal to member states to "deny safe haven to those members of the previous Iraqi regime who are alleged

111 Eyal Benvenisti, "Agora: Future Implications of the Iraq Conflict: Water Conflicts During the Occupation of Iraq" 97 AJIL 860 at 863.

112 Security Council Resolution 1483, para 8.

113 Resolution 1483, para 8.

114 Resolution 1483, para 4. Accordingly, the UN Charter forms part of the applicable law in Iraq, as the Coalition Authority is bound by its principles.

to be responsible for crimes and atrocities and to support actions to bring them to justice".[115]

A significant innovation in Resolution 1483 is the creation of the office of UN Special Representative for Iraq. The Special Representative has an important role in overseeing compliance with the law of occupation, and as a representative of the international community, is independent of the occupying powers. The text of the resolution and the characterisation of the role of the UN and its Special Representative has been criticised however. Benvenisti suggests that it is "a rather convoluted and unsatisfactory way to inject the issue of human rights into the fray of occupation policies".[116] He does however commend the Security Council for creating the office of UN Special Representative to Iraq, noting that it is the first time the UN has had an independent supervisory role during a belligerent occupation.[117] Tragically, just months after his appointment to the position, Special Representative Sergio Vieira de Mello was killed on 19 August 2003 when the UN Headquarters in Baghdad was destroyed in a suicide bomb attack. Several resistance groups opposed to the occupation claimed responsibility for the attack.[118] De Mello was not replaced, and UN staff in Iraq were withdrawn to UN offices in Cyprus and Jordan, where they remain. The absence of a UN Special Representative has significantly diminished the capacity of the UN to fulfil its Security Council mandated role in Iraq.

Control over Iraq's oil revenue

In the lead up to the invasion of Iraq there was considerable speculation over the Coalition's intentions with regard to Iraq's oil and associated revenue. Resolution 1483 provides that oil revenue is to be paid into a Development Bank account for Iraq and disbursed at the direction of the Authority in consultation with an Iraq interim administration.[119] This revenue is to be used for the purposes of "the economic reconstruction and repair of Iraq's infrastructure". This will include repairs to plant and equipment in Iraqi oil fields. Funds are also to be used "in a transparent manner to meet the humanitarian needs of the Iraqi people", "for the continued disarmament of Iraq", and to meet "the costs of civil administration".[120] Surplus funds are to be held in trust for the people of Iraq pending the installation of a representative government.[121] The legality of oil contracts entered into by the Coalition Provisional Authority goes beyond the scope of this paper, but has been considered by others.[122]

115 Resolution 1483, para 3.

116 Eyal Benvenisti, "Agora: Future Implications of the Iraq Conflict: Water Conflicts During the Occupation of Iraq" 97 AJIL 860 at 863.

117 Eyal Benvenisti, "Agora: Future Implications of the Iraq Conflict: Water Conflicts During the Occupation of Iraq" 97 AJIL 860 at 863.

118 Three resistance groups have claimed responsibility for the bombing: Hafs el-Masri Brigades, the Armed Vanguards of the Second Muhammad Army, and Muhammad's Army.

119 Resolution 1483, paras 12 and 13.

120 Resolution 1483.

121 Resolution 1483, paras 11–14.

122 See for example: Pieter H.F. Bekker "The Legal Status of Foreign Economic Interests in Occupied Iraq" http://www.asil.org/insights/insigh114.htm July 2003. Bekker notes that "the legal status of contracts concluded during an occupation and exceeding the length of the occupation is uncertain, especially if such contracts relate to the occupied state's natural resources".

Powers and obligations of the occupying forces in Iraq

Duty to restore and maintain law and order

When legitimate power passes to the occupier, the latter must "take all measures in his power to restore and ensure as far as possible public order and safety while respecting . . . the laws in force in the country".[123] This obligation is contained in both treaty[124] and customary law,[125] however it does not arise until an occupying power has achieved "effective control".[126] The question of when effective control has actually been achieved is therefore of vital importance in determining at what point occupying forces are obliged to maintain and restore law and order. According to Human Rights Watch, "Under customary international law, this duty begins once a stable regime of occupation has been established, but under the Geneva Conventions, the duty attaches as soon as the occupying force has any relation with the civilians of that territory, that is, at the soonest possible moment—a principle that finds reflection in U.S. military policy."[127] The International Committee of the Red Cross asserts that "There is no intermediate period between what might be termed the invasion phase and the inauguration of a stable regime of occupation. Even a patrol which penetrates into enemy territory without any intention of staying there must respect the Conventions in its dealings with the civilians it meets."[128] US military doctrine requires that the protections relating to occupation apply "as far as possible in areas through which troops are passing and even on the battlefield" (Field Manual, 27–10, p. 138, para. 352).

The importance of preparation for the assumption of the obligation to maintain order was also highlighted by human rights NGOs in the lead up to the invasion of Iraq. Human Rights Watch contended that international law requires that:

> . . . the United States and its allies . . . use their own personnel to secure public order as they advance through the country . . . [and further that the Coalition] be prepared to mobilize and adequately train local military, and eventually police, personnel for such responsibilities. These forces must follow directly on those that displace existing authorities, to leave no intermediate period for reprisal and revenge.[129]

---

123 Art 43 The Hague Regulations IV (1907). See also Hague Regulations (IV) of 1907 art. 43; 4th Geneva Convention, art. 27.

124 Art 43 The Hague Regulations IV (1907).

125 Both the Hague Regulations IV (1907) and the 4th Geneva Convention have entered into custom. See also Bulman, T.P. "A Dangerous Guessing Game Disguised as Enlightened Policy: United States Law of War Obligations during Military Operations other than War" *Military Law Review* Vol 159 152.

126 Kelly, M.J. *Restoring and Maintaining Order in Complex Peace Operations: The Search for a Legal Framework* Kluwer p185.

127 "International Humanitarian Law Issues in a Potential War in Iraq", Human Rights Watch Briefing Paper, February 20, 2003 http://www.hrw.org/backgrounder/arms/iraq0202003.htm accessed 26 May 2003. Cf. Hague Regulation (Arts 42, 43); Fourth Geneva Convention (Art 6); ICRC Commentary on the Fourth Geneva Convention, p 60 ("There is no intermediate period between what might be termed the invasion phase and the inauguration of a stable regime of occupation. Even a patrol which penetrates into enemy territory without any intention of staying there must respect the Conventions in its dealings with the civilians it meets.")

128 Commentary Art. 6 Convention (IV) relative to the Protection of Civilian Persons in Time of War. Geneva, 12 August 1949 <http://www.icrc.org/ihl.nsf/0/030537c0a8ee01dfc12563cd0042a6be?OpenDocument> date accessed 15 April 2004.

129 "International Humanitarian Law Issues In A Potential War In Iraq", Human Rights Watch Briefing Paper, February 20, 2003 http://www.hrw.org/backgrounder/arms/iraq0202003.htm accessed 26 May 2003. Note: There is little doubt that if the Coalition had in place sufficient numbers of properly trained

Legal scholars have long asserted that where belligerent forces intend to occupy an enemy's territory, they must be in a position to make their authority felt and their protection effective within that newly occupied territory.[130] The scale of looting and lawlessness in the immediate aftermath of the invasion is indicative of the Coalition's failure to meet these preconditions—particularly in Baghdad and other parts of the "Sunni Triangle". This constituted an egregious error by the occupying powers and one that cannot lightly be brushed aside.[131] It also raises questions about whether there is effective occupation of some Iraqi towns (such as Fullujah) when occupation forces are unwilling to enter and maintain order in these centres of resistance to the occupation. The apparent complicity of some Iraqi police and security personnel in attacks upon civilians, and the refusal of Iraqi military units to fight resistance forces in Fullujah adds to doubts that these towns are "effectively occupied".[132]

Where force commanders exercise effective control over an area of territory and have the capacity to act to restore or maintain order—and fail to do so—this would constitute a violation of the obligation of the occupier.[133] It should be emphasised that where an occupying area has been unable to exercise effective control over an area, the obligation to restore and maintain order does not arise. In Fullujah and other towns in the "Sunni Triangle", the intensity of resistance attacks upon Coalition forces has at various times prevented US troops from exercising effective control over those towns. Accordingly it can be argued that the obligations under the law of occupation do not apply during these periods.

The frequency and sustained nature of resistance attacks upon Coalition military targets, humanitarian agencies and Iraqi "collaborators" clearly poses questions about the ability of occupying powers to fulfil their duty to maintain law and order in parts of Iraq. A detailed analysis of the resistance movements in Iraq and their causes goes beyond the scope of this paper. However a number of issues may be flagged for present purposes. Firstly, there is little doubt that armed resistance in the Sunni triangle is attributable not only to former members of the Iraqi secret service and foreign mudjahadin, but also to members of the disbanded Iraqi Army.[134] One consequence of the CPA's decision to disband the Iraqi Army was that hundreds of thousands of armed and trained Iraqi men were left unemployed and without an income. This undoubtedly fuelled armed resistance to the occupiers.[135] Many Iraqi soldiers—particularly those from Sunni towns including Tikrit and Fullujah—

and equipped personnel in Baghdad and other cities and towns when the regime was displaced, the widespread looting, lawlessness and criminal activity could have been much less, and public order more effectively maintained. This issue is explored further later.

130 Morgan and Baly p 182.

131 James Fallows, "Blind Into Baghdad: The inside story of a historic failure" 2004 *The Atlantic* January/February 2004 http://www.theatlantic.com/issues/2004/01/fallows.htm date accessed 17 March 2004.

132 "2 American Civilians Killed in Iraqi Ambush" Rajiv Chandrasekaran, Washington Post Foreign Service, March 11, 2004 http://www.washingtonpost.com/wp-dyn/articles/A47999-2004Mar10.html.

133 Kelly, M.J. *Restoring and Maintaining Order in Complex Peace Operations: The Search for a Legal Framework* Kluwer, pp185–188.

134 See: *Saddam's Revenge*, a film by Antonio Rados.

135 Fallows has noted that the Future of Iraq Project, the Army War College and other organisations had warned against disbanding the Iraqi army: "Blind Into Baghdad: The inside story of a historic failure" 2004 *The Atlantic* January/February 2004 http://www.theatlantic.com/issues/2004/01/fallows.htm date accessed 17 March 2004.

were intensely loyal to the Ba'ath regime. With their social and economic status threatened by foreign occupation, it was inevitable that some former soldiers would hide weaponry and execute armed attacks upon the occupiers.

Secondly, the arrest and detention of dozens of foreign nationals implicated in resistance attacks and suicide bombing activities that have cost the lives of hundreds of Iraqi civilians suggests inadequate efforts were made by Coalition forces to secure Iraqi borders during the invasion and early stages of the occupation of Iraq. While some of these foreign groups may have been allowed into Iraq by the Ba'ath regime before the war, others have been able to enter during the occupation. Failure to prevent the infiltration of foreign fighters is indicative of general failures by the Coalition to provide adequate security to the Iraqi population. One may ask "How can occupiers be expected to maintain security in an environment where some resisters are well armed and prepared to engage in suicide bombing and self-annihilation tactics?" Occupiers are expected to fulfil their obligations under the law of occupation. If they are unable to do so, they have a number of options: (1) end their occupation and withdraw from the territory, (2) declare certain portions of the occupied territory to be under the effective control of other belligerents, (3) negotiate the transfer of control over the territory to local inhabitants—preferably under UN auspices, or (4) hand over control of the territory to a UN peacekeeping force. To their credit, the occupying powers in Iraq appear to have accepted that prolonged foreign occupation is untenable. In November 2003—during a period of sustained and devastating resistance attacks upon Coalition forces, humanitarian workers and Iraqi civilians—the Coalition accelerated its plans for a transition from foreign occupation to Iraqi self-government, agreeing to a transfer of sovereignty on 30 June 2004.

Without security other obligations cannot be fulfilled

Restoration of security is a primary objective of any occupying force, for without it other obligations such as the provision of clean water, electricity and other basic necessities cannot be fulfilled. In the period since the collapse of the Ba'ath regime, security has not yet been restored in many parts of Iraq. In Baghdad, US forces still retreat behind the walls of presidential palaces and military compounds before dark in order to avoid attack by groups resisting the occupation. Attacks upon Coalition forces are frequent, and have on occasion been met by the use of lethal force by US troops. US soldiers have on occasion fired into crowds of protestors,[136] raising concerns in some areas about whether US forces are providing public security or undermining it. The International Committee of the Red Cross has noted that:

> Achieving security must be in conformity with international human rights law standards. These standards apply to all those acting under US authority including members of the US and Coalition armed forces Iraqi Police and international law enforcement officers.[137]

136 "U.S. Troops Fire on Iraq Protesters Again" http://www.guardian.co.uk/worldlatest/story/0,1280,–2622272,00.html Wednesday April 30, 2003, date accessed 26 June 2003.

137 "The War in Iraq and International Humanitarian Law" Human Rights Watch "<http://www.hrw.org/campaigns/iraq/ihlfaqoccupation.htm> (last updated on 16 May 2003); (date accessed 18 June 2003).

Similar concerns were raised during the early stages of British occupation of Southern Iraq, although these concerns appear to have eased over time.[138] In May 2003 Alex Renton, a spokesman for Oxfam speaking from the Iraqi town of Nasiriyah, observed:

> The question of security is fundamental . . . as is the problem of looting. We did actually manage to repair the water system in Nasiriyah, only to see it looted a couple of days later.[139]

Respect for public and private property

Occupying powers (belligerent occupying forces) must respect both the lives and private property rights of occupied peoples. Private property cannot be confiscated,[140] and pillage is formally forbidden.[141] Occupying forces have an obligation to prosecute those who steal private property—whether the offenders are soldiers of an occupying power, or members of the local population.[142] However, they also have considerable latitude under international law in the use of public buildings and other property of an occupied territory—including cash funds that are the property of the state.[143] Depots of arms, means of transport, stores and supplies, vessels, and weapons belonging to private individuals may all be seized and used during a military occupation.[144] There is however an obligation to restore property and provide compensation ". . . when peace is made".[145] In the context of occupied Iraq, these rights and obligations (and all others attaching to occupying forces under treaty and customary law) must however be read subject to the provisions of Security Council Resolution 1483. This resolution is silent on the question of the liability of occupying forces to pay compensation for damage or loss of property, yet paragraph 5 does call upon "all concerned to comply fully with their obligations under international law including in particular the Geneva Conventions of 1949 and the Hague Regulations of 1907". Accordingly, Coalition forces remain liable under principles of state responsibility to meet the costs of repair or replacement of property seized during the occupation. These costs may not be recovered from the proceeds of sale of Iraqi oil or other assets belonging to the people of Iraq, but must be met by the occupying powers themselves.

138 During the first eight weeks of the military occupation of Southern Iraq by British troops, the people of Basra remained fearful for their lives and property. "Basra: British Troops Fail to Provide Security" Human Rights Watch 3 June 2003 <http://hrw.org?press/2003/06/iraq060303.htm> date accessed 12 June 2003; "Basra: Crime and Insecurity under British Occupation" *Human Rights Watch* Vol. 15 No. 6 (E) June 2003.

139 Ed Vulliamy, "Gun gangs rule streets as US loses control" Sunday May 25, 2003 The Observer <http://www.observer.co.uk/Print/0,3858,4676629,00.html> date accessed 18 June 2003.

140 Art 46 The Hague Regulations IV (1907) See also Art 53 4th Geneva Convention.

141 Art 47 The Hague Regulations IV (1907).

142 Art 56 Para 2 The Hague Regulations IV (1907).

143 Art 53 The Hague Regulations IV (1907).

144 Art 53 The Hague Regulations IV (1907).

145 Art 53 The Hague Regulations IV (1907).

Religious and cultural property

Television footage of the looting of the National Museum in Baghdad in April 2003 raised international concern about the protection of cultural property in Iraq. A series of Hague Conventions[146] provide a regime for the protection of cultural heritage. Under Art 56 of the 1907 Hague Regulations:

> the property of municipalities, institutions dedicated to religion, charity and education, the arts and sciences, even when State property, shall be treated as private property. All seizure of, destruction or wilful damage done to institutions of this character, historic monuments, works of art and science, is forbidden, and should be made the subject of legal proceedings.[147]

The Hague Regulations of 1907 and the Hague Convention for the Protection of Cultural Property in the Event of Armed Conflict [1954] form part of customary law, however subsequent protocols do not yet enjoy such status. The US is yet to ratify *any* of the international instruments pertaining to the Protection of Cultural Heritage, although it has signed the Hague Convention for the Protection of Cultural Property in the Event of Armed Conflict [1954]. It has neither signed nor ratified any of the other UN era instruments pertaining to the protection of cultural heritage. Australia ratified the 1954 Hague Convention in 1984, but is yet to ratify either Protocol. The United Kingdom has not ratified any of these three instruments. However, Iraq, Australia and the United Kingdom have all ratified the Paris Convention on the Means of Prohibiting and Preventing the Illicit Import, Export and Transfer of Ownership of Cultural Property [1970], which entered into force in 1972. Accordingly, all belligerent powers except the US have treaty obligations to prevent the illegal export of cultural heritage. However their obligations with respect to the comprehensive protection of cultural heritage during conflict are more limited.

Some of these gaps in the protection of cultural property have been filled by Resolution 1483. The occupying powers and forces serving under them[148] are bound under Resolution 1483 by significant obligations with respect to cultural property. The preamble to Resolution 1483 stresses "the need for respect for the archaeological, historical, cultural, and religious heritage of Iraq, and for the continued protection of archaeological, historical, cultural, and religious sites, museums, libraries, and monuments". Paragraph 7 of the operative part of the resolution imposes direct obligations on the occupying powers. It requires that

---

146 The Hague Regulations IV (1907); Hague Regulations for the Protection of Cultural Property in the Event of Armed Conflict, 14 May 1954; Regulations for the Execution of the Convention for the Protection of Cultural Property in the Event of Armed Conflict (1954); Protocol for the Protection of Cultural Property in the Event of Armed Conflict, The Hague (1954); Second Protocol to the Hague Regulations for the Protection of Cultural Property in the Event of Armed Conflict, The Hague (26 March 1999). The Second Protocol which aims to further strengthen the legal regime for the protection of cultural property in the event of armed conflict is yet to enter into force and has not been signed by the US, the UK, Australia or Iraq. For ratification details for each of these instruments see UNESCO website: http://www.unesco.org/culture/laws/hague/html_eng/protocol2.shtml> date accessed 1 July 2003, last update: 21 January 2003.

147 Art 56 The Hague Regulations IV (1907).

148 The Preamble to Resolution 1483 expressly recognised the UK and the US as occupying powers in Iraq. However troops from other states including Australia, Poland, and Spain arguably are or have been exercising the powers of an occupying army. Troops from these states have responsibility for providing security in designated geographical areas of Iraq. Whether they can be described as occupying powers or merely states that are fulfilling a role delegated by the US and the UK is a matter for conjecture.

> ... all Member States take appropriate steps to facilitate the safe return to Iraqi institutions of Iraqi cultural property and other items of archaeological, historical, cultural, rare scientific, and religious importance illegally removed from the Iraq National Museum, the National Library, and other locations in Iraq since the adoption of resolution 661 (1990) of 6 August 1990, including by establishing a prohibition on trade in or transfer of such items and items with respect to which reasonable suspicion exists that they have been illegally removed.

The occupying powers in Iraq have obviously been in the prime position to facilitate the recovery of cultural property, and have done so through the interception of goods at international border posts, and the collection of stolen artefacts during searches of vehicles and homes.

Administration of public property and institutions

Occupying powers have obligations regarding the protection and administration of public assets. As trustees rather than owners of public property, occupying powers must "safeguard the capital of these properties".[149] Accordingly, the failure to prevent the wanton destruction of public property by saboteurs in areas under occupation, may amount to a breach of these obligations. Occupiers also have an obligation to administer public property in accordance with the rules of usufruct. This means that while they may enjoy the profits and advantages of public property during occupation, Coalition forces (and others using public property upon the direction of the Authority) must not damage or alter such property in any way.[150]

Protection of the basic human rights of occupied peoples

Treaty law on occupation expressly includes a number of human rights guarantees. Occupying forces have a duty to treat *all* people humanely—including civilians, combatants and persons in detention. Detainees are entitled to this right whether or not they are afforded POW status.[151] Furthermore, detainees are not to be subjected to physical or moral coercion to obtain information.[152] Torture, mutilation and corporal punishment are also specifically prohibited.[153] Other prohibited conduct includes the extermination of protected persons and the imposition of physical suffering.[154] Accordingly, the use of torture or physical and moral coercion in an attempt to obtain information relating to the location of weapons of mass destruction (WMDs), members of Hussein's ruling elite or resistance fighters and munitions would be illegal. The delivery of detainees to third states that are amenable to the use of torture as a means of obtaining information is also illegal. Such conduct violates both the prohibition on forcible transfers,[155] and the prohibition on the use of torture—the latter being a non-derogable norm of *jus cogens*. The imposition of

149 Art 55 The Hague Regulations IV (1907) and Art 53 4th Geneva Convention.
150 Art 55 The Hague Regulations IV (1907).
151 Common Art 3 Geneva Conventions I–IV (1949).
152 Art 31, 4th Geneva Convention.
153 Art 33, 4th Geneva Convention.
154 Art 32, 4th Geneva Convention.
155 Art 49, and Art 147, 4th Geneva Convention. The prohibition on forcible transfers is discussed below.

collective penalties,[156] the taking of hostages, and acts of reprisal by occupying forces for attacks on their troops are all prohibited under the laws of armed conflict.[157] Occupying powers must also comply with their obligations under general human rights instruments where these have either been ratified by the occupying power or the occupied state, or have entered into customary law.[158]

Transfer of protected persons

The forcible transfer of protected persons (including POWs and "unlawful combatants") from occupied territory to the territory of the Occupying Power—or any other country—is prohibited regardless of motive.[159] However, as with many Geneva Convention prohibitions, there are significant caveats which weaken this general prohibition.[160] In the context of forcible transfers, evacuations are permitted "if the security of the population or imperative military reasons do demand".[161] However, "such evacuations shall not involve the displacement of protected persons outside the bounds of the occupied territory except when for material reasons it is impossible to avoid such displacement. Persons thus evacuated shall be transferred back to their homes as soon as hostilities in the area in question have ceased."[162] Any transfer by the Coalition of detainees from Iraq to Guantanamo Bay would violate the laws of occupation. Ultimately Coalition forces in Iraq did not follow the Afghanistan precedent of sending detainees to Cuba, choosing instead to intern them in Iraq. The requirement that prisoners of war may only be interned within the occupied territory in which they were captured, extends to former Ba'ath regime officials—including Saddam Hussein.

Duty to protect women

There are specific duties upon occupying powers to protect women during occupation.[163] Women must be especially protected against any attack "to their honour—in particular from rape, enforced prostitution or any form of indecent assault".[164] The

156 Collective penalties include the punishment of a person or people for the actions of others.

157 Art 33, 4th Geneva Convention.

158 The US has ratified the International Convention on the Prevention and Punishment of the Crime of Genocide (1988), the International Covenant on Civil and Political Rights (1992), the Convention Against Torture and Other Cruel, Inhuman or Degrading Treatment or Punishment (1994), and the International Convention on the Elimination of All Forms of Racial Discrimination (1994) but is yet to ratify the Statute on the International Criminal Court, the United Nations Convention on the Elimination of All Forms of Discrimination Against Women, and the Torture Protocol. The UK has ratified all of these instruments.

159 Art 49, 4th Geneva Convention. This article reflects the concern of the drafting states to prevent a repetition of the forcible transfer of peoples that occurred in World War II. During World War II, millions of Jews (and others) were forcibly removed from their homes, stripped of their property, relocated to concentration camps outside their home countries and transported to their deaths in Nazi gas chambers as part of Hitler's Final Solution.

160 For a discussion of this and other weaknesses in the protections afforded under the Geneva Conventions see, Goodman D.P. "The Need for Fundamental Change in the Law of Belligerent Occupation" 37 Stan. L. Rev. 1573.

161 Art 49, 4th Geneva Convention

162 Art 49, 4th Geneva Convention.

163 Art 46, Hague Regulations and Art 27, 4th Geneva Convention.

164 Art 46, Hague Regulations and Art 27 2nd para, 4th Geneva Convention.

obligation of Coalition forces to protect women is of particular importance given reports of a significant increase in rape and other serious human rights abuses since the fall of the Hussein regime.[165] Women are staying at home due to their fear of being kidnapped or assaulted by men with guns, and also because of the absence of any effective system of justice.[166] Evidence of serious sexual crimes against women in Baghdad has been documented by human rights groups including Human Rights Watch.[167]

Obligations regarding hospitals, public health and humanitarian assistance

Occupying powers have strenuous obligations to provide for the health of occupied peoples, including those in detention.[168] These obligations include requirements to implement preventative measures to:

(a) combat the spread of contagious diseases and epidemics, and
(b) ensure and maintain the cooperation of national and local medical and hospital establishments and services, and public health and hygiene in the occupied territory.[169]

Coalition forces were put on notice regarding these obligations by various NGOs prior to the invasion of Iraq.[170] Resolution 1483 urges all states (not just the occupiers) to provide humanitarian aid in Iraq. It calls upon all Member States to "... help meet the humanitarian and other needs of the Iraqi people by providing food [and] medical supplies".[171] Paragraph 14 provides that "... the Development Fund for Iraq shall be used in a transparent manner to meet the humanitarian needs of the Iraqi people ...".

However the principal obligation remains with the occupiers to meet the basic needs of the occupied population. The 4th Geneva Convention places the onus on occupying states to (among other things):

i) ensure the food and medical supplies of the population,[172]

165 "Iraqi women forced to veil" http://news.bbc.co.uk/2/hi/middle_east/2986962.stm last updated: 13 June 2003, date accessed 12 July 2003.

166 See Carol Morello "Women living in fear" 20 May 2003 http://www.amanjordan.org/english/daily_news/wmview.php?ArtID=1528 date accessed 12 June 2003.

167 "Climate Of Fear: Sexual Violence And Abduction Of Women And Girls In Baghdad" http://hrw.org/reports/2003/iraq0703/ date accessed 17 July 2003. This report is based on research conducted by Human Rights Watch in Baghdad, Iraq, from 27 May 2003 to 20 June 2003.

168 Art 56, 4th Geneva Convention. See also "Letter dated 8 May 2003 from the Permanent Representatives of the United Kingdom of Great Britain and Northern Ireland and the United States of America to the United Nations addressed to the President of the Security Council" (S/2003/538). This letter is referred to in Resolution 1483. In it, the Coalition partners in Iraq declared that they would "strictly abide by their obligations under international law, including those relating to the essential humanitarian needs of the people of Iraq". Source: <http://wwww.reliefweb.int/w/Rwb.nsf/0/d948088248b5662bc1256d260032d662?OpenDocument> date accessed 11 July 2003.

169 Art 56, 4th Geneva Convention.

170 "U.S. unprepared for humanitarian obligations of Iraq occupation" 10 Mar 2003 Refugees International http://www.reliefweb.int/w/rwb.nsf/0/90e440064d17d39f85256ce50061cb80?OpenDocument date accessed 12 June 2003.

171 Paragraph 2.

172 However there is a caveat: the provisions of the population need only be provided by the occupying forces "to the fullest extent of the means available to it" Art 55, 4th Geneva Convention. See also Commentary.

ii) agree to relief schemes,[173] and
iii) allow free passage of consignments of food, medical supplies and clothing.[174]

Replacement of public officials and judicial officers

Occupying powers are prohibited from altering the status of judges or public officials in occupied territories.[175] However, somewhat incongruously they are permitted to remove public officials from their posts.[176] Accordingly, US proposals to purge the Iraqi legal system of judges loyal to Saddam Hussein[177] are permissible under the laws of occupation. Such action may also be said to be necessary in order to further the objectives of Security Council Resolution 1483 which calls for a "representative government based on the rule of law that affords equal rights and justice to all Iraqi citizens"[178] as well as "international efforts to promote legal and judicial reform".[179]

The removal of judges who have played a role in the apparatus of cruel and oppressive regimes has historical precedent. In post-war Germany, the allies agreed to remove members of the previous regime from public office.[180] The Potsdam Declaration (Tripartite Agreement by the United States, the United Kingdom and Soviet Russia concerning Conquered Countries, August 2, 1945) provided that:

> All members of the Nazi party who have been more than nominal participants in its activities and all other persons hostile to Allied purposes shall be removed from public and semi public office and from positions of responsibility in important private undertakings. Such persons shall be replaced by persons who, by their political and moral qualities, are deemed capable of assisting in developing genuine democratic institutions in Germany.

In contrast to the position adopted by the occupying powers in Iraq, the victorious allies of World War II did not consider themselves constrained by the existing laws of occupation in post-War Germany and Japan. They embarked on a major overhaul of the institutions of both states, including their constitutions, which were rewritten by the occupiers.[181]

173 Art 59, 4th Geneva Convention.

174 Art 59, 4th Geneva Convention.

175 Art 54, 4th Geneva Convention.

176 Art 51, 4th Geneva Convention.

177 "Iraq Gets Court Reform; U.S. Soldier Dies" http://news.findlaw.com/ap_stories/i/1107/6-17-2003/20030617160012_47.html 17 June 2003, date accessed 12 July 2003.

178 Preamble Resolution 1483.

179 Paragraph 8(i) Resolution 1483.

180 However the Allies did not consider that the Hague Regulations applied to the occupations of Germany or Japan.

181 In both cases, international law was incorporated into the domestic law of the occupied states. See: Grundgesetz "Basic Law" (German Constitution) (May 23, 1949), Art 25: "The general rules of public international law form part of the Federal law. They take precedence over the laws and directly create rights and duties for the inhabitants of the Federal territory"; and the Constitution of Japan (November 3, 1946), Art 98: "This Constitution shall be the supreme law of the nation and no law, ordinance, imperial rescript or other act of government, or part thereof, contrary to the provisions hereof, shall have legal force or validity. 2) The treaties concluded by Japan and established laws of nations shall be faithfully observed."

Modification of the penal laws of occupied territory

As noted above, the penal laws of an occupied territory remain in force unless suspended or repealed by the occupying power.[182] The latter course may be adopted where the penal laws constitute a threat to the security of the occupying power, or is an obstacle to the application of the 4th Geneva Convention. Occupying powers can also implement provisions which are essential to enabling the occupying power to fulfil its convention obligations to:

1. maintain the orderly government of the territory;
2. ensure the security of the Occupying Power;
3. ensure the security of the members and property of the occupying forces or administration; and
4. maintain and secure the establishments and lines of communication used by the occupying powers.[183]

Resolution 1483 calls upon the Authority "... consistent with the Charter of the United Nations and other relevant international law, to promote the welfare of the Iraqi people through the effective administration of the territory".[184] It also emphasises the importance of accountability for crimes and atrocities committed by the previous Iraqi regime.[185] The Authority's mandate under the resolution could be interpreted in a variety of ways. On the one hand it may be argued that the abolition and replacement of the Iraqi legal system and other essential organs of the state is precluded under both the law of occupation, and Resolution 1483—which does not specifically authorise such change. On the other hand, one can point to resolution references to the need for judicial and legal reform, and argue that the good governance of the territory may demand that the legal system be rapidly overhauled. Such reform may be necessary so that the thousands of detainees may be afforded their rights to be released and/or brought to trial without undue delay. Paragraph 4 of the resolution arguably provides a basis for the alteration of the existing legal system by the Authority, if without such reform, the Authority is impeded in its efforts to fulfil its obligations under the resolution.[186]

Vetting of the Iraqi judiciary has been necessary to ensure that judicial officers who may have been complicit in crimes committed by members of the Ba'ath regime do not preside over cases involving the very persons they collaborated with, and to restore public confidence in the judiciary. However the wholesale replacement of the Iraqi legal system would have been unnecessary and a violation of the law of occupation.[187] By contrast, the creation of the Central Criminal Court of Iraq to deal

182 Art 64, 4th Geneva Convention.

183 Art 64, 4th Geneva Convention.

184 Para 4 Resolution 1483.

185 Preamble and Para 4 Resolution 1483.

186 Para 4 of Resolution 1483 "Calls upon the Authority, consistent with the Charter of the United Nations and other relevant international law, to promote the welfare of the Iraqi people through the effective administration of the territory, including in particular working towards the restoration of conditions of security and stability and the creation of conditions in which the Iraqi people may freely determine their own political future". The Preamble and Paras 3, 4 and 8 of Resolution 1483 spell out the powers and obligations of the occupying forces in Iraq.

187 Art 54 of the 4th Geneva Convention precludes the alteration of the status of judges. By implication the total overhaul of an existing legal system (except those aspects that offend the norms of civilised society) exceeds the authority of an occupying power under the Geneva Conventions.

with "those serious crimes that most directly threaten public order and safety"[188] is permissible, as occupying forces are required to maintain public order and security.[189] The complete replacement of Iraq's existing criminal code (the 1969 Iraqi Penal Code 3rd Edition) could only be justified if the existing legal system represented a real obstacle to the application of the 4th Geneva Convention.[190] This is not the case. To date, the CPA has repealed and amended some provisions contained within Iraqi criminal statutes, however it has not sought to replace the entire Iraqi Penal Code.[191]

Prior to the invasion of Iraq, the Working Group on Transitional Justice (a group affiliated with the US State Department's *Future of Iraq Project*) conducted a comprehensive 12-month review of the Iraqi legal system and considered methods of reform.[192] Over 40 distinguished Iraqi expatriate jurists, judges, lawyers and professors (now living in England, the Emirates and the Unites States) contributed to the review which culminated in a 700 page report.[193] However, according to Professor Cherif Bassiouni,[194] the Department of Justice threw "all that overboard" and sent a group of six distinguished US federal judges to reform the Iraqi legal system.[195]

Bassiouni observed in May 2003, that "Iraq had a well-established legal system

188 Order 13 The Central Criminal Court of Iraq (Revised—3rd Ed) 18 June 2003 <http://www.cpa-iraq.org/regulations/CPAORD13_revised.pdf> date accessed 16 April 2004.

189 Order 13 The Central Criminal Court of Iraq (Revised—3d Ed) 18 June 2003 http://www.cpa-iraq.org/regulations/CPAORD13_revised.pdf date accessed 16 April 2004.

190 Art 64, 4th Geneva Convention.

191 See CPA Orders 7 and 13 http://www.cpa-iraq.org/regulations.

192 "The New Iraq" News Hour May 13, 2003 date accessed 12 June 2003 <http://www.pbs.org/newshour/bb/middle_east/jan-june03/iraq_5-13.html>.

193 5 April 2003 by Ralph Dannheisser. Former Iraqi Jurists Propose Plan for Post-Saddam Legal System http://usinfo.state.gov/regional/nea/iraq/text2003/0405law.htm. The report proposes a three-tiered approach to justice in Iraq. This involves the establishment of a Special Iraqi Court (in Iraq) to deal with major international crimes such as war crimes, genocide and crimes against humanity, secondly the prosecution of serious violations of domestic law in ordinary Iraqi courts, and thirdly the establishment of a truth and reconciliation commission to deal with offences carrying a maximum penalty of less than five years' imprisonment. Professor Cherif Bassiouni [interview] "The New Iraq" News Hour May 13, 2003 date accessed 12 June 2003 <http://www.pbs.org/newshour/bb/middle_east/jan-june03/iraq_5–13.html>.

194 Professor Bassiouni was a nominee for the 1999 Nobel Peace Prize for his contribution to the establishment of the International Criminal Court. He has been a law professor at DePaul University College of Law for more than three decades, is president of DePaul's International Human Rights Law Institute (IHRLI) which serves as an umbrella for several DePaul initiatives including the Weapons Control Center, the Rule of Law program, and the Human Rights in the Americas Project. Bassiouni is a world-renowned scholar who has authored and edited 60 books on United States criminal law, international and comparative criminal law, and some 200 articles published in law journals in the US and other countries. Source: Pace Law School http://www.law.pace.edu/news/sloan00.html date accessed 27 June 2003.

195 "The New Iraq" News Hour May 13, 2003 date accessed 13 May 2003 <http://www.pbs.org/newshour/bb/middle_east/jan-june03/iraq_5–13.html>. See also "The Transition to Democracy in Iraq", The working document of the Conference of the Iraqi Opposition, November 2002, Chapter 6 "Reform of the Law and Order System" www.iraqiaffairs.org/pages/res14.htm date accessed 14 July 2003. Jay Garner supported the Future of Iraq Project but has stated that it was dismissed by the Pentagon. See: Frontline documentary "Truth, War and Consequences", http://www.pbs.org/wgbh/pages/frontline/shows/truth/interviews/garner.html date accessed 14 March 2004.

. . . for all practical purposes as good a legal system as all of those in the Arab world and many in Europe as well".[196]

> Hussein . . . subverted the judges, subverted the laws by adding amendments . . . as well as by special decrees of the Revolutionary Command Council. The legal system simply became an instrument of tyranny. What needs to be done is to not rebuild the legal system from scratch but to remove all these encumbrances.[197]

Duties owed to detainees alleged to have violated the laws of armed conflict

All persons detained by occupying forces are entitled to humane treatment—regardless of how they are categorised by the occupying power.[198] The Geneva Conventions place ultimate responsibility for the treatment of POWs squarely upon the government of the occupying power. Responsibility does not begin and end with the officer in charge of the detainees, but rests with the occupying powers themselves.[199] The requirement that POWs be treated humanely includes a prohibition upon their confinement "except when indispensable for safety and only while those circumstances continue to exist".[200] Occupying powers must also respect the basic rights of those accused of violating the laws of armed conflict.[201] These rights include the guarantee of a fair trial and counsel of the defendant's choice.[202] Sentence may only be pronounced after a trial by competent courts of the occupying power.[203] There are also significant restrictions on the use of the death penalty by courts in occupied territory.[204] The death penalty may only be invoked upon conviction of adult persons for espionage, serious acts of sabotage or intentional offences which have caused the death of one or more persons. However such offences must have been punishable by death under the law of the occupied territory in force before the occupation began. This penalty may not be invoked against a person who was under the age of 18 at the time of the offence. The US is therefore precluded from executing child soldiers who are arrested during armed conflict or the subsequent occupation of Iraq.[205]

---

196 "The Iraq legal system was based on the Egyptian legal system which was based on the French legal system. The Iraqi civil code was authored by an Egyptian scholar in the late 1940s or early 1950s. It has a very good secularised legal system. The state department spent a whole year with over 40 distinguished Iraqi expatriate jurists—judges, lawyers, professors who lived in England, the Emirates and the United States who worked for a whole year to prepare a review of all the Iraqi laws and how to reform them . . .". [Cherif Bassiouni] "The New Iraq" News Hour May 13, 2003 URL: <http://www.pbs.org/newshour/bb/middle_east/jan-june03/iraq_5–13.html> date accessed 13 May 2003.

197 Cherif Bassiouni "The New Iraq" News Hour [last updated May 13, 2003] <http://www.pbs.org/newshour/bb/middle_east/jan-june03/iraq_5–13.html> date accessed 13 May 2003.

198 Common Art 3 Geneva Conventions (1949).

199 Art 4 Hague Regulations 1907

200 Art 5 Hague Regulations 1907.

201 For a comprehensive list of basic rights under international law see the *International Covenant of Civil and Political Rights* (1966) and the fundamental guarantees, set out in Art 75 (1) of 1977 Additional Protocol 1.

202 "International Humanitarian Law Issues In A Potential War In Iraq", Human Rights Watch Briefing Paper, 20 February 2003 http://www.hrw.org/backgrounder/arms/iraq0202003.htm accessed 26 May 2003.

203 Art 71, 4th Geneva Convention.

204 Art 68, 4th Geneva Convention.

205 Art 68 Para 5, 4th Geneva Convention. This prohibition stand regardless of whether the child soldiers are classified as lawful or unlawful combatants.

ACCOUNTABILITY FOR VIOLATIONS OF THE LAW OF OCCUPATION

Military justice during occupation: crimes committed by the occupiers

Persons captured or detained for involvement in planning or carrying out attacks upon occupying forces (e.g. acts of sabotage) may be put on trial by the occupying power. However such persons must be provided with the safeguards of a proper trial and defence.[206] There is a substantial jurisprudence pertaining to military tribunals, a discussion of which goes beyond the scope of this paper. The 4th Geneva Convention permits the prosecution of persons who violate the laws of occupation and the laws of armed conflict generally, before military tribunals. The rules pertaining to the conduct of military trials contained within US Department of Defense Military Commission Order No. 1 and subsequent orders, do not appear to afford accused persons their full entitlements under international law. As a consequence, these orders have met with significant criticism.[207] The proposed tribunals appear to have been designed with terror suspects—rather than alleged war criminals—in mind. Accordingly, concerns have been raised that these or similar such tribunals may be used to deal with "unlawful combatants" in Iraq. One category of detainees that may be targeted by a US military tribunal are those alleged to have been involved in the planning of suicide bombing missions against Coalition troops, or attacks on oil pipelines. While such tactics are permissible during armed conflict (and persons involved in such attacks during a military occupation may be deemed patriots by the ousted government) those who engage in such attacks may nevertheless be punished by the occupying powers.[208] The 4th Geneva Convention prescribes spying, sabotage and being "a person under definite suspicion of activity hostile to the security"[209] as conduct for which trial and punishment by the occupier are permissible. However, as noted above, all such persons must also be afforded their rights under the 4th Geneva Convention, including the right to a fair and regular trial.[210] It is this writer's view that the Bush Administration's rules of procedure for the conduct of military tribunals do not satisfy the minimum requirements of international law. Accordingly, the right to a fair and regular trial cannot be guaranteed under this system of justice.

Grave breaches of the Geneva Conventions

In addition to prosecuting those who violate the laws of occupation, occupying powers may put on trial persons who commit grave breaches of the Geneva Conventions. In fact they are required by law to take measures to bring to justice those

206 See for example: Art 105, 4th Geneva Convention.

207 See for example: Broomes, John W. "Maintaining Honor in Troubled Times: Defining the Rights of Terrorism Suspects Detained in Cuba" (2002) 42 Washburn L.J. 107.

208 Art 5, 4th Geneva Convention.

209 Art 5, 4th Geneva Convention.

210 Art 5 Paras 2 & 3, 4th Geneva Convention.

who have committed such breaches.[211] All states party to the Geneva Conventions are obliged to pass legislation ensuring that effective penal sanctions are in place to enable the prosecution of grave breaches of the Conventions.[212] There are also obligations to search for persons who have committed grave breaches, and to bring them before the state's courts. However, any such prosecutions must be in accordance with the minimum requirements for the conduct of trials set out in the Geneva Conventions. In the event that former members of the Ba'ath regime are captured in foreign states, it is likely that they would be handed over for trial in the Iraqi Special Court[213]—a court specifically established to deal with grave crimes committed by the Ba'ath regime.

Examples of violations of the duties of belligerents[214]

Failure to prevent or stop looting

Questions have been raised about potential violations of international law by Coalition forces on account of the failure to prevent looting or properly secure many sites of cultural, religious, scientific and economic importance. Of particular concern has been the absence of measures to protect sites containing dangerous materials—including nuclear facilities.[215] Does the duty to maintain public order and safety include a requirement that a large invading force deploy sufficient personnel and resources to prevent anarchy, lawlessness and looting within occupied cities and towns? The US and its Coalition allies clearly had the military resources to secure ministry buildings, the national museum and other key government facilities upon the fall of Baghdad. Whether sufficient troops could or should have been sent to guard these buildings is a contentious issue. US soldiers were obviously ordered to secure and protect the Ministry of Oil, while other government buildings were looted around it. Failure to prevent the Ministries of Education, and Trade and Industry in Baghdad from being looted and burnt out suggests that Coalition forces have violated the laws of occupation. As noted above, Coalition forces should have anticipated and been prepared for the rapid descent into lawlessness upon the collapse of the regime. They are therefore responsible for failing to prevent looting and crime waves in Iraqi cities. Assertions to the contrary are undermined by the

---

211 Grave breaches include wilful killing, torture or inhumane treatment, unlawful transfer or unlawful confinement of protected persons, wilfully depriving a protected person to the rights of fair and regular trial prescribed in the Convention, taking hostage, and extensive destruction and appropriation of property not justified by military necessity: Art 147, 4th Geneva Convention.

212 Art 145, 4th Geneva Convention.

213 The Iraqi Special Court has its own statute that has been endorsed by the CPA and the IGC. See: CPA Order 48 dated 10/12/03 http://www.cpa-iraq.org/regulations.

214 For an analysis of Iraqi violations of the Law of War see: "Why do States Violate The Law of War? A Comparison of Iraqi Violations in Two Gulf Wars" Lt Robert A. Bailey, 27 Syracuse Journal of International Law and Commerce 103.

215 For example there is concern at the potential looting of nuclear material from the Tuwaitha nuclear research facility which was looted in early May 2003. "Concern Over Iraq Nuke Looting" Vienna, Austria, 5 May 2003 http://www.cbsnews.com/stories/2003/05/05/iraq/main552369.shtml date accessed 26 June 2003.

pre-war warnings of many NGOs, retired military officers and interest groups, including those mentioned above.[216]

Violations regarding conditions of detention

The detention of up to 3,000 Iraqis in uncomfortable conditions (including hooding, gagging and tying of detainees' hands) at US detention camps close to Baghdad airport suggests further breaches of international humanitarian law by Coalition forces.[217] Many of the detainees were civilians. It has been alleged that some were beaten by US soldiers.[218] This treatment violates convention rights including the right to be treated humanely. Red Cross officials were denied access to detainees for a long period of time.[219] This raises questions about non-compliance by US forces in Baghdad with Art 30 of the 4th Geneva Convention. This article provides for Red Cross visits to protected persons (including detainees) and requires occupying powers to facilitate "as much as possible" visits to protected persons.

Rights of "unlawful combatants" (including members of resistance movements)

As noted above in the context of military tribunals, those detained in Iraq on suspicion of involvement in terrorism must be brought before a properly constituted court in accordance with international law. Indefinite or prolonged detention without charge or trial is not sanctioned by either Resolution 1483 or the treaties on the law of occupation. Coalition forces have the capacity and the duty to bring so called "unlawful combatants" before a competent tribunal to determine their status. They should do so as soon as is practicable. Those who are classified by the tribunal as prisoners of war may be detained until the end of hostilities. Those who are suspected of involvement in the commission of war crimes, crimes against humanity, or other crimes against domestic or international law (including terrorism) should be promptly charged and brought to trial. Detainees who do not fall into either of the above categories are entitled to immediate release by the tribunal. While the detention of those who have prepared for, planned or engaged in acts of violence in occupied Iraq is justified under Resolution 1483 in order to restore "conditions of security and stability",[220] and also under the treaty law on occupation, the occupying

216 See also: Urban Warfare Considerations by C. L. Staten, Sr. National Security Analyst Emergency Response & Research Institute Chicago, IL; Understanding and Combating Irregular and Guerrilla Forces During A "Conventional War" In Iraq [posted 29 March 2003] [date accessed 12 June 2003] <http://www.emergency.com/2003/urban_warfare_considerations.htm>. See also: Red Cross says Coalition forces are responsible for law and order in occupied Baghdad, Friday, April 11, 2003 http://www.redding.com/news/apafternoonupdate/past/20030411aptop066.shtml date accessed 27 June 2003.

217 Ed Vulliamy "Red Cross denied access to PoWs" May 25, 2003 The Observer <http://www.observer.co.uk/Print/0,3858,4676630,00.html> date accessed 12 June 2003.

218 "There is circumstantial evidence that (Iraqis detained in Baghdad) . . . are being gagged and hooded, in the manner of the Afghans and other captives held at Guantanamo Bay in Cuba—treatment in itself questionable under international law." Sunday May 25, 2003 The Observer "Red Cross denied access to PoWs" <http://www.observer.co.uk/Print/0,3858,4676630,00.html> date accessed 12 June 2003; "Red Cross denied access to PoWs" Ed Vulliamy, Sunday May 25, 2003 The Observer <http://www.observer.co.uk/Print/0,3858,4676630,00.html> date accessed 12 June 2003.

219 Ed Vulliamy "Red Cross denied access to PoWs" May 25, 2003 The Observer <http://www.observer.co.uk/Print/0,3858,4676630,00.html> date accessed 12 June 2003.

220 Para 4 Security Council Resolution 1483 (2003).

powers are still obliged to afford detainees their rights under international law. Those who the Coalition does not intend to put on trial must be released at the end of the occupation or handed over to Iraqi authorities for prosecution or release. This issue is discussed in the next paragraph. Those who are to be put on trial in military tribunals or Iraqi courts should be afforded the right to trial as soon as is practicable.

Release of POWs at the end of hostilities

Article 118 of the 3rd Geneva Convention provides that:

> Prisoners of war shall be released and repatriated without delay after the cessation of active hostilities.

There has been much speculation that the US's failure to make a formal declaration ending hostilities was a calculated strategy and one designed to justify the non-release of enemy prisoners of war.[221] In a carefully worded statement on 1 May 2003, President Bush declared: "Major combat operations in Iraq have ended . . . the United States and our allies have prevailed. And now our Coalition is engaged in securing and reconstructing that country."[222] Once hostilities have come to an end, occupying forces are precluded from detaining both POWs and enemy civilians, unless they are suspected of committing grave breaches of the Conventions or other crimes against Iraqi or international law. Enemy civilians and soldiers who are not suspected of such behaviour should be immediately released and permitted to leave the territory under occupation.[223]

Prosecution of grave breaches of the Geneva Conventions

President Bush has indicated that Coalition members intend to prosecute those responsible for war crimes committed during the current conflict and the 1991 Gulf War.[224] Coalition forces have an obligation to arrest, detain and bring to justice persons in Iraq who are suspected of committing war crimes and crimes against humanity. However at least one man suspected of killing thousands of Shi'ite Iraqis has been mistakenly released by US forces.[225]

---

221 Pentagon Enemy Prisoner of War Briefing from Kuwait City, Thursday, May 8, 2003 http://www.defenselink.mil/transcripts/2003/tr20030508–0160.html accessed 9 June 2003.

222 "President Bush Announces Combat Operations in Iraq Have Ended" Office of the Press Secretary May 1, 2003 <http://www.whitehouse.gov/news/releases/2003/05/iraq/20030501–15.html> date accessed 16 June 2003.

223 For a discussion of the obligations of belligerent forces to enemy civilians during hostilities see Dr. Walter L. Williams, Jr. "The freedom of civilians of enemy nationality to depart from territory controlled by a hostile belligerent" 100 (1983) Mil. L. Rev. 135 at 143–145.

224 "Anybody who wants to harm American troops will be found and brought to justice," Bush www.guardian.co.uk/worldlatest/story/0,1280,–2861991,00.html date accessed 5 July 2003.

225 Mohammed Jawad al-Neifus was released (in error) from the Bucca Internment facility in Umm Qasr on May 18 after being captured April 26 in the city of Hilla, not far from a recently discovered mass grave containing the remains of thousands of Shi'ites who were slaughtered after rising up against Saddam Hussein's regime after the 1991 war: Jim Mannion "US says suspect in murder of Iraq Shiites released in error" <http://www.lebanon.com/news/local/2003/5/30.htm> [posted 30 May 2003]; [date accessed 18 June 2003] "U.S. casualties prompt Iraq security crackdown" <http://www.cnn.com/2003/WORLD/meast/05/30/sprj.irq.main/> [Saturday, May 31, 2003]; [date accessed 18 June 2003] "Iraq killings suspect freed 'in error' <http://news.bbc.co.uk/2/hi/middle_east/2950398.stm> [posted Friday, 30 May 2003]; [date accessed 18 June 2003].

In order to comply fully with their obligations under the Conventions, Coalition forces must make all reasonable efforts to ensure that all of those responsible for crimes against humanity and war crimes in Iraq are prosecuted. This may require the arrest and prosecution of not only Iraqis but also foreign fighters and Coalition troops themselves. Occupying forces exercise martial law in occupied territory. They are unlikely to surrender their own soldiers to local courts. The CPA took matters a step further by conferring upon Coalition forces local immunity from criminal, civil and administrative legal process. In a Public Notice dated 26 June 2003, the CPA made clear that Coalition military and civilian personnel are subject to the exclusive jurisdiction of the state contributing them to the Coalition. Consequently, if Coalition troops are to be brought to justice for crimes committed in Iraq, it will be under the military law of the relevant Coalition force.

DOES THE INTERNATIONAL LAW OF OCCUPATION OFFER AN ADEQUATE LEGAL FRAMEWORK FOR REGULATION OF BELLIGERENT OCCUPATIONS IN THE 21st CENTURY?

The law of occupation forms an integral part of a wider body of law—international humanitarian law. The philosophical rationale for international humanitarian law is the pursuit of Henry Dunant's ideal of the protection of victims during war. The recent conflict in Iraq has cast the spotlight upon the obligations that states assume when they embark upon the belligerent military occupation of a foreign state. Senior officials in the US State Department and Pentagon were clearly aware of the law of occupation, yet the invasion of Iraq was authorised without commanders on the ground being provided with a coherent plan for the occupation phase. This showed reckless indifference to both the challenges that confronted their own soldiers, as well as the obligations owed to the people of Iraq. While military historians are likely to describe the post-conflict phase of Operation Iraqi Freedom as a debacle—and weighty reports will inevitably be written on the "Lessons Learned in Iraq"—what do these mistakes tell us about the current state of the law of occupation? Do recent events in Iraq point to the need for a review of the law of occupation? If so, which aspects need to be re-examined? Do the obligations of occupiers need to be refined? Do the issues of compliance with (and enforcement of) the law of occupation need to be addressed in concrete terms through further codification of the law?

Is further codification of the law of occupation necessary?

In discussing these questions, it is important to observe that the failure of an occupier to comply with certain obligations does not undermine the authority of the law itself. However lessons learnt during an occupation may inform debate on possible reform of the law of occupation. One shortcoming of the law of occupation highlighted during the belligerent occupation of Iraq is the lack of clarity of certain treaty provisions in defining the nature and scope of obligations and duties of occupying forces. The applicable treaties are often silent on fundamental problems that can and do arise in the administration of occupied territory. For instance, how far does the obligation to provide basic necessities for the civilian population extend? Are the occupiers obliged to provide employment or social security payments to those whose livelihoods have been destroyed as a result of attacks launched by the occupiers during the invasion phase (or even the occupation phase) of military operations? Does any such entitlement extend to those who have lost their employment due to structural changes imposed by the occupiers? Must all of the infrastructure damaged or destroyed during the conflict be repaired or replaced? Should the occupiers be responsible for the repair of property damaged by acts of sabotage planned or carried out by the inhabitants of the territory prior to the occupation? Must the occupiers repair damage caused by remnants of the former regime or other resistance forces *during* the occupation? What about infrastructure that is undamaged but dilapidated due to pre-war neglect?

The answer to these questions is not found in the text of the applicable treaties. The answers will depend upon: (i) the length of the occupation, (ii) how one interprets the applicable treaty provisions on occupation, and (iii) human rights obligations under treaty law of the respective occupying power.

As a matter of common sense, protection of the civilian population requires restoration of basic services. This will often require the repair, maintenance and even replacement of public infrastructure. Providing security to the public, and maintaining law and order, may be facilitated by the payment of pensions for the elderly and the infirm, and social security payments to those who are unemployed—particularly where unemployment is a direct consequence of the invasion and/or occupation. Another option is large-scale job creation programmes including public works schemes for the unemployed. Unfortunately these suggestions are not codified in the applicable treaties. Consequently, the extent of the occupier's responsibilities in these areas is a matter to be determined in the exercise of the occupier's discretion.[226] Clearly, the treaties on occupation were not drafted with either (i) modern social security schemes or (ii) complex and prolonged occupations, in mind. Notwithstanding the need for flexibility in international instruments to take into account contrasting situations, there is a need for partial revision of this body of law to provide greater guidance to occupiers on their obligations. Nevertheless care must be taken to ensure sufficient flexibility is retained in the relevant provisions so that changing circumstances and needs may be taken into account.

The Security Council as reformer of the law of occupation

The further codification of the law of occupation would likely be a lengthy and uncertain process. A simpler, faster and more flexible alternative involves leaving the question of the nature and scope of the obligations of occupying powers to the Security Council to determine on a case by case basis. This option would allow the Security Council to address the specific needs of a particular occupation through comprehensive and tailor made resolutions. Such resolutions may address matters not expressly covered by the law of occupation. This is the approach that was taken by the Security Council in Resolution 1483. The UN Charter establishes that a resolution of the Security Council has primacy over treaty provisions in the event of

226 Geneva Convention IV Arts 55 (duty to provide food and medical supplies) and 59 (relief schemes) do not specify whether pensions and social security benefits must be paid to the aged, the infirm and unemployed.

a conflict between the two.[227] Accordingly, the Security Council does have the authority to tailor resolutions to meet the needs of the occupiers and the occupied in specific military occupations. If however the Security Council does not address a salient issue, one must have recourse to the relevant treaty law on occupation.

Although attractive from the perspective of enabling issues not addressed in the law of occupation to be incorporated in a binding resolution, this approach is not without its problems. Firstly, permanent members of the Security Council can veto such resolutions. Accordingly, those states holding the power of veto may prevent the council from imposing obligations upon occupying powers beyond those prescribed in the law of occupation. Secondly, a two-tiered approach to the law of occupation could emerge, whereby permanent members of the Security Council—and their favourites—may face less onerous obligations as occupiers than states that do not enjoy such power or favour. This situation could arise when permanent members of the council exercise their power of veto to defeat substantive resolutions of the council. The veto is a formidable weapon which hovers over the deliberations of the Security Council like an invisible Sword of Damocles. Its mere existence is sufficient to prevent matters that clearly constituted a threat to international peace and security from being placed on the agenda of the Security Council. The Chinese invasion, occupation and annexation of Tibet, and Russia's invasion and occupation of Chechnya are two salient illustrations of this problem. Thirdly, even where Security Council resolutions are not vetoed, permanent members who are themselves occupiers of foreign states have an unfair advantage in the negotiation of the terms of resolutions that clarify the nature and scope of the obligations and duties of occupying powers. Fourthly, as the August 2003 bombing of the UN headquarters in Baghdad so powerfully demonstrated, close cooperation between the UN and an occupying force that has invaded a country in violation of international law may expose UN staff to the danger of being targeted by resistance groups who view UN personnel as collaborators with the enemy. Fifthly, the credibility of the UN may be undermined by the passage of resolutions that endorse the belligerent occupation of sovereign states—particularly in cases where the occupation was brought about through military intervention that was not itself expressly authorised by the Security Council.

Notwithstanding these concerns, this writer is of the view that both approaches set out above need to be adopted. Namely:

1. the law of occupation needs to be further codified to fill in existing gaps, and
2. Security Council resolutions should be passed to further prescribe the rights and obligations of the occupiers and the occupied in the context of specific foreign occupations.

An imperfect yet historic beginning: Security Council Resolution 1483

Resolution 1483 is the first Security Council resolution to provide a detailed framework for the governance of a belligerent occupation. It is arguably the most

227 Art 103 of the Charter provides that: "In the event of a conflict between the obligations of members of the United Nations under the present Charter and their obligations under any other international agreement, their obligations under the present charter shall prevail."

comprehensive and innovative Security Council mandate on the governance of an occupied territory ever issued by the UN. It is unique for other reasons as well. Firstly it expressly provides that the occupying powers are to comply with the treaty law on occupation. Secondly the belligerent occupying powers in Iraq voted in favour of the resolution—which is itself a landmark achievement. Thirdly it makes clear the intention of the Council that the entire resolution be read and interpreted in accordance with relevant provisions of The Hague Regulations and the 4th Geneva Conventions. Although by no means a perfect resolution,[228] the attention paid to matters such as accountability for crimes of the former regime, humanitarian aid, effective government, and recognition of the sovereign rights of the Iraq people, reflects not only the importance the Security Council placed on these matters, but also the acquired experience of the Council in the authorisation and supervision of peace operations over the past 50 years.

One matter that was not addressed by the Council in Resolution 1483 is the issue of enforcement. Where a state fails to comply with its obligations under international law, the questions of compliance and enforcement arise. The process of enforcement of the laws of occupation is essentially left to occupying powers.[229] A number of issues arise in this context:

1. Accountability for violations of the law of occupation by:
   a. the inhabitants of the occupied territory, and
   b. the occupiers themselves.
2. State responsibility of occupying powers for failure to meet their obligations under the law of occupation.

At the cessation of hostilities, the occupying powers are obliged to bring those who have violated the laws of armed conflict to justice. They are usually willing and able to put inhabitants of the occupied territory on trial for crimes against the occupying forces. In the case of violations of the laws of armed conflict by the military personnel of occupying forces, the investigation and prosecution of war crimes and other breaches of international law is usually left to the military authorities of the occupying power(s). As noted above, it is likely that war crimes and crimes against humanity committed by Iraqi forces will be dealt with by either Coalition military tribunals in Iraq or Iraqi domestic courts or tribunals established by an Iraqi administration. By contrast, crimes committed by Coalition forces will be dealt with under the domestic military law of the applicable Coalition force, unless the occupying states were willing to hand over those charged with war crimes to the International Criminal Court.

The issue of state responsibility for violations of the law of occupation is more problematic. Other than the International Criminal Court—a tribunal with limited jurisdiction—there are no compulsory treaty mechanisms enabling neutral states to prosecute occupying powers for violations of the laws of occupation.[230] The

228 For criticisms of the resolution see for example Eyal Benvenisti, "Agora: Future Implications of the Iraq Conflict: Water Conflicts During the Occupation of Iraq" 97 AJIL 860.

229 This situation is unsurprising given the influence at the preparatory conventions to these treaties of powerful states who were more likely to be occupiers than the occupied.

230 There are of course other mechanisms by which individuals and states may be held accountable for violations of international law in the course of a military occupation. These include an Ad Hoc tribunal established by the Security Council or the International Criminal Court. Prosecutions in such cases

International Court of Justice may only exercise jurisdiction where the states party to the dispute have granted the court jurisdiction to determine such disputes, or otherwise give their consent. In light of the adverse findings against the US in *Nicaragua v United States of America,*[231] the occupying powers in Iraq are unlikely to consent to the ICJ handling disputes involving potential violations of international law in Iraq. Consequently, the occupying powers may never have to account for their conduct in occupied Iraq before a properly constituted international tribunal or court. A detailed discussion of the efficacy of the law of occupation is something that falls outside the scope of this paper. Suffice it to say, Coalition accountability for non-compliance with their obligations and duties under international law is a question that is likely to be the subject of ongoing public and academic discussion.

CONCLUSION

The belligerent occupation of Iraq has cast the spotlight on a fundamentally important—yet often overlooked—branch of public international law. The law of occupation delineates the duties and responsibilities of both the occupiers and the occupied. In doing so, it has an important role to play in enhancing the efficacy of international humanitarian law during the military occupation of sovereign states. The US and UK are to be commended for acknowledging the applicability and binding nature of this body of law. In doing so they have recognised that even those who consider themselves "liberators" have responsibilities as occupiers. Recognition of the binding nature of the law of occupation is important for many reasons. Foremost is that it helps to promote compliance with its norms by occupying forces.

While the law of occupation provides an internationally recognised legal framework for the governance of occupied territory, it is by no means "all things to all people". This is clearly not a body of law that guarantees effective accountability in the event of human rights violations by occupying forces. By its nature, it vests military power and hence the levers of justice in the hands of the occupiers. Different states have differing human rights obligations and different mechanisms for dealing with breaches of human rights by their citizens—be they military personnel or civilians. In some cases this may mean that an occupying power may take little or no action against one of its citizens for human rights violations in occupied territory. While reflective of the realities of martial law (and the need for occupying forces to provide security and restore order), the absence of an effective and independent enforcement system within the law of occupation does not sit comfortably with notions of universal human rights protection. Reform of the law of occupation is therefore warranted, with the principal aims being: 1. to strengthen enforcement mechanisms, 2. to promote compliance, and 3. afford greater protection of the rights of civilians during military occupations.

would only be necessary if the occupying powers were not willing or able to bring their own citizens to justice for crimes committed in Iraq. However given the US's failure to ratify the Rome Statute, and its insistence on the passage of Security Council Resolution 1422 (passed in July 2002 and renewed as Resolution 1487 in June 2003) which grants immunity to personnel involved in United Nations missions who are not from State Parties to the ICC Statute, it is improbable that US soldiers would be brought to justice in that forum.

231 Judgment, Merits ICJ Reports 1986.

Recent events in Iraq have graphically demonstrated the difficulties that can beset a belligerent occupying army. In areas where the presence of foreign troops is unwelcome, the challenges inherent in fulfilling basic obligations may be formidable. The dangers involved in seeking to provide security, maintain law and order, and coordinate reconstruction work have been illustrated by the constant stream of attacks by resistance fighters on Coalition vehicles and compounds since the fall of the Ba'ath regime. The rising death toll among occupying forces has done little to strengthen the resolve of the occupiers to investigate crimes allegedly committed by their own soldiers. In these circumstances, it is inevitable that a perception will emerge among some members of the occupied population that violations of basic human rights are committed by the occupying army with impunity. For as long as the law of occupation provides a legal framework that is essentially self-regulatory, such perceptions are likely to continue. The existing norms reflect reluctance by those states that negotiated the relevant treaties to relinquish sovereignty rights to an independent umpire. Subsequent state practice has not significantly altered this position. However the post-World War II gains of the human rights movement, the burgeoning jurisprudence on international criminal law, and the momentum for universal justice fostered by the entry into force of the Rome Statute of the International Criminal Court, may provide the impetus required for states to embark upon a review of the current law of occupation. What is needed is 1. greater clarity of the nature and scope of the rights and duties of the occupiers and the occupied, and 2. effective accountability mechanisms. The obstacles that lie in the path to gaining the requisite consensus among states to implement such reforms are formidable. Firstly, states that may expect to find themselves in the role of occupiers may be reluctant to assume increasingly onerous and expensive obligations. On the other hand, many states may be unwilling to do anything that may be seen to encourage or condone the belligerent invasion and occupation of sovereign states. The difficulties inherent in achieving consensus on the nature and scope of the rights and duties of occupiers have been magnified by 1. the refusal of the majority of sovereign states to endorse the war in Iraq and 2. concerns that some counter-terrorism strategies may involve belligerent occupation and the violation of state sovereignty. Ultimately however, the reforms advocated above are in the interests of both groups. If implemented,[232] they could provide a legal framework that may facilitate a greater level of compliance by occupying forces, while also deterring reckless or impulsive acts of aggression by states.

232 These reform objectives could be implemented by a number of methods. One option is through the further codification of the law of occupation. Codification could be undertaken through Security Council endorsement of a modern code on occupation, or through the entry into force of a new or revised multilateral treaty on occupation. The later approach allows maximum participation in the development of the code by all interested states and international organisations. Preliminary steps to the implementation of such a treaty could include extensive deliberations between states and NGOs such as the Red Cross. Whether powerful states would be prepared to endorse a code that expands upon the rights of occupied peoples and strengthens the obligations of occupying forces is a matter for conjecture. In light of the current US administration's refusal to ratify the Rome Statute of the International Criminal Court and its general reluctance to embrace multilateral treaties, there must be doubt as to whether the US would endorse a treaty that could render its soldiers, military commanders and political leaders liable for violations of the laws of occupation. However as the entry into force of the Rome Statute of the International Criminal Court has shown, where there is substantial international support for the progressive development of international law, resistance by a few states—even powerful states—may not be sufficient to prevent such advances.

THE LANGUAGE OF INTERNATIONAL TRADE LAW: PROBLEMS OR SALVATION?

*Dr Bruno Zeller**

INTRODUCTION

This paper does not look at language as a tool of drafting legal texts or for that matter language in a literary sense. It is, rather, inward looking and will focus on the construction of international conventions, specifically the CISG. It is hoped that it will stimulate discussion and contributes towards the recognition of a "global language" necessary for the success of any international uniform law.

This is of special interest and importance with the emergence of a global community of courts.[1] This has been assisted by a constitutional cross-fertilisation as courts are starting to cite each other's precedents.[2] This has been made easier by municipal courts agreeing that a domestic litigant cannot be guaranteed to be able to sue in his own jurisdiction if he engages in trans-national business.[3]

A desire to cooperate has not only been expressed on a political level but has also penetrated the legal dispute settlement process. The international law of dispute settlement is transcending the phase of mere cooperation.[4]

The creation and ratification of international conventions possibly has assisted in this process. Arguably, a global jurisprudence could be the outcome and this has already been shown to be achievable, especially in the case of the CISG. Of importance therefore is that a rhetorical community with its own language and concepts needs to be formed to facilitate the internationalisation of law.

This paper argues that the CISG has managed to introduce a language which spans all legal families. Furthermore the language is conducive to introduce concepts which are also universal in character. In sum the CISG has managed to use language and concepts which

> take into account the different social, economic and legal systems [and therefore] contribute to the removal of legal barriers in international trade and promote the development of international trade.[5]

Arguably the CISG has overcome inherent domestic problems of language and concepts. It has done so by recognising that articles and concepts must be drafted in such a way that they are adaptable to change, are capable of adjustments and are not "caught" in legal phrases, which become frozen in history.[6] Significantly, Rabel

---

* Senior lecturer, Victoria University, Melbourne.

1 See A. Slaughter, "A Global Community of Courts" 44 Harv. Int'l L.J. 191.

2 Slaughter at 193.

3 Slaughter at 209.

4 A. Peters, "International Dispute Settlement: A Network of Cooperative Duties" EJIL (2003) Vol 14 No 1, 1, at 1.

5 Preamble, Convention for the International Sale of Goods, CISG.

6 E. Rabel, "Der Entwurf eines einheitlichen Kaufgesetzes" Rabels Zeitschrift 9 (1935) 1, at 2.

argued that an international trade law cannot be derived from domestic principles, which are unique and more importantly are built on concepts and expressed in a language which is focused on that particular country's history.[7] In other words municipal concepts and language must be "unpacked" and written in such a way that it becomes universally acceptable by creating its own history.

The section below maps the territory this paper will explore. The paper goes on to examine the problems confronted by the drafters of the convention and explains how language and concepts are used to overcome these obstacles. The paper then demonstrates that the CISG has been interpreted and applied uniformly and hence has achieved its stated goals as expressed in the preamble.

MAPPING THE TERRITORY

Rabel,[8] as early as the 1930s, recognised that municipal laws are not very useful in regulating international trade. Very simply, differences among legal traditions are sometimes irreconcilable and furthermore an international sale is not merely a domestic sale with incidental foreign elements.[9] One of the proposed solutions was to unify choice of law rules. However this would not achieve coherence as these rules are highly intricate and as Kötz observed these issues are the "nuclear physics of jurisprudence".[10] Compared to domestic trade, international trade operates in alien legal and cultural environments where foreign languages could be spoken and special attention must therefore be given to communication. Rabel clearly envisaged that the best solution is the creation of a uniform international legal system and in 1938 he published the first coherent international sales law.[11]

The success of an international sales law can only be claimed if international uniformity of laws can be achieved. Uniformity of law though must go beyond the text and must also include the application of the stated law within a broad international community. Arguably the most successful international trade law so far is the United Nations Convention on Contracts for the International Sale of Goods (CISG). The success in the introduction of the convention, which is currently ratified in 68 countries, is due to the ability to achieve a uniform application. Uniformity of international application is the stated goal of the CISG and for that purpose domestic rules are displaced and substituted with one international rule.

The Preamble restates the attempt of unification by pointing out that:

> ... the adoption of uniform rules which govern contracts for the international sale of goods and take into account the different social, economic and legal systems would contribute to the removal of legal barriers in international trade and promote the development of international trade.[12]

---

7 Ibid at 5.

8 Ibid.

9 B. Audit, "The Vienna Sales Convention and the Lex Mercatoria" in Lex Mercatoria and Arbitration, Carbonneau ed, 1990, 171, at 174.

10 H. Kötz, "Allgemeine Rechtsgrundsätze als Ersatzrecht", Rabels Zeitschrift, 34 (1970), at 663.

11 Rabel above n 6.

12 Preamble CISG above n 5.

Basically the CISG is concerned with three aspects: the adoption of uniform rules, a contribution towards the removal of legal barriers in international trade and the promotion and development of international trade.

In essence, the question is whether the CISG is capable of achieving the stated goals, which in turn depend on a uniform interpretation in all member states. In other words the CISG must be interpreted uniformly in all member states. To achieve such a goal its language and concepts must be written in such a way that they are able to be universally understood. This is specifically important as the CISG spans several legal and economic systems. Importantly the preamble urges the reader to take "into account the different social, economic and legal systems" and therefore interpreters must be sensitive to these differences. This is reinforced within the CISG, specifically when interpreting and applying Art. 8. Article 8 urges the parties to interpret intent according to "the understanding a reasonable person of the same kind as the other party would have in the same circumstances".

Just to be sensitive to differences, whether cultural or legal, is of little value if the most important factor, namely the deeply political nature of uniformity of a convention, is not solved. As an example, the Romanian delegate in the debate in the sixth Committee of the General Assembly noted that:

> . . . it was necessary to establish rules that would facilitate commercial transactions on the basis of respect for sovereignty and national independence, non-intervention in the domestic affairs of States and mutual benefit . . .[13]

Two obvious solutions to achieve uniformity would have been to either introduce a definition section into the convention or create an international tribunal similar to WTO legislation to solve potential disputes.

First the convention did not vest interpretational authority with an international tribunal, nor has any editorial board been created to amend the CISG as the need arises.[14] Two examples to the contrary can be quoted. First, in the United States an editorial board meets regularly with a view to amend, if necessary, the Uniform Commercial Code (UCC). Secondly the European Court of Justice interprets the Brussels Convention on Recognition and Enforcement of Judgments and its decisions are binding on all member states of the EC. The obvious advantage not to have similar practices in place is the fact that it has a bearing on the sovereignty of contracting States. The alternative would have been politically unacceptable. It is doubtful if many States would have accepted the CISG if a court like the European Court of Justice would have influenced domestic law of contracting States with its decisions.

A very good example should be noted. In 1992, Switzerland had the opportunity to join the European Economic Zone (EWR), which would have been the first step in joining the EC.[15] The Swiss rejected the initiative and in 1999 the seven bilateral agreements with the EC were accepted by parliament and ratified by referendum in 2000. The main reason for the 1992 rejection was the fact that the contract with the

13 Item 88, From Summary Records, 21 U.N. GAOR C.6 (947th–955th mtgs) U.N. Doc.A./6594.

14 P. Koneru, "The International Interpretation of the UN Convention on the Contracts for the International Sale of Goods: An Approach based on General Principles" (1997) 6 Minnesota Journal of Global Trade 105, 105.

15 *Neue Zürcher Zeitung*, "Gleichwertigkeit der Rechtssysteme, Die Bilateralen Abkommen mit der EU" September 16, 1999 [http://www.nzz.ch].

EWR contained an automatic right to changes in law. If the EC changes legal rules, these changes apply automatically to all member states.[16] Even in retrospect, it is still recognised that a loss of sovereign self-determination was unacceptable, as Switzerland would have been subjected to rule from Brussels.[17] The 2000 acceptance was heavily influenced by the fact that Switzerland has no obligation to adjust or accept EU legal changes.[18] The loss of sovereignty influenced Switzerland to reject such a partnership and would do so again. By analogy, the same arguments would be advanced by many states if the CISG would have interpretational authority vested in an international tribunal.

Secondly, the convention could have included a definitional section to explain significant terms. However this option was not taken up; instead the drafters chose to introduce general principles as well as limited definitions within the text of the CISG. As an example, Art. 14 states that: "A proposal for concluding a contract addressed to one or more specific persons constitutes an offer . . ." The reader therefore cannot rely on a self contained text where words are given a limited but technical meaning; instead the CISG

> encourages a broad and conversational interpretation of the words of the text, leading to greater depth and complexities in the interpretation of individual provisions.[19]

As a solution, the drafting of the CISG was driven by the idea that unification of rules requires the use of a common legal language in its formation.[20] This was achieved by a three-pronged solution. First, language was chosen which is devoid of technical legal terms; secondly, concepts were introduced which are not based on municipal practices. Thirdly and most importantly, the CISG introduced an interpretative article into its regime, namely Art. 7.

Article 7 states:

> (1) In the interpretation of this Convention, regard is to be had to its international character and to the need to promote uniformity in its application and the observance of good faith in international trade.
>
> (2) Questions concerning matters governed by this Convention which are not expressly settled in it are to be settled in conformity with the general principles on which it is based or, in the absence of such principles, in conformity with the law applicable by virtue of the rules of private international law.

Arguably Art. 7 is the single most important article of the CISG. Karollus certainly thinks that this is the case when he notes that the CISG "is well on the way to becoming the Magna Carta of international trade".[21]

If the success of this article and indirectly the CISG could be measured by its adoption into other conventions then it has achieved its objective. Article 7 has been

---

16 Ibid.

17 *Neue Zürcher Zeitung.*, "Die Bilateralen Verträge im Vergleich zum EWR-Beitritt". November 8, 2000 [http://www.nzz.ch].

18 Ibid.

19 A.H. Kastely, "Unification and Community: A Rhetorical Analysis of the United Nation Sales Convention", 8 Nw. J. Int'l. L and Bus. (1988) 574, at 580.

20 M. Bonell, "The UNIDROIT Initiative for the Progressive Codification of International Law", (1978) 27 International and Comparative Law Quarterly, 413.

21 M. Karollus, "Judicial Interpretation and Application of the CISG in Germany 1988–1994", (1995) Cornell Review of the Convention on Contracts for the International Sale of Goods 51, 68.

included fully or partially in several other international conventions and model laws. The UNCITRAL Draft Convention on Assignment in Receivables Financing has included Art. 7 fully.

The UNIDROIT Convention on International Factoring used Art. 7 but provided that "regard is to be had to its object and purpose as set forth in the preamble".[22] Such an inclusion builds on Art. 7 by stressing that the method of interpretation needs to be focused on the "Four Corners" of the Convention. The Draft UNIDROIT Convention on International Interest in Mobile Equipment[23] follows the combined approach taken by Art. 7.[24]

The UNIDROIT Principles of International Commercial Contracts (PICC) and the Principles of European Contract Law (PECL) both included sections on interpretation, which relied heavily on Art. 7 of the CISG. The significance of this development is twofold. First, the CISG has influenced the drafting of interpretational articles in conventions and restatements of varying subject matters. This suggests that the inclusion of Art. 7 must be regarded as a general principle of international law. Secondly, it is argued that there is common intention to create a methodology for an interpretation and supplementation contained in Art. 7, which has created a core consensus in drafting future conventions or model laws.

LANGUAGE AND CONCEPTS

Introduction

The mere fact that a convention has been written and ratified by diverse countries does not in itself guarantee the desire and purpose to be uniform. The text of the convention must be capable of being understood and applied in a uniform manner. Such uniformity is only possible if it addresses the needs of a community that creates a legal system of its own. Kastely suggested that the CISG introduced a rhetorical community in which the readers

> first assent to the language and values of the text itself, and then use the language and values to inform their relations with one another.[25]

The convention has unique values when compared with domestic law. It has a common language reflecting values which are understood irrespective of the cultural or legal background of those who apply the convention because the CISG defines the values of its own community.

In contrast, it has been suggested that international laws in general and the CISG in particular "lack a common legal theory and practice upon which judges and practitioners can rely".[26] Arguably this appears to be true but needs to be distinguished from another view which states that:

---

22 Art. 6 UNIDROIT Convention on International Factoring.

23 Rome, February 12, 1999 Art. 6(2).

24 M. Gebauer, "Uniform Law, General Principles and Autonomous Interpretation" (2000) 4 Uniform Law Review 683, 696.

25 A.H. Kastely above n 19, at 574.

26 F. Diedrich, "Maintaining Uniformity in International Uniform Law Via Autonomous Interpretation: Software Contracts and the CISG", (1996) 8 Pace International Law Review 303, 303.

> ... The uniform law from the very moment of its coming into operation starts to differ from itself. Every judge in every country is a sovereign interpreter of the text, and the judge became a judge by learning the system of law of his own country. And as the speediest bird is unable to fly out of itself, so the judge is unable to forget the law that he has learned. Divergent or contradictory interpretations, like the application of rules of different countries, lead to different judgment.[27]

Reczei assumes that judges and arbitrators are trapped in municipal thinking. Such an opinion unfortunately reflects the inability to move away from domestic language and values and to realise that an international text cannot "borrow" language or values from one particular system only.

The difference between the two opinions is illustrated by the fact that Diedrich recognises that uniformity and predictability are possible to achieve. It requires that a common legal theory and practice supported by a common language can be established. Supportive evidence that a common legal theory and practice is possible can be found in the original 1935 proposal of a Unified Sales Law. A comparison with the CISG indicates that the basic structure of the two laws shows remarkable similarities.[28] Rabel indicated that a unification of law is only successful if a compromise is achieved. He suggested that such compromise could be achieved through comparative studies especially between the Anglo-American system on one hand and the Continental systems including Japan and South America on the other.[29] Rabel showed a remarkable insight by isolating the necessary key criteria by which international uniformity can be achieved. If it is further considered that the lack of acceptance of the international community of the UNIDROIT rules was due to the perception that it had a European dominance in production and content,[30] the question must be asked: are concepts and language so intertwined that one cannot exist without the other? The answer must be yes.

It is language which creates particular words, which in turn give rise to concepts. Concepts cannot exist without a history or heritage. It is argued that the CISG—through the choice of language—has drafted concepts which create a common legal theory and practice. Such a theory is not national but international in character. It is understood by the international community. In sum, an international community has been created,[31] united by the use of a common legal language, which finds expression in unique concepts.

The foundation of every domestic legal system is that laws are an expression of the culture of a society. A society or community gives meaning to concepts, which are unique to a particular municipal community. By analogy, the CISG has created a community, namely the international business community, which also is bound together by a common language and common concepts. The CISG therefore is capable of creating a common legal theory and practice as envisaged by Diedrich.

---

27 L. Reczei, "Process and Value of the Unification of Commercial Law: Lessons for the Future Drawn from the Past 25 years" (1992) in 25th UNCITRAL Congress 5, 6.

28 E. Rabel, above n 6. Rabel, in his article, included the full text of the proposed unified law. It is instructive to compare the CISG with the original proposal.

29 Ibid 6.

30 J. Honnold, "The Draft Convention on Contracts for the International Sale of Goods: An Overview", (1979) 27 American Journal of Comparative Law, 223, at 223 and 225.

31 Kastely above n 19, at 575.

Reczei on the other hand assumes that judges by definition are trapped in municipal thinking and practices. This paper shows that judges are not unduly trapped in municipal thinking and practice because the CISG has been written in such a way that its language and concepts are international in character. Furthermore once the internationality is recognised the judiciary has adapted to the sea change in legal thinking. As an example, in *Rheinland Versicherungen v Atlarex S.r.l.*[32] the Tribunale di Vigevano referred to no fewer than 42 foreign cases in support of its decision, and demonstrated successfully that a *de facto* supranational *stare decisis* is in existence.

In order to create a legal theory and practice, a common tool needs to be applied to the CISG. That particular tool to interpretation is Art. 7, the interpretative article. It is the key that opens the door to a common unified approach to the interpretation and application of the CISG. By applying this interpretative article, a common interpretive practice supported by case law has been created, which takes on the function of a common legal theory.

It is possible there will be divergent judgments if Art. 7 is not understood and applied correctly. Reczei had a particular point of time in mind, namely the point of introduction of a unified system of law. It would be difficult to argue that an international unified system of law would not suffer from divergent decisions at the beginning. By analogy, the United Nations Security Council and General Assembly asked for Advisory Opinions of the International Court of Justice as a basis to form decisions. Uncertainties, which required opinions, are typically clustered within the first 10 years of the Court's existence with only a handful of comparable advice sought in the following 30 years.[33]

In sum it can be argued that the constitutive nature of language and of a particular text must be evaluated and any analysis must focus "attention on the nature of the community formed by a text, on its points of coherence and on its potential vulnerabilities".[34]

Multilingual implications

Domestic legislation needs to consider the choice and clarity of words. International legislation, in addition, needs to consider the effects of translation on the meaning of words, as most conventions unfortunately are not only written in one language alone. This gives rise to a new method of interpretation when meaning must be given to a word that is unclear. A consultation of a translation of the same word or article in different languages is needed to find a possible answer to the original question.

Article 3(1) can be used to illustrate this. The particular issue is that the buyer can supply a "substantial" part of material. What is the meaning of substantial?

32 Vigevano, 12 July 2000, Italy, [http://www.cisgw3.law.pace.edu/caseds/000712i3.html] last update November 20, 2000.

33 E. De Wet, "Judicial Review of the United Nations Security Council and General Assembly through Advisory Opinions of the International Court of Justice" (2000) 3 Schweizerische Zeitschrift für Internationales und Europäisches Recht, 237, 270.

34 Kastely above n 19, at 575.

The German and French translations of the CISG are *Wesentlich,* and *un part essentielle. Wesentlich* does not match exactly the French or English translation. It corresponds better with *un part essentielle,* rather than the English "substantial". It is not debated that substantial or essential can be used to translate *Wesentlich.* However several German legislations using *Wesentlich* use the translation of "essential".[35] Hence to look at "substantial" as found in Art. 3(1), the word essential must be kept in mind and may help to overcome any ambiguities which may otherwise arise.

There is another factor which is important, namely which is the authentic language of the text? Texts which are not authentic cannot be used authoritatively and may be given only persuasive status. The authentic texts of the CISG are Arabic, Chinese, English, French, Russian and Spanish. All other languages are not authentic as they are official translations only. Considering that all meetings in Vienna were conducted in English or French, these languages should be given priority over other authentic texts as they best represent the intentions of the representatives at the 1980 Diplomatic Conference.[36] Hence looking at the above comparison between the English, French and German translations, the German would carry less weight than the other two. It must also be noted that even between the authentic translations of the CISG, solutions to unclear meanings of words are difficult especially if differences need to be understood which are of a conceptual nature.

Yet even within one language, difficulties may arise. The German text is not only the translation between English and German but also the result of a joint drafting of Austria, Germany, the former German Democratic Republic and Switzerland. As such it could be argued that within the German-speaking group of nations a translation was achieved which takes into consideration the "heritage of legal doctrine". However, equally well, one may argue that:

> [it] can lead to an inevitable choice between precise adherence to the original text in the translation, with the risk that the rendering of the translation is inelegant or out of harmony with linguistic usage, or a freer rendering which responds to the structure and usage of the second language but at the sacrifice of legal accuracy.[37]

Rabel anticipated such a problem in translation and suggested that the translation of difficult passages should not be according to legislative language (*Gesetzessprache*) but according to legal language *(Rechtssprache).*[38]

The conclusion which can be drawn is that words to be included into a unified law have to be chosen very carefully. Only through a careful choice of words can problems be minimised, which otherwise may eventuate in translations not only of the words but also of the concepts which are expressed by the words in question.

---

35 The same translation was used in M.J. Raff, "German Real Property Law and the Conclusive Land Title Register" (1999) (unpublished PhD thesis, the University of Melbourne (on file with author) (translation of German Civil Code concerning the words *wesentliche Bestandteile*).

36 F. Diedrich, above n 26, at 318.

37 R.M. Goode, "Reflections on the Harmonization of Commercial Law" (1991) 1 Uniform Law Review 71, n 36.

38 E. Rabel, above n 6, at 7.

Concept of choice of words

The approach to the choice of words as required above also fits into the policy of uniform interpretation as it views words not in a national but international context. It also overcomes the problem Honnold describes as literary "deconstruction".[39]

Such considerations make the choice of words harder and require a special solution. The drafters of the CISG solved this particular problem and consciously "rooted out words with domestic legal connotations in favour of non-legal earthy words to refer to physical acts".[40] In sum the CISG must and has used words that refer to typical events of international transactions and "in which the community can conceive relationships and resolve conflicts".[41]

To illustrate the above point a question could be asked, namely how does the CISG define goods? Article 2 does not describe positively the meaning of goods. It states and lists exclusions. At first glance the solution to the definition of goods is everything not excluded in Art. 2. This is not very satisfactory but on further reading of the CISG a more narrowly defined description can be elicited. Article 35 mentions goods as required by the contract and "which are contained or packaged" in the manner required by the contract.[42] Article 46(3) requires that, if goods do not conform to the contract, the seller can remedy the lack of conformity by "repair".[43] Articles 85 to 88 regulate the preservation of goods and Art. 87 specifically mentions "warehousing" of goods. What conclusions can be drawn from this? If there is uncertainty as to whether a particular item can be classified as goods, a court can ask additional questions such as whether the item in question is movable, tangible property that can be packaged, repaired if necessary and warehoused if necessary.

Another example is the passing of risk.[44] In domestic legislation whenever passing of risk is examined, words are used such as "title or property" passes to the buyer or seller. The CISG on the other hand uses the words "[goods] handed over"[45] or "[goods] taken over".[46] Such phraseology helps in the determination of the meaning of words and hence articles. The CISG repeats in essence what one of the great judges namely Lord Mansfield C.J. in 1761 observed:

> The daily negotiations and property of merchants ought not to depend upon subtleties and niceties, but upon rules easily learned and easily retained because they are the dictate of common sense.[47]

The trend to use "non-legal earthy words" is not only limited to international conventions. Within domestic law such moves are becoming well established. The Income Tax Assessment Act 1997 (Cth), as one of its aims, is rewriting the Income Tax Assessment Act 1936 (Cth). The purpose is "[to] rewrite the law with a better

39 J. Honnold, "Uniform Laws for International Trade: Early 'Care and Feeding' for Uniform Growth", (1995) 1 International Trade and Business Law Journal 1, fn 6.

40 Ibid 2.

41 Kastely above n 19, at 579.

42 CISG above n 5, Art. 35.

43 Ibid Art. 46(3).

44 CISG above n 5, Chapter IV.

45 Ibid Art. 67(1), 68.

46 Ibid Art. 69(1) and (2).

47 *Hamilton v. Mendes* (1761), 2 Bur. 1214.

structure and [therefore] make it easier to understand".[48] However despite the recognition of the shortfall in ULIS, namely its European orientation, another problem of ULIS has not been corrected. The problem is that despite efforts of the working parties the words and concepts remained in essence of Anglo or Western European origin. The reason is understandable as at its conception and final draft in 1980 the most important trading nations understood or were part of the Anglo Western European cultural sphere of influence.

However it must be said that currently other cultural groups, such as countries where shariah law is dominant, are making efforts to reconcile their domestic laws with the CISG and other international conventions where compatibility cannot be achieved otherwise.[49]

CONCEPTS AND LANGUAGE

The CISG has included concepts into its regime through the incorporation of principles pursuant to Art. 7(2). The problem is how can principles transcend national borders? In essence, to understand the transnational need for sales laws a

> . . . study not of contract law, but rather of contract practice, is the key to understanding the economic properties of contracting that are necessary to work out sensible uniform laws for commercial purposes.[50]

What then is the difference between "contract law" and "contract practice"? It is implicit in the description that contract law is tied to a system of law based on a national or domestic body of law. Through that particular municipal system, contract law would have evolved based on known and understood principles. However, contract practices are looking beyond a legal system and the law in general. Practices transcend legal, social and economic thoughts and processes and have become universal. That is, they are common elements, which transcend borders.

It might be argued that once contract practices have been identified, an international law can be put into practice. Looking at this question, Honnold asks:

> Can clear, predictable international law be made from the divergent rules of dozens of domestic legal systems, rules built with local idioms for which there are no equivalent terms in other languages?[51]

The answer he noted is "unhappily no, but that is not the end of the story".[52] It must be remembered that any kind of legal regulation is a potential source of unpredictability but the transnational nature of international business provides an additional source or dimension to the difficulty of securing predictability.[53]

---

48 Woellner, Barkoczy, Murphy, *2000 Australian Taxation Law* (10th ed, 1999) 24.

49 At a recent conference organised between Victoria University, Melbourne and the International Islamic University of Kuala Lumpur several as yet unpublished papers were delivered which argued that shariah law is compatible with the CISG on most aspects.

50 R. Amissah, "The Autonomous Contract, Reflecting the Borderless Electronic Commercial Environment in Contracting", Electronic Handel (1996) [http://www.cisg.law.pace.edu/cisg/biblio/amissah2.html].

51 J. Honnold, "Goals of Unification—Process and value of the unification of commercial law: lessons for the future drawn from the past 25 years" (1992) 25th UNCITRAL Congress, 11, 11.

52 Ibid.

53 R. Amissah, above n 50, 16.

Drobnig illustrates the transnational nature of international business by pointing to the fact that it is bound up with the Roman division between *leges* and *jus*. Such a distinction was also used within Art. 7(2) of the CISG.[54] Drobnig observed that:

> it is almost of the essence of general principles of law that they are not laid down by any legislative action. They are nowhere readily formulated—rather they have to be elaborated.[55]

The translation of words from one language into another one which form parts of concepts or principles is also fraught with difficulty. Kastely states:

> [W]ords used in one language . . . carry implications different from those in another . . . The terms "offer" and "acceptance" provide powerful examples of this. In English these words carry a rich heritage of legal doctrine, and their equivalents in the Western European languages have similar depth . . . Yet the translations of these words used in the other official versions, such as Chinese and Arabic, do not carry similar implications . . .[56]

As stated above, the CISG uses "non-legal earthy words" but care must also be taken that these words do not disguise domestic concepts, which could be unknown to the other party. Two examples are illustrative. The notion of consideration, vital in common law, is totally absent in the CISG. The convention also eliminated the French concept of *delivrance* which combines both delivery and conformity.[57] The word which instead was chosen is *livraison* or in English "delivery". These words convey the same connotation or concept. Other concepts such as "offer and acceptance" or contractual commitment could not be avoided. These are essential in any contract irrespective of where these concepts are used. As a solution, the CISG has explained the concept of contractual commitment within the text of the convention rather than give a specific rule of offer and acceptance.

It is argued that because of the particular choice of words, legislative interpretation requires an approach different from the one traditionally adopted by the legal profession. Indeed, to appreciate the full meaning of words and to resolve many ambiguities, they must be read within the context of the CISG.[58] In other words, the meaning must be elicited within the "Four Corners" of the convention. The reason is that the convention, due to language constraints, incorporated concepts into the text as principles. Some principles are clearly stated, such as the principle of good faith, but others are contained within the four corners of the convention. Not only principles but also simpler concepts such as definitional questions are interspersed within the convention.

Kastely has put special emphasis on four values, which are included but are not exclusive in the CISG. They are contractual commitment, forthright communication between parties, good faith and trust and the forgiveness of human error.[59]

One of the more interesting articles in connection to forthright communication between parties is Art. 8. In brief Art. 8 states:

54 U. Drobnig, "General Principles of European Contract Law" in P. Sarcevic and P. Volken (eds), *International Sale of Goods, Dubrovnik Lectures* (1985) 306.

55 Ibid 310.

56 A.H. Kastely, above n 19, at 593.

57 B. Audit above n 9, at 180.

58 Ibid.

59 Kastely above 19, at 580.

> (1) For the purposes of this Convention statements made by and other conduct of a party are to be interpreted according to his intent where the other party knew or could not have been unaware what the intent was.
>
> (2) If the preceding paragraph is not applicable, statements made by and other conduct of a party are to be interpreted according to the understanding that a reasonable person of the same kind as the other party would have had in the same circumstances.
>
> (3) In determining the intent of a party or the understanding a reasonable person would have had, due consideration is to be given to all relevant circumstances of the case including the negotiations, any practices which the parties have established between themselves, usages and any subsequent conduct of the parties.

The CISG follows a subjective approach to the interpretation of contracts. Only if the subjective intent of parties cannot be elicited pursuant to Art. 8(1) will the objective approach as set out in Art. 8(2) and (3) be followed.

In the United States it is now well established that the parol evidence rule is "trumped" by Art. 8. It certainly makes the rule as to what evidence is applicable clearer and more concise by inquiring into the intent of the parties and not just merely relying on a contract as evidenced in writing. In international trade a clear and simple rule is of the essence. As shown above the formalistic approach of the CISG allows a conclusion to be reached in a clear and more predictable manner. Such a methodology is justified in international trade where finality in a simple form is important. Cost considerations of the "tyranny of distance" require simple solutions. In domestic sales, on the other hand, rules must "capture the complex developments [of domestic law] over [many] years".[60] If one looks at the jurisprudence in common law on the principle of mistake and the parol evidence, it is no wonder that the international business community has great difficulty understanding the "complex developments" in this area. International trade in a global environment cannot function effectively without predictable and clear rules. *MCC-Marble*[61] illustrates this point well. The facts of the case are simple enough. Despite the signing of a contract, the clauses contained within that written document were not considered to be binding as the parties could demonstrate that a contrary subjective intent was established.

MCC-Marble's opinion

> ... reveals a court striving to transcend its background in domestic U.S. law, energetic in pursuing an international perspective on the Convention's meaning, and informed, thoughtful and coherent in its grasp of CISG provisions and their meaning.[62]

The court stated that "contrary to the result of the objective approach which is familiar practice in United States courts",[63] the CISG appears to permit a

60 R.E. Speidel, "Warranties of Quality in Revised Article 2, Sales and the Convention on contracts for the International Sale of Goods" (1999) 14 Journal of Contract Law, 15 at 27.

61 144 F.3d 1384 (11th Cir. (Fla.) 1998) [http://cisgw3.law.pace.edu/cases/980629u1.html] last update February 27, 2001.

62 H.M. Flechtner, "The U.N. Sales Convention (CISG) and MCC-Marble Ceramic Center Inc. v Ceramica Nuova D'Agostino, S.p.A.. The Eleventh Circuit Weighs in on Interpretation, Subjective Intent, Procedural Limits to the Convention's Scope and the Parol Evidence Rule", 18 Journal of Law and Commerce (1999), 259, 260.

63 *MCC-Marble*, above n 61, 1387 n. 8 and 1388 n.11.

"substantial inquiry into the parties' subjective intent, even if the parties did not engage in any objectively ascertainable means of registering this intent".[64] This particular decision indicates that there is no uncertainty in the law despite the opinions of some writers that the CISG engages in the use of "indefinite legal concepts".[65]

However it cannot be argued that the CISG is genuinely free from national connotations, and therefore truly an instrument of an international community. As the CISG is a deeply political document, some countries, despite objections of others, introduced petty and nationalistic elements into the convention. Article 28 is such an example. It states that if a party is entitled to require performance of an obligation of another party "a court is not bound to enter a judgement for specific performance unless the court would do so under its own law in respect of similar contracts of sale not governed by this convention".[66] Despite the objections of other delegates, the United States and the United Kingdom won the concession and had their amendments included into Art. 28.[67] It appears that this inclusion is based largely on historical reasons. The right to obtain specific performance is uncongenial to common law lawyers.[68] It is significant that the United Kingdom took a leading role in the development of the CISG and then turned around and did not ratify the instrument. It appears that one of the stumbling blocks or criticism of the CISG is that it does not match up to English standards of precision and drafting.[69] Such views exhibit the inability to understand the necessity to write the CISG in a "new language" and with "new concepts" as it addresses an international community and not a domestic one. It appears that the UK has not grasped the significance of an international community and still remains in isolation.

As Art. 28 only states that a court "is not bound", it could be argued that courts therefore can implement the remedy of specific performance pursuant to Art. 46(1) despite the fact that its domestic courts would not do so under their own laws. If a court would do so it would interpret Art. 28 narrowly and within the four corners of the CISG. In other words, the spirit of the CISG and specifically the mandate of Art. 7 would induce a court to remain within the international community and look at concepts within that particular framework. Significantly only one case, taking Art. 28 into consideration, has been reported[70] whereas 32 cases deal with Art. 46 only. The court in this case correctly looked at the CISG, first namely Art. 46(1), which provides that the buyer may require the seller to perform its obligation. The judge, pursuant to Art. 28, consulted domestic law and found that replaceability is a

65 A. Williams, Forecasting the Potential Impact of the Vienna Sales Convention on International Sales Law in the United Kingdom, [http://www.cisgw3.law.pace.edu/cisgt/biblio/williams.html].

64 Ibid 1387 and 1388.

66 Art. 28 CISG.

67 See Report of the Working Group, 6th session U.N. Document A/CN.9/100; see also report on Art. 28 in U.N. Doc.A/CONF.97/11.

68 A. Garro, "Reconciliation of Legal Traditions in the U.N. Convention on Contracts for the International Sale of Goods", 23 International Lawyer (1989) 443, at 452.

69 A. Williams, above n 65.

70 *Magellan International Corporation v Salzgitter Handel GmbH*, U.S. District Court, Northern District of Illinois, 99 C 5153, [http://www.cisg.law.pace.edu/wais/db/cases2/991207u1.html] last update May 13, 2002.

practical matter. The court came to the conclusion that both the UCC as well as Art. 46(1) must be consulted to come to a proper conclusion.

CONCLUSION

How successful is the CISG? Unfortunately the whole international rhetorical community has not embraced the CISG with equal enthusiasm and therefore the success of the CISG has been mixed. Judges and arbitrators have understood the language and concepts of the CISG and the jurisprudence exhibits a remarkable uniformity. However anecdotally many legal advisors still suggest to their clients not to include the CISG into their legal dealings. Therefore Reczei in his assessment would have been correct if he suggested that "legal advisers [but not judges] are unable to forget the law that they have learned".[71]

However from an institutional point of view, the CISG has been successful. It has been ratified by 68 countries and has become the de facto sales law in Europe. Arguably England, the last bastion of conservatism in its slow approach to "europeasation", will also ratify through necessity the CISG. The CISG has spawned many model laws such as the European Principles of Contract Law and many conventions have adopted Art. 7, either totally or in parts. It has been shown that the CISG, through its choice of words and concepts, has created a language that is common to its rhetorical community, and hence forms the basic element on which an interpretation of detailed provisions of the text can rely. Article 7 injects that particular loyalty to an international community.[72] Arguably readers and users of the CISG are aware that linguistic and conceptual differences between an international document and domestic law require a different mind set when interpreting the CISG.

UNCITRAL in its 33rd session regarding future work in the field of electronic commerce referred to the CISG and concluded that:

> ... [it] was felt to constitute a readily acceptable framework for on-line contracts dealing with the sale of goods.[73]

Such a conclusion shows that the language and concepts of the CISG are "timeless" and are expressed in such a way that not only the international community understand its language but it is broad enough to absorb a changing business and technological environment. The CISG is a living document as its language is adaptable and the concepts international in character. It has successfully avoided ethnocentric interpretation and application. The working party specifically examined the formation of the contract and noted that the advantage of looking at the CISG is that the convention has

> ... demonstrated their workable character in an international environment ... due to their ability to transcend the traditional differences in the approaches taken by civil and common law.[74]

71 Reczei above n 27.

72 Kastely above n 19, at 582.

73 Working Group on Electronic Commerce 38th session. 12–23 March 2001. U.N. Document A/CN/9/WG.IV/WP.91 at 1.

74 Working Group at 40.

In sum it would be difficult to argue that a document—written more than 20 years ago—and which is looked upon as capable of absorbing changes necessitated by electronic commerce is not written in a truly international language. It must be pointed out that many domestic laws are in need of amendments to absorb the changes, which the CISG is capable of without a rewrite of the rules. There is truly nothing more convincing than the above observations.

A PEACE PLAN FOR THE BATTLE OF THE FORMS

Andre Corterier

INTRODUCTION—A PROPOSAL FOR PEACE

One of the more enduring fields of contention in trade law is known as "the Battle of the Forms".[1] It arises when merchants exchange letters, emails or forms which at first glance seem to establish a contract but which include—or incorporate by reference—mutually contradictory or at least widely varying standard terms. The root cause of the Battle of the Forms is—as with many battles—a misunderstanding. It is not a misunderstanding between the merchants involved. Rather, it is a misunderstanding between the merchants and their lawyers: merchants, in seeking to structure their transactions more efficiently, seek the aid of lawyers to draft a set of standard terms suitable for them. These terms, or a reference to them, then tend to be included in every future letter sent by the merchants in question. In legal analysis, to this point, every statement which includes a reference to such terms is understood to also say "but only under the following conditions" (followed by the standard terms as conditions). The parties continue to act, however, as merchants do, plying their trade unfettered by the fine print they now include with their correspondence. This is rarely a problem—should the other party also employ standard terms, then it does so because it, too, is a merchant. Both sides act in pursuit of what they perceive as mutual gain, while writing their orders and order confirmations on documents which include their pre-printed legal boilerplate. Most times, they then perform as agreed and nothing more comes of it. When legal difficulties arise, however, it is again lawyers who scrutinize their correspondence. They then often find a discrepancy between the apparent contract formed by the correspondence, on its face, and the conflicting standard terms both sides attempted to include in it. And it appears as though we, as a profession, are prepared to disregard the apparent agreement between the merchants more easily than our colleagues' work.

My suggestion, then, is that this is wrong. It is the merchants who make individual declarations which they have thought about at the time and with which they seek to bring about a legal result: a binding contract. Their legal boilerplate is attached to these statements, expressing a preferred way of dealing. It is not meant to prevent formation of a contract or to delay its formation to some as yet unknown date in the future, at which lawyers will decide that a contract was formed through one subsequent act or another. In actual fact, two merchants sought to deal with one another. They agreed on something. And it is this meeting of the minds which leads to a contract.

1 For a more in-depth treatment of the phenomenon, see e.g. Symposium, "Battle of the Forms", 4 Canad. Bus. L. J. 261 (1980).

SITUATION REPORT

Except where otherwise stated, this article focuses on what appears to be the most common occurrence of the Battle of the Forms: "The routine exchange of Order and Acknowledgment forms without attention or objection to the discrepancies between the terms printed on their forms."[2] As a point in case, I will illustrate this approach in the purview of the United Nations Convention on Contracts for the International Sale of Goods (CISG).[3] The CISG was created to promote legal certainty in international trade.[4] However, years after its creation, there is still nothing new on the "Battle of the Forms" front.[5] The main contenders for a way of dealing with this conflict, the "Last Shot Theory" and the "Knock Out Rule" (see below), both have pros and cons, though neither is able to convince a sufficiently large following to secure victory. The reason for this is that both of these approaches are victim to the same misconception: to give equal weight to every word of a declaration. To do so, however, is to allow form to defeat function. Just because the words are included in the same document they do not necessarily all carry the same weight.

When faced with standard terms, the parties themselves do not give equal weight to every word in each other's statements. Rather, they concentrate on the matters of the deal which are truly important to them, while generally ignoring the minutiae dealt with by each other's standard terms.[6] This explains why parties so often believe that they have entered into a contract, only to have lawyers tell them that by virtue of their own standard terms, formation of a contract was prevented. Lawyers—especially, judges and arbitrators—need to be more respectful of the parties' actual intentions when interpreting their statements (according to Art. 8 CISG). Parties that wish to enter into a contract even though their standard terms collide are free to do so. They are even free to do so without fixing which terms should apply. And there is nothing in the CISG which prevents this.

The battlefield

The primary reason to employ standard terms is efficiency.[7] If every little thing involved in a transaction had to be individually negotiated every time a contract

2 Honnold, *Uniform Law for International Sales*, 3rd ed. (1999), Art. 19 at 165.

3 An overview of the treatment of this problem by various rules of domestic law can be found in von Mehren, "The 'Battle of the Forms' ", 38 Am. J. Comp. L. 265 (1990).

4 Honnold, Art. 7 at 96; Bonell, in: Bianca/Bonell, *Commentary on the International Sales Law* (1987), Introduction at 1.1; Siehr, in: Honsell et al., "Kommentar zum UN-Kaufrecht" [Commentary on the UN Sales Law], (1997), Preamble at 11; Ferrari, in: Schlechtriem/Schwenzer, Art. 7 at 4; Bailey, "Facing the Truth: Seeing the Convention on Contracts for the International Sale of Goods as an Obstacle to a Uniform Law of International Sales", 32 Cornell Int'l L. J. 273 at 292 (1999).

5 This may be an overstatement: Murray ("The Definitive Battle of the Forms: Chaos Revisited?", in 20 J. Law & Commerce 1 (2000)) etc. have addressed the problem in the context of the CISG, though without having found or proposed a solution; others have proposed novel approaches to resolve the disagreement, though without addressing the problem of the *apparent* agreement, see e.g. Rühl, "The Battle of the Forms: Comparative and Economic Observations", 24 Penn. J. Int'l Econ. L. 189 (2003).

6 Compare Ont. L. Ref. Com., I Sale 81 n. 25.

7 Honnold, Art. 19 at 165.

was entered into, many businesses operating with small margins of profit per transaction could not function.[8] Thus, standard terms were created to reduce the amount of negotiation spent on a single contract. In fact, it seems that these days everybody employs them. In some jurisdictions, especially where the Last Shot Theory is widely followed, this has led to some people finding themselves in front of a court only to be told that they had, by taking delivery or some other such action, agreed to someone else's standard terms in their entirety. It wasn't long before so-called "exclusion clauses" began to appear.[9] These seek to state, in a party's standard terms, that a contract will only be entered into according to these standard terms, and none other. Some courts have been willing to take this at face value and arrived at the conclusion that no contract had been formed at all, although the parties had clearly reached an agreement based on which they had exchanged goods.

The end result, so far, seems to be that all traders now need to be very careful not to be "trapped" by someone else's standard terms. This increases the amount of attention to detail parties must spend per contract, and thus efficiency is defeated.

The combatants

Until now, international jurisprudence has applied two very different theories in order to solve these problems. There is no decisive prevalence of either one of them so far,[10] leaving the parties in a position where risk assessment is extremely difficult.

The Last Shot (Theory)

The earlier attempt at a solution, generally traced to the common law, is known as the "Last Shot Theory".[11] It treats every statement made with reference to conflicting standard terms as a rejection of the earlier (counter-) offer, combined with a counter-offer. The last offer thus made is treated as having been implicitly accepted when a party acts in regard to the transaction without making reference to its own standard terms. Thus, through sending goods or taking delivery of them, a party is treated as having accepted the "Last Shot" fired by the other party. Application reveals a number of flaws, most of which are recognized even by its proponents.

In the context of the CISG, Art. 19 CISG[12] is often considered to mandate this

8 Compare Ont. L. Ref. Com., I Sale 81 n. 25.

9 Empirically, I have found exclusion clauses even in "example standard terms" offered online, without regard to the business which might wish to employ these.

10 "It is fortunate that problems arising out of the 'battle of the forms' do not arise more frequently for legal science has not yet found a satisfactory way to decide what the parties have 'agreed' when they have consummated a transaction on the basis of the routine exchange of inconsistent forms", Honnold, Art. 19 at 165; compare Schlechtriem, in: Schlechtriem/Schwenzer, Art. 19 at 20.

11 See, e.g., Symposium, "Battle of the Forms", 4 Canad. Bus. L.J. 261 (1980).

12 Below, n.13.

approach.[13] The reasoning is based on the "mirror rule", according to which an acceptance must mirror the offer to lead to a binding contract. It follows that the incongruity regarding the standard terms of the acceptance in the above example disqualifies the acceptance as such. Instead, it is construed as a rejection of the terms offered, combined with a counter-offer (which then incorporates the standard terms of the counter-offering party). The same fate awaits each and every subsequent declaration making reference to standard terms. Thus, a contract *cannot* be concluded through the exchange of correspondence as long as both sides include references to colliding standard terms. According to this theory, should the parties move forward with their transaction, it is not pursuant to a contract already formed, rather they conclude the contract through an implicit acceptance (often in conjunction with shipping or acceptance of the goods), on the basis of the last (counter-) offer made, thus incorporating the standard terms to which a reference was made last.

The well-known flaw of this theory is that the formation of a legally binding contract (and, especially, its content) is more the result of chance than it is of a meeting of the minds. The parties may believe a contract already formed and continue their correspondence (on their standard stationery, mentioning their standard terms) only to fix side issues such as the colour of the goods. According to the Last Shot Theory, however, they are still rejecting offers and making counter-offers. Only when, during the performance of the transaction, a party takes an action without making reference to its standard terms (such as shipping the goods or taking delivery), this action becomes an (implicit) acceptance. Thus the declarations of intent of offer and acceptance are attributed to actions which are actually performed by the parties with a view to what they consider a "done deal". It is often surprising for parties to hear that, for example, they accepted some else's standard terms by accepting the delivered goods, when all they meant to do was to take custody of the goods. They meant to take over the goods from the shipping company, as they felt required to do pursuant to a contract which both the recipient and the sender of the goods considered to exist already.

Associated problems (agency, validity of acceptance, unjust enrichment)

Close inspection of the Last Shot Theory's ramifications elicits another problem concerning the action which the Last Shot Theory would label an implicit acceptance of the last counter-offer. Whether it is handing the goods over to the shipping agent or taking custody of them: these are actions which tend to be taken by employees

13 This approach, in the context of the CISG, is favoured by, inter alia: Farnsworth, in: Bianca/Bonell, Art. 19 at 2.5; Blodgett, "The UN Convention on the Sale of Goods and the 'Battle of the Forms' ", in: 18 Colo. Law. 423 at 426 (1989); Dessemontet, "La Convention des Nations Unies du 11 Avril 1980 sur les Contrats de Ventes Internationales de Marchandises" [The United Nations Convention of 11 April 1980 on Contracts for the International Sale of Goods], in Dessemontet (ed.), *Contrats de vente internationale;* [International Sales Contracts] (1991), 47, at 54 et seq.; Enderlein/Maskow/Strohbach, *Internationales Kaufrecht* [International Sales Law] (1991), Art. 19 at 10; Herber/Czerwenka, *Internationales Kaufrecht, Kommentar zu dem Übereinkommen der Vereinten Nationen vom 11. April 1980 über Verträge über den internationalen Warenkauf* [International Sales Law, Commentary on the Convention of the United Nations of 11 April 1980 on Contracts for the International Sale of Goods] (1991), Art. 19 at 18; Kelso, "The United Nations Convention on the International Sale of Goods: Contract Formation and the Battle of the Forms", in: 21 Columb. J. Transnat'l L. 529 at 553 (1982/3); Winship, "Formation of International Sales Contracts under the 1980 Vienna Convention", in: 17 Int'l Law. 1 at 12 (1983).

not empowered to enter into contracts on behalf of their employing merchant. The employee is neither so empowered by virtue of its employment contract, nor does the other party have reason to assume such power. While the employer has likely told the employee (how) to take shipments, this was not meant as a blanket licence to accept offers. The resulting problems are, of course, outside of the scope of the CISG (according to Art. 4 (a)). Thus, even if one were to follow the assumptions required by the Last Shot Theory, this would lead to the application of principles of private international law, and through these to the application of one national law or another. Under German law, for example, the results would reach beyond considerations of the general principles of agency. Not only would the person in question not be empowered to represent its principal, more vitally it would lack the intent to make such a representation when undertaking the action in question. Under German law, if an action or statement is made without the will to declare something legally relevant, then, should the action or statement be construed as legally relevant, the resulting contract is easily invalidated. Again, questions of validity lie outside the scope of the CISG.

As the likelihood of a valid acceptance slims, another problem is raised: if the goods are shipped and received without a contract in existence, the recipient is unjustly enriched. Without a sales contract having been in existence at any point in time, the resulting unjust enrichment must again be resolved by resorting to principles of private international law, and thence by national law. And at least under German law, the one causing another to be unjustly enriched is in an unfavourable position to regain its loss if it caused the enrichment knowing that no legal cause existed.[14]

Bad faith

Another unfortunate development due to the widespread acceptance of the Last Shot Theory is that some merchants have become aware of the odd interpretation of their statements by lawyers. They thus seek to snare the other side of a transaction into—apparently—accepting their standard terms by sending superfluous letters making reference to their standard terms in an attempt to get the last shot in. Needless to say, they do this knowing that the other party believes a contract to be in existence already, so they are not actually making counter-offers, but merely going through motions which they hope may be rewarded in a court of law.

The outlook becomes no less bleak where both parties involved have become "wise". The resulting tit-for-tat of superfluous correspondence shows clearly that the contractual items which matter to the parties have been settled already, and thus that a contract was formed already. Both parties are ready to go ahead with the transaction, even though they are not yet certain whose standard terms may be found to govern it. The behaviour of parties engaged in such a bizarre lottery is markedly different from that evidenced by parties which actually care about their

14 Section 814 of the Bürgerliches Gesetzbuch (BGB) [German Civil Code] states: "Das zum Zwecke der Erfüllung einer Verbindlichkeit Geleistete kann nicht zurückgefordert werden, wenn der Leistende gewusst hat, dass er zur Leistung nicht verpflichtet war . . ." ["What has been granted in order to fulfil an obligation cannot be reclaimed when the grantor knew that he was not obliged . . ."].

standard terms enough to let them make or break a contract: the latter merchants mention the problem by name, ensuring that an understanding is reached on the clauses that shall govern the contract. Each time the parties do not attempt to reach a clear agreement on the terms of the contract once a divergence between their standard terms is apparent, they show that such divergence is secondary in importance and are willing to contract regardless of such differences.

The willingness of the Last Shot Theory's proponents to assign implied declarations to subsequent actions remains astonishing: first, even though the content of the initial correspondence evidences the belief of a party that it has already entered into a contract, the Last Shot Theory nevertheless takes the boilerplate references to its standard terms to mean that this party is rejecting, time and again, offers made to it. Then, once performance of the envisioned contract begins, all of a sudden the party is considered to be willing to not only derogate from its own provisions supposedly so staidly held on to in the past, but to bow to another party's provisions, without further ado, and without even stating so expressly. As any acceptance, even one made implicitly, needs to reach the offeror, proponents of the Last Shot Theory require yet an additional leap of faith: one needs to assume that, between the parties who supposedly valued their fine print so highly, the offeror has—somehow—impliedly offered the possibility to the offeree to accept without notice to the offeror, and that the offeree now—again implicitly—accepts this offer.

In the end, analysed according to the Last Shot Theory, a typical transaction with colliding general conditions goes through the following sequence: the offeror makes an initial offer, including its standard terms. The offeree rejects this offer because it conflicts with its own standard terms, and makes a counter-offer (the content of which is the same amount of the same products for the same price, but with the offeree's standard terms). This counter-offer is again rejected. The parties may or may not send further correspondence, all of which are offers, all of which are rejected because they do not conform to the offeree's standard terms. Then, one party sends goods to the other party (without having entered into a contract) and thereby impliedly offers the opportunity to accept the current proposal, and to do so without ever informing the sender that a contract has, in fact, been entered into. The recipient then accepts the goods and unilaterally bows to the other party's general conditions—without telling the other party so.

This interpretation of events ignores the meeting of the minds which the parties shared when they exchanged their initial correspondence. At least in the ambit of the CISG, it is also against the law: Art. 8(2) CISG requires that "statements made by and other conduct of a party are to be interpreted according to the understanding that a reasonable person of the same kind as the other party would have had in the same circumstances" (more about correct interpretation below). Such interpretation of the train of events given above would hardly show that the party accepting the goods wishes to thereby declare acceptance of a contract. Moreover, in the light of its past (alleged) insistence on its own standard terms, there is no basis upon which to assume that it now wishes to accept another's standard terms in their totality. If its continued references to its own terms really were (as it is popularly construed) evidence of an unwillingness to budge from them, there is no reason to assume that those standard terms have suddenly become less important. Nevertheless, adherents of the Last Shot Theory propose that a *reasonable business person* must conclude from the acceptance of delivered goods that the recipient thereby, implicitly, declares that the recipient wishes to enter into a contract, to submit to the sender's standard terms in their entirety, and to accept the sender's (again implicitly made) offer to accept without notice to the sender. The number of assumptions layered on top of one another on behalf of the recipient has been criticized as much as the assumption that a merchant would send goods without a contract in existence on the chance that this "offer" will be accepted, while waiving the right of being told whether it is in fact accepted.

As one can see, the Last Shot Theory was born from a too-strict adherence to the mirror image rule. Using such a strict measurement of the declarations' content, one could not find matching declarations, and thus one needed to find an acceptance elsewhere. As the declaration with which the offeree meant to accept was considered insufficient, one turned to an action less fraught with apparent ambiguity, though devoid of declarative intent.

The Knock Out (Rule)

The view favoured by academia in Europe is the so-called "Knock Out" Rule and applies neither set of standard terms fully. It works on the basic assumption that when the parties exchange goods, both parties' activities clearly show that they feel bound by a contractual obligation to do so. Ergo, a contract has been entered into. Since this view does not identify the declarations which actually formed the contract, it needs to employ some detours to identify the content of the obligations entered into. The starting point is the basic form of the contract in question—under the CISG a sales contract—in its appearance under the law, which will be modified as far as the parties have agreed on a deviation from the law. Such a deviation will therefore be entered into (only) by corresponding standard terms. Conflicting terms (as well as terms derogating from the law which appear only in one side's form) will be disregarded, they "knock" each other "out". The Knock-Out Rule deduces the cause from its symptom: both parties have performed; *ergo* a contract has been formed. Because their declarations seem to be conflicting, they have to meet on middle ground.

One basic flaw of this approach is its sole reliance on the exchange of goods. While the parties will believe a contract to be in existence already, either party can still back out of the contract as long as the goods have not been delivered (something which is also true for the Last Shot Theory). Another criticism usually levelled at this approach is its apparent conflict with Art. 19 CISG, which is widely understood to mandate the application of the Last Shot Theory.

This theory evidences the same root cause for the problem: lawyers are unable or unwilling to find declarations giving rise to a contract in the declarations which led the parties themselves to believe that a contract was formed. Recognizing that neither the declarations made subsequent to the ones the parties considered offer and acceptance nor subsequent actions, properly analysed, will amount to offer and acceptance, this theory looks elsewhere to find a contract. As their declarations do not suffice, an exchange of goods—which the parties would obviously not effect in the absence of a contract—is relied upon to show the existence of a contract. Still—the parties believed a contract to be in existence prior to the exchange of goods. And if the parties agree that they have a contract, then they do, for their agreement on this is what gives rise to the contract. Yet the Knock Out Rule is unable to satisfactorily cope with a change of mind of one party before or during the transaction.

REALITY CHECK

Both of the above theories fail to reflect real life. If we assume for the moment that small businesses are at either end of a transaction and that the first exchange of letters has just taken place, how would the relevant parties judge their actions? If the ordering merchant asked the employee in charge of procurement whether the required goods had been secured, what would the employee say? "Yes, the order has just been confirmed"—or something to that effect. At the recipient end, an employee would likely feel confident enough to tell the merchant that a buyer had been found for x amount of goods.

Neither of them would be wrong—the order *has* been confirmed, and in the usual course of events the goods *will* be shipped due to that order. The buyer will pay, too. At least, that is the intent of the parties involved at the time they exchanged these letters. There is a meeting of the minds here, and the object of a contract is to protect the parties against a subsequent change of mind by the other party. The consensus achieved between the parties in this hypothetical example should be so protected. However, none of the current theories does so: according to the Last Shot Theory, the order confirmation was a rejection combined with a counter-offer which as of yet has not been accepted; according to the Knock Out Rule, without a transaction to prove a contract, there isn't one.

REASONABLE INTERPRETATION

So the problem persists. It seems time to take a fresh look at the problem, and the governing law, to see whether one cannot find a solution, after all. The problem seems to hinge on the merchants' willingness to believe that a contract was formed, even though their standard terms state something else, and lawyers' unwillingness to follow such a leap of faith. How is it, then, that merchants arrive at the idea of a formed contract, and how is this reflected by the law?

To answer this question, proper methodology requires that we first identify the declarations which might form a contract. And it is then necessary to establish their actual content. This is a question of the proper interpretation of declarations. The parameters of interpretation of declarations are laid out by the applicable law. In the CISG, these are found in and around Art. 8 CISG. Neither the Last Shot Theory nor the Knock Out Rule correctly apply this part of the law.

The rules of engagement

To properly judge the legal relevance of the exchange of letters containing conflicting standard terms, it is vitally important that one examines the relevant provisions of the applicable law.

Freedom of contract: Art. 6 CISG

First, it bears keeping in mind that the parties' will reigns supreme in their formation of the contract.[15] Thus, where the parties have intended to do something other than what the law provides for, their common intent supersedes the law.

The contract

Even under the aegis of the CISG, a contract[16] is formed through offer[17] and acceptance.[18] In Battle of the Forms cases, the original communication is generally structured by the offeror to be an offer as defined in Art. 14 CISG. Subsequent letters and actions, on their own, are generally not: it is only by interpretation in regard of the original statement that the Last Shot Theory manages to qualify them as subsequent "offers", with the difficulties entailed therein outlined above.

The express mention of "conduct . . . indicating assent to an offer" as constituting acceptance under Art. 18 CISG is sometimes regarded as specifically mandating that taking custody of a shipment etc. are acceptances as defined in Art. 18 CISG. Nevertheless, taking custody of a shipment only indicates assent to an offer if it is clear at the time that the making of the shipment constitutes an offer and that taking custody of it is meant to accept this offer. If the shipment is received on the assumption that a contract exists, taking custody of the goods only indicates that the assumed contract is meant to be honoured, not that an offer is meant to be accepted. See p. 192 et seq.

Qualified assent: Art. 19 CISG

The rule of Art. 19(I) CISG is often cited as the reason why within the scope of the CISG—unfair as it may or may not be—the last shot rule should be applied, supposedly having black letter law in its favour. This approach misconstrues the function of Art. 19 CISG, however: Art. 19 CISG is not actually a rule of interpretation. The provision is found in Part II of the convention, entitled "Formation of Contract". This part of the convention deals with how contracts are formed (offer and acceptance), for how long an offer is valid, under which conditions it can be retracted, etc. The rules governing the interpretation of declarations are found in Part I of the convention, Chapter 2: Art. 7 CISG deals with the interpretation of the convention, Art. 8 CISG governs the interpretation of declarations, Art. 9 CISG deals with trade usages. Art. 19 CISG merely lays out the consequences of an exchange of declarations when these have a certain content. Indeed, it was suggested in the

15 Art. 6 CISG: "The parties may ... derogate from or vary the effect of any of [the Convention's] provisions."

16 Art. 23 CISG: "A contract is concluded at the moment when an acceptance of an offer becomes effective . . ."

17 Art. 14 CISG: "A proposal for concluding a contract . . . constitutes an offer if it is sufficiently definite and indicates the intention of the offeror to be bound in case of acceptance. . . ."

18 Art. 18 CISG: "A statement made by or other conduct of the offeree indicating assent to an offer is an acceptance. Silence in and of itself does not amount to an acceptance."

working group to add a provision (to what became Art. 14 CISG) to address the inclusion of standard terms. This was rejected with the argument that the draft already contained provisions dealing with the interpretation of a contract.[19] The question of what the content of a declaration is, and thus whether or not a certain declaration actually falls into the ambit of Art. 19 CISG, must be answered before turning to Art. 19 CISG.[20] This can only be done through proper interpretation of said declarations, which is governed by Art. 8 CISG.[21]

Interpretation

According to Art. 8 CISG,[22] declarations are to be interpreted according to the actual intent of the declaring party inasmuch as the intent was clear to *the other party*. The same is true for actions possibly containing implicit declarations.

The paramount parameters in interpreting a declaration, thus, are two aspects: firstly, the intent of the declaring party, and secondly whether the receiving party "could not have been unaware" of said intent (Art. 8 I CISG). Only if such intention-based interpretation is impossible, according to para. 2 of Art. 8 CISG, a reasonable person test is to be employed. In either case, the current negotiations and their past and previous conduct have to be taken into account (Art. 8 III CISG).

The roadmap to peace

Thus, it is only proper interpretation of the statements meant by the parties to give rise to a contract which will tell us whether a contract was concluded and, if so, when it was concluded and what provisions it entails.

---

19 UNCITRAL-Yearbook IX (1978) p. 81 n. 278.

20 It bears noting that a provision dealing specifically with standard terms had been proposed during the eighth session of the working group on contract formation, Jan 4–14 1978, but was deleted before going before the commission and was not considered by the Diplomatic Conference; compare Honnold, *Documentary History of the Uniform Law for International Sales* (1989), 263 et seq., 283. The proposed provision would have effectively restated the knock-out rule. It was argued, however, that a material alteration in a purported acceptance should terminate an offer and be treated as a counter-offer, whether such alterations were in a printed form or elsewhere. However, not only are no reasons for this view offered in the record, such an understanding of Art. 19 CISG does nothing to prevent the parties from imposing their own views on contract formation, as illustrated below.

21 Compare Neumayer/Ming, *Convention de Vienne sure les Contrats de Vente Internationale de Marchandises* [Vienna Convention on Contracts for the International Sale of Goods] (1993), Art. 7 at 1.

22 Art. 8 CISG:
"(1) For the purposes of this Convention statements made by and other conduct of a party are to be interpreted according to his intent where the other party knew or could not have been unaware what that intent was.
(2) If the preceding paragraph is not applicable, statements made by and other conduct of a party are to be interpreted according to the understanding that a reasonable person of the same kind as the other party would have had in the same circumstances.
(3) In determining the intent of a party or the understanding a reasonable person would have had, due consideration is to be given to all relevant circumstances of the case including the negotiations, any practices which the parties have established between themselves, usages and any subsequent conduct of the parties."

Interpretation of the offer

Offer according to Art. 8(1)

People talking to one another invariably include in their statements issues that are more important to them than others and some that are less important—the trick being, of course, to know which is which. Written statements are not that much different: even the initial correspondence (say, an order) of a party including a reference to standard terms already shows a hierarchy within the declaration: the party addresses certain details of the specific transaction in a way quite specifically tailored to the situation at hand, usually while employing stationery referring to standard terms in small print on its back.

The way in which this statement is delivered shows the difference between the two parts: the offer made (on the front) is the product of a business decision by the offeror. The standard terms are terms of dealing which the offeror, on the advice of its lawyer, would prefer to deal under and therefore includes by way of reference. Exclusion clauses in the standard terms notwithstanding, the offeror usually does not wish to forego this deal just because certain minutiae in the standard terms do not exactly correspond with their approximations in the offeree's standard terms. This seems even more unlikely with regard to the fact that the offeror can anticipate that its standard terms will likely conflict with those of the offeree.

A different question is whether the offeree knows of this intent or, failing that, cannot be unaware of that intent. It is impossible to say that this is always the case. Thus, Art. 8(1) does not suffice to answer this. One must then turn to Art. 8(2)—interpretation from the vantage point of a reasonable business person. Thus, while certain facts speak for the intent of the offeror to assign reduced weight to its standard terms, whether or not the offeree gathers such intent from the offer is, failing specific knowledge, a matter of interpretation from the vantage point of a reasonable business person.

Offer according to Art. 8(2)

If one looks at the meaning a reasonable business person would derive from the first letter, the difference in importance between the two parts of the letter is obvious. However, it would likely be too far reaching to assume from this that the standard terms are of no relevance whatever and that the sender was merely going through the motions. There are, after all, some business people who take certain clauses very seriously. When the only thing by which the recipient can gauge the offeror's intent is that one letter, a reasonable business person can only guess how important they are. They would seem not to be terribly important for this individual transaction, as one might assume that the offeror would state so specifically in such cases. While this is not necessarily true, the recipient will likely continue based on the assumption that the fine print is of lesser importance—and send an acceptance.

Seeing how often these problems occur before the courts, it would seem that this is the usual consequence. One needs to keep in mind, however, that at this point in time, the offeree is on shaky ground with its belief—the offeror could still turn out to be one of the few individuals who do take their standard terms seriously.

Once the offeree has communicated its own stance on the issue and its understanding of the offer, subsequent conduct of the offeror (see below) will show whether this was the case.

The crux of the matter: interpretation of the acceptance

Acceptance according to Art. 8(1)

If the acceptance of a business offer including standard terms also sports such a standard reference to (conflicting) standard terms, then by a plain meaning analysis the declaration made is contradictory. This means that the statement, on its face, makes no sense: it includes, on the one hand, an acceptance of the offer made (which did include the offeror's standard terms) and, on the other hand, rejects the offer pursuant to its exclusion clause. The statement thus states both "yes" *and* "no".

The importance of this realization cannot be overstressed. The standard "acceptance" in a Battle of the Forms scenario is nonsensical on its face: it says "yes" as it is specifically written as an answer to the offer. Nothing in the specifically written part indicates anything but consent. Yet, it also makes reference to standard terms which say "no" to the same offer. It's a "yes" making reference to a "no". It has the effect of stating: "I accept the offer. Please also note that I reject the offer." Generally, such a self-contradictory statement would have to be considered void. The truth, however, is that the parties did have the intent to declare something and neither party is unaware of this fact.

How, then, to reconcile this contradiction? The standard way to reconcile this has been to assume that the offeree meant not both "yes" and "no", but meant to say, "yes, but . . .", that is, meant to say "yes, I'd like to take that offer, BUT only under the following conditions". Exposure to the Last Shot Theory and the Mirror Rule has so ingrained this reflex in us that most of us on first glance no longer realize that the statement portrayed above is nonsensical the way it is actually written. Interpreting this as a "yes, but . . ." kind of statement, of course, necessarily leads to the conclusion pointed out by Art. 19 CISG. It bears pointing out again, however, that Art. 19 CISG really does no more than state that a "yes, but . . ." statement does not lead to the conclusion of a (thus modified) contract. The crux of the matter, though, is the question whether this statement can really be so interpreted. Would a party aware of the conflicting standard terms and meaning to make a counter-offer simply state "yes" to the offer, including a reference to conflicting terms, trusting the recipient of the message (or a court) to understand that it was meant as a "yes, but . . ."? A reasonable merchant doubtless would not. A reasonable merchant who understood and appreciates the difference in standard terms and seeks to establish which standard terms will govern a transaction, will explicitly state the problem and seek to come to an agreement. That the offeree does not do so is something the recipient, as a reasonable merchant, must consider when interpreting such statements (and usually does).

As far as Art. 8(1) CISG is concerned, however, we are still interpreting according to the actual intent of the party. Typically, the declaring party's actual intent is not to declare "yes, but . . .". It merely wants to accept the offer made, and simply disregards the fact that their standard terms may (under the law) inhibit their ability to do so due to their exclusion clauses or material differences. Clearly, the drafter of the standard terms wished to ensure that contracts would be entered into only pursuant to them. The merchant employing them, however, has a business to run. The simple fact is that in markets where all parties employ standard terms, all parties would have to starve if all parties insisted on all of them.[23] So they generally do not.[24]

This bears repetition: the actual intent of a party which sends what appears to be an acceptance on its face, but contains conflicting standard terms, is not to reject and counter-offer, but to accept—disregarding what Art. 19 CISG may have to say on the matter just as the apparent conflict in the standard terms is disregarded.

Three questions thus arise:

1) Is that the understanding the recipient will (or should) have?
2) If so, is such an acceptance effective?
3) If so, what then are the contractual terms? (See below.)

If it is known that the "acceptance" was so understood, its interpretation is finished and one can turn to the offeror's subsequent conduct (below). If such knowledge is unavailable, as it generally is in a court of law, one must turn to Art. 8(2) to find what the offeror ought to have understood.

Acceptance according to Art. 8(2)

That the Battle of the Forms enters the courts so often shows that business people in the position of the recipient of such a statement *in fact* usually treat the statement as an acceptance. Factually, thus, the recipient will value the accepting part of the offeree's message above the rejecting standard terms on its back. A question one may have to ask, then, is if this is reasonable. The answer is yes: one has to keep in mind that interpretation of the message must ask which understanding a reasonable person *of the same kind* as the recipient would derive from it (Art. 8(2) CISG). Thus the question is not what a lawyer (with famous affinity for small print) would understand from the message, but what a (reasonable) merchant would think. A reasonable merchant, of course, understands the prevalence of standard terms as well as the fact that a merchant who writes a letter which, on its face, accepts an offer, means to accept it regardless of conflicting standard terms.

Can this acceptance be understood to accept unconditionally? No. There is no reason to support a "first shot rule". While the fact that the discrepancy was disregarded which exists between a statement on its face and included standard terms tells the recipient that the standard terms are of lesser importance, the fact that they were still included also tells the recipient that they are not of no concern at all. What, then, is the receiving merchant to make of this? It would appear that while the offeree employs standard terms and has an interest in continuing to do so, it is unwilling to let these stand in the way of the envisioned transaction—or else would have drawn notice to that fact. What is more, apparently the offeree understood the inclusion of the offeror's standard terms in the offer to be of a similar nature. For had the offeree understood the offeror's standard terms to make or break a possible contract, this matter would again have been addressed explicitly.

23 Compare Ont. L. Ref. Com., I Sale 81 n. 25.

24 *Ibid.*

Having found declarations of intent which, properly interpreted, actually mirror one another, the question remains whether there is anything in the convention which prevents these statements from forming a contract.

In most cases, the—for lawyers, surprising—result is what the parties in question believe at the time, also: that a contract has indeed been formed. This is what they expressed and the legal result, once their statements are properly interpreted, will match this expression. It can be stated at this point, then, that under the CISG, in a Battle of the Forms scenario where both parties seemingly disregard their standard terms unless and until a problem with the transaction arises, a contract is formed through the initial offer and acceptance. For the content of such contracts, see below.

One may argue that this would seem to be a problem for those rare merchants to whom their own standard terms matter greatly. Enough so, in fact, that they will let their inclusion in their contracts make or break a deal. Such merchants would respond to the reception of such an "acceptance" not with an ambiguous letter or by establishing a letter of credit or shipping goods, but by pointing this problem out to the offeree.[25]

In fact, after the offeree has sent its acceptance, we know only that the offeree in fact understood the offer to place secondary importance on its standard terms. Once the acceptance is received, this understanding of the offer by the offeree is also known to the offeror. We do not yet know whether this understanding was correct. Which leads to the role of subsequent behaviour in the interpretation of such declarations.

Interpretation of offer and acceptance in the light of subsequent behaviour

According to Art. 8(3) CISG, the circumstances of the case, as well as the parties' subsequent behaviour, are to be considered in determining the content of their initial declarations. After the reception of the "acceptance", that is, the order confirmation, the only thing that is *known* is that the initial order was understood to give secondary weight to the standard terms accompanying it and that the recipient similarly gives secondary weight to its own standard terms, based on the fact that the conflict between their standard terms goes unremarked. Whether the offer was *meant* the way it was understood is not—yet—entirely clear.

Equal weight (or lack thereof) to the standard terms of "offer" and "acceptance"

If the offeror—as is usually the case in these scenarios—also included its own standard terms only as a matter of general business, not letting them stand in the way of what looks like a beneficial contract, then the offeror will continue to act as people usually do in these scenarios: the discrepancy between their standard terms will continue to go unremarked. Additional letters may be sent (not addressing the problem of apparently conflicting standard terms), goods may be sent or a letter of

---

25 Compare John O. Honnold's statement: " '[G]ood faith probably would be promoted by a liberal application of provisions like Articles 19(2) and 21(2), which require a party to inform another who is known to be subject to a misapprehension." Honnold, Art. 7 at 95.

credit opened. In each case the silence on the issue of conflicting standard terms speaks loudly: it proclaims that, exclusion clauses notwithstanding, the parties are happy with the exchange of offer and acceptance as they stand and are willing to let them stand as they are. Thus the contract is formed through the initial exchange of offer and acceptance, because both are intended to form a contract irrespective of possibly conflicting standard terms. That this is true for the acceptance is obvious from its form alone: it seeks to accept (not modify), without regard to the conflicting standard terms it introduces. That this is also true for the original offer becomes obvious from the offeror's subsequent behaviour, in which it acts in a fashion which shows that it considers a contract to be formed.

This is markedly different from the common analysis under a "Last Shot Rule" point of view. In such an analysis, the subsequent behaviour would be interpreted as an implicit statement in itself, even though the party in question does not intend to state something with its behaviour. With the approach suggested here, the offeror's subsequent behaviour is interpreted in line with reality: as evidence of the party's original intent.

This bolsters the understanding one would have gleaned from the parties' communication until then regardless: they have struck a deal, though they have left a number of details undecided. But this is no different when parties conclude contracts without standard terms—the possibility to conclude a contract without fixing every little detail exists, and both merchants and private parties can avail themselves of this possibility. Even parties who generally include standard terms which do fix all the little details have the freedom to do so. Neither party is bound by its stationery or its standard terms. And when parties who have a different way in which they generally fix those details conclude a contract without deciding on the differences, then that is what they have done: they have concluded a contract without deciding on the differences between their standard terms. Art. 6 of the CISG specifically allows the parties to derogate from the provisions of the CISG, and Art. 19 CISG is not exempt from this.

Actual adherence to standard terms by the offeror

But what if the hierarchy evident in the initial order was *mis*understood to mean a lesser importance of the standard terms? The hypothetical offeror who cares deeply about contracting *only* to its own standard terms would be faced with an acceptance which clearly does not understand how important the offeror's standard terms are to the offeror. What would a *reasonable* merchant do in this position? It would be reasonable to inquire whether the conflicting standard terms had been overlooked. It would be reasonable to declare unequivocally that a contract would be entered into *only* according to the terms of the offeror, in a message which states so as its main content, rather than as an add-on to something else. This could be done via email, fax or phone. It would *not* be reasonable to send another message which again only made reference to conflicting standard terms, the way it was sent before, as this did not lead the other party to understand this—a fact which is now *known* to the offeror. By the same token it would not be reasonable to go forward with a part of the transaction once this misunderstanding is known.

The reasonableness—or lack thereof—of the offeror's behaviour is, of course, very relevant in the interpretation of its subsequent conduct, as such is the general yardstick—according to Art. 8(2) CISG—by which statements and conduct are interpreted when actual intent is not known.

So it is at this point that the rare offeror who really does wish to stick to its standard terms effectively changes the interpretation of its earlier statements through its subsequent conduct. While it may at first seem odd that the content of a declaration changes after it has been made—and received—the consideration of subsequent behaviour in the interpretation of a declaration necessarily includes this possibility.

Once both parties are—at least legally—aware of the conflicting standard terms and their respective exclusion clauses, any further actions which fail to address this apparent disagreement are indicative of an actual agreement already reached. For it is the only logical action once such an open disagreement is recognized: if both the offeror and the offeree really did wish to conclude only according to their standard terms or not conclude at all, the next letter would either attempt to clarify this or read something like "We are sorry that we could not agree." If that is the case, interpretation of the statements (with regard to subsequent conduct) is easy—clearly, the standard terms were meant to be an integral part of the statements.

If the subsequent actions are anything else—discussions about time and place of delivery (if these weren't part of the offer), an enlargement of the order, a confirmation, then—whether these additional messages contain references to standard terms or not—the parties show that they have agreed, that a deal is more important to both of the parties than their standard terms. Subsequent messages may continue to contain references to standard terms, but this will be ignored by the parties as it was before. This treatment should be reflected in their analysis.

The role of Art. 19 CISG

Some may insist that the way to this interpretation of the parties' declarations is barred by Art. 19 CISG. Art. 19(1) mandates that a "reply to an offer which purports to be an acceptance but contains additions, limitations or other modifications is a rejection of the offer and constitutes a counter-offer". The question which first needs to be answered in this regard, however, as pointed out above, is whether the modifications etc. found in the reply's standard terms are actually meant to be contained in the "acceptance". As shown above, they are generally not meant to be included, at least in so far as they would prevent formation of a contract.

Art. 19(2) CISG not only specifically allows modification of a contract where modifications are immaterial, it creates in this regard a regime which mirrors that which follows from the interpretation of offer and acceptance suggested above: should the receiving party give great(er) weight to the clauses in question, it is up to the receiving party to give notice of this difference in opinion, thereby preventing the formation of a contract with such modifications. If the receiving party makes no such objection, the contract is formed in the modified fashion suggested by the offeree. The same result follows from the interpretation of the Battle of the Forms scenario suggested here: the initial acceptance shows that the conflicting standard terms were not understood to be so material as to prevent the formation of a contract. Should the offeror disagree, it is up to the offeror to state so—explicitly.

The approach suggested here therefore does not require a major change in methodology—it requires only that one take a serious look at the declarations made by the parties and at the meaning the parties meant to assign to them, rather than focus on the fine print, in order to find that, in treating their standard terms as not material (that is, as not material enough to prevent formation of a contract), the parties act in accordance with Art. 19(2) CISG.

Art. 19(3) CISG would seem, at first glance, to prevent such a treatment of the declarations made, as it states that terms relating to a number of issues often addressed in standard terms "are considered to alter the terms of the offer materially". The reason for this would seem to be that with an offer which does not contain terms relating to, e.g., the extent of liability of one party to the other, an acceptance which contains an exclusion of liability would lead to a contract containing such an exclusion of liability unless the offeror objected "without undue delay". Such a result would indeed make for a bad rule. And this effect is the primary reason for Art. 19(3): by virtue of it, no party will be bound by materially differing terms in a purported acceptance simply because it neglected to scrutinize its terms thoroughly.

In the context of the Battle of the Forms, however, both parties employ standard terms. Neither can expect to have its own terms govern the transaction in its entirety unless an explicit agreement is reached about this, and the parties both employ these terms knowing—and not caring—that the other party's terms may differ. Thus the parties treat even such provisions as immaterial which Art. 19(3) CISG considers to be material.

What is often overlooked in this context is that the parties are free to do this: according to Art. 6 CISG, the parties are free to "derogate from or vary the effects of *any* of [the Convention's] provisions".[26] Thus, when the parties treat their standard terms as not material enough to prevent formation of a contract, then they are not.

CONTENT OF THE CONTRACT

The question of what content the contract so formed would have, is again answered by the application of the rules of interpretation and has, in effect, already been answered above. Primarily, the contract concerns those things the parties included in the individual parts of their declarations with which the parties have formed what they consider the contract.

As far as their standard terms are concerned, interpretation as above has shown that in the scenarios discussed here, both of the parties wish to include their standard terms *as far as they do not prevent formation of a contract*. This primarily concerns application of the mirror rule: obviously, where both sets of standard terms contain identical terms, these are included in the contract as well.

At the other end of the spectrum there are terms which have a corresponding term in the other set of standard terms which makes a different stipulation concerning the same matter. Clearly, as with the Knock Out Rule, these are *not* included in the contract. As the parties have made their preferences clear and differ in them, no agreement is reached regarding these terms.

26 Of course, just as offer and acceptance can be made implicitly, so an implicit derogation from a rule can be made implicitly, through conduct, compare Schlechtriem, etc. (Art. 6).

Less straightforward is the treatment of such standard terms which do not find an analogous expression in the other party's standard terms. The party who included in its standard terms would like to have it included, but will waive it if it would prevent formation of the contract. Obviously, if the other party has a different idea in this regard and no agreement has been reached, as with standard terms which do have a corresponding clause in the other set, the clause cannot be included. But how should one interpret silence in this regard? Where a party's standard terms are silent on an issue, that party's "standard terms" are the terms of the law.[27] Thus the guiding inquiry is whether the other party's standard terms materially deviate from the provisions of the law.

Art. 19 CISG gives guidance[28] as to which standard terms of either party may be included in the contract and which ones are not. The relevant paragraphs are 2 and 3:

> (2): However, a reply to an offer which purports to be an acceptance but contains additional or different terms which do materially alter the terms of the offer constitutes an acceptance, unless the offeror, without undue delay, objects orally to the discrepancy or dispatches a notice to that effect. If he does not so object, the terms of the contract are the terms of the offer with the modifications contained in the acceptance.
>
> (3): Additional or different terms relating, among other things, to the price, payment, quality and quantity of the goods, place and time of delivery, extent of one party's liability to the other or the settlement of disputes are considered to alter the terms of the offer materially.

Thus, any standard terms which are considered material under Art. 19(3) CISG are not part of the contract. These standard terms would prevent the formation of the contract and have therefore, implicitly, been waived. All non-material terms under this analysis may be included in the contract.

This does not contravene the interpretation above which arrived at the conclusion that the parties treated none of their standard terms as material. In the exchange of declarations it became clear that none of the parties considered any of their standard terms material enough to prevent formation of a contract. As Art. 6 CISG gives the party sufficient autonomy to do this, none of their clauses are material enough to prevent formation of the contract.

A different question is which of these clauses will be incorporated into the contract. Parties who do not employ standard terms leave every issue they haven't discussed to the law. Parties who employ standard terms but do not negotiate in detail which of them should apply, leave this decision to the law. Thus, Art. 19 CISG is the proper guideline to decide which of the standard terms will be included. Those which would ordinarily prevent formation of a contract will not be included. The remainder of terms which only one party uses will be.[29]

---

27 BGH [German Federal Supreme Court, decision of 9 January 2002] NJW 2002; 1651, 1653 = CISG-online 651.

28 Admittedly, this guideline still leaves much room for interpretation; compare, inter alia, Schlechtriem in Schlechtriem/Schwenzer, Art. 19 at 8 et seq.

29 One aspect of this is that a party's standard terms which are more lenient towards the other party than that party's own standard terms may be more easily qualified as a non-material alteration, as in LG Baden-Baden [Appellate Court of Baden-Baden, decision of 14 August 1991] RIW 1992, 62 et seq. = CISG-online 24.

THE RULE OF REASON

The approach suggested here, then, is as follows. In the exchange of order and confirmation without regard to the apparent conflict between the standard terms included by both, a contract is formed when the confirmation, by failure to mention the conflict, is shown not to consider the conflict significant and the subsequent conduct of the offeror shows that the offer similarly did not consider its standard terms material enough to prevent formation of a contract.

The content of such a contract includes the items explicitly agreed to by both parties and such terms featured only on one side's standard terms which are immaterial under Art. 19(2) CISG. In all other respects, the provisions of the law govern, as the parties have not agreed to differ from them.

INTERNATIONAL ARBITRATION MOOT

The Twelfth Annual Willem C. Vis International Commercial Arbitration Moot, 2004–2005

Nicholas John Collie, Thomas William Fitzgerald, Katherine Mary Hevron, Madge Puja Mukund, Michael Edward Taylor and Gabriël Adelin Moens

INTRODUCTION

For the second time, a team from the University of Notre Dame Australia, Perth participated in the prestigious Willem C. Vis International Commercial Arbitration Moot, held in Vienna, Austria in April 2005. Willem C. Vis (1924–93) was a world-recognised expert in international commercial transactions and dispute settlement procedures. The University of Notre Dame Australia was one of 158 law schools throughout the world that participated in the Moot. The team consisted of Nicholas John Collie, Thomas William Fitzgerald, Katherine Mary Hevron, Madge Puja Mukund, and Michael Edward Taylor. They were coached by Professor Gabriël A. Moens, Head, Graduate School of Law. At the time of publication of this Review, Professor Moens is the Dean of Law at Murdoch University, Perth.

The Willem C. Vis Moot brings together students from diverse cultures through a common endeavour: the training of law leaders of tomorrow in principles of international commercial law and techniques of international commercial arbitration. The Moot is organised by the Institute of International Commercial Law at the Pace University School of Law, New York and is sponsored by various international commercial arbitration institutions, including UNCITRAL. The goals of the Moot are described in Volumes II and III of *International Trade and Business Law Annual* (1996) 2 ITBLA 229; (1997) 3 ITBLA 277). It suffices for the purposes of this Introduction to emphasize that the Moot stimulates the study of international commercial law, especially the United Nations Convention on Contracts for the International Sale of Goods, 1980 (CISG) and various arbitration rules. The Moot offers participants an opportunity to interpret these texts in the light of different legal systems and to develop an expertise in advocating a position before an arbitral panel composed of arbitrators from different legal systems. The Moot Problem in the 2004–05 competition involved a controversy arising out of a hypothetical international sale of goods subject to the CISG and the Swiss Arbitration Rules.

Nicholas Collie and Thomas Fitzgerald presented the arguments to panels consisting of three arbitrators. They proceeded to the Semi-Finals where they were defeated by Stetson University. The students also received prizes for best oralist and their Memorandum for the Respondent received an Honorary Mention for Best Memorandum. In the next sections, the 2004–05 Moot problem and its clarifications are reproduced. This is followed by the School's Memorandum for the Respondent. The problem, clarifications and the memorandum are useful resources in the teaching of the CISG, and of international commercial arbitration law. They also serve as a historical record of the Twelfth Willem C. Vis International Commercial Arbitration Moot 2004–05.

TWELFTH ANNUAL WILLEM C. VIS INTERNATIONAL COMMERCIAL ARBITRATION MOOT

Vienna, Austria
March 18 to 24 2005

Organized by:
Institute of International Commercial Law
Pace University School of Law
78 North Broadway
White Plains, NY 10603
USA

and

SECOND ANNUAL WILLEM C. VIS (EAST) INTERNATIONAL COMMERCIAL ARBITRATION MOOT

Hong Kong
April 5 to 10, 2004

Organized by:
The Chartered Institute of Arbitrators (East Asia Branch)
Hong Kong International Arbitration Centre
38/F, Two Exchange Square
Central, Hong Kong SAR

and

City University School of Law
83 Tat Chee Avenue
Kowloon Tong, Hong Kong SAR

THE PROBLEM

Table of Contents

Horace Fasttrack
Advocate at the Court
75 Court Street
Capitol City, Mediterraneo
Tel. (0) 146–9845
Telefax (0) 146–9850

2 July 2004

Arbitration Secretariat
Chamber of Commerce and Industry of Geneva
4, Boulevard du Théâtre
P.O. Box 5039
CH-1211 Geneva 11
Switzerland

Dear Sirs:

I represent the Mediterraneo Confectionary Associates, Inc. which, pursuant to Article 7 of the Arbitration Rules of the Chamber of Commerce and Industry of Geneva, hereby submits its request for arbitration against the Equatoriana Commodity Exporters, S.A. in five copies.

Payment will be made for the administrative costs and the provisional advance on the arbitrator's costs as provided in Article 35 upon receipt of your invoice.

Sincerely yours,

(Signed)
Horace Fasttrack
Counsel for Mediterraneo Confectionary Associates, Inc.

Encl: Request for arbitration with exhibits

Chamber of Commerce and Industry of Geneva

Request for Arbitration

Mediterraneo Confectionary Associates, Inc.
Claimant

v.

Equatoriana Commodity Exporters, S.A.
Respondent

The Claimant, Mediterraneo Confectionary Associates, Inc., hereby requests that the dispute between it and the Respondent, Equatoriana Commodity Exporters, S.A., that is set forth below be submitted to arbitration under the Geneva Arbitration Rules, as provided in the contract between them.

STATEMENT OF CASE

I. Parties

1. Mediterraneo Confectionary Associates, Inc. is a corporation organized under the laws of Mediterraneo. It has its principal office at 121 Sweet Street, Capitol City, Mediterraneo. The telephone number is (0) 555–1235 and the fax number is (0) 555–1237. Mediterraneo Confectionary Associates, Inc. is a producer of various confectionary items. To produce the confectionaries it uses large quantities of cocoa among other ingredients. The confectionaries are sold throughout Mediterraneo and are exported to neighboring countries.

2. Equatoriana Commodity Exporters, S.A. is a corporation organized under the laws of Equatoriana. It has its principal office at 325 Commodities Avenue, Port City, Equatoriana. The telephone number is (0) 487–2314 and the fax number is (0) 487–2320. Equatoriana Commodity Exporters, S.A. is a trader in commodities, including cocoa. Although it largely trades commodities produced in Equatoriana, it also trades commodities produced in other countries.

II. Facts

3. On 19 November 2001 Mr. Harold Smart, account executive for Equatoriana Commodity Exporters, S.A., telephoned Mr. James Sweet, commodity buyer for Mediterraneo Confectionary Associates, Inc., and offered to sell cocoa to it. The two companies have done business together on a number of occasions over the years. At the end of the telephone conversation it was agreed that Equatoriana Commodity Exporters, S.A. would sell 400 metric tons of cocoa beans to Mediterraneo Confectionary Associates, Inc. During the period January–February 2002 Equatoriana Commodity Exporters, S.A. was to fix a delivery date that would be between the months of March to May 2002. The price was set at the current market price on 19 November 2001 of USD .5628 per pound, which was equivalent to USD 1,240.75 per metric ton. (One metric ton equals 2204.6 pounds.) The total contract price for the 400 metric tons was USD 496,299.55.

4. Mr. Smart sent a fax that day (Claimant's Exhibit No. 1) confirming the telephone conversation, a copy of which was mailed with a written contract enclosed. (Claimant's Exhibit No. 2)

5. On 24 February 2002, towards the end of the period during which Equatoriana Commodity Exporters, S.A. was required to name a shipping date for the cocoa, Mr. Smart wrote to Mr. Sweet. He referred to the storm that had hit the cocoa producing area in Equatoriana on 14 February 2002, a fact that had been widely reported in the cocoa industry. He went on to say that the extent of the damage was not yet known and that the Equatoriana Government Cocoa Marketing Organization had announced that no cocoa would be released for export through at least the month of March. (Claimant's Exhibit No. 3)

6. Mr. Sweet replied to Mr. Smart on 5 March 2002. (Claimant's Exhibit No. 4) He pointed out that the contract did not call for Equatoriana Commodity Exporters, S.A. to deliver cocoa from Equatoriana. The cocoa could come from anywhere; the source was irrelevant to Mediterraneo Confectionary Associates, Inc. Although he indicated that Mediterraneo Confectionary Associates, Inc. was not under immediate pressure to receive the cocoa, it would be later in the year. If the cocoa had not been delivered by then, Mediterraneo Confectionary Associates, Inc. would have to look elsewhere and would look to Equatoriana Commodity Exporters, S.A. to reimburse it for any additional costs it might incur.

7. During the following month there were several telephone calls in which Mr. Sweet constantly inquired as to when Equatoriana Commodity Exporters, S.A. would fix a date for delivery of the cocoa. This was followed by a letter dated 10 April 2002 from Mr. Sweet to Mr. Smart in which he said that Mediterraneo Confectionary Associates, Inc. expected Equatoriana Commodity Exporters, S.A. to deliver all of the cocoa by the end of May 2002. (Claimant's Exhibit No. 5)

8. Finally, on 7 May 2002 Mr. Smart sent a telefax indicating that 100 tons would be shipped later that month. (Claimant's Exhibit No. 6) They were shipped on 18 May 2002, received and paid for at the contract rate of USD 1,240.75 per metric ton, for a total of USD 124,075.

9. Although Mr. Sweet called Mr. Smart a number of times during the months of June and July inquiring as to the date when the additional 300 tons of cocoa would be delivered, there was no further written correspondence until 15 August 2002 when Mr. Sweet wrote to Mr. Smart. (Claimant's Exhibit No. 7) In this letter he wrote that Mediterraneo Confectionary Associates, Inc. would soon need to receive delivery of the remaining 300 tons of cocoa. He reiterated what he had written in his letter of 5 March 2002 (Claimant's Exhibit No. 4) that, if Equatoriana Commodity Exporters, S.A. would not be able to fulfill its obligation, Mediterraneo Confectionary Associates, Inc. would purchase elsewhere and hold Equatoriana Commodity Exporters, S.A. liable for any extra expense that might be incurred.

10. Nothing was heard from Equatoriana Commodity Exporters, S.A. in reply during the following six weeks. Finally, on 24 October 2002 Mediterraneo Confectionary Associates, Inc. purchased 300 tons of cocoa beans from Oceania Produce Ltd. at the then current market price of USD 2,205.26. It notified

Equatoriana Commodity Exporters, S.A. of the purchase by fax and letter on 25 October 2002 and stated that a claim for the excess amount it had paid would be made by counsel. (Claimant's Exhibit No. 8) The indicated letter was sent by Mr. Horace Fasttrack to Mr. Albert Tender, President, Equatoriana Commodity Exporters, S.A. on 11 November 2002. (Claimant's Exhibit No. 9)

11. Two days later, on 13 November 2002, Mr. Smart wrote to Mr. Sweet that Equatoriana Commodity Exporters, S.A. would have been prepared to deliver the 300 tons of cocoa beans. In that letter Mr. Smart asserted that the contract had not been "terminated" by Mediterraneo Confectionary Associates, Inc. but had been breached by the cover purchase. Mr. Smart stated that he had been instructed to state that Equatoriana Commodity Exporters, S.A. would not pay the USD 289,353 claimed by Mediterraneo Confectionary Associates, Inc. (Claimant's Exhibit No. 10)

12. Since Equatoriana Commodity Exporters, S.A. claimed that the contract had not been "terminated" by Mediterraneo Confectionary Associates, Inc., in an abundance of caution on 15 November 2002 Mr. Horace Fasttrack, counsel for Mediterraneo Confectionary Associates, Inc., wrote to Equatoriana Commodity Exporters, S.A. formally avoiding the contract. (Claimant's Exhibit No. 11)

13. During the subsequent year and a half there have been negotiations to attempt to reach a settlement, but no agreement has been reached.

III. Arbitration Clause, Applicable Law

14. The arbitration clause in the contract is as follows:

"Any disputes arising with respect to or in connection with this agreement shall be finally decided by three arbitrators in accordance with the Rules of Arbitration of the Chamber of Commerce and Industry of Geneva. The arbitration shall take place in Vindobona, Danubia and shall be in English."

15. Danubia has adopted the UNCITRAL Model Law on International Commercial Arbitration without amendment.

16. Danubia, Equatoriana and Mediterraneo are party to the Convention on the Recognition and Enforcement of Foreign Arbitral Awards.

17. Both Equatoriana and Mediterraneo are party to the United Nations Convention on Contracts for the International Sale of Goods and have made no declarations or reservations. Therefore, the Convention applies pursuant its Article 1(1)(a).

IV. Legal Conclusions

18. The Geneva Chamber of Commerce and Industry has jurisdiction over this arbitration.

19. Equatoriana Commodity Exporters, S.A. was obligated by its cocoa contract 1045 dated 19 November 2001 to notify Mediterraneo Confectionary Associates, Inc. during the months of January or February 2002 of the place where and the date when it would deliver 400 tons of cocoa, such delivery to take place during the

months March to May 2002 at the Seller's choice. It failed to give the notice of a delivery date in January or February 2002 as it was required to do. Finally, on 18 May 2002 it made a partial delivery of 100 of the 400 tons. During the next two months there were repeated telephonic and written inquiries as to when the remaining 300 tons would be delivered. The final written inquiry was 15 August 2002. Equatoriana Commodity Exporters, S.A. was informed that Mediterraneo Confectionary Associates, Inc. was running low on supplies and would soon have to purchase elsewhere. Equatoriana Commodity Exporters, S.A. did not reply. By at least 24 October 2002 Equatoriana Commodity Exporters, S.A. was in fundamental breach of contract. Mediterraneo Confectionary Associates, Inc. was consequently authorized to make a cover purchase, which it did at the prevailing market price.

V. Relief Requested

20. Mediterraneo Confectionary Associates, Inc. requests the tribunal to find:

- that it has jurisdiction over this dispute;

- that Equatoriana Commodity Exporters, S.A. was in fundamental breach of its cocoa contract 1045 dated 19 November 2001 with Mediterraneo Confectionary Associates, Inc. by at least 24 October 2002 in that it had failed to deliver 300 tons of the 400 tons of cocoa, which it was required by the contract to do during the months of March to May 2002;

- that Mediterraneo Confectionary Associates, Inc. was justified in making a cover purchase of 300 tons of cocoa at the then current market price on 24 October 2002.

21. Consequently, Mediterraneo Confectionary Associates, Inc. requests the tribunal to order:

- Equatoriana Commodity Exporters, S.A. to pay Mediterraneo Confectionary Associates, Inc. the sum of USD 289,353, being the difference between the contract price for the 300 tons of cocoa of USD 372,225 (USD 1,240.75 per ton) and the cover price of USD 661,578 (USD 2,205.26 per ton);

- Equatoriana Commodity Exporters, S.A. to pay interest at the prevailing market rate in Mediterraneo on the said sum from 24 October 2002 until the date of payment;

- Equatoriana Commodity Exporters, S.A. to pay the costs of arbitration as well as the attorney's fees incurred by Mediterraneo Confectionary Associates, Inc. in this arbitration pursuant to Article 36 of the Arbitration Rules.

(Signed)
Horace Fasttrack
Counsel

2 July 2004

Claimant's Exhibit No. 1

Equatoriana Commodity Exporters, S.A.
325 Commodities Avenue
Port City, Equatoriana
Telephone: (0) 487–2314
Fax (0) 487–2320

19 November 2001

Mr. James Sweet
Mediterraneo Confectionary Associates, Inc.
121 Sweet Street
Capitol City, Mediterraneo

By Fax and post

Dear Mr. Sweet:

I wish to confirm our telephone conversation of today. As agreed, Equatoriana Commodity Exporters, S.A. will sell, and Mediterraneo Confectionary Associates, Inc. will purchase, 400 metric tons of cocoa beans on the usual terms at USD 1,240.75 per metric ton. In January–February 2002 Equatoriana Commodity Exporters, S.A. will fix a delivery place and date for the beans, which will be between the months of March to May 2002.

A contract embodying these terms will accompany the posted copy of this letter.

Sincerely yours,

(Signed)
Harold Smart
Account Executive

Claimant's Exhibit No. 2

Contract: Cocoa 1045

SOLD BY: Equatoriana Commodity Exporters, S.A.
TO: Mediterraneo Confectionary Associates, Inc.

Four hundred (400) metric tons net of cocoa beans (in original shipping bags of average weight(s) customary for the Growth), deliverable, at the seller's option, at one of the customary delivery points for the country, between the first and last days of March to May 2002 inclusive; the delivery within such time is to be at seller's option, upon notice to the buyer during the months of January to February 2002.

The Cocoa is to be of standard Grade and Count.

Deviations of up to one percent (1%) in weight are without price allowance. The contract price will be adjusted at the contract rate per pound for deviations in weight of more than one percent.

The price is USD 1,240.75 per metric ton (USD .5628 per pound) for a total of USD 496,299.55. Payment due on notification of loading.

Delivery will be in one or more installments at the option of Seller.

Transportation from delivery point will be arranged by the Seller upon Buyer's request with all costs at the charge of the Buyer.

Any disputes arising with respect to or in connection with this agreement shall be finally decided by three arbitrators in accordance with the Rules of Arbitration of the Chamber of Commerce and Industry of Geneva, Switzerland. The arbitration shall take place in Vindobona, Danubia and shall be in English.

(Signed)
Harold Smart
Account Executive
Equatoriana Commodity Exporters, S.A.

(Signed)
James Sweet
Commodity Buyer
Mediterraneo Confectionary Associates, Inc.

19 November 2001

23 November 2001

Claimant's Exhibit No. 3

Equatoriana Commodity Exporters, S.A.
325 Commodities Avenue
Port City, Equatoriana
Telephone: (0) 487–2314
Fax (0) 487–2320

24 February 2002

Mr. James Sweet
Mediterraneo Confectionary Associates, Inc.
121 Sweet Street
Capitol City, Mediterraneo

By Fax and post

Dear Mr. Sweet:

I wish to confirm our telephone conversation of today. As has been widely reported, the storm that hit the cocoa producing areas in Equatoriana on 14 February 2002 has caused extensive damage to the crop that was ready for harvesting. It is still not clear just how much crop has been lost and how much may have suffered damage that will reduce its quality below international standards.

The Equatoriana Government Cocoa Marketing Organization has announced that no cocoa will be released for export through at least the month of March. As soon as I have more information I will be sure to let you know.

Sincerely yours,

(Signed)
Harold Smart
Account Executive

Claimant's Exhibit No. 4

Mediterraneo Confectionary Associates, Inc.
121 Sweet Street
Capitol City, Mediterraneo
Telephone (0) 555–1235
Telefax number (0) 555–1237

5 March 2002

Mr. Harold Smart
Equatoriana Commodity Exporters, S.A.
325 Commodities Avenue
Port City, Equatoriana

Post and Fax (0) 487–2320

Re: Your Cocoa Contract 1045

Dear Mr. Smart:

I refer to our telephone conversation of earlier today. To reiterate, we are very concerned as to whether you will be able to fulfill your agreement to ship to us the 400 metric tons of cocoa that was agreed.

It is irrelevant that there has been an unexpected shortfall in the Equatoriana cocoa crop due to the storm in mid-February or that the Equatoriana Government Cocoa Marketing Organization will not release cocoa for export through at least this month. The contract did not provide specifically for Equatoriana cocoa and the source is completely irrelevant to us.

Although we are not under immediate pressure to receive the contracted cocoa, we will be later this year. Naturally, we would then have to look elsewhere for the cocoa if Equatoriana Commodity Exporters, S.A. has not lived up to its agreement. If that were to happen, we would look to you for reimbursement of any additional costs that we might incur.

Sincerely yours,

(Signed)
James Sweet
Commodity Buyer

Claimant's Exhibit No. 5

Mediterraneo Confectionary Associates, Inc.
121 Sweet Street
Capitol City, Mediterraneo
Telephone (0) 555–1235
Telefax number (0) 555–1237

10 April 2002

Mr. Harold Smart
Equatoriana Commodity Exporters, S.A.
325 Commodities Avenue
Port City, Equatoriana

Post and Fax (0) 487–2320

Re: Your Cocoa Contract 1045

Dear Mr. Smart:

We have spoken on the telephone several times now in regard to the failure of Equatoriana Commodity Exporters, S.A. to fix a delivery date by the end of February. It is now almost the middle of April and all you have been able to tell me is that you expect the Equatoriana Government Cocoa Marketing Organization to begin releasing cocoa soon for export, though you doubt that you would be able to deliver more than an installment on the contract in the near future.

Naturally we will be happy to receive whatever you are able to send us, but we expect you to deliver the entire 400 metric tons you agreed to deliver and to do it by the end of May.

I look forward to receiving from you a more specific indication as to when and how much you will be delivering.

Sincerely yours,

(Signed)
James Sweet
Commodity Buyer

Claimant's Exhibit No. 6

Equatoriana Commodity Exporters, S.A.
325 Commodities Avenue
Port City, Equatoriana
Telephone: (0) 487–2314
Fax (0) 487–2320

7 May 2002

Mr. James Sweet
Mediterraneo Confectionary Associates, Inc.
121 Sweet Street
Capitol City, Mediterraneo

By Fax and post

Re: Cocoa contract 1045

Dear Mr. Sweet:

This is to confirm our telephone conversation of today in which I informed you that the Equatoriana Government Cocoa Marketing Organization had released to us a small amount of cocoa for export. Consequently, we will ship 100 tons Equatoriana cocoa to you this month.

We are expecting a loading date of 18 May. As soon as I have more specific details I will let you know.

I apologize for the delay in fulfilling our contract. The market for cocoa in Equatoriana is very difficult at present, but we look forward to shipping you the remaining 300 tons in the very near future.

Sincerely yours,

(Signed)
Harold Smart
Account Executive

Claimant's Exhibit No. 7

Mediterraneo Confectionary Associates, Inc.
121 Sweet Street
Capitol City, Mediterraneo
Telephone (0) 555–1235
Telefax number (0) 555–1237

15 August 2002

Mr. Harold Smart
Equatoriana Commodity Exporters, S.A.
325 Commodities Avenue
Port City, Equatoriana

Post and Fax (0) 487–2320

Re: Your Cocoa Contract 1045

Dear Mr. Smart:

It is now five and a half months past the time that Equatoriana Commodity Exporters, S.A. was obligated to notify us of the shipping date for the 400 metric tons of cocoa you sold to us and two and a half months after the end of the contract period for shipping it. All we have seen so far are the 100 tons shipped in May. Therefore, you continue to owe us 300 tons.

We can understand the problems you may be facing but they are your problems, not ours. Our contract was for cocoa, not for Equatoriana cocoa. The price of USD 1,240.75 per ton was the market price when the contract was made last November. The market has been rising steadily and is now in the range of USD 1,900 to USD 2,000 per ton. Let us hope it does not rise any further.

It is obvious that, if we do not receive notification from you soon when you will be shipping the remaining 300 tons, we will have to purchase elsewhere. Our stocks are lower than we are comfortable with. If we are forced to purchase elsewhere, we will hold you responsible for our extra costs. If the market continues to rise, and there is some reason to believe that it will, those extra costs will be considerable.

Sincerely yours,

(Signed)
James Sweet
Commodity Buyer

Claimant's Exhibit No. 8

Mediterraneo Confectionary Associates, Inc.
121 Sweet Street
Capitol City, Mediterraneo
Telephone (0) 555–1235
Telefax number (0) 555–1237

25 October 2002

Mr. Harold Smart
Equatoriana Commodity Exporters, S.A.
325 Commodities Avenue
Port City, Equatoriana

Post and Fax (0) 487–2320

Re: Your Cocoa Contract 1045

Dear Mr. Smart:

I am sure that this letter will not be a surprise to you or to your colleagues at Equatoriana Commodity Exporters, S.A.

We have waited patiently for you to deliver to us the 300 tons of cocoa still outstanding on your cocoa contract 1045 dated 19 November 2001. Delivery was due at the latest 31 May of this year and it is now late October. Since Equatoriana Commodity Exporters, S.A. has shown no intention of delivering to us and we were facing the likelihood of running out of supplies if we waited any longer, yesterday we contracted to buy 300 tons of cocoa.

It is no news to you that the price of cocoa has been increasing almost constantly during the past year. We purchased at the current market price of USD 2,205.26.

You may wish to inform your president, Mr. Tender, that in due course he will receive a letter from our legal counsel making demand on Equatoriana Commodity Exporters, S.A. for USD 289,353. That is the amount that we had to pay for the cocoa beyond the contract price at which you had contracted to supply us.

I am authorized to say that this situation, serious as it is, does not detract from our desire to continue the business relationship we have had with you in the past.

Sincerely yours,

(Signed)
James Sweet
Commodity Buyer

Claimant's Exhibit No. 9

Horace Fasttrack
Advocate at the Court
75 Court Street
Capitol City, Mediterraneo
Tel. (0) 146–9845
Telefax (0) 146–9850

11 November 2002

Mr. Albert Tender, President
Equatoriana Commodity Exporters, S.A.
325 Commodities Avenue
Port City, Equatoriana

Post and Fax (0) 487–2320

Re: Your Cocoa Contract 1045

Dear Mr. Tender:

I represent the Mediterraneo Confectionary Associates, Inc. in regard to the failure of Equatoriana Commodity Exporters, S.A. to deliver 300 tons of the 400 tons of cocoa you agreed to sell to it.

Your contract called for the delivery of 400 tons of cocoa during the months March to May 2002 at a price of USD 1,240.75 per metric ton. You delivered 100 tons on 18 May 2002. In spite of repeated telephone calls and a number of letters requesting information as to when the remaining 300 tons of cocoa would be shipped by Equatoriana Commodity Exporters, S.A. no further shipment of cocoa has been made.

Consequently, on 24 October 2002 Mediterraneo Confectionary Associates, Inc. purchased 300 tons of cocoa at the current market price of USD 2,205.26. The total purchase price was, therefore, USD 661,578. I enclose a copy of the cover contract. The contract price that Mediterraneo Confectionary Associates, Inc. was obligated to pay you for the 300 tons was USD 372,225.

I hereby make demand upon Equatoriana Commodity Exporters, S.A. to pay Mediterraneo Confectionary Associates, Inc. the sum of USD 289,353, representing the extra expense that it has suffered through your failure to fulfill your obligations under the referenced contract.

Sincerely yours,

(Signed)
Horace Fasttrack

Encl: Oceania Contract for cocoa [Not included in Moot Problem]

Claimant's Exhibit No. 10

Equatoriana Commodity Exporters, S.A.
325 Commodities Avenue
Port City, Equatoriana
Telephone: (0) 487–2314
Fax (0) 487–2320

13 November 2002

Mr. James Sweet
Mediterraneo Confectionary Associates, Inc.
121 Sweet Street
Capitol City, Mediterraneo

By Fax and post

Re: Cocoa contract 1045

Dear Mr. Sweet:

We are in receipt of your letter to me of 25 October 2002 and of the letter of 11 November 2002 from Mr. Horace Fasttrack to Mr. Tender.

It is unfortunate that you did not give us more specific knowledge ahead of time that you were planning to purchase the cocoa elsewhere. There had been rumors for some time that the Equatoriana Government Cocoa Marketing Organization was planning to release additional cocoa. Undoubtedly you were aware of them, since they had been reported widely.

Those rumors have now been confirmed. Since our contract 1045 had never been terminated by you, we would have been able to ship to you the necessary 300 tons within the next several weeks. You have made no complaint that the delay has caused you any supply problems as yet or any extra expense, except for your action in unnecessarily purchasing cocoa at the price current several weeks ago.

Your actions in purchasing the cocoa elsewhere at a much higher price than that in our contract and demanding from us the difference constituted a breach of the contract on your part. Under the circumstances, I have been instructed to inform you that Equatoriana Commodity Exporters, S.A. sees no reason why it should pay to Mediterraneo Confectionary Associates, Inc. the USD 289,353 mentioned in your letter to me and in that of Mr. Fasttrack to Mr. Tender.

Sincerely yours,

(Signed)
Harold Smart
Account Executive

Claimant's Exhibit No. 11

Horace Fasttrack
Advocate at the Court
75 Court Street
Capitol City, Mediterraneo
Tel. (0) 146–9845
Telefax (0) 146–9850

15 November 2002

Mr. Albert Tender, President
Equatoriana Commodity Exporters, S.A.
325 Commodities Avenue
Port City, Equatoriana

Post and Fax (0) 487–2320

Re: Your Cocoa Contract 1045

Dear Mr. Tender:

Equatoriana Commodity Exporters, S.A. has forwarded to me the letter dated 13 November 2002 from Mr. Harold Smart, an Account Executive with your company, and Mr. James Sweet of Mediterraneo Confectionary Associates, Inc.

The referenced letter is essentially in response to my letter to you of 11 November 2002 in which I made demand on Equatoriana Commodity Exporters, S.A. to pay the sum of USD 289,353 to Mediterraneo Confectionary Associates, Inc. to compensate it for the extra amount it was required to pay for the 300 tons of cocoa that your company failed to deliver.

In the course of his letter, Mr. Smart states that Equatoriana Commodity Exporters, S.A. had not been given specific notice that Mediterraneo Confectionary Associates, Inc. would be purchasing cocoa elsewhere to fill its needs. That is clearly not the case. I refer you in particular to Mr. Sweet's letter of 15 August 2002 to Mr. Smart.

Furthermore, in his letter Mr. Smart suggests that the cocoa contract had not been terminated. The contract was terminated automatically by the failure of Equatoriana Commodity Exporters, S.A. to deliver the cocoa for such a long period later than it was contractually obligated to do. However, in an abundance of caution I wish now to state clearly that the Mediterraneo Confectionary Associates, Inc. considers the referenced contract to be terminated.

I call upon you to promptly pay the sum of USD 289,353 to Mediterraneo Confectionary Associates, Inc.

Sincerely,

(Signed)
Horace Fasttrack

SWISS CHAMBERS' ARBITRATION

Chambers of Commerce and Industry of Basel Berne Geneva Lausanne Lugano Zurich www.swissarbitration.ch

FedEx

Horace Fasttrack, Esq.
Advocate at the Court
75 Court Street
Capitol City
Mediterraneo

Case no 30000–2004

Geneva, July 6, 2004

Re: Mediterraneo Confectionary Associates Inc. versus Equatoriana Commodity Exporters SA

Dear Sir,

We acknowledge receipt of your Notice of arbitration received by the Chamber of commerce and industry of Geneva on July 5, 2004.

This matter has been filed under reference **case number 30000–2004** and we would appreciate if you were kind enough to state the complete reference in all future correspondence.

For your information, the Chamber of commerce and industry of Geneva as well as the Chambers of commerce of Basel, Bern, Ticino, Vaud and Zurich have adopted the new Swiss Rules of International Arbitration ("Swiss Rules"), enclosed herewith, which entered into force on January 1st, 2004. The Swiss Rules unify and harmonize the arbitration rules of the above-mentioned Chambers of Commerce and replace the Chambers' existing Rules in the field of international arbitration.

Pursuant to Article 1, paragraph 3 of the Swiss Rules, these Rules shall apply to all arbitral proceedings in which the Notice of Arbitration is submitted after January 1st, 2004.

According to Section 1.1. of Appendix B of the Swiss Rules, you are invited to pay the amount of **Swiss francs 4'500,**—on the account of the CCIG with UBS SA, Rue du Rhône 8, 1204 Genève, number HU108533.1, with the reference "*Arbitration case 30000–2004*".

Please be advised that, in accordance with Section 1.3 of Appendix B, the Chamber will not proceed with the arbitration unless and until this payment is made, which means that the Notice of arbitration will be forwarded to the Respondent only when this payment has been received.

The Arbitral Tribunal shall determine any further administrative costs that may be due to the Chambers at a later stage of these proceedings (Article 38(f) and Section 2.3 of Appendix B of the Swiss Rules).

Feel free to contact us should you need further information.

Yours faithfully,

(signed)
Daniela Jobin
Member of the Arbitration Committee

Enclosure : Swiss Rules of International Arbitration

Chamber of Commerce and Industry of Geneva • Boulevard du Théâtre 4 • 1204 Geneva
Tel. +4122 819 91 11 • Fax +4122 819 91 36 • arbitration@ccig.ch

Horace Fasttrack
Advocate at the Court
75 Court Street
Capitol City, Mediterraneo
Tel. (0) 146–9845
Telefax (0) 146–9850

12 July 2004

Mme Daniela Jobin
Chamber of Commerce and Industry of Geneva
4, Boulevard du Théâtre
P.O. Box 5039
CH-1211 Geneva 11
Switzerland

Re: Case no 30000–2004

Mediterraneo Confectionary Associates Inc. versus Equatoriana Commodity Exporters SA

Dear Mme Jobin:

Thank you for your letter of 6 July 2004 acknowledging receipt of the request for arbitration in the above referenced case.

Per your instructions the sum of CHF 4.500 has been transferred to the account of CCIG with UBS SA, Rue du Rhône 8, 1204 Genève, number HU108533.1, with the reference "*Arbitration case 30000–2004*". I attach a copy of the transfer order.

I await your further information as to the progress of the request.

Yours sincerely,

(Signed)
Horace Fasttrack

SWISS CHAMBERS' ARBITRATION

Chambers of Commerce and Industry of | Basel, Berne, Geneva, Lausanne, Lugano, Zurich | www.swissarbitration.ch

FedEx

Horace Fasttrack, Esq.
Advocate at the Court
75 Court Street
Capitol City
Mediterraneo

FedEx

Equatoriana Commodity Exporters SA
325 Commodity Avenue
Port City
Equatoriana

Case no 30000–2004

Geneva, July 16, 2004

Re: Mediterraneo Confectionary Associates Inc. versus Equatoriana Commodity Exporters SA

Dear Sirs,

We thank Mediterraneo Confectionary Associates Inc. for the payment of CHF 4'500, representing the Registration Fee, received on July 15, 2004, as well as for the Notice of arbitration filed against Equatoriana Commodity Exporters SA on July 5, 2004.

This case has been filed under reference **case no 30000–2004**, which the parties are kindly invited to mention in all future correspondence.

The Respondent will find herewith a copy of the Notice of arbitration together with the exhibits and a copy of the Swiss Rules of International Arbitration.

The Respondent is advised that the Chamber of commerce and industry of Geneva as well as the Chambers of commerce of Basel, Bern, Ticino, Vaud and Zurich have adopted the new Swiss Rules of International Arbitration ("Swiss Rules"), which entered into force on January 1st, 2004. The Swiss Rules unify and harmonize the arbitration rules of the above-mentioned Chambers of Commerce and replace the Chambers' existing Rules in the field of international arbitration.

Pursuant to Article 1, paragraph 3 of the Swiss Rules, these Rules shall apply to the present arbitral proceedings, since the Notice of Arbitration was submitted after January 1st, 2004.

The Respondent is hereby invited to file its Answer to the Notice of arbitration **within thirty days from receipt of this notification** in accordance with Article 3, paragraphs 7–10 of the Swiss Rules.

Chamber of Commerce and Industry of Geneva • Boulevard du Théâtre 4 • 1204 Geneva
Tel. +4122 819 91 11 • Fax +4122 819 91 36 • arbitration@ccig.ch **1/2**

The Chamber notes that the amount of the claim is USD 289'353. Under Articles 6, paragraph 4 and 42, paragraph 2 of the Swiss Rules, disputes involving amounts (claim and counterclaim) which do not exceed CHF 1'000'000, are subject to the Expedited Procedure before a sole arbitrator.

Hence, the parties are invited to state **within 30 days from receipt of this letter** whether, for the event that there would be no counterclaim, or that the amount of the counterclaim together with the amount of the claim would not exceed CHF 1'000'000, they would agree to a single arbitrator (see Art. 42, paragraph 2(c) Swiss Rules).

Such consent would not bind the parties in the event that the threshold of CHF 1'000'000 is exceeded. Upon receipt of the Answer to the Notice of arbitration, the Chamber will then be in possession of all the necessary elements to proceed with the constitution of either a one-person or a three-member arbitral tribunal. The Chamber will thus provide new time-limits for the designation of the sole arbitrator by mutual agreement, or the co-arbitrators in case of a three-member arbitral tribunal.

We nevertheless draw your attention to the fact that, in the event that the parties do not agree on the appointment of a sole arbitrator, i.e. if the dispute is to be referred to a three-member arbitral tribunal, the fees of the tribunal are most likely to be higher than those of a sole arbitrator. In fact, the fees of the arbitrators shall be calculated in accordance with Section 2.8 of Appendix B (cf. Article 42, paragraph 2(c) of the Swiss Rules).

Finally, the Chamber notes that the Agreement to Arbitrate provides for the seat of the arbitration in Vindobona, Danubia, i.e. outside of Switzerland. Please be advised that, at this juncture, Article 1, paragraph 2 of the Swiss Rules requires that the seat be in Switzerland. However, on July 6, 2004, the Swiss Chambers decided to amend Article 1, paragraph 2 of the Swiss Rules to allow the seat of the arbitration to be fixed abroad. The amended provision reads as follows:

"The parties are free to designate the seat of the arbitration in Switzerland or elsewhere."

In view of the imminent entry into force of this new provision (on August 1st, 2004), the Special Committee of the Swiss Chambers has decided to conduct this arbitration with the seat in Vindobona, Danubia, as from the date it was filed.

We look forward to hearing from you and remain

Yours faithfully,

(signed)
Daniela Jobin
Member of the Arbitration Committee

Enclosures :– Notice of arbitration and exhibits, for the Respondent
– Swiss Rules for the Respondent

Chamber of Commerce and Industry of Geneva • Boulevard du Théâtre 4 • 1204 Geneva
Tel. +4122 819 91 11 • Fax +4122 819 91 36 • arbitration@ccig.ch **2/2**

Horace Fasttrack
Advocate at the Court
75 Court Street
Capitol City, Mediterraneo
Tel. (0) 146–9845
Telefax (0) 146–9850

21 July 2004

Mme Daniela Jobin
Chamber of Commerce and Industry of Geneva
4, Boulevard du Théâtre
P.O. Box 5039
CH-1211 Geneva 11
Switzerland

Re: Case no 30000–2004

Mediterraneo Confectionary Associates Inc. versus Equatoriana Commodity Exporters SA

Dear Mme Jobin:

Thank you for your letter of 16 July 2004 in regard to the above referenced case.

We appreciate that you have brought to our attention the desirability of having a single arbitrator rather than three, as provided in the arbitration clause. Although it will be more expensive to have three arbitrators, we would prefer it.

Article 7 of the Swiss Rules provides that, if we could not agree with Equatoriana Commodity Exporters, S.A. on a sole arbitrator within thirty days, the choice of the arbitrator would be made by "the Chambers", which I understand to mean the Arbitration Committee representing all six chambers of commerce and industry. Rather than risk the possibility that we and Equatoriana Commodity Exporters, S.A. would not be able to agree on a sole arbitrator within the thirty days, we would prefer to follow the procedure in Article 8 and in the arbitration clause. That would permit us to appoint one of the three arbitrators, which we feel is important enough to bear the extra cost.

Yours sincerely,

(Signed)
Horace Fasttrack

Joseph Langweiler
Lawyer
14 Capitol Boulevard
Oceanside, Equatoriana

10 August 2004

Mme Daniela Jobin
Chamber of Commerce and Industry of Geneva
4, Boulevard du Théâtre
P.O. Box 5039
CH-1211 Geneva 11
Switzerland

Re: Case no 30000-2004

Mediterraneo Confectionary Associates Inc. versus Equatoriana Commodity Exporters SA

Dear Mme Jobin:

I acknowledge receipt of your letter of 16 July 2004 addressed to Equatoriana Commodity Exporters, S.A. and the enclosed notice of arbitration and the statement of claim by Mediterraneo Confectionary Associates, Inc.

I represent Equatoriana Commodity Exporters, S.A. in this dispute.

In accord with your letter and the Swiss Rules there is enclosed the Answer to the claim brought by Mediterraneo Confectionary Associates, Inc. The Answer also contains a counter-claim brought on the basis of Article 21(5) of the Swiss Rules.

A transfer of CHF 4.500 has been made to the account of the CCIG with UBS SA, Rue du Rhône 8, 1204 Genève, number HU108533.1, with the reference "*Arbitration case 30000-2004*".

We understand that Mr. Horace Fasttrack has written you that he would prefer that the dispute be settled by a tribunal of three arbitrators rather than by one arbitrator as you had proposed. We are in agreement with him, and for the reasons he gave you.

I look forward to hearing from you further in this matter.

Sincerely yours,

Joseph Langweiler

Encl: Answer and counter-claim
Copy transfer order [Not included in the Moot Problem]

Swiss Chambers' Arbitration

Case no 30000-2004

Re: Mediterraneo Confectionary Associates Inc. versus Equatoriana Commodity Exporters SA

Answer to Notice of Arbitration and Counter-Claim

STATEMENT OF CASE

I. Parties

1. Mediterraneo Confectionary Associates, Inc., the Claimant, is a corporation organized under the laws of Mediterraneo. It has its principal office at 121 Sweet Street, Capitol City, Mediterraneo. The telephone number is (0) 555–1235 and the fax number is (0) 555–1237. Mediterraneo Confectionary Associates, Inc. is a producer of various confectionary items. To produce the confectionaries it uses large quantities of cocoa and sugar among other ingredients. The confectionaries are sold throughout Mediterraneo and are exported to neighboring countries.

2. Equatoriana Commodity Exporters, S.A., the Respondent, is a corporation organized under the laws of Equatoriana. It has its principal office at 325 Commodities Avenue, Port City, Equatoriana. The telephone number is (0) 487–2314 and the fax number is (0) 487–2320. Equatoriana Commodity Exporters, S.A. is a trader in commodities, including cocoa and sugar. It trades primarily commodities produced in Equatoriana, although on occasion it trades commodities produced in other countries.

II. Facts—Transaction

3. The transaction in regard to our cocoa contract 1045 dated 19 November 2001 took place as described in the Claimant's Request for Arbitration, paragraphs 3 through 11. Equatoriana Commodity Exporters, S.A. agrees that there was a letter dated 15 November 2002 from Mr. Horace Fasttrack, counsel for Mediterraneo Confectionary Associates, Inc. that stated Mediterraneo Confectionary Associates, Inc. was avoiding the contract. (Claimant's Exhibit No. 11) Equatoriana Commodity Exporters, S.A. does not know the motivation for the letter.

III. Legal Argument

A. Equatoriana Commodity Exporters, S.A. is not liable for the late delivery

1. Contract anticipated sale of cocoa from Equatoriana

4. The statement to be found in the letter from Mr. Sweet to Mr. Smart dated 5 March 2002 (Claimant's Exhibit No. 4) that "The contract did not provide specifically for Equatoriana cocoa . . ." is misleading. It is correct that the written contract did not provide "specifically" for Equatoriana cocoa, but there is no doubt that both Mr. Sweet and Mr. Smart contracted in regard to cocoa from Equatoriana. As is indicated

by the name of the Respondent, Equatoriana Commodity Exporters, S.A., the Respondent's business is essentially the exportation of commodities from Equatoriana. Only a small portion of its business involves the sale of commodities produced in other countries.

5. It is highly relevant that every sale of cocoa by Equatoriana Commodity Exporters, S.A. to Mediterraneo Confectionary Associates, Inc. has been of cocoa that was produced in Equatoriana. It may well be true, as that letter goes on to say, that "the source is completely irrelevant to us", i.e. to Mediterraneo Confectionary Associates, Inc., at the time that Mr. Sweet wrote the letter. It was not so completely irrelevant at the time of contracting.

6. Equatoriana is not a major producer of cocoa and its cocoa is not of the highest quality. Consequently, Equatoriana cocoa sells at a discount to cocoa from most other producing countries. Although Equatoriana cocoa is not regularly traded on either the New York Board of Trade or on Euronext LIFFE in London, as is true of a few other small producers of cocoa, provision is made in their rules governing pricing for such producers. On the New York Board of Trade cocoa futures are traded in dollars per metric ton. Only a small portion of the futures contracts result in physical delivery of cocoa. Respondent's Exhibit No. 1 contains an extract from the New York Board of Trade Cocoa Rules that shows that, when a contract results in physical delivery, cocoa from countries in Group A is delivered at a premium of USD 160 per metric ton. Cocoa from countries in Group B is delivered at a premium of USD 80 per metric ton while cocoa from countries in Group C is delivered at par. It will be noticed that cocoa from Equatoriana would be included in Group C.

7. Respondent's Exhibit No. 2 shows the same phenomenon in London in the Euronext LIFFE Cocoa Futures Contract, Exchange Contract No. 401. There are two principal differences between it and the New York Board of Trade Rules, besides the fact that the contracts are denominated in pounds sterling. The first is that there are five categories of sources for cocoa instead of three. The second is that differentiation in price between cocoa from different sources is expressed in terms of a discount from the exchange contract price rather than as a premium. Equatoriana cocoa would fall into the lowest price category in London as in New York.

8. The price for the cocoa sold by Equatoriana Commodity Exporters, S.A. to Mediterraneo Confectionary Associates, Inc. in contract 1045 dated 19 November 2001 was priced in US dollars. Respondent's Exhibit No. 3 shows the monthly prices for cocoa in US cents per pound as shown on the website of the International Cocoa Organization. The International Cocoa Organization is an inter-governmental organization created under the auspices of the United Nations. Multiplying the price for the month of November 2001 as shown in Respondent's Exhibit No. 3 by 2204.6 (the number of pounds in a metric ton) shows that the price per metric ton was USD 1,240.75, the price at which the cocoa was sold in contract 1045 between the two parties. The fact that there was no deviation from the basic price indicates that the contract envisaged cocoa coming from a country in category C in the New York Board of Trade Cocoa Rules or the fifth category in the Euronext LIFFE Cocoa Futures Contract, Exchange Contract No. 401. As noted above, those categories included cocoa from Equatoriana and almost no other sources.

2. Equatoriana Commodity Exporters, S.A. was prohibited from fulfilling the contract within the period provided in the contract

9. As noted in Mr. Smart's letter of 24 February 2002, (Claimant's Exhibit No. 3) subsequent to the storm that hit the cocoa growing area of Equatoriana on 14 February 2002, the Equatoriana Government Cocoa Marketing Organization announced that no cocoa would be released for export through at least the month of March. The embargo on export of cocoa continued until early November 2002, except for a small amount released in May 2002. It was from that May release that Equatoriana Commodity Exporters, S.A. was able to deliver 100 tons on 18 May 2002 to Mediterraneo Confectionary Associates, Inc. Since there was a governmental prohibition against exporting cocoa from February to November 2002, under Article 79 of the United Nations Convention on Contracts for the International Sale of Goods (CISG) Equatoriana Commodity Exporters, S.A. is exonerated from liability for failure to deliver the remaining 300 tons during that period.

B. Mediterraneo Confectionary Associates, Inc. was not justified in avoiding the contract

10. The contract signed in November 2001 called for delivery during the months March to May 2002. It is clear that timely performance was not of importance to Mediterraneo Confectionary Associates, Inc. and there could be no fundamental breach unless the delay was extraordinarily long or the buyer had fixed "an additional period of time of reasonable length for performance by the seller of his obligations" in accordance with Article 47 of the CISG. If it had and Equatoriana Commodity Exporters, S.A. had not delivered during that period (even if exonerated from liability under Article 79), Mediterraneo Confectionary Associates, Inc. would have been authorized to avoid the contract.

11. No additional period of time was fixed by Mediterraneo Confectionary Associates, Inc., as called for by Article 47. The last communication from them prior to their purchase of replacement cocoa on 24 October 2002 and the purported avoidance of the contract on 11 November 2002 was the letter from Mr. Sweet of 15 August 2002. In that letter all that he said was that they would need the cocoa "soon". It is unfortunate that Mediterraneo Confectionary Associates, Inc. did not at least contact Equatoriana Commodity Exporters, S.A. immediately before they purchased the cocoa elsewhere. As stated in the letter of Mr. Smart of 13 November 2002, (Claimant's Exhibit No. 10) there had been rumors for some time that the Equatoriana Government Cocoa Marketing Organization was planning to release additional cocoa, which it did on 13 November. It would then have been possible for Equatoriana Commodity Exporters, S.A. to deliver the remaining 300 tons.

C. Damages claimed by Mediterraneo Confectionary Associates, Inc. are incorrect

12. As a subsidiary and partial defense to be considered only if the Tribunal should find that Mediterraneo Confectionary Associates, Inc. has a claim for damages. Equatoriana Commodity Exporters, S.A. contests the calculation of damages presented by Mediterraneo Confectionary Associates, Inc. in its claim. The price of cocoa, like that of many other commodities, is often very volatile. Therefore, it matters from which date damages are measured. As noted in the claim, Mediterraneo

Confectionary Associates, Inc. purchased 300 tons of cocoa on 24 October 2002 at a time when the market price was at almost a historic high of 100.03 cents per pound, (Respondent's Exhibit No. 3) or USD 2,205.26 per metric ton for a total contract price of USD 661,578. Also, as noted in the claim, on 15 November 2002 Mr. Fasttrack, counsel for Mediterraneo Confectionary Associates, Inc., purported to avoid the contract. On that date the price for cocoa had gone down to 82.29 cents per pound, or USD 1,814.17 per metric ton. If the 300 tons of cocoa had been purchased on the date Mediterraneo Confectionary Associates, Inc. purported to avoid the contract, it would have paid USD 544,251. The amount it paid would have been USD 172,026 more than the contract price in cocoa contract 1045 instead of USD 289,353 as claimed.

IV. Counterclaim

A. Facts

13. On 20 November 2003 Equatoriana Commodity Exporters, S.A. sold 2,500 metric tons of sugar to Mediterraneo Confectionary Associates, Inc. (Respondent's Exhibit No. 4) The price was USD. 07 per pound or USD 154.32 per metric ton, for a total contract price of USD 385,805. The contract was FOB (Incoterms 2000) Port Hope, Oceania. Delivery to the carrier, Oceania Shipping Lines, was made in conformity with the contract on 4 December 2003. The sugar was loaded on the vessel, Oceania Condor, on 8 December 2003.

14. Mediterraneo Confectionary Associates, Inc. claimed that when the sugar arrived in Mediterraneo it was wet and had become contaminated and could no longer be used for confectionary purposes. (Respondent's Exhibit No. 5) Consequently, it has refused to pay the contract price.

15. According to FOB (Incoterms 2000), section B5 "The buyer must bear all risks of loss of or damage to the goods from the time they have passed the ship's rail at the named port of shipment." Confectionary Associates, Inc., therefore, bore the risk of loss during transit. The sugar was in good condition when turned over to the Oceania Shipping Lines for carriage to Mediterraneo as shown by the receipt issued by it. (Respondent's Exhibit No. 6) If there was water damage to the sugar, it was after the risk of loss had passed to Mediterraneo Confectionary Associates, Inc. The water damage is not the responsibility of Equatoriana Commodity Exporters, S.A. and Mediterraneo Confectionary Associates, Inc. is obligated to pay the contract price.

16. Since the contract called for payment ten days subsequent to delivery in Port Hope, Oceania, in accord with Article 78 of the United Nations Convention on Contracts for the International Sale of Goods Mediterraneo Confectionary Associates, Inc. is obligated to pay interest on the outstanding price from 18 December 2003.

B. Arbitration Clause

17. The contract contained an arbitration clause calling for arbitration by three arbitrators in accordance with the Rules of Arbitration of the Oceania Commodity Association. However, the Tribunal has jurisdiction to consider this dispute

pursuant to Article 21(5) of the Swiss Rules, which provides: "The arbitral tribunal shall have jurisdiction to hear a set-off defence even when the relationship out of which this defence is said to arise is not within the scope of the arbitration clause or is the object of another arbitration agreement or forum-selection clause."

V. Relief Requested

18. Equatoriana Commodity Exporters, S.A. requests the Tribunal to find:

In regard to cocoa contract 1045

- That the contract was for the sale of cocoa from Equatoriana;
- That Equatoriana Commodity Exporters, S.A. was impeded through no fault of its own from delivering during the period February to November 2002 more than 100 tons of the 400 tons contracted;
- That Mediterraneo Confectionary Associates, Inc. did not fix a period for delivery pursuant to Article 47 CISG for Equatoriana Commodity Exporters, S.A. to deliver the 300 tons of cocoa not yet delivered;
- That Mediterraneo Confectionary Associates, Inc. was not authorized under Article 49 CISG to avoid the contract;
- That, if the Tribunal were to find that Mediterraneo has the right to damages from Equatoriana Commodity Exporters, S.A., the damages should be measured by the difference between the contract price and the market price on 15 November 2002 and not by the larger difference between the contract price and the price paid by Mediterraneo Confectionary Associates, Inc. in the substitute transaction.

In regard to sugar contract 2212

- That the Tribunal has jurisdiction to consider the counter-claim;
- That any damage that may have occurred to the sugar happened after the risk of loss had passed to Mediterraneo Confectionary Associates, Inc.;
- That Mediterraneo Confectionary Associates, Inc. is obligated to pay the full contract price of USD 385,805 for the sugar.

19. Therefore, Equatoriana Commodity Exporters, S.A. requests the Tribunal to:

In regard to cocoa contract 1045

- Dismiss the claim for damages in totality brought by Mediterraneo Confectionary Associates, Inc.;
- Alternatively and only if it finds that Mediterraneo has a claim for damages, find that the damages are limited to USD 172,026.

In regard to sugar contract 2212

- Order Mediterraneo Confectionary Associates, Inc. to pay the full contract price of USD 385,805;
- Order Mediterraneo Confectionary Associates, Inc. to pay interest on the price of USD 385,805 from 18 December 2003 to the date of payment.

In regard to the arbitration

- Order Mediterraneo Confectionary Associates, Inc. to pay all costs of the arbitration, including the costs for legal representation and assistance incurred by Equatoriana Commodity Exporters, S.A. in this arbitration, in accord with Article 38 of the Swiss Rules.

(Signed)
Counsel

10 August 2004

Respondent's Exhibit No. 1

NYBOT®
Extract from Cocoa Rules
(Full text of the Cocoa Rules can be found at http://www.nybot.com/. Click on Rulebooks. Chapter 9 of the NYBOT® Rules governs Cocoa Futures and Options)

Rule 9.18. Grading Cocoa

(a) All Cocoa to be delivered in Exchange-Segregated Lots must be certified as deliverable with respect to Growth, Description, Condition, Count and Grade in accordance with the provisions of this Rule.

(b) The Growth, Description, Condition, Count and Grade of Cocoa which may be delivered on an Exchange Futures Contract are as follows:

(i) *Growth and Description*

The following Growths and Descriptions of Cocoa, as such Growths and Descriptions may from time to time be known in the trade, may be delivered at the premiums or at par as indicated below:

Group A—Addition of $160—per metric ton

Ghana—Main Crop Nigeria—Main Crop
Ivory Coast—Main Crop Sierra Leone—Main Crop
Lome—Main Crop

Group B—Addition of $80—per metric ton

Arriba (Ecuador) Ivory Coast Panama
Bahai (Brazil) Jamaica Salvador
Cameroon Indonesia-Java Samoa
Sri Lanka Liberia—Main Crop San Thome
Chiapas (Mexico) Masie Nguema Surinam
Costa Rican (Fernando Poo) Tabasco (Mexico)
Ghana—Mid-Crop New Guinea Trinidad
Grenada New Hebrides Venezuela
Guatemala Nicaragua Victoria (Brazil)
Hispaniolas (Dominican Republic) Nigeria—Light Crop Zaire
Honduras

Group C—At Par

Bolivia
Haiti
Indonesia-Sulawesi
Malaysia
Para (Brazil)
Peru
Sanchez (Dominican Republic) and all other growths not presently specified above.

Respondent's Exhibit No. 2

LIFFE

EXCHANGE CONTRACT NO. 401

COCOA FUTURES CONTRACT

CONTRACT TERMS—Issue Date: 11 October 2001

ADMINISTRATIVE PROCEDURES—Issue Date: 7 December 2000

4.08 A Seller shall deliver under a Contract a Delivery Unit which exclusively contains Cocoa from a single Origin stated from time to time to be in the following Origin Groups. A Delivery Unit delivered under a Contract shall be subject to the discount stated in respect of the following Origin Groups, or such other discount as may be prescribed by the Board from time to time.

(a) Origin Group 1: Cocoa delivered from one of the following Origins shall not be subject to a discount: Ghana; Cote d'Ivoire; Nigeria; Sierra Leone; Togo; Cameroon; Equatorial Guinea; Democratic Republic of Congo (formerly known as Zaire); Western Samoa; Grenada Fine Estates; Trinidad & Tobago Plantation; and Jamaica.

(b) Origin Group 2: Cocoa delivered from one of the following Origins shall be subject to a discount of £25 per tonne: Sao Tome and Principe; and Sri Lanka.

(c) Origin Group 3: Cocoa delivered from one of the following Origins shall be subject to a discount of £50 per tonne: Brazil Bahia Superior; Brazil Vitoria Superior; Ecuador; and Papua New Guinea.

(d) Origin Group 4: Cocoa delivered from the following Origin shall be subject to a discount of £75 per tonne: Malaysia.

(e) Origin Group 5: Cocoa delivered from any other Origin shall be subject to a discount of £100 per tonne.

Respondent's Exhibit No. 3

Monthly Average Cocoa Prices[a/ b/] 1971–2004

Year	Jan	Feb	Mar	Apr	May	Jun	Jul	Aug	Sep	Oct	Nov	Dec
US cents/ pound												
1971	27.23	25.48	24.47	24.76	23.16	24.04	25.89	26.91	25	22.47	21.96	21.79
1972	24.26	24.94	26.12	26.37	27.87	28.19	29.24	31.04	32.85	33.02	32.51	33.37
1973	32.47	33.87	38.3	42.73	53.03	58.02	70.3	64.22	60.25	58.72	51.87	51.74
1974	50.89	58.38	67.39	82.6	82.71	70.28	71.67	73.48	72.35	79.18	75.59	64.36
1975	67.19	67.84	62.64	56.2	48.01	44.9	52.85	53.25	52.47	56.7	55.99	59.83
1976	63.7	65.04	64.17	74.32	80.2	87.26	88.75	96.23	108.41	117.39	132.67	134.92
1977	156.45	173.15	182.92	162.66	171.53	192.84	197.84	180.02	174.65	167.48	157.87	144.87
1978	135.08	128.14	153.35	156.1	142.19	135.68	143.47	152.43	170.09	173.57	182.77	179.03
1979	165.77	158.85	154.02	147.29	152.32	157.82	147.47	142.18	146.13	138.72	136.77	144.52
1980	143.63	146.78	140.18	131.97	117.24	113.27	111.77	104.85	108.2	104.54	98.57	95.7
1981	94.94	92.57	95.97	95.69	87.68	75.31	92.91	101.92	106.01	98.55	93.28	95.46
1982	99.25	94.67	88.35	79.17	77.79	71.29	71.59	70.74	76.48	74.29	69.91	74.55
1983	80.93	88.1	84.34	85.15	93.67	104.22	104.45	104.46	96.98	95	100.68	115.25
1984	118.93	113.28	115.04	115.05	121.45	112.72	100.54	100.41	104.83	102.39	102.29	97.09
1985	100.68	103.12	101.26	101.64	96.57	94.88	100.24	103.21	106.24	107.19	104.22	107.93
1986	105.4	100.63	95.58	90.25	86.44	86.48	91.74	93.79	100.08	94.03	91.65	89.65
1987	89.66	88.83	91.16	93.88	93.82	90.74	95.93	91.7	90.16	86.73	87.91	86.05
1988	89.5	81.6	76.44	74.8	77.42	73.67	72.95	65.67	56.21	59.16	66.96	68.12
1989	65.17	67.23	63.9	58.57	54.78	56.8	61.02	58.29	51.75	48.25	45.79	44.01
1990	45.12	46.56	51.32	60.58	65.61	60.08	61.04	58.53	62.21	59.31	61.32	58.69
1991	56.36	55.1	54.9	51.97	48.18	47.21	46.75	51.66	57.8	58.97	59.68	61.99
1992	58.17	54.1	51.19	47.37	45.15	43.66	50	53.43	51.03	48.58	48.8	46.98
1993	46.97	45.22	44.24	45.92	45.24	44.78	48.1	49.76	57.51	58.63	60.29	61.47
1994	57.33	55.74	59.29	56.36	62.5	66.18	70.41	70.37	67.4	65.68	65.18	63.48
1995	66.63	68.51	67.36	66.64	65.56	65.19	61.87	64.09	63.36	63.26	65.16	62.54
1996	61.21	62.14	60.72	66.06	69.13	69.74	67.84	68.03	66.96	67	66.65	66.88
1997	64.8	62.27	69.11	71.26	71.14	76.58	76.08	74.94	80.27	78.99	76.87	78.8
1998	75.67	74.43	77.98	78.31	81.39	78.1	77.67	76.37	76.54	74.68	72.34	68.71
1999	66.01	63.89	59.57	53.8	48.2	52.7	50.5	47.92	48.14	46.33	41.84	41.67
2000	41.63	38.97	42.32	41.34	41.23	42.71	42.49	39.82	40.06	39.83	36.33	36.45
2001	43.84	52.48	51	49.06	48.97	44.1	43.87	46.91	46.26	49.21	56.28	60.64
2002	62.79	67.67	72.21	71.18	72.82	75.24	84.76	88.93	98.16	100.03	82.29	91.75
2003	99.1	101.57	90.48	87.44	79.37	71.63	70.78	71.28	74.01	67.22	68.54	73.81
2004	73.68	71.17	68.24	65.2	64.13	63.86	70.74	78.44				

a/ The table is taken from the web site of the International Cocoa Organization, http://www.icco.org/prices/pricesave.htm. The daily price for cocoa beans is calculated using the average of the quotations of the nearest three active future trading months on the London Cocoa Terminal Market and on the New York Coffee, Sugar and Cocoa Exchange at the time of the London close.

b/ To determine the price in US dollars per metric ton, multiply by 2204.6

Respondent's Exhibit No. 4

Contract: Sugar 2212

SOLD BY: Equatoriana Commodity Exporters, S.A.
TO: Mediterraneo Confectionary Associates, Inc.

2,500 metric tons of sound Raw Centrifugal Cane Sugar in bulk at 7 cents net cash U.S. currency per pound (USD 154.32 per metric ton) based on 97 degrees average polarization with standard adjustment for other grades. Total contract price USD 385,805 payable ten days after delivery.

The sugar delivered under this contract shall have been manufactured no earlier than twelve (12) calendar months preceding the delivery month specified below. Seller shall be responsible for all expenses pertaining to delivery and loading of sugar into the vessel, including freight taxes and other taxes of the country of origin of any nature. Normal pilotage, wharfage charges, customs fees and similar charges pertaining to the entry or exit of the vessel at loading port are for the account of the Buyer. Sugar delivered shall be free and clear of all liens and claims of any kind. The sugar delivered shall be freely available for export.

Delivery during December 2003 to be made by Oceania Sugar Producers, FOB (Incoterms 2000) Port Hope, Oceania to Buyer's nominated vessel.

Any disputes arising with respect to or in connection with this agreement shall be finally decided by three arbitrators in Port Hope, Oceania in accordance with the Rules of Arbitration of the Oceania Commodity Association in English.

(Signed)
Equatoriana Commodity Exporters, S.A.

20 November 2003

(Signed)
Mediterraneo Confectionary Associates, Inc.

21 November 2003

Respondent's Exhibit No. 5

Mediterraneo Confectionary Associates, Inc.
121 Sweet Street
Capitol City, Mediterraneo
Telephone (0) 555–1235
Telefax number (0) 555–1237

19 December 2003

Mr. Gerold Hunt
Equatoriana Commodity Exporters, S.A.
325 Commodities Avenue
Port City, Equatoriana

Post and Fax (0) 487–2320

Re: Your Sugar Contract 2212

Dear Mr. Hunt:

This is to confirm our telephone conversation of today. The shipment of sugar under your contract 2212 arrived on Monday, 15 December. It was soaked and has become contaminated. It obviously cannot be used at all for the confectionary purposes for which it was purchased and we are of the opinion that it cannot be used for human consumption at all.

From all appearances the sugar became fouled prior to loading into the containers. Under the circumstances we will not be paying the purchase price. Moreover, we would like to know what you wish to be done with the sugar.

Sincerely,
(Signed)
Robert Sawyer

Respondent's Exhibit No. 6

OCEANIA SHIPPING LINES

CARGO RECEIPT

Goods: 2,500 metric tons bagged sugar

Received from: Oceania Sugar Producers

Condition: Apparent good condition

Purpose: Stuff into container for shipment

Vessel: Oceania Condor

Sailing date:

Destination: Capitol City, Mediterraneo

Notify party: Mediterraneo Confectionary Associates, Inc.
Telephone: (0) 555–1235

(Signed)

4 December 2003

THIS IS NOT A SHIPPING DOCUMENT

SWISS CHAMBERS' ARBITRATION

Chambers of Commerce and Industry of Basel Berne Geneva Lausanne Lugano Zurich www.swissarbitration.ch

FedEx

Horace Fasttrack, Esq.
Advocate at the Court
75 Court Street
Capitol City
Mediterraneo

FedEx

Joseph Langweiler, Esq.
Lawyer
14 Capitol Boulevard
Oceania
Equatoriana

Case no 30000–2004

Geneva, August 13, 2004

Re: Mediterraneo Confectionary Associates Inc. versus Equatoriana Commodity Exporters SA

Dear Sirs,

We acknowledge receipt of the Answer to the Notice of arbitration and Counterclaim received from Equatoriana Commodity Exporters SA by fax on August 10, 2004, and by mail on August 12, 2004, a copy of which is enclosed herewith for the Claimant.

We thank the Respondent for the payment of the amount of CHF 4'500 representing the fees for the Counterclaim, received on August 12, 2004.

In view of the Notice of arbitration and of the Counterclaim, the amount in dispute does not exceed CHF 1'000'000. Pursuant to Article 42, paragraph 2(a) of the Swiss Rules, the arbitral proceedings shall therefore be conducted in accordance with the **Expedited Procedure**.

In view of the letter received from the Claimant on July 21, 2004 (a copy of which is enclosed herewith for the Respondent) and of the Respondent's Answer to the Notice of arbitration, the parties have not agreed to designate a sole arbitrator. The arbitration will thus be subject to a tribunal composed of three members as provided in the arbitration clause, and the fees of the three arbitrators will be computed in accordance with Section 2.8 of Appendix B (cf. Article 42, paragraph 2(c) of the Swiss Rules).

Each party is now invited to designate its arbitrator by **August 31st, 2004**, pursuant to Article 8, paragraph 1 of the Swiss Rules. Failing such designation, the Chamber shall appoint the arbitrator(s) in accordance with Article 8, paragraph 2 of the Rules.

The parties are kindly advised that all designations of arbitrators by the parties are subject to confirmation by the Chamber, pursuant to Article 5 of the Swiss Rules.

Finally, the Chamber notes that the counterclaim appears to arise out of a different contract than the claim, which contract contains an arbitration agreement referring to the Rules of Arbitration of the Oceania Commodity Association. If appropriate, it will be for the arbitral tribunal to rule on its jurisdiction (Article 21, paragraph 5) over the counterclaim.

Yours faithfully,

(Signed)
Daniela Jobin
Member of the Arbitration Committee

Enclosures: – Answer and Counterclaim, for the Claimant
– Copy of the letter by Claimant of July 21, 2004, for the Respondent

Chamber of Commerce and Industry of Geneva • Boulevard du Théâtre 4 • 1204 Geneva
Tel. +4122 819 91 11 • Fax +4122 819 91 36 • arbitration@ccig.ch **2/2**

Horace Fasttrack
Advocate at the Court
75 Court Street
Capitol City, Mediterraneo
Tel. (0) 146–9845
Telefax (0) 146–9850

31 August 2004

Mme Daniela Jobin
Chamber of Commerce and Industry of Geneva
4, Boulevard du Théâtre
P.O. Box 5039
CH–1211 Geneva 11
Switzerland

Re: Case no 30000–2004

Mediterraneo Confectionary Associates Inc. versus Equatoriana Commodity Exporters SA

Dear Mme Jobin:

I acknowledge your letter of 13 August 2004 enclosing the answer and counter-claim of Equatoriana Commodity Exporters, S.A.

Enclosed is the Answer to the counter-claim. There will indeed be a challenge to the jurisdiction of the tribunal to hear the counter-claim.

As you have requested, Dr. Claimant Arbitrator is hereby nominated to serve as the claimant appointed arbitrator. Dr. Claimant Arbitrator has his office at 423 River St. Riverside, Mediterraneo. A copy of his curriculum vitae is attached.

Sincerely yours,

(Signed)
Horace Fasttrack

Encl: Dr. Claimant Arbitrator, curriculum vitae [Not included in Moot Problem]

Swiss Chambers' Arbitration

Case no 30000–2004

Re: Mediterraneo Confectionary Associates Inc. versus Equatoriana Commodity Exporters SA

Answer to Counter-Claim

I. Transaction

1. The intended purchase of 2,500 metric tons of sugar from Equatoriana Commodity Exporters, S.A. took place as described in the counter-claim. As set forth in the letter from Mr. Robert Sawyer to Mr. Gerold Hunt of Equatoriana Commodity Exporters, S.A. dated 19 December 2003, when the sugar arrived it was unusable for human consumption. Attached as Claimant's Exhibit No. 12 is the report by the surveyor.

II. Legal Argument

A. The Tribunal lacks jurisdiction to hear the counter-claim

2. The contract contained an arbitration clause calling for arbitration in Port Hope, Oceania in accordance with the Rules of Arbitration of the Oceania Commodity Association. The reason for choosing arbitration before the Oceania Commodity Association was that the sugar was supplied by Oceania Sugar Producers and delivered to the carrier in Port Hope, Oceania. Furthermore, the Oceania Commodity Association is specialized in commodity arbitrations.

3. There would normally be no question of jurisdiction under the Swiss Rules given the arbitration clause in the contract. The only basis for jurisdiction is Article 21(5), which provides "The arbitral tribunal shall have jurisdiction to hear a set-off defence even when the relationship out of which this defence is said to arise is not within the scope of the arbitration clause or is the object of another arbitration agreement or forum-selection clause."

4. Article 21(5) cannot give jurisdiction to the Tribunal to consider the dispute between Mediterraneo Confectionary Associates, Inc. and Equatoriana Commodity Exporters, S.A. Mediterraneo Confectionary Associates, Inc. and Equatoriana Commodity Exporters, S.A. never agreed to the provision. When they entered into cocoa contract 1045 they contracted for the Rules of Arbitration of the Chamber of Commerce and Industry of Geneva. Those Rules to which they agreed, which are still in existence and apply to domestic Swiss arbitrations, contain no provision of this type that purports to give a tribunal organized under the Swiss Rules jurisdiction even though the dispute "is the object of another arbitration agreement or forum-selection clause." While Mediterraneo Confectionary Associates, Inc. does not object to the general application of the Swiss Rules considered as a new version of the Geneva Rules as applicable to international arbitrations, it does object to the application of Article 21(5).

B. Article 21(5) covers only set-off defences and not counter-claims

5. Article 21(5) states that it applies to set-off defences. It does not say that it gives jurisdiction to the Tribunal to consider counter-claims. Equatoriana Commodity Exporters, S.A. itself labels its discussion of the dispute in regard to sugar contract 2212 as a counter-claim. It thereby recognizes that its claim in regard to that contract cannot be heard by this Tribunal. If it wishes to institute an arbitration, it must do so as provided in the arbitration clause, namely under the rules of the Oceania Commodity Association.

6. If the tribunal rules that it does have jurisdiction, the maximum extent of relief that Equatoriana Commodity Exporters, S.A. could receive would be a set-off against the recovery that will be awarded Mediterraneo Confectionary Associates, Inc. in its claim.

C. The sugar was unfit for human consumption

7. As noted above, when the sugar arrived, it was unfit for human consumption. As a consequence of the fundamental breach of contract by Equatoriana Commodity Exporters, S.A., Mediterraneo Confectionary Associates, Inc. is not obligated to pay the purchase price.

III. Plea

8. Mediterraneo Confectionary Associates, Inc. requests the Tribunal to declare
   - that it has no jurisdiction to consider the counter-claim;
   - that, if it has jurisdiction, it would only be to consider the assertions of Equatoriana Commodity Exporters, S.A as a set-off defense and not as a counter-claim;
   - that, if it has jurisdiction, Mediterraneo Confectionary Associates, Inc. is not obligated to pay the price for the sugar because it was unfit for human consumption when it was delivered.

(Signed)
Horace Fasttrack

31 August 2004

(Claimant's Exhibit No. 12)

[Damage report by surveyor. Not included in the Problem.]

Joseph Langweiler
Lawyer
14 Capitol Boulevard
Oceanside, Equatoriana

31 August 2004

Mme Daniela Jobin
Chamber of Commerce and Industry of Geneva
4, Boulevard du Théâtre
P.O. Box 5039
CH–1211 Geneva 11
Switzerland

Re: Case no 30000–2004

Mediterraneo Confectionary Associates Inc. versus Equatoriana Commodity Exporters SA

Dear Mme Jobin:

I wish to acknowledge receipt of your letter of 13 August 2004 in which you invite the two parties to this arbitration to designate an arbitrator by 31 August 2004.

I should like to inform you that the respondent designates Mr. Respondent Arbitrator, 114 Seaview St., Oceanside, Equatoriana, as the respondent nominated arbitrator.

Sincerely,

(Signed)
Joseph Langweiler

Encl. CV Mr. Respondent Arbitrator [Not included in Moot Problem]

SWISS CHAMBERS' ARBITRATION

Chambers of Commerce and Industry of | Basel Berne Geneva Lausanne Lugano Zurich | www.swissarbitration.ch

FedEx

Dr. Claimant Arbitrator, Esq.
423 River St.
Riverside
Equatoriana

Case no 30000–2004

Geneva, September 3, 2004

Re: Mediterraneo Confectionary Associates Inc. versus Equatoriana Commodity Exporters SA

Dear Sir,

We are pleased to inform you that you have been designated by the Claimant as arbitrator in the above-mentioned case, in which the Chamber of commerce and industry of Geneva is the administrating institution.

The arbitration shall be conducted under the Swiss Rules of International Arbitration, a copy of which is enclosed herewith for your information.

The parties are the following:

Mediterraneo Confectionary Associates, Inc
121 Sweet Street
Capitol City
Mediterraneo

Claimant, represented by

Horace Fasttrack, Esq.
Advocate at the Court
75 Court Street
Capitol City
Mediterraneo
Tel. : + 0 146 9845 / Fax : + 0 146 9850

versus

Equatoriana Commodity Exporters SA
325 Commodity Avenue
Port City
Equatoriana

Respondent, represented by

Joseph Langweiler, Esq.
Lawyer
14 Capitol Boulevard
Oceania
Equatoriana

The claim is based on a contract of purchase of cocoa beans signed by the parties in 2001. The agreement to arbitrate refers to the Chamber of Commerce and Industry of Geneva and the seat of the arbitration is in Vindobona, Danubia. The claim amounts to USD 289'353.

The Respondent has filed a counterclaim, based on a contract of purchase of sugar signed in 2003. The counterclaim amounts to USD 385'805. The agreement to arbitrate refers to the Rules of arbitration of the Oceania Commodity Association, with the seat of the arbitration in Port Hope.

In view of the amount in dispute, the provisions of Article 42 paragraph 2 of the Swiss Rules are applicable to the arbitral proceedings, which shall be conducted in accordance with the **Expedited Procedure**. Consequently, the award shall be made within six months from the date when the Chamber transmitted the file to the Arbitral Tribunal (Art. 42 paragraph 1 (d)).

For your information, the Respondent has designated Dr. Respondent Arbitrator, in Oceanside, Equatoriana, as co-arbitrator.

In order to allow the Arbitration Committee to confirm you as arbitrator pursuant to Article 5, paragraph 1 of the Swiss Rules, we kindly invite you to confirm that you are willing and able to accept the appointment. In this respect, we thank you in advance for completing and returning the attached consent and statement of independence, together with your curriculum vitae.

We look forward to receiving the above in order to be in a position to confirm you soon as arbitrator for the Claimant.

Finally, we would like to stress that prior to your confirmation and receiving the file, you should not take any action in this arbitration.

Please do not hesitate to contact us, should you need further information.

Yours faithfully,

(signed)
Daniela Jobin
Member of the Arbitration Committee

Enclosures – Swiss Rules of International Arbitration
– Statement of independence

CC to the parties

[A similar letter was sent to the arbitrator designated by the Respondent]

SWISS CHAMBERS' ARBITRATION

Chambers of Commerce and Industry of Basel, Berne, Geneva, Lausanne, Lugano, Zurich www.swissarbitration.ch

Arbitration No: 30000–2004

CONSENT TO APPOINTMENT

and

STATEMENT OF INDEPENDENCE

Name:

(1) I hereby consent to my appointment as arbitrator in this arbitration.

(2) I undertake to act in accordance with the Swiss Rules of International Arbitration applicable to this arbitration.

(3) I declare that I am, and shall remain, impartial and independent of the parties.

(4) **(Please delete whichever of the following two statements does not apply)**

(i) I further declare that to the best of my knowledge, there are no circumstances, past or present, likely to give rise to justifiable doubts as to my impartiality or independence.

(ii) In accordance with Art 9, paragraph 2 of the Swiss Rules I wish to disclose the following circumstances: **(Use separate sheet.)** To the best of my belief, these circumstances do not impair my impartiality or independence.

(5) I undertake to disclose to the Chamber of Commerce and to all parties, any circumstances arising in the future which are likely to give rise to justifiable doubts as to my impartiality or independence, until the arbitration is concluded.

Signed: Date: ________________________

Chamber of Commerce and Industry of Geneva • Boulevard du Théâtre 4 • 1204 Geneva
Tel. +4122 819 91 11 • Fax +4122 819 91 36 • arbitration@ccig.ch **3/3**

Dr. Claimant Arbitrator
423 River St.
Riverside, Mediterraneo

6 September 2004

Mme Daniela Jobin
Chamber of Commerce and Industry of Geneva
4, Boulevard du Théâtre
P.O. Box 5039
CH-1211 Geneva 11
Switzerland

Re: Case no 30000–2004

Mediterraneo Confectionary Associates Inc. versus Equatoriana Commodity Exporters SA

Dear Mme. Jobin:

I acknowledge receipt of your letter of 3 September 2004 in which you inquire whether there are any circumstances likely to give rise to justifiable doubts as to my impartiality or independence as arbitrator in the above-referenced matter.

There are no such circumstances and I shall be privileged to receive confirmation from the Swiss Chambers of my nomination as an arbitrator. A completed copy of the form you sent me is attached.

Yours sincerely,

(Signed)
Claimant Arbitrator

Encl. Consent to appointment form

[A similar letter was received from Mr. Respondent Arbitrator.]

SWISS CHAMBERS' ARBITRATION

Chambers of Commerce and Industry of Basel Berne Geneva Lausanne Lugano Zurich www.swissarbitration.ch

FedEx

Dr Claimant Arbitrator, Esq.
423 River Street
Riverside
Mediterraneo

FedEx

Respondent Arbitrator, Esq.
114, Seaview St.
Oceanside
Equatoriana

Case no 30000–2004

Geneva, September 13, 2004

Re: Mediterraneo Confectionary Associates Inc. versus Equatoriana Commodity Exporters SA

Dear Sirs,

Thank you for your letters of September 6, 2004.

I have the pleasure to inform you that the Arbitration Committee has confirmed you as co-arbitrators in the matter mentioned above, pursuant to Article 5 of the Swiss Rules. You will find enclosed a copy of your respective statements of independence.

In accordance with Article 8, paragraph 2 and Article 42, paragraph 1(a) of the Swiss Rules, you are invited, **within fifteen days from receipt of this letter** to designate the presiding arbitrator. Failing such designation, the Chamber shall appoint the presiding arbitrator.

We thank you in advance and remain

Yours faithfully,

(signed)
Daniela Jobin
Member of the Arbitration Committee

Encl.: – Copy of your respective statement of independence [not included in Moot Problem]

CC to the parties

Chamber of Commerce and Industry of Geneva • Boulevard du Théâtre 4 • 1204 Geneva
Tel. +4122 819 91 11 • Fax +4122 819 91 36 • arbitration@ccig.ch **1/1**

Dr. Claimant Arbitrator
423 River St.
Riverside, Mediterraneo

16 September 2004

Mme Daniela Jobin
Chamber of Commerce and Industry of Geneva
4, Boulevard du Théâtre
P.O. Box 5039
CH-1211 Geneva 11
Switzerland

Re: Case no 30000–2004

Mediterraneo Confectionary Associates Inc. versus Equatoriana Commodity Exporters SA

Dear Mme. Jobin:

Upon the receipt of your letters confirming our appointment as arbitrators in the above referenced case, Mr. Respondent Arbitrator and I conferred by telephone in regard to the naming of the presiding arbitrator. We have agreed to designate Professor Presiding Arbitrator. We have discussed his designation as presiding arbitrator with him and he is in agreement. Professor Presiding Arbitrator is a well known arbitrator in Danubia and he has presided over a number of international arbitrations.
I attach a copy of his curriculum vitae.
His address is Schiedsgericht Strasse 36, Vindobona, Danubia.

Yours sincerely,

(Signed)
Claimant Arbitrator

Encl. CV Professor Presiding Arbitrator [Not included in Moot Problem.]

[A letter was sent to Professor Presiding Arbitrator requesting a statement as to his impartiality and independence similar to that sent to the two party designated arbitrators and he sent the requested statement.]

SWISS CHAMBERS' ARBITRATION

Chambers of Commerce and Industry of Basel, Berne, Geneva, Lausanne, Lugano, Zurich — www.swissarbitration.ch

FedEx	**Professor Presiding Arbitrator, Esq.** Schiedsgericht Strasse 36 Vindobona, Danubia
FedEx	**Dr Claimant Arbitrator, Esq.** 423 River Street Riverside, Mediterraneo
FedEx	**Respondent Arbitrator, Esq.** 114, Seaview St. Oceanside, Equatoriana
Case no 30000–2004	Geneva, September 22, 2004

Re:* *Mediterraneo Confectionary Associates Inc. versus Equatoriana Commodity Exporters SA

Dear Sirs,

I thank Prof. Presiding Arbitrator for his letter of September 21, 2004, a copy of which is enclosed herewith for the co-arbitrators.

I have the pleasure to inform you that the Arbitration Committee has confirmed Prof. Presiding Arbitrator as Chairman of the arbitral tribunal, pursuant to Article 5 of the Swiss Rules. Thus, I am pleased to provide you with the file, including all relevant documents transmitted by the parties.

In accordance with Article 41 paragraph 1 of the Swiss Rules, you are now invited to request the parties to pay the deposit on the cost of the arbitration. We thank you in advance for providing the Chamber with a copy of such request.

We take this opportunity to remind you that the Agreement to arbitrate provides that the arbitration is subject to the **Expedited Procedure**, pursuant to Article 42 paragraph 1 of the Swiss Rules.

Finally, the Arbitration Committee would be most grateful if you could provide it with a copy of the time-tables containing the steps of the proceedings (Art. 15 paragraph 3 of Swiss Rules).

We thank you in advance for your kind cooperation and remain

Yours faithfully,

(signed)

Daniela Jobin
Member of the Arbitration Committee

Chamber of Commerce and Industry of Geneva • Boulevard du Théâtre 4 • 1204 Geneva
Tel. +4122 819 91 11 • Fax +4122 819 91 36 • arbitration@ccig.ch **1/1**

SWISS CHAMBERS' ARBITRATION

Chambers of Commerce and Industry of Basel Berne Geneva Lausanne Lugano Zurich

www.swissarbitration.ch

FedEx

Horace Fasttrack, Esq.
Advocate at the Court
75 Court Street
Capitol City
Mediterraneo

FedEx

Joseph Langweiler, Esq.
Lawyer
14 Capitol Boulevard
Oceania
Equatoriana

Case no 30000–2004 Geneva, September 22, 2004

Re Mediterraneo Confectionary Associates Inc. versus Equatoriana Commodity Exporters SA

Dear Sirs,

Please be advised that, according to Article 5 of the Swiss Rules, the Arbitration Committee has confirmed Professor Presiding Arbitrator as Chairman of the arbitral tribunal.

The parties will find enclosed herewith a copy of the statement of independence received from Prof. Presiding Arbitrator, together with his curriculum vitae.

The Arbitration Committee transmitted today the file to the arbitral tribunal, as mentioned in our letter of this day to the arbitrators, a copy of which is attached herewith for your information.

The parties are invited to communicate henceforth directly with the arbitral tribunal.

Yours faithfully,

(signed)
Daniela Jobin
Member of the Arbitration Committee

Enclosure: – Copy of the letter from Prof. Presiding Arbitrator [Not enclosed in Moot Problem]
– Copy of our letter of this day to the parties

Chamber of Commerce and Industry of Geneva • Boulevard du Théâtre 4 • 1204 Geneva
Tel. +4122 819 91 11 • Fax +4122 819 91 36 • arbitration@ccig.ch **1/1**

Swiss Chambers' Arbitration

Case no 30000–2004

Mediterraneo Confectionary Associates Inc. versus Equatoriana Commodity Exporters SA

Procedural Order No. 1

1. The Arbitral Tribunal, composed of Mr.______, Dr.______, and myself as chairman, has authorized me in conformity with the Swiss Rules for International Arbitration, Article 31(2) to make procedural rulings alone.

2. On 30 September 2004____________________, counsel for the Claimant, Mediterraneo Confectionary Associates, Inc.,________________________, counsel for the Respondent, Equatoriana Commodity Exporters, S.A. and I had a conference call in which we discussed the procedures that should be followed in the arbitration. Because of the special nature of this Moot arbitration, it was agreed that the objections raised by Mediterraneo Confectionary Associates, Inc. to the counter-claim filed by Equatoriana Commodity Exporters, S.A. would be considered at the same time as the substantive claim of Mediterraneo Confectionary Associates, Inc.

3. Counsel agreed that the Tribunal might be able to decide the claim presented by Mediterraneo Confectionary Associates, Inc. on legal issues alone, without the need for an extensive procedure to determine facts beyond those already set forth in the Statement of Claim and the Statement of Defense.

4. In regard to the counter-claim, it will first be necessary to decide whether the tribunal should consider it on the merits and, if so, whether the relief granted to Equatoriana Commodity Exporters, S.A. should be limited to a set-off to any relief granted to Mediterraneo Confectionary Associates, Inc. in its claim. If the tribunal does decide to consider the counter-claim on the merits, it would be necessary at a later time to engage in a more detailed examination of the condition of the sugar at the time the risk of loss passed from Equatoriana Commodity Exporters, S.A. to Mediterraneo Confectionary Associates, Inc.

5. As noted above, it is not expected that there will need to be an extensive procedure to determine facts at this stage of the arbitration. Those factual issues that may need to be developed at this first stage of the arbitration will be determined in accordance with the procedures found in the Rules of the Twelfth Annual Willem C. Vis International Commercial Arbitration Moot. In accordance with those Rules questions may be submitted to Professor Eric Bergsten, preferably by e-mail at eric.bergsten@chello.at, by Friday, 22 October 2004. The answers are expected to be distributed to all parties by 29 October 2004.

6. It was agreed that the memoranda should be prepared by Mediterraneo Confectionary Associates, Inc. for submission by e-mail by 9 December 2004 followed by hard copy in the required number to arrive by 15 December 2004. Equatoriana Commodity Exporters, S.A. is to submit its memorandum by e-mail by 27 January 2005 followed by hard copy in the required numbers to arrive by 1 February 2005.

7. The memoranda should discuss the following issues. In regard to cocoa contract 1045:

- Whether Equatoriana Commodity Exporters, S.A. was excused from delivering the 300 tons by reason of the embargo placed on the export of cocoa by the Equatoriana Government Cocoa Marketing Organization from mid-February to early November 2002;

- If Equatoriana Commodity Exporters, S.A. is not excused, whether Mediterraneo Confectionary Associates, Inc. can claim damages for the late or nondelivery; and

- If Mediterraneo Confectionary Associates, Inc. can claim damages, the proper amount of those damages.

The memoranda should not discuss whether pre-award or post-award interest can be claimed by Mediterraneo Confectionary Associates, Inc. There should also be no discussion of the allocation of the costs of arbitration.

8. In respect of sugar contract 2212, the memoranda should discuss whether the tribunal has jurisdiction to consider the counter-claim. The memoranda should also discuss whether, if the tribunal has jurisdiction to consider the counter-claim, the recovery would be limited to a set-off against any recovery that Mediterraneo Confectionary Associates, Inc. might recover in regard to the cocoa contract.

9. Oral arguments will be scheduled in the month of March 2005 in Vienna and in April in Hong Kong. All participants in the Vienna arguments will be invited to a welcoming event followed by a reception on the evening of Friday, 18 March 2005. Arguments will take place beginning the following morning, Saturday, 19 March 2005. Participants will also be invited to a welcoming party sponsored by the Moot Alumni Association on Thursday evening, 17 March 2005. Participants in the Hong Kong arguments will receive their schedule at a later time.

(Signed)
President of the Tribunal

1 October 2004

Swiss Chambers' Arbitration

Case no 30000–2004

Mediterraneo Confectionary Associates Inc. versus Equatoriana Commodity Exporters SA

Procedural Order No. 2

Following the procedure agreed upon by the parties and set forth in Procedural Order No. 1, the parties have submitted a number of requests for clarifications. The responses to those requests are set forth below.

Legal Rules and Arbitration

1. Are Danubia, Equatoriana, Mediterraneo and Oceania common law or civil law countries?

Equatoriana and Oceania are civil law. Mediterraneo and Danubia are common law and English speaking.

2. What is the period of limitations (prescription) for bringing a contractual claim in the relevant legal system?

Equatoriana, Mediterraneo and Oceania are all party to the Convention on the Limitation Period in the International Sale of Goods. The Convention can be found on the UNCITRAL web site. The period of limitation in the Convention is four years.

3. Is Oceania a party to the Convention on the Recognition and Enforcement of Foreign Arbitral Awards?

Yes.

4. Do the Rules of Arbitration of the Oceania Commodity Association contain any provision on counter-claims or set-offs?

The provision is identical to Article 19(3) of the UNCITRAL Arbitration Rules.

"In his statement of defence, or at a later stage in the arbitral proceedings if the arbitral tribunal decides that the delay was justified under the circumstances, the respondent may make a counter-claim arising out of the same contract or rely on a claim arising out of the same contract for the purpose of a set-off."

5. Was the adoption of the Swiss Rules of International Arbitration and their replacement for international arbitration of the arbitration rules of the six chambers of commerce, including Geneva, publicized?

The adoption of the Swiss Rules was well publicized in interested circles and known by lawyers who engage in international commercial arbitrations. The arbitration rules of each of the six chambers of commerce, including Geneva, continue to be valid for domestic Swiss arbitrations.

6. Would there be a significant difference between arbitration in a specialized body such as the Oceania Commodity Association and a body for international commercial arbitration in general, as provided in the Swiss Rules?

Commodity exchanges and many trade associations have an associated arbitration facility for disputes arising in the particular exchange or trade. Those arbitration facilities would be subject to the same arbitration law as any other arbitration facility in the same country. They would have their own rules and arbitrators would almost always come from the members of the exchange or participants in the trade concerned. The use of the associated arbitration facility is required for exchange traded contracts under the rules of commodity exchanges such as the New York Board of Trade and LIFFE and for contracts between members of many trade associations. Specialized arbitration facilities are particularly useful when the dispute is in regard to the quality of the commodities delivered or where specialized practices in the trade are concerned. Where the dispute involves general questions of law or trade practices, specialized arbitration facilities have no particular advantage over arbitration institutions for international commercial arbitration in general. Of course, where the parties have a choice of arbitration institution, the choice is normally made in the underlying contract at the time of sale and not later when the nature of the dispute is known.

The two parties in this case do not belong to any association that would require arbitration in any particular arbitration institution. Cocoa and sugar are the only two commodities sold by Equatoriana Commodity Exporters, S.A. to Mediterraneo Confectionary Associates, Inc. and all the contracts had the same arbitration clauses as found in the two contracts in question.

Cocoa contract

7. Did the various persons involved in this case act within the scope of their authority?

Yes. It might be mentioned that the arbitral center always demands a written power of attorney of the legal representatives of the parties. Those documents were submitted but are not included in the case file.

8. Does Equatoriana often experience storms in the cocoa growing area?

Storms occur in Equatoriana, as they do in most places. The storm on 14 February 2002 was the first storm in 22 years that had caused damage to the cocoa trees. The damage in 1980 was not extensive.

9. Were cocoa growing areas in other countries affected by the storm?

No.

10. When was the export ban ordered and when did it end?

The first order was on 22 February 2002 and covered the month of March 2002. On 20 March 2002 the order was extended until further notice. The export ban was rescinded on 12 November 2002.

11. What is the authority and procedures of the Equatoriana Government Cocoa Marketing Organization?

The Organization is an official entity. It has a monopoly on the purchase of cocoa from the producers. It does not sell to buyers outside Equatoriana. There are a few local users of the cocoa beans that purchase from the Organization, but the vast majority of the cocoa is sold to exporters, such as Equatoriana Commodity Exporters. The Organization stores the cocoa in its warehouses. When an exporter enters into an export contract it places an order with the Organization for an equivalent amount. Delivery to the ultimate purchaser is made directly from the Organization's warehouse on the delivery date or during the delivery period, March to May 2002 in this case. The usual procedure was followed in respect of cocoa contract 1045 up to the export embargo.

12. Could Equatoriana Commodity Exporters, S.A. have petitioned against the export embargo or asked for an exemption from it?

There was no legal procedure available for Equatoriana Commodity Exporters, S.A. to protest the export embargo. It could always have asked for an exemption. It did not do so. Several other exporters did ask for exemptions and all were rejected.

13. How long has Equatoriana Commodity Exporters, S.A. been in business and do they have a good reputation?

It has been in business since 1961 and it has a good reputation.

14. Has Equatoriana Commodity Exporters, S.A. ever supplied anyone with cocoa beans that did not originate in Equatoriana?

No. As indicated in both the Statement of Claim and the Statement of Defense, on occasion it trades commodities produced in other countries. It could do so with cocoa beans, but it never has. The sale of cocoa beans represents about 20 per cent of its total business.

15. Was cocoa contract 1045 on a standard form of Equatoriana Commodity Exporters, S.A.?

Yes. Equatoriana Commodity Exporters, S.A. adapted the contract form from the form to be found in the New York Board of Trade Cocoa Rules 9.03.

16. To what did the words "usual terms" refer to in Claimant's Exhibit No. 1?

They referred to the contract form as used in contract 1045, which had been used in all previous cocoa contracts.

17. What do the words "at par" mean as used in the New York Board of Trade Cocoa Rules (Respondent's Exhibit 1) in regard to Group C?

Contracts are traded on the New York Board of Trade, and on LIFFE in London, for future delivery of cocoa among members of the exchange. The contracts are absolutely standardized except for the price. The New York Cocoa Rules call for the following procedure. At specified periodical intervals the contracts that each member has purchased are set off against contracts that the member has sold. A member that has sold more contracts than he has purchased must be prepared to deliver physical cocoa to a member that has bought more contracts than he has sold. Only about two per cent of the contracts result in physical delivery of cocoa. The cocoa that is to be delivered is already in a warehouse licensed by the exchange. In fulfillment of an exchange traded contract the seller can deliver cocoa produced anywhere that he has stored in a warehouse. Nevertheless, since cocoa from places listed in Group A is of a higher quality, the buyer must pay the seller USD 160 per metric ton in addition to the price for the contract. If cocoa from a place listed in Group C is delivered, no additional payment need be made. It will be noted that Group C includes a number of named countries and "all other growths not presently specified above." Cocoa from Equatoriana is not specified, so it would fall within Group C.

The prices for any given commodity—here cocoa—paid on the major exchanges establish the world-wide market price for that commodity. Contracts such as cocoa contract 1045 are negotiated on the basis of the prices for cocoa being paid on the exchange, though they often vary from that price for specific reasons, such as the quantity purchased. Similarly, the price in those individually negotiated contracts will reflect what is to be found in the exchange rules, namely that the cost of cocoa from places listed in Group A in the New York rules is higher than for cocoa from places in Group C.

18. What do the words "standard grade and count" mean?

Reference is made to the full text of NYBOT[fi] Cocoa Rule 9.18 at the URL noted in Respondent's Exhibit No. 1 for an explanation.

19. Did Mediterraneo Confectionary Associates, Inc. know that the cocoa delivered in its previous contracts with Equatoriana Commodity Exporters, S.A. came from Equatoriana?

Yes. Origin was always known since it was the buyer's responsibility to arrange for the carriage of the goods. Moreover, the bags in which the cocoa was packed indicated their origin.

20. Did either country, Mediterraneo or Equatoriana, have any regulations that would have required that the cocoa be of Equatoriana origin?

No.

21. Was anything said in the telephone call of 5 March 2002, referred to in Mr. Sweet's letter of 5 March 2002, in regard to a date by which delivery had to be made?

No, other than that Mediterraneo Confectionary Associates, Inc. expected delivery during the contractual period, which would not expire for almost three months.

22. Was there any communication between Mediterraneo Confectionary Associates, Inc. and Equatoriana Commodity Exporters Mr. Sweet's letter of 15 August 2002 and the purchase of the 300 tons of cocoa on 24 October 2002?

There was one telephone call from Mr. Smart to Mr. Sweet on 29 September 2002 in which he said that there was no indication as yet as to when the export ban would be rescinded. Mr. Sweet reiterated the concerns expressed in his letter of 15 August 2002.

23. Has there ever been a legal dispute between Mediterraneo Confectionary Associates, Inc. and Equatoriana Commodity Exporters or unilateral avoidance of the contract?

No.

24. What are the yearly requirements for cocoa of Mediterraneo Confectionary Associates, Inc.?

Its yearly requirements average 1,500 metric tons. The 400 metric tons contracted for would, therefore, equal slightly over its average requirements for three months. By the time of its purchase of 300 metric tons on 24 October 2002 it had slightly more than 100 metric tons in inventory. Around the end of November it would have had to cease producing certain of its products unless it had received additional cocoa. All that it purchases is used in its confectionary business. It never purchases cocoa for resale.

25. Could Mediterraneo Confectionary Associates, Inc. have purchased the 300 tons from a different supplier at a lower price?

There were a multitude of suppliers from whom the cocoa could have been purchased. The purchase was at the then current market price and it is doubtful that a lower price could have been found. Mediterraneo Confectionary Associates, Inc. had purchased from Oceana Produce Ltd. in the past at the market price.

The chart from the International Cocoa Organization in Respondent's Exhibit No. 3 shows the average price paid for cocoa during a given month. It does not show the daily fluctuations. For the purposes of this arbitration (Moot) the prices shown in the chart for any given month are considered to represent the market price for cocoa purchased on any given day during that month.

26. Was the cocoa purchased in the cover contract of the same grade as that from Equatoriana?

Yes.

27. Did the cover purchase price include the transport costs?

In both the contract with Equatoriana Commodity Exporters, S.A. and in the cover contract the transport costs were the responsibility of the buyer. Those costs were slightly higher in the cover contract, but they were not included in the claim. The possibility of including them now is subject to Swiss Rules, Article 20.

28. How much cocoa was released to Equatoriana Commodity Exporters, S.A. by the Equatoriana Government Cocoa Marketing Organization in May?

The Organization required each exporter to submit the contracts they had entered into. The Organization then released specific amounts for each of those contracts. It released 100 metric tons for the contract with Mediterraneo Confectionary Associates, Inc.

29. Could Mediterraneo Confectionary Associates, Inc. have known about the plans of the Organization to terminate the export ban before it purchased the 300 replacement tons?

The rumors that it would do so were circulating in interested circles in Equatoriana and in the cocoa industry world-wide. However, a small purchaser, such as Mediterraneo Confectionary Associates, Inc., would not necessarily have heard them. If called on to do so, the relevant personnel for Mediterraneo Confectionary Associates, Inc. would testify that they did not know of the rumors.

Sugar

30. Was sugar contract 2212 on a standard form of Equatoriana Commodity Exporters, S.A.?

Yes.

31. Why did the sugar contract provide that delivery would be made by Oceania Sugar Producers?

As described in the Statement of Defence, paragraph 2, Equatoriana Commodity Exporters, S.A. trades primarily commodities produced in Equatoriana, although on occasion it trades commodities produced in other countries. On this occasion it sold sugar produced in Oceania. Shipment of the sugar to Mediterraneo Confectionary Associates, Inc. was directly from Oceania by the party that had sold the sugar to Equatoriana Commodity Exporters, S.A.

32. How trustworthy is the statement on the cargo receipt that the sugar was in "apparent good condition" when it was received by Oceania Shipping Lines?

The first issue is whether the tribunal has jurisdiction in regard to the sugar contract. That is to be considered in the memoranda and the oral hearings during the Moot. Only if the tribunal has jurisdiction will the tribunal consider the merits of the dispute at a time subsequent to the Moot. If the sugar was as bad on arrival as claimed, the dispute would revolve around the question of which party bore the risk of loss at the time the deterioration occurred. According to FOB Incoterms 2000, A5 on Transfer of Risks:

> "The seller must, subject to the provisions of B5, bear all risks of loss of or damage to the goods until such time as they have passed the ship's rail at the named port of shipment."

As stated in the Statement of Defence, para. 15, FOB Incoterms 2000, B5 provides that the buyer bears the risk of loss once the goods have passed the ship's rail. In addition, the buyer bears the risk of loss in two situations that are not relevant to the facts in regard to this sugar contract. It will be noted that the cargo receipt states only that the carrier has received the sugar but not that it has yet been loaded on a ship. If the deterioration occurred prior to loading, the seller bears the risk of loss. If the deterioration occurred after loading, the buyer bears the risk of loss. The time of the passage of the risk of loss from seller to buyer is an important factor in each of the thirteen different Incoterms 2000.

(Signed)
President of the Tribunal

30 October 2004

LIST OF ABBREVIATIONS

§	Section
&	and
AAA Rules	American Arbitration Association International Arbitration Rules, 1993
AC	Appeals Court
AG	Amtsgericht
Art.	Article
CA	Court of Appeal/Cour d'appel
CCIG	Rules of Arbitration of the Chamber of Commerce and Industry of Geneva 1992
CENTRAL	Center for Transnational Law, List of Principles, Rules and Standards of the Lex Mercatoria
cf.	compare with
C.I.L.L.	Construction Industry Law Letter
CISG	The United Nations Convention on Contracts for the International Sale of Goods 1980
2nd Cir.	United States Court of Appeals, Second Circuit
CL	Claimant (Stockholm Memorandum)
CLOUT	Case Law on UNCITRAL Texts
Co.	Company
Corp.	Corporation
CLR	Commonwealth Law Reports
Ct.	Court
ECE	Equatoriana Commodity Exporters, S.A.
ed.	Editor *or* Edition
eds.	Editors
et al.	And others
FCA	Federal Court of Australia
FOB	Free on Board (Incoterms 2000)
HCA	High Court of Australia
HL	House of Lords
Inc.	Incorporated
IBA	International Bar Association
ICC	International Chamber of Commerce
ICC Rules	Rules of Arbitration of the International Chamber of Commerce 1998
i.e.	id est (that is)
KG	Kantonsgericht
LCIA Rules	London Court of International Arbitration Rules 1998
LIFFE	London International Financial Futures and Options Exchange

LG	Landesgericht
Ltd.	Limited
MCA	Mediterraneo Confectionary Associates, Inc.
Model Law	UNCITRAL Model Law on International Commercial Arbitration 1985
New York Convention	Convention on the Recognition and Enforcement of Foreign Arbitral Awards, 1958
No.	Number
NYBOT	New York Board of Trade
OGH	Oberster Gerichtshof (Austria)
OLG	Oberlandesgericht
para.	Paragraph
PILR	Pace International Law Review
Pty.	Proprietary
QBD	High Court of Justice (Queen's Bench Division)
RAOCA	Rules of Arbitration of the Oceania Commodity Association
RE	Respondent (Stockholm Memorandum)
SBGH	Schweizeriches Bundesgericht
S.p.A.	Società per azioni
S.r.l.	Società a responsabilità limitata
Swiss Rules	Swiss Rules of International Arbitration 2004
TC Vaud	Tribunal Cantonal Vaud
UNCITRAL	United Nations Commission on International Trade Law
UNIDROIT	International Institute for the Unification of Private Law
US	United States Supreme Court Reports
v.	versus
VCLT	Vienna Convention on the Law of Treaties
vol.	Volume
WIPO	World Intellectual Property Organization
YCA	Yearbook of Commercial Arbitration

LIST OF AUTHORITIES

AMERASINGHE, C.F. — *Jurisdiction of International Tribunals*. The Hague: Kluwer Law International, 2003.
(Cited as Amerasinghe)

BABIAK, A. — "Fundamental Breach Under the UN CISG" 6 *Temple International and Comparative Law Journal* 113–143.
(Cited as Babiak)

BELL, A.S. — "Jurisdiction and Arbitration Agreements in Transnational Contracts" (1996) 11 *Journal of Contract Law* 53–72.
(Cited as Bell)

BERG, A. — "Arbitration: Legal Set-Off and Enforcing Admitted Claims" (2000) 2 *Lloyd's Maritime and Commerical Law Quarterly* 153–160.
(Cited as Berg)

BERGER, K.P. — "Set-Off in International Economic Arbitration" (1999) 15 (1) *Arbitration International* 53–84.
(Cited as Berger (1999))

BIANCA, C.M. & M.J. BONELL (EDS). — *Commentary on the International Sales Law: The 1980 Vienna Sales Convention*. Milan: Giuffrè, 1987.
(Cited as Bianca & Bonell)

BINDER, P. — *International Commercial Arbitration in UNCITRAL Model Law Jurisdictions: An International Comparison of the UNCITRAL Model Law on International Commercial Arbitration*. London: Sweet & Maxwell, 2000.
(Cited as Binder)

BONELL, M.J. (ED). — *A New Approach to International Commercial Contracts: The UNIDROIT Principles of International Commercial Contracts*. The Hague: Kluwer Law International, 1999.
(Cited as Bonell)

BORN, G.B. — *International Commercial Arbitration*. The Hague: Kluwer Law International, 2001.
(Cited as Born)

BOUT, P. — "Trade Usages: Article 9 of the Convention on Contracts for the International Sale of Goods" *Pace Essay Submission* (1998).
URL: *http://www.cisg.law.pace.edu/cisg/biblio/bout.html*
(Cited as Bout)

BRANSON, D.J. & R.E. WALLACE. — "Court-Ordered Consolidated Arbitrations in the United States: Recent Authority Assures Parties the Choice" (1998) 5 (1) *Journal of International Arbitration* 89–94.
(Cited as Branson & Wallace)

BRIDGE, M. — *The International Sale of Goods*. Oxford: University Press, 1999.
(Cited as Bridge)

Burger, L. "The New Swiss Rules of International Arbitration: A Comparative Analysis" (2004) 19 *Mealey's International Arbitration Report* 1–7.
(Cited as Burger)

Burnett, R. *The Law of International Business Transactions* 3rd ed. New South Wales: Federation Press, 2004.
(Cited as Burnett)

Bydlinski, F. "Das Allgemeine Vertragsrecht" *Das UNCITRAL-Kaufrecht im Vergleich zum österreichischen Recht* (Doralt, P. ed., 1985) 52–63.
(Cited as Bydlinski)

Carbonneau, T.E. *Cases and Materials on the Law and Practice of Arbitration* 3rd ed. Huntington NY: Juris Publishing, 2002.
(Cited as Carbonneau)

Carr, I. *International Trade Law*. London: Cavendish Publishing Ltd, 1996.
(Cited as Carr)

Chengwei, L. *Remedies for Non-performance: Perspectives from CISG, UNIDROIT Principles & PECL* 2003.
Reproduced at URL: *http://www.cisg.law.pace.edu/cisg/biblio/chengwei.html*
(Cited as Chengwei)

Chui, J.C. "Consolidation of Arbitral Proceedings and International Commercial Arbitration" (1990) 7 (2) *Journal of International Arbitration* 53–76.
(Cited as Chui)

Coe, J.J. *International Commercial Arbitration: American Principles and Practices in a Global Context*. New York: Transnational Publishers, Inc., 1997.
(Cited as Coe)

Craig, W.L. "Uses and Abuses of Appeal from Awards" (1988) 4 *Arbitration International* 174–227.
(Cited as Craig)

Craig, W., Park, W. & J. Paulsson. *Annotated Guide to the 1998 ICC Arbitration Rules*. Dobbs Ferry: Oceana Publications Inc, 1998.
(Cited as Craig, Park & Paulsson)

D'Arcy, L., Murray, C. & B. Cleave. *Schmitthoff's Export Trade* 10th ed. London: Sweet & Maxwell, 2000.
(Cited as Schmitthoff)

Dand, R. *The International Cocoa Trade*. Cambridge: Woodhead Publishing Ltd, 1999.
(Cited as Dand)

Day, D.M. *The Law of International Trade*. London: Butterworths, 1981.
(Cited as Day)

DECLERCQ, P.J.M. — "Modern Analysis of the legal effect of Force Majeure clauses in situations of Commercial Impracticability" (1995) 15 *Journal of Law and Commerce* 213–255.
(Cited as Declercq)

DERAINS, Y. & E. SCHWARTZ. — *A Guide to the New ICC Rules of Arbitration*. The Hague: Kluwer Law International, 1998.
(Cited as Derains & Schwartz)

DERHAM, R. — "Recent Issues in Relation to Set-off" (1994) 68 *Australian Law Journal* 331–362.
(Cited as Derham (1994))

DERHAM, S.R. — *Set Off* 2nd ed. Oxford: Clarendon Press, 1996.
(Cited as Derham (1996))

DIMATTEO, L.A. ET AL. — "The Interpretative Turn in International Sales Law: An Analysis of Fifteen Years of CISG Jurisprudence" (2004) *Northwestern Journal of International Law and Business* 299–440.
(Cited as DiMatteo et al.)

DIPALMA, M. — "*Nachfrist* under National Law, the CISG, and the UNIDROIT and European Principles: A Comparison" (1999) 5 (1) *International Contract Adviser* 28–38.
URL: *http://www.cisg.law.pace.edu/cisg/biblio/DiPalma.html*
(Cited as DiPalma)

DORE, I.I. — *Theory and Practice of Multiparty Commercial Arbitration with Special Reference to the UNCITRAL Framework*. London: Graham Trotman Publishing, 1990.
(Cited as Dore (1990))

DORE, I.I. — *Arbitration and Conciliation Under the UNCITRAL Rules: A Textual Analysis*. Dordrecht: Martinus Nijhoff Publishers, 1986.
(Cited as Dore 1986)

EL-SAGHIR, H. — "Commentary of Fundamental Breach—Guide to Article 25"
URL: *http://www.cisg.law.pace.edu/cisg/text/peclcomp25.html*
(Cited as El-Saghir)

ENDERLEIN, F. & D. MASKOW. — *International Sales Law*. New York: Oceana Publications, 1992.
(Cited as Enderlein & Maskow)

FISHER, S. — "A Comparative Analysis of Sellers' and Buyers' Remedies Under the Vienna Sales Convention with Australian Law" presented at *ALTA Conference, Queensland University of Technology, July 1992*.
(Cited as Fisher)

FLECHTNER, H. — "Remedies Under the New International Sales Convention: The Perspective from Article 2 of the U.C.C." (1988) 8 *Journal of Law and Commerce* 53–108.
URL: *http://www.cisg.law.pace.edu/cisg/text/flecht25.html*.
(Cited as Flechtner)

Fox, W.F.	*International Commercial Agreements: A Functional Primer on Drafting, Negotiating and Resolving Disputes*. Deventer: Kluwer Law and Taxation Publishers, 1988. (Cited as Fox)
Gabriel, H.	*Practitioner's Guide to the Convention on Contracts for the International Sale of Goods (CISG) and the Uniform Commercial Code (UCC)*. New York: Oceana Inc., 1994. (Cited as Gabriel)
Gaillard, E. & J. Savage (Eds).	*Fouchard Gaillard Goldman on International Commercial Arbitration*. The Hague: Kluwer Law International, 1999. (Cited as Gaillard & Savage)
Galston, N. (Ed).	*International Sales: The United Nations Convention on CISG*. New York: Matthew Bender, 1984. (Cited as Galston)
Garnett, R. et al.	*A Practical Guide to International Commercial Arbitration*. Dobbs Ferry: Oceana Publishing, Inc., 2000. (Cited as Garnett et al.)
Gillies, P. & G. Moens (Eds).	*International Trade and Business: Law, Policy and Ethics*. Sydney: Cavendish Publishing (Australia) Pty Ltd., 1998. (Cited as Gillies & Moens)
Hanotiau, B.	"Complex Multicontract-Multiparty Arbitrations" (1998) 14 *Arbitration International* 369–394. (Cited as Hanotiau)
Herrera Petrus, C.	"Spanish Perspectives on the Doctrines of Kompetenz-Kompetenz and Separability: A Comparative Analysis of Spain's 1988 Arbitration Act" (2000) *American Review of International Arbitration* 397–427. (Cited as Herrera Petrus)
Holtzmann, H. & J. Neuhaus.	*A Guide to the UNCITRAL Model Law on International Commercial Arbitration: Legislative History and Commentary*. Deventer: Kluwer Law and Taxation Publishers, 1989. (Cited as Holtzmann & Neuhaus)
Honnold, J.O.	*Uniform Law for International Sales Under the 1980 United Nations Convention* 2nd ed. Deventer: Kluwer Law and Taxation Publishers, 1991. (Cited as Honnold (1991))
Honnold, J.O.	*Uniform Law for International Sales Under the 1980 United Nations Convention* 3rd ed. Deventer: Kluwer Law International, 1999. (Cited as Honnold (1999))
Huber, S. & E. Trachte-Huber.	*Arbitration. Cases and Materials*. Cincinnati: Anderson Publishing Co, 1998. (Cited as Huber & Trachte-Huber)
Jarvin, S.	"The Sources and Limits of the Arbitrator's Powers" (1986) 2 *Arbitration International* 140–163. (Cited as Jarvin)

KAROLLUS, M. — "Judicial Interpretation and Application of the CISG in Germany 1988–1994" (1995) *Cornell Review of the Convention on Contracts for the International Sale of Goods* 51–94.
(Cited as Karollus)

KARRER, P. — "Jurisdiction on Set-off Defences and Counterclaims" (2001) 67 *Arbitration: the Journal of the Chartered Institute of Arbitrators* 176–178.
(Cited as Karrer)

KIMBEL, E. — "*Nachfrist* Notice and Avoidance under the CISG" (1999) 18 *Journal of Law and Commerce* 301–331.
URL: *http://www.cisg.law.pace.edu/cisg/biblio/kimbel.html*
(Cited as Kimbel)

KRITZER, A. — *International Contract Manual: Guide to Practical Application of the United Nations Convention on Contracts for the International Sale of Goods*. Boston: Kluwer Law and Taxation Publishers, 1993.
(Cited as Kritzer)

LAMM, C.B. & G. SPOORENBERG. — "The Enforcement of Foreign Arbitral Awards Under the New York Convention, Recent Developments" presented at *ICC Conference on International Arbitration 5 November 2001.*
(Cited as Lamm & Spoorenberg)

LEBOULANGER, P. — "Multi-contract Arbitration" (1996) 13 *Journal of International Arbitration* 43–99.
(Cited as Leboulanger)

LOOKOFSKY, J. — *Understanding the CISG in the USA* 2nd ed. The Hague: Kluwer Law International, 2004.
(Cited as Lookofsky)

LORENZ, A. — "Fundamental Breach Under the CISG".
URL: *http://www.cisg.law.pace.edu/cisg/biblio/lorenz.html*
(Cited as Lorenz)

MAGNUS, U. — "Wesentliche Fragen des UN-Kaufrechts" (1999) 3 *Zeitschrift für Europäisches Privatrecht*, 642–663.
(Cited as Magnus (1999))

MAGNUS, U. — "General Principles of UN-Sales Law" (1997) 3 *International Trade and Business Law Annual*, 33–56.
(Cited as Magnus (1997))

MARASINGHE, L. — *Contract of Sale in International Trade Law*. Singapore: Butterworths Asia, 1992.
(Cited as Marasinghe)

MCCRACKEN, S. — *The Banker's Remedy of Set Off*. London: Butterworths, 1998.
(Cited as McCracken)

MELVILLE, M.L. — "The Nature of Fundamental Breach" (1980) 130 *National Law Journal*, 307–310.
(Cited as Melville)

MICHIDA, S.	"Cancellation of Contract" (1979) 27 *The American Journal of Comparative Law* 279–289. (Cited as Michida)
MO, J.	*International Commercial Law* 3rd ed. Australia: Butterworths, 2003. (Cited as Mo)
MURRAY, J.E.	"An Essay on the Formation of Contracts and Related Matters Under the United Nations Convention on Contracts for the International Sale of Goods" (1988) 8(11) *Journal of Law and Commerce* 11. (Cited as Murray)
NICHOLAS, B.	"*Force Majeure* and Frustration" (1979) 27 *American Journal of Comparative Law* 231–245. (Cited as Nicholas)
NICKLISCH, F.	"Multi-Party Arbitration and Dispute Resolution in Major Industrial Projects" (1994) 11(4) *Journal of International Arbitration*, 57–72. (Cited as Nicklisch)
NYGH, P.E. & P. BUTT (EDS).	*Butterworths Australian Legal Dictionary*. Sydney: Butterworths, 1997. (Cited as Nygh & Butt)
PACE INTERNATIONAL LAW REVIEW (ED).	*Review of the Convention on Contracts for the International Sale of Goods*. The Hague: Kluwer Law International, 1999. (Cited as PILR 1999)
PACE INTERNATIONAL LAW REVIEW (ED).	*Review of the Convention on Contracts for the International Sale of Goods*. The Hague: Kluwer Law International, 1999. (Cited as PILR 2000)
PERILLO, J.	"Hardship and its Impact on Contractual Obligations: A Comparative Analysis" in Saggi, *Conferenze E Seminari*: Rome, 1996. URL: *http://www.crdcs.org/frames20.htm* (Cited as Perillo)
PERALES VISCASILLAS, M.	"El Contrato de Compraventa Internacional De Mercancias (Convención de 1980)". URL: *http://www.cisg.law.pace.edu/cisg/biblio/perales1.html* (Cited as Perales Viscasillas)
PETER, W.	"Some Observations on the New Swiss Rules of International Arbitration" (2004) *ASA Special Series* No.22. (Cited as Peter)
PILIOUNIS, P.	"The Remedies of Specific Performance, Price Reduction and Additional Time (*Nachfrist*) under the CISG: Are these worthwhile changes or additions to English Sales Law?" (2000) 12 *Pace International Law Review* 1–46. URL: *http://www.cisg.law.pace.edu/cisg/biblio/piliounis.html* (Cited as Piliounis)

PLATTE, M.	"When Should an Arbitrator Join Cases?" (2002) 18(1) *Arbitration International* 67–76. (Cited as Platte)
RAUH, T.	"Legal Consequences of Force Majeure Under Swiss, English & United States Law" 25 (1996) *Denver Journal of International Law & Policy* 151. (Cited as Rauh)
REDFERN, A. & M. HUNTER.	*Law and Practice of International Commercial Arbitration* 3rd ed. London: Sweet & Maxwell, 1999. (Cited as Redfern & Hunter)
RIMKE, J.	"Force majeure and hardship: Application in international trade practice with specific regard to the CISG and the UNIDROIT Principles of International Commercial Contracts" (2000) *Pace Review of the Convention for the International Sale of Goods*, Kluwer 197–243. URL: *http://www.cisg.law.pace.edu/cisg/biblio/rimke.html* (Cited as Rimke)
ROSEN, J.A.	"Arbitration Under Private International Law: The Doctrines of Separability and Competence de la Competence" (1994) 17 *Fordham International Law Journal* 599–666. (Cited as Rosen)
ROSETT, A.	"A Critical Reflection on the United Nations Convention on Contracts for the International Sale of Goods" (1984) 45 *Ohio State Law Journal* 265–305. (Cited as Rosett)
RUBINO-SAMMARTANO, M.	"Multi Party Arbitration" (1981) 9 (xi) *International Business Lawyer* 436. (Cited as Rubino-Sammartano (1981))
RUBINO-SAMMARTANO, M.	*International Arbitration Law*. Deventer: Kluwer Law and Taxation Publisher, 1990. (Cited as Rubino-Sammartano (1990))
SACCO, R. & G. DE NOVA.	*Il Contratto*. Tomo secondo, Torino: VTET, 1993. (Cited as Sacco & De Nova)
SANDERS, P.	*The Work of UNCITRAL on Arbitration and Conciliation*. The Hague: Kluwer Law International, 2001. (Cited as Sanders)
SASSOON, D.	*British Shipping Laws (vol. 5) C.I.F. and F.O.B. Contracts* 2nd ed. London: Stevens & Sons, 1975. (Cited as Sassoon)
SCHERER, M.	"New Rules of International Arbitration in Switzerland" (2004) 4 *International Arbitration Law Review* 119–125. (Cited as Scherer)
SCHLECHTRIEM, P. (ED).	*Commentary on the UN Convention on the International Sale of Goods (CISG)*. Oxford: Clarendon Press, 1998. (Cited as Schlechtriem (1998))

SCHLECHTRIEM, P. — *Uniform Sales Law—The UN Convention on Contracts for the International Sale of Goods*. Vienna: Manz, 1986.
(Cited as Schlechtriem (1986))

SCHNEIDER, M.E. — "Multi-Fora Disputes" (1990) 6 *Arbitration International* 101–121.
(Cited as Schneider)

SCHULZ, A. — "Report on the Second Meeting of the Informal Working Group" (2003) *Hague Conference on Private International Law* 1–20.
(Cited as Schulz)

SECRETARIAT COMMENTARY. — *Guide to Article 49.*
URL: *http://www.cisg.law.pace.edu/cisg/text/peclcomp49.html*
(Cited as Secretariat Commentary on Article 49)

SECRETARIAT COMMENTARY. — *Guide to CISG Article 79.*
URL: *http://www.cisg.law.pace.edu/cisg/text/secomm/secomm–79.html*
(Cited as Secretariat Commentary on Article 79)

SEKOLEC, J. — "International Dispute Resolution: Areas Where Further Research may be Useful" (2003) 20 (1) *Journal of International Arbitration* 35–66.
(Cited as Sekolec)

SUTTON, J.S. — "Measuring Damages Under the United Nations Convention on the International Sale of Goods" (1989) 50 *Ohio State Law Journal* 737.
(Cited as Sutton)

TIEDER, B. — "Factors to Consider in the Choice of Procedural and Substantive Law in International Arbitration" (2003) 20 (4) *Journal of International Arbitration*, 393–407.
(Cited as Tieder)

UNCITRAL — "Analytical commentary on draft text of a model law on international commercial arbitration: report of the Secretary-General" (A/CN.9/264).
(Cited as UNCITRAL Commentary A/CN.9/264)

UNIDROIT PRINCIPLES — UNIDROIT Principles of International Commercial Contracts, Rome: International Institute for the Unification of Private Law, 2004.
(Cited as UNIDROIT Principles 2004)

VAN DER WALT, M. — "The Clarification of Equitable Set-Off" (1998) 72 *The Australian Law Journal* 516–539.
(Cited as Van Der Walt)

VAN HOUTTE, H. — *The Law of International Trade* 2nd ed. London: Sweet & Maxwell, 2002.
(Cited as Van Houtte)

WALDRON, A.J. "Set-Off and Counterclaim—the Necessary Connection" (1990) *Lloyd's Maritime and Commercial Law Quarterly* 472–478.
(Cited as Waldron)

WEBER-STECHER, U. "Swiss Rules of International Arbitration" (2004).
URL: *www.wengerlaw.ch/downloads/publications/pdf/en/wv-swiss_ rules.pdf*
(Cited as Weber-Stecher)

WOOD, P. *English and International Set-Off*. London: Sweet & Maxwell, 1989.
(Cited as Wood)

YEARBOOK COMMERCIAL ARBITRATION *Yearbook Commercial Arbitration* (1989) (XIV), 187.
(Cited as YCA (1989))

ZELLER, B. *Guide to Article 47 & 49 (1)(b).*
URL: *http://www.cisg.law.pace.edu/cisg/text/peclcomp47.html*
(Cited as Zeller)

ZIMMERMANN, R. *Comparative Foundations of A European Law of Set-Off and Prescription*. Cambridge: Cambridge University Press, 2002.
(Cited as Zimmermann)

LIST OF CITED CASES

Australia

Friedlander v. The Bank of Australasia [1909] High Court of Australia, 8 CLR 85.

Radio 2UE Sydney Pty Ltd v. Stereo FM Pty Ltd (1982) Federal Court of Australia, 44 Australian Law Reports 557.

Austria

Internationales Schiedsgericht der Bundeskammer der gewerblichen Wirtschaft SCH-4366 of 15 June 1994.

URL: *http://cisgw3.law.pace.edu/cases/940615a3.html*

Oberster Gerichtshof 10 Ob 518/95 of 6 February 1996.

URL: *http://www.cisg.law.pace.edu/cases/960202a3.html*

Oberster Gerichtshof 6 Ob 311/99z of 9 March 2000.

URL: *http://cisgw3.law.pace.edu/cases/000309a3.html*

Oberster Gerichtshof 1 Ob 292/99v of 28 April 2000.

URL: *http://www.cisg.law.pace.edu/cases/000428a3.html*

France

M. Caiato Roger v. La Société française de factoring international factor France "S.F.F." (SA), Cour d'appel Grenoble 93/4126 of 13 September 1995.

URL: *http://www.cisg.law.pace.edu/cases/950913f1.html*

M. Marques Roque Joachim v. La Sarl Holding Manin Rivière, Cour d'appel Grenoble 93/4879 of 26 April 1995.

URL: *http://www.cisg.law.pace.edu/cases/950426f2.html*

SARL BRI Production "Bonaventure" v. Société Pan African Export, Cour d'appel Grenoble, decision of 22 February 1995.

URL: *http://cisgw3.law.pace.edu/cases/950222f1.html*

Germany

Amtsgericht Alsfeld 31 C 534/94 of 12 May 1995.

URL: *http://www.cisg.law.pace.edu/cases/950512g1.html*

Amtsgericht Oldenburg in Holstein 5 C 73/89 of 24 April 1990.

URL: *http://cisgw3.law.pace.edu/cases/900424g1.html*

Bundesgerichtshof VII ZR 51/95 of 3 April 1996.

URL: *http://cisgw3.law.pace.edu/cases/960403g1.html*

Landgericht Frankfurt 3/11 0 3/91 of 16 September 1991.

URL: *http://cisgw3.law.pace.edu/cases/910916g1.html*

Landgericht Hamburg 5 O 543/88 of 26 September 1990.

URL: *http://www.cisg.law.pace.edu/cisg/wais/db/cases2/900926g1.html*

Landgericht Heidelberg O 42/92 KfH I of 3 July 1992.
URL: *http://www.cisg.law.pace.edu/cases/920703g1.html*
Landgericht München 10 O 5423/01 of 20 February 2002.
URL: *http://cisgw3.law.pace.edu/cases/020220g1.html*
Oberlandesgericht Bamberg 3 U 83/98 of 13 January 1999.
URL: *http://www.cisg.law.pace.edu/cases/990113g1.html*
Oberlandesgericht Düsseldorf 6 U 228/92 of 18 November 1993.
URL: *http://cisgw3.law.pace.edu/cases/931118g1.html*
Oberlandesgericht Düsseldorf 17 U 146/93 of 14 January 1994.
URL: *http://www.cisg.law.pace.edu/cases/940114g1.html*
Oberlandesgericht Düsseldorf 6 U 119/93 of 10 February 1994.
URL: *http://cisgw3.law.pace.edu/cases/940210g2.html*
Oberlandesgericht Düsseldorf 6 U 87/96 of 24 April 1997.
URL: *http://cisgw3.law.pace.edu/cases/970424g1.html*
Oberlandesgericht Frankfurt 5 U 15/93 of 18 January 1994.
URL: *http://www.cisg.law.pace.edu/cases/940118g1.html*
Oberlandesgericht Frankfurt am Main 5 U 164/90 of 17 September 1991.
URL: *http://www.cisg.law.pace.edu/cisg/wais/db/cases2/910917g1.html*
Oberlandesgericht Hamburg 5 U 224/93 of 14 December 1994.
URL: *http://www.cisg.law.pace.edu/cases/941214g1.html*
Oberlandesgericht Hamburg 1 U 167/95 of 28 February 1997.
URL: *http://www.cisg.law.pace.edu/cases/970228g1.html*
Oberlandesgericht Hamburg 1 U 143/95 and 410 O 21/95 of 4 July 1997.
URL: *http://www.cisg.law.pace.edu/cases/970704g1.html*
Oberlandesgericht Hamm 11 U 41/97 of 5 November 1997.
URL: *http://www.cisg.law.pace.edu/cases/971105g1.html*
Oberlandesgericht Koblenz 2 U 1230/91 of 17 September 1993.
URL: *http://www.cisg.law.pace.edu/cases/930917g1.html*
Oberlandesgericht Köln 29 U 202/93 of 22 February 1994.
URL: *http://www.uncitral.org/english/clout/abstract/abstr9.htm*
Oberlandesgericht Köln 16 U 77/01 of 14 October 2002.
URL: *http://cisgw3.law.pace.edu/cases/021014g1.html*
Oberlandesgericht München 7 U 4419/93 of 2 March 1994.
URL: *http://cisgw3.law.pace.edu/cases/940302g1.html*
Oberlandesgericht München 7 U 1720/94 of 8 February 1995.
URL: *http://www.cisg.law.pace.edu/cases/950208g1.html*
Oberlandesgericht München 7 U 4427/97 of 11 March 1998.
URL: *http://www.cisg.law.pace.edu/cases/980311g1.html*
Oberlandesgericht Saarbrücken 1 U 69/92 of 13 January 1993.
URL: *http://www.cisg.law.pace.edu/cases/930113g1.html*

Hungary

Arbitration Court of the Chamber of Commerce and Industry of Budapest VB 97142 of 25 May 1999.
URL: *http://cisgw3.law.pace.edu/cases/990525h1.html*

ICC Awards

ICC Arbitration Case No. 122/85 of 1987.
ICC Arbitration Case No. 3540 of 1980.
ICC Arbitration Case No. 5713 of 1989.
ICC Arbitration Case No. 7197 of 1992.
ICC Arbitration Case No. 7645 of 1995.
ICC Arbitration Case No. 8128 of 1995.
ICC Arbitration Case No. 8574 of 1996.
URL: *http://www.cisg.law.pace.edu/cases/968574i1.html*
ICC Arbitration Case No. 8740 of 1996.
URL: *http://www.cisg.law.pace.edu/cases/968740i1.html*

Russian Federation

Russian Federation Chamber of Commerce and Industry, 155/1994 of 16 March 1995.
URL: *http://www.cisg.law.pace.edu/cisg/wais/db/cases2/950316r1.html*
Tribunal of International Commercial Arbitration at the Russian Federation Chamber of Commerce and Industry 54/1999 of 24 January 2000.
URL: *http://cisgw3.law.pace.edu/cases/000124r1.html*
Tribunal of International Commercial Arbitration at the Russian Federation Chamber of Commerce and Industry 406/1998 of 6 June 2002.
URL: *http://www.cisg.law.pace.edu/cases/000606r1.html*

Switzerland

Amtsgericht Zweibrücken 1C 216/92 of 14 October 1992.
FCF S.A. v. Adriafil Commerciale S.r.l., Bundesgericht 4C.105/2000 of 15 September 2000.
URL: *http://cisgw3.law.pace.edu/cases/000915s2.html*
Handelsgericht Zürich HG 95 0347 of 5 February 1997.
URL: *http://cisgw3.law.pace.edu/cases/970205s1.html*
Kantonsgericht Freiburg Apph 27/97 Apph 10667 of 23 January 1998.
URL: *http://www.cisg.law.pace.edu/cisg/wais/db/cases2/980123s1.html*
Komplex v Voest-Alpine Stahl SBGH (Federal Tribunal) of 14 June 1990.
Tribunal Cantonal Vaud 01 93 1061 163/96/BA of 1996.
URL: *http://www.cisg.law.pace.edu/cisg/wais/db/cases2/960311s2.html*

United Kingdom

Brauer & Co v. James Clark (1952) House of Lords, All England Reports (2) 497.

C. Czarnikow Ltd. v. Centrala Handlu Zagranicznego ("Rolimpex") (1978) 2 Lloyd's Reports 305.

Glencore Grain v. Agros Trading Co. Court of Appeal (Civil Division) [1999] 2 Lloyd's Reports 410.

National Carriers Ltd. v. Panalpina (Northern) Ltd. (1981) Appeals Court, 675.

Ranko Group v. Antarctic Maritime SA The "Robin" QBD (Commercial Crt) Unreported of 12 June 1998.

Taylor Woodrow Civil Engineering v. Hutchison IDH Development Ltd QBD, [1998] C.I.L.L. 1434

Winterfield v. Bradnum (1878) 3 High Court of Justice, QBD 324.

United States of America

Compania Espanola de Petroleos, S.A. v. Nereus Shipping, S.A. 527 Federal Reporter (2nd Series) 966, 2d Cir (1975).

Delchi Carrier S.p.A v Rotorex Corp. 10 Federal Reporter (3rd Series) 2d Cir. (1994).

URL: *http://www.cisg.law.pace.edu/cases/940909u1.html*

Raw Materials Inc. v. Manfred Forberich GmbH & Co., KG U.S. District Court, Northern District of Illinois, Eastern Division 03 C 1154 of 6 July 2004.

URL: *http://cisgw3.law.pace.edu/cases/040706u1.html*

Thomson-CSF, SA v. American Arbitration Association 64 Federal Reporter (3rd Series) 773 2d Cir. (1995)

LIST OF LEGAL AUTHORITIES

American Arbitration Association International Arbitration Rules, 1 September 2000 (AAA Rules)

CENTRAL List of Lex Mercatoria Principles, Rules and Standards (CENTRAL List of Principles)

Chamber of Commerce and Industry of Geneva Arbitration Rules, 1 January 1992 (CGIG Rules)

Convention on the Recognition and Enforcement of Foreign Arbitral Awards, New York, 10 June 1958 (New York Convention)

International Bar Association Rules of Ethics for International Arbitrators (IBA)

International Chamber of Commerce, Paris, 1 January 1998 (ICC Rules)

London International Financial Futures and Options Exchange, Exchange Contract 401 Cocoa Futures Contract, 11 October 2001 (LIFFE Contract 401)

London Court of International Arbitration Rules, 1 January 1998 (LCIA Rules)

New York Board of Trade, Cocoa Rules (NYBOT Rules)

Swiss Rules of International Arbitration, 1 January 2004 (Swiss Rules)

UNCITRAL Model Law on International Commercial Arbitration, 21 June 1985 (Model Law)

UNCITRAL Arbitration Rules, 1976 (UNCITRAL Rules)

UNIDROIT Principles of International Commercial Contracts, Rome, 2004 (UNIDROIT Principles 2004)

United Nations Convention on Contracts for the International Sale of Goods, Vienna, 11 April 1980 (CISG)

Vienna Convention on the Law of Treaties, Vienna, 23 May 1969 (VCLT)

STATEMENT OF PURPOSE

The Respondent, Equatoriana Commodity Exporters, S.A. (ECE) has prepared this Memorandum in compliance with the Arbitral Tribunal's Procedural Order No. 1, issued on 1 October 2004.

It is argued that:

- The Arbitral Tribunal has jurisdiction to hear ECE's counterclaim;
- ECE's late delivery of 300 tons of cocoa beans is excusable under The United Nations Convention on Contracts for the International Sale of Goods (CISG);
- The Claimant, Mediterraneo Confectionary Associates, Inc. (MCA) is not entitled to claim damages for ECE's late delivery of 300 tons of cocoa beans; and
- MCA cannot claim damages under Article 74 CISG in the amount of US$289,353

In relation to each of these four issues, ECE summarises the arguments made by MCA in the Memorandum for the Claimant prepared by Stockholm University. Where ECE refers to an issue which is not addressed in the Memorandum for the Claimant, the heading pertaining to that issue is followed by [NEW ARGUMENT]. In arguing these propositions, ECE will demonstrate the legal and factual bases for its claim, and will respond to MCA's arguments.

In accordance with Procedural Order No.1, the substantive issues of the dispute will be argued at the same time as the jurisdictional issues and there will be no discussion of arguments in relation to interest or the allocation of the costs of arbitration.

The references to books or articles in the Arguments of this Memorandum are comprised of the surname of the author followed by the page number or paragraph number. References to cases include the name of the case, the relevant court and the year of the judgment. The full citations to references are listed in the List of Authorities and List of Cited Cases.

ARGUMENTS

I. THE JURISDICTION OF THE ARBITRAL TRIBUNAL TO HEAR *ECE*'S COUNTERCLAIM

1. The President of the Arbitral Tribunal, in his Procedural Order No. 1 of 1 October 2004, has requested a discussion of whether this Tribunal has authority to consider the counterclaim by Equatoriana Commodity Exporters, S.A. (ECE, Respondent) against Mediterraneo Confectionary Associates (MCA, Claimant). In this part of the Memorandum, ECE argues that (1) the Tribunal has authority to rule on its own jurisdiction, (2) the Tribunal has jurisdiction to hear ECE's claim for the purpose of a set-off defence, (3) the Tribunal's jurisdiction is not limited to a set-off defence but can be extended to ECE's counterclaim, and (4) a decision by the Tribunal to hear ECE's counterclaim will not affect the enforceability of the Tribunal's Award.

1. The Arbitral Tribunal has authority to rule on its own jurisdiction [NEW ARGUMENT]

2. This dispute concerns two contracts for the supply of commodities used in the production of confectionery products entered into by MCA and ECE: Sugar Contract 2212 and Cocoa Contract 1045. The Rules of Arbitration of the Oceania Commodity Association (RAOCA) govern Sugar Contract 2212 [*Respondent's Exhibit No. 4; Answer to Notice of Arbitration and Counter-Claim, 13*]. The Chamber of Commerce and Industry of Geneva Arbitration Rules (CCIG) were originally chosen by MCA and ECE as the arbitral rules applicable to Cocoa Contract 1045 [*Claimant's Exhibit No. 2; Request for Arbitration, 3*]. However, on 1 January 2004, the new Swiss Rules of International Arbitration (Swiss Rules) succeeded the CCIG in the field of international arbitration [*Letter of Daniela Jobin to Horace Fasttrack, 6 July 2004*; cf. *Burger, 1; Weber-Stecher, 2*].

3. Article 21(1) Swiss Rules stipulates: "The arbitral tribunal shall have the power to rule on objections that it has no jurisdiction, including any objections with respect to the existence or validity of the arbitration clause or of the separate arbitration agreement." This Article gives the Tribunal the authority to rule on its own jurisdiction to resolve the disputes relating to Cocoa Contract 1045 and Sugar Contract 2212 [cf. *ICC Rules 15(1); AAA Rules 15(1); LCIA Rules 23.1; Amerasinghe, 130; Craig, Park & Paulsson, 59; Derains & Schwartz, 99–102; Herrera Petrus, 397; Rosen, 607; Tieder, 399*].

2. The Arbitral Tribunal has jurisdiction to hear the dispute arising out of Sugar Contract 2212 for the purpose of a set-off defence

4. Although MCA "does not object to the general application of the Swiss Rules to international arbitrations" [*Claimant's Memorandum, para. 68*; cf. *Answer to Counter-Claim, 4*], it objects to the specific application of Article 21(5) to confer authority on the Arbitral Tribunal to hear the dispute arising out of Sugar Contract 2212 [*Answer to Counter-Claim, 4; Claimant's Memorandum, para. 64–70*]. This Article states: "The arbitral tribunal shall have jurisdiction to hear a set-off defence even when the relationship out of which this defence is said to arise is . . . the object of another arbitration agreement." In responding to MCA's objection, ECE argues that Article 21(5) Swiss Rules gives the Arbitral Tribunal jurisdiction to hear the dispute arising out of Sugar Contract 2212 [*Answer to Notice of Arbitration and Counter-Claim, 17*] because (1) Article 21(5) applies to Sugar Contract 2212, and (2) ECE's claim satisfies the requirements of a set-off in Article 21(5), or (3) ECE's claim satisfies the requirements of an "equitable" set-off.

2.1 *Article 21(5)* Swiss Rules *applies to Sugar Contract 2212*

5. MCA's objection to the jurisdiction of the Arbitral Tribunal to hear ECE's counterclaim is based on the ground that the operation of Article 21(5) Swiss Rules would supplant RAOCA's rule on set-off which, unlike Article 21(5), limits a set-off to "a claim arising out of the same contract" [*Procedural Order No. 2, Clarification 4*; cf. *Claimant's Memorandum, para. 67*]. However, this argument is erroneous because, at law, Article 21(5) Swiss Rules applies to Sugar Contract 2212 for three reasons. These reasons, collectively, mandate the application of this Article: (a) the Swiss Rules in their entirety apply to the original claim arising out of Cocoa Contract 1045, (b) Article 21(5) Swiss Rules has automatically supplanted the set-off provision in

RAOCA and (c) MCA is estopped from claiming that the set-off provision in Article 21(5) Swiss Rules does not apply to Sugar Contract 2212.

(a) The *Swiss Rules* in their entirety apply to the original claim arising out of Cocoa Contract 1045

6. Article 1(1) Swiss Rules confirms that, "These Rules shall govern international arbitrations, where an agreement to arbitrate refers to these Rules, or to the arbitration rules" of the Chamber of Commerce and Industry of Geneva, among others. In addition, Article 1(3) Swiss Rules stipulates that, "These rules shall come into force on January 1st, 2004 and, unless the parties have agreed otherwise, shall apply to all arbitral proceedings in which the Notice of Arbitration is submitted on or after that date" [cf. *Peter, 3–4*]. The Swiss Rules in their entirety apply to disputes arising out of Cocoa Contract 1045 because (i) the arbitration between MCA and ECE is an international arbitration since MCA has its place of business in Mediterraneo, and ECE is located in Equatoriana [*Request for Arbitration, 1–2; Answer to Notice of Arbitration and Counter-Claim, 1–2*], (ii) the arbitration agreement in Cocoa Contract 1045 refers to the CCIG [*Request for Arbitration, 14*], and (iii) MCA submitted its Notice of Arbitration on 2 July 2004. Hence, the Swiss Rules in their entirety are the applicable procedural rules in the arbitration arising out of Cocoa Contract 1045 and the Arbitral Tribunal has jurisdiction to hear the cocoa dispute.

(b) Article 21(5) *Swiss Rules* has automatically supplanted the set-off provision in *RAOCA*

7. RAOCA contains a provision identical to Article 19(3) UNCITRAL Arbitration Rules [*Procedural Order No. 2, Clarification* 4], which provides that "the respondent may . . . rely on a claim arising out of the same contract for the purpose of a set-off." MCA argues that RAOCA's set-off provision applies to Sugar Contract 2212, and therefore prevents the Arbitral Tribunal from hearing the dispute arising out of that contract [*Claimant's Memorandum, para. 73*]. This argument, in essence, is based on the ground that MCA and ECE subjected Sugar Contract 2212 to a specific set-off regime which is different from that contained in Article 21(5) Swiss Rules. This reasoning might be valid if the original claim had been raised under Sugar Contract 2212. In such a case RAOCA's set-off provision would prevail because RAOCA's procedural rules would govern the arbitration proceedings. However, the original claim has been raised under Cocoa Contract 1045 and the Swiss Rules are the rules applicable to the arbitration arising under that contract. Article 21(5) Swiss Rules specifically gives this Tribunal the power to hear a set-off defence where it is "the object of another arbitration agreement" [cf. *Hanotiau, 379; Peter, 8*]. Therefore, Article 21(5) Swiss Rules, by its operation, automatically supplants RAOCA's set-off provision.

8. MCA has argued that the imposition of Article 21(5) Swiss Rules "on parties who expressly chose the application of rules not containing such a competence for the arbitral Tribunal will lead to inequity" [*Claimant's Memorandum, para. 69*]. However, at law, arbitration may be subject to arbitral rules, which were not envisaged by the parties when they entered into their contract. The validity of this view is illustrated by *Komplex v. Voest-Alpine Stahl* [*(1990), SBGH*] where a Federal Tribunal held that an ICC arbitration agreement "was governed by the revised ICC

Rules and not by the Rules in force when the arbitration agreement was concluded" [*Scherer, 121*; cf. *Taylor Woodrow Civil Engineering v. Hutchison IDH Development Ltd (QBD, 1998); Ranko Group v. Antarctic Maritime SA (QBD, 1998)*]. Indeed, "The rules of arbitration service-providers, are—just like legislation—subject to periodical amendments to reflect developing practice and expectations of users" [*Scherer, 121*]. Such an adaptation occurred on 1 January 2004 when the Swiss Rules replaced the CCIG for international arbitrations. Hence, the operation of Article 21(5) Swiss Rules supplants the set-off provision in RAOCA to give the Arbitral Tribunal jurisdiction to hear the dispute arising out of Sugar Contract 2212.

(c) *MCA* is estopped from claiming that the set-off provision in Article 21(5) *Swiss Rules* does not apply to Sugar Contract 2212

9. MCA is estopped from claiming that the set-off provision in Article 21(5) Swiss Rules does not apply to Sugar Contract 2212 because MCA implicitly consented to the application of this Article when it failed to object promptly to its operation. MCA formulated its objection to Article 21(5) in its Answer to Counter-Claim of 31 August 2004 [*Answer to Counter-Claim, 4*]. However, MCA had been aware since 6 July 2004 that the Swiss Rules would apply to the dispute arising out of Cocoa Contract 1045 when it received a letter from the Chamber of Commerce and Industry of Geneva stating that, "the Chamber of commerce and industry of Geneva as well as the Chambers of commerce of Basel, Bern, Ticino, Vaud and Zurich have adopted the new Swiss Rules of International Arbitration" [*Letter from Daniela Jobin, 6 July 2004*]. The letter further outlined that, in accordance with Article 1(3), the Swiss Rules would apply to all international arbitrations "in which the Notice of Arbitration is submitted after January 1st, 2004" unless the parties have agreed otherwise. MCA failed to object to the application of Article 21(5) Swiss Rules at this time, thereby implicitly consenting to its operation. Thus, MCA's objection on 31 August 2004 came after MCA had consented to the application of the Swiss Rules. Therefore, MCA's objection to the application of Article 21(5) Swiss Rules to prevent this Arbitral Tribunal from assuming jurisdiction to hear the dispute arising out of Sugar Contract 2212 is untimely.

10. MCA's implicit consent to the applicability of Article 21(5) Swiss Rules is further demonstrated by payment of the arbitration fee to the Chamber of Commerce and Industry of Geneva [*Letter from Horace Fasttrack, 12 July 2004*; cf. *Born, 190; Thomson-CSF, SA v. American Arbitration Association (2nd Circ., 1995)*]. MCA had ample opportunity to examine the Rules before it paid the arbitration fee because it received a copy of the Swiss Rules on 6 July 2004 [*Letter from Daniela Jobin, 6 July 2004*]. Furthermore, MCA made specific reference to Article 7 and Article 8 Swiss Rules in its letter of 21 July 2004 to the Chamber of Commerce and Industry of Geneva [*Letter to Daniela Jobin, 21 July 2004*]. This reference indicates that MCA was aware that the Swiss Rules had succeeded the CCIG in international arbitrations and that it was relying on these Rules to resolve the dispute arising out of Cocoa Contract 1045. Thus, MCA's payment of the arbitration fee without comment and subsequent reliance on Article 7 and Article 8 Swiss Rules demonstrate MCA's implicit consent to the application of Article 21(5) Swiss Rules, thereby extending the jurisdiction of the Tribunal to hear disputes arising out of other contracts.

2.2 ECE's *claim satisfies the requirements of a set-off under Article 21(5)* Swiss Rules

11. A set-off is essentially a cross-claim by a respondent, which can be used to reduce his liability wholly or partially in respect of a claimant's original claim [*Derham (1996), 1; Berg, 154*]. ECE argues that its claim arising under Sugar Contract 2212 qualifies as a set-off under Article 21(5) Swiss Rules by (a) discussing the requirements of a set-off under Article 21(5) Swiss Rules, and (b) revealing how MCA's debt under Sugar Contract 2212 satisfies these requirements, thereby giving the Arbitral Tribunal jurisdiction to hear the dispute arising out of Sugar Contract 2212.

(a) A set-off under Article 21(5) *Swiss Rules* must be liquidated and due and payable

12. Although "set-off defence" is not defined in Article 21(5) Swiss Rules, its procedural meaning in the context of the dispute between MCA and ECE may be gleaned from ICC Case No. 3540 [*(1980)*; cf. *Magnus (1997), 47; KG Freiburg (1998), Apph 10667; TC Vaud (1996), 01 93 1061; OLG München (1998,) 7 U 4427/97; OLG Hamm (1997), 11 U 41/97; OLG Koblenz (1993), 2 U 1230/91; ICC No. 5713, (1989)*]. The arbitral tribunal noted that, where the set-off defence arises out of different contracts, the defence is, in essence, subject to two interrelated cumulative conditions: (i) the claim of the party who relies on the set-off defence must be liquidated, i.e. certain or ascertainable and (ii) the claim must be mature, i.e. due and payable. The arbitral tribunal also emphasised in ICC Case No. 3540 the usefulness of the *lex mercatoria* to strengthen its understanding of the set-off defence in the context of different contracts.

13. A modern articulation of the *lex mercatoria* is provided by the UNIDROIT Principles of International Commercial Contracts 2004 (UNIDROIT Principles 2004), which may be used "to interpret or supplement international uniform law instruments" [*Bonell, 5*; cf. *Redfern & Hunter, 124; CENTRAL List of Principles; UNIDROIT Principles 2004, 1*]. Article 8.1(b) of these Principles requires that the obligation of the party who relies on the set-off defence "is ascertained as to its existence and amount and performance is due." This Article accords with the view that, where a set-off defence is claimed under obligations arising out of different contracts, the "invariable and universal requirement" is that the claim "must be liquidated and . . . must be due and payable" [*Wood, 1140*; cf. *Berg, 155; Glencore v. Agros (CA, 1999)*]. Hence, ECE's claim under Sugar Contract 2212 will come within the "set-off" provision of Article 21(5) Swiss Rules if it satisfies the conditions that (i) its exact value is certain or easily ascertainable and (ii) is due and payable.

(b) *MCA*'s debt under Sugar Contract 2212 is liquidated and due and payable

14. Sugar Contract 2212 provided that delivery of the sugar was to be made in accordance with the FOB Incoterm [*Respondent's Exhibit No. 4*]. Under FOB Rules A4 and B4, delivery occurs when the goods are loaded on the nominated vessel at the named port of shipment [*Bridge, 111; Carr, 35; Day, 45; Marasinghe, 129*]. The sugar was loaded on the Oceania Condor on 8 December 2003 [*Answer to Notice of Arbitration and Counter-Claim, para. 13*]. Once delivery has occurred, the buyer has an obligation under FOB Rule B1 to pay the purchase price in accordance with the contract [*Day, 52*]. Sugar Contract 2212 stipulated that the total contract price of US$385,805 was "payable ten days after delivery" [*Respondent's Exhibit No. 4*]. This contractual obligation is not dependent upon the inspection of the goods by the buyer [*Sassoon, 415; Schmitthoff, 16*]. Hence, MCA's liquidated debt of US$385,805 became due and payable on 18 December 2003. As such, ECE is entitled to rely on MCA's debt for the purpose of giving the Arbitral Tribunal jurisdiction to hear the set-off defence arising out of Sugar Contract 2212.

2.3 Alternatively, ECE's *claim satisfies the requirements of an "equitable" set-off because Cocoa Contract 1045 and Sugar Contract 2212 share the same "economic purpose"* [NEW ARGUMENT]

15. The defence of "equitable" set-off, unlike the set-off defence provided for in Article 21(5) Swiss Rules, only requires that the debt to be set off is closely related to the original claim; it does not require the debt to be liquidated, due and payable [*Van der Walt, 517; Zimmermann, 61*]. Therefore, if the Arbitral Tribunal were to decide that ECE's claim arising under Sugar Contract 2212 does not satisfy the requirements of a set-off defence in Article 21(5) Swiss Rules, the Tribunal is still authorised to hear ECE's claim because Cocoa Contract 1045 and Sugar Contract 2212 share the same "economic purpose". In such a case, the Tribunal has jurisdiction to hear the dispute arising out of both contracts, "but only if the cross-demands are so closely connected that it would be unjust or inequitable for one party to proceed with his claim without giving credit for the other" [*Derham (1994), 332;* cf. *Berg, 154; Waldron, 477*].

16. Where there is an economic and functional link between contracts, these agreements "should not be regarded as autonomous agreements" [*Leboulanger, 72;* cf. *Platte, 47*]. This approach is supported in ICC Case No. 122/85 in which the tribunal indicated that, while there was no formal link between the two contracts, it was evident that they were substantially interdependent. The tribunal stated that the two contracts were a part of the same economic relationship because "without the materials which claimant undertook to supply, defendant was unable to carry out the manufacture of the heat exchangers" [*YCA, (1989), 189*]. As such, the arbitral tribunal was justified in assuming jurisdiction to hear both disputes.

17. MCA contracted with ECE for the supply of cocoa and sugar, which are both used in the production of confectionery goods [*Answer to Notice of Arbitration and Counter-Claim, para. 1; Respondent's Exhibit No. 5*]. The cocoa from Cocoa Contract 1045 and the sugar from Sugar Contract 2212 thus share the same economic purpose. Hence, MCA's contention that "Cocoa Contract 1045 and Sugar Contract 2212 are not part of a greater agreement between the parties" [*Claimant's Memorandum, para. 66*] is unconvincing. As both contracts support the production of confectionery goods, the relationship between ECE and MCA was, in essence, a business relationship with a single economic purpose [*Claimant's Exhibit No. 8*]. Therefore, the Arbitral Tribunal has jurisdiction to hear ECE's claim arising under Sugar Contract 2212 for the purpose of hearing an "equitable" set-off defence.

3. The jurisdiction of the Tribunal is not limited to a set-off defence but can be extended to *ECE*'s counterclaim

18. MCA opposes the extension of the Arbitral Tribunal's jurisdiction to ECE's counterclaim on the ground that a set-off and a counterclaim are two distinct concepts. In particular, MCA submits that the two concepts are inherently distinct because, allegedly, a counterclaim is procedural in nature while a set-off is substantive [*Claimant's Memorandum, para. 84*]. MCA further contends that, if the Tribunal were to assume jurisdiction to consider the counterclaim, ECE's set-off should be limited to any recovery that MCA might be awarded under Cocoa Contract 1045 [*Claimant's Memorandum, para. 86*]. By way of response, ECE argues that (1) its set-off defence can be extended to a counterclaim for legal reasons, (2) policy reasons support the extension of set-off to a counterclaim, and (3) the extension of ECE's set-off defence to a counterclaim results in its ability to recover more than MCA might be awarded under Cocoa Contract 1045.

3.1 ECE*'s set-off defence under Article 21(5)* Swiss Rules *can be extended to a counterclaim for legal reasons*

19. ECE's set-off defence under Article 21(5) Swiss Rules can be extended to a counterclaim because the legal principles pertaining to counterclaim and set-off are virtually identical. Like a set-off, a counterclaim is a cross-claim by a respondent against the claimant, heard in the same proceedings as the original claim [*McCracken, 115; Rubino-Sammartano (1990), 336; Wood, 241*]. Hence, both set-off and counterclaim can be used as procedural devices [*Berger, 55–58*]. Every set-off can be pleaded as a counterclaim, although not every counterclaim can be pleaded as a set-off [*Wood, 245*].

20. The conceptual similarity between set-off and counterclaim is recognised by a number of writers [*Berger, 58; Dore (1986), 57*]. For example, Wood states that, "Mutual counterclaims for money are now only a hair's-breadth away from set-off" [*Wood, 13;* cf. *Karrer, 117*] and also suggests that, "A set-off can always be pleaded as a counterclaim if the party so wishes" [*Wood, 244*]. This is further evidenced by the fact that Halsbury's Laws of England considers the two issues to be so closely related that set-off is dealt with under the heading of "Set-Off and Counterclaim" [*McCracken, 115*].

21. Set-off and counterclaim are deemed so similar in international arbitration that many of the arbitration rules, including the UNCITRAL Arbitration Rules (Article 19(4) and Article 18(2)) and the WIPO Arbitration Rules (Article 42(c)), require the same basic procedure to be followed for establishing the factual existence of a claim when raising either a counterclaim or a set-off [*Berger, 59*]. Similarly, although the UNCITRAL Model Law on International Commercial Arbitration (Model Law) "no longer refers expressly to counter-claims . . . a provision referring to [set-off] would apply . . . to a counter-claim" [*UNCITRAL Commentary A/CN.9/264, 128;* cf. *Binder, 28–29*].

22. Thus, counterclaim and set-off are very similar legal concepts which, especially in international arbitrations, are often raised for the same purpose or overall aim of including a cross-claim in an established arbitration hearing. "Set-off in international economic arbitration is therefore sometimes regarded as a 'counterclaim in disguise' " [*Berger, 58*]. Accordingly, the set-off defence in Article 21(5) Swiss Rules can be extended legally to ECE's counterclaim to give the Arbitral Tribunal jurisdiction to hear the dispute arising out of Sugar Contract 2212.

3.2 *Policy reasons support the extension of* ECE's *set-off to a counterclaim*

23. A decision by the Arbitral Tribunal to extend ECE's set-off to a counterclaim is justifiable on policy grounds because Cocoa Contract 1045 and Sugar Contract 2212 form one "economic and operational unit hidden behind a multi-contract façade, that actually amounts to one fundamental relationship" [*Leboulanger, 46–47*; cf. *Platte, 72; Respondent's Memorandum, para. 15–17*]. In such a case, an extension of the Tribunal's jurisdiction can occur without the consent of one party where the disputes heard by the Tribunal arise out of the same principal economic relationship [*Gaillard & Savage, para. 519–525; Platte, 6; Schneider, 103*]. In particular, ECE argues that the extension of the set-off defence in Article 21(5) to a counterclaim will (i) ensure the efficient conduct of the arbitration process and (ii) serve to avoid contradictory findings [cf. *Bell, 63; Branson & Wallace, 90; Huber & Trachte-Huber, 533; Nicklisch, 69; Platte, 78; Compania Espanola de Petroleos, S.A. v. Nereus Shipping, S.A. (2nd Circ., 1976)*].

24. Firstly, ECE and MCA consented to the authority of the Arbitral Tribunal to determine the dispute arising out of Cocoa Contract 1045. Both parties have elected an arbitrator, agreed upon the seat of arbitration and the broad procedure to be followed in the determination of this dispute. As such, the parties' consent indicates that this Arbitral Tribunal meets the requirements of impartiality and independence as required by Article 9 Swiss Rules. In this light, the extension of the Tribunal's jurisdiction to hear ECE's counterclaim arising out of Sugar Contract 2212 will avoid "the constitution of unnecessary tribunals and will thus reduce arbitral fees" [*Leboulanger, 63*; cf. *Platte, 78; Chui, 55*]. The existence of this Tribunal makes it unnecessary to convene another tribunal for the resolution of disputes arising out of Sugar Contract 2212. MCA's contention that "The Tribunal will not gain procedural efficiency by trying this issue" [*Claimant's Memorandum, para. 76*] is misguided because MCA and ECE will save time and money if the Arbitral Tribunal allows both disputes to be heard at the same time. Indeed, the assumption of jurisdiction by the Arbitral Tribunal over Sugar Contract 2212 is likely to reduce costs, provide for a speedy resolution of the dispute and make "proceedings more efficient" [*Platte, 78*].

25. Secondly, if the Arbitral Tribunal only allows the set-off defence, but not the counterclaim, then ECE will need to apply to the Oceania Commodity Association, under RAOCA, for the outstanding amount owed under Sugar Contract 2212. This creates the undesirable possibility of two arbitral tribunals rendering contradictory awards. This contradiction "may give rise to serious problems at the enforcement stage" because contradictory awards "cannot be reconciled by courts examining their merits or their reasoning" [*Leboulanger, 63*; cf. *Chui, 56; Rubino-Sammartano (1981), 436*]. The Arbitral Tribunal cannot avoid this contradiction by refusing to hear both the set-off defence and the counterclaim because ECE's claim satisfies the requirements of a set-off under Article 21(5) Swiss Rules [*Respondent's Memorandum, para. 11–14*]. Therefore, procedural concerns mandate the conferral of jurisdiction on the Arbitral Tribunal to hear ECE's counterclaim at the same time as the cocoa dispute is heard.

3.3 The extension of ECE*'s set-off defence to a counterclaim results in its recovery of more than* MCA *might be awarded under Cocoa Contract 1045*

26. A counterclaim, unlike a set-off defence, is not limited to the amount of the original claim, but allows full recovery of the amount requested in the counterclaim. Despite MCA's insistence that "the relief awarded to RE should be limited to a set-off against any recovery CL might recover" [*Claimant's Memorandum, para. 86*], a counter-claimant is allowed to claim damages in excess of the original claimant's damages because a counterclaim is not raised as a defence to the original claim [*Schulz, 18; Sekolec, 46; Wood, 242; Winterfield v. Bradnum (QBD, 1878)*]. ECE's claim is for US$385,805, which exceeds the maximum amount requested by MCA, namely US$289,353 [*Request for Arbitration, 18; Answer to Notice of Arbitration and Counter-Claim, 18*]. Therefore, the extension of Article 21(5) to a counterclaim enables ECE to recover more than MCA might be awarded under Cocoa Contract 1045.

4. The Arbitral Tribunal's award will be enforceable under the New York Convention and the Model Law

27. MCA suggests that a decision by the Arbitral Tribunal to hear ECE's counterclaim arising under Sugar Contract 2212 "will . . . raise concern as to the recognition and enforcement of the award" [*Claimant's Memorandum, para. 80*]. This suggestion is based on the argument that the Tribunal's award will violate the Convention on the Recognition and Enforcement of Foreign Arbitral Awards (New York Convention) and the Model Law. Article V(1)(c) New York Convention stipulates that the recognition and enforcement of an arbitral award may be refused if "The award deals with a difference not contemplated by or not falling within the terms of the submission to arbitration." Article V(1)(d) provides that an award may be set aside if "the arbitral procedure was not in accordance with the agreement of the parties" [cf. *Dore (1990), 84*]. Article 34(2)(a)(iii)–(iv) Model Law contains almost identical language [*Coe, 513; Holtzmann & Neuhaus, 911; Sanders, 57*].

28. Despite MCA's concerns, the Arbitral Tribunal's jurisdiction to hear ECE's counterclaim or set-off defence will not compromise the validity of the Tribunal's award. Indeed, Article 21(5) Swiss Rules, by its operation, extends the jurisdiction of the Arbitral Tribunal to the dispute arising out of Sugar Contract 2212. Hence, the arbitral procedure accords with the parties' arbitration agreement. Furthermore, ECE's counterclaim comes "within the terms of the submission to arbitration" because the dispute relating to Sugar Contract 2212 is a dispute "arising with respect to or in connection with" [*Claimant's Exhibit No. 2*] the arbitration agreement contained in Cocoa Contract 1045. This connection stems from the fact that Cocoa Contract 1045 and Sugar Contract 2212 serve the same economic purpose [*Respondent's Memorandum, para. 15–17*]. Accordingly, a decision by this Tribunal to hear ECE's counterclaim will not violate any of the provisions, contained in either the New York Convention or the Model Law, governing the enforceability of arbitral awards.

29. Additionally, "the arbitrator's authority to determine his own jurisdiction is not dependent on the question whether the award will be enforceable or not" [*Jarvin, para. 37*]. As such, the issue of the enforceability of an award should not limit an arbitrator's decision to assume jurisdiction over a dispute. Finally, domestic courts are reluctant to interfere with the decisions of an arbitral tribunal because of the policy requirements that arbitral awards be certain and final [*Carbonneau, 582; Craig, 179–180; Garnett et al., 101; Lamm & Spoorenberg, 3*]. Accordingly, MCA's argument that the extension of the Tribunal's jurisdiction to hear ECE's claim "jeopardizes the award" [*Claimant's Memorandum, para. 79*] is erroneous and should not influence the Arbitral Tribunal's decision to hear ECE's counterclaim.

II. *ECE*'S LATE DELIVERY OF 300 TONS OF COCOA BEANS IS EXCUSABLE UNDER THE *CISG*

30. In his Procedural Order No. 1, the President of the Arbitral Tribunal has requested an examination of whether the embargo placed on the export of cocoa beans by the Equatoriana Government Cocoa Marketing Organization from 22 February 2002 to 12 November 2002 excused ECE from delivering 300 tons of cocoa beans [*Procedural Order No. 1, para. 7; Procedural Order No. 2, Clarification 10*]. In this part of the Memorandum, ECE argues that its late delivery of the remaining 300 tons of cocoa beans was excusable because (1) MCA contracted to purchase Equatoriana cocoa beans and (2) ECE's failure to deliver cocoa beans is excusable under Article 79 CISG.

1. *MCA* contracted to purchase Equatoriana cocoa beans

31. MCA argues that, "The language of the contract is of primary importance to determine whether the parties agreed on a specific origin for the goods" [*Claimant's Memorandum, para. 3*] and that "the contract between the parties is a contract for general goods and not specifically for cocoa from Equatoriana" [*Claimant's Memorandum, para. 11*]. In responding to these claims, ECE argues that (1) Cocoa Contract 1045 was validly concluded on 19 November 2001, (2) the express terms of the contract do not reveal the origin of the cocoa beans, and (3) the implied terms of the contract reveal that MCA contracted to purchase Equatoriana cocoa beans.

1.1 Cocoa Contract 1045 was validly concluded on 19 November 2001

32. On 19 November 2001, Mr. Harold Smart, account executive for ECE, telephoned Mr. James Sweet, commodity buyer for MCA, offering to sell MCA 400 metric tons of cocoa beans at US$1240.75 per metric ton [*Request for Arbitration, 3*]. Mr. Sweet accepted this offer. During their conversation Mr. Smart and Mr. Sweet referred to the contract goods as "cocoa beans". The terms of the oral contract were confirmed by Mr. Smart by fax [*Claimant's Exhibit No. 1*] and evidenced by the written contract sent the same day [*Claimant's Exhibit No. 1; Claimant's Exhibit No. 2*]. The subsequent fax and written evidence of the oral contract sent by ECE stated that the cocoa beans would be sold according to the "usual terms" [*Claimant's Exhibit No. 1*] and would be of "standard grade and count" [*Claimant's Exhibit No. 2*].

33. This oral contract complies with the United Nations Convention on Contracts for the International Sale of Goods (CISG), which provides the substantive law applicable to Cocoa Contract 1045 [*Request for Arbitration, 17*]. Indeed, Article 11 CISG states that a contract "need not be concluded in . . . writing and is not subject to any other requirements as to form" [cf. *Enderlein & Maskow, 73–74; Gillies & Moens, 13; Honnold (1999), 135; Schlechtriem (1998), 85*]. Mr. Smart's offer was "sufficiently definite" because it identified the goods and fixed the quantity and the price in accordance with Article 14(1) CISG [*Bydlinski, 52–63; Enderlein & Maskow, 84; Honnold (1999), 197; Karollus, 60; Lookofsky, 46–47; Schlechtriem (1998), 105*]. Mr. Sweet's acceptance accords with Article 18(2) CISG because Mr. Smart's oral offer was "accepted immediately" during the telephone conversation [cf. *Enderlein & Maskow, 95; Honnold (1999), 176; Lookofsky, 53*]. Thus a valid oral contract was formed under the CISG from which the Arbitral Tribunal can determine the express terms of the contract.

1.2 The express terms of Cocoa Contract 1045 do not reveal the origin of the cocoa beans

34. An express term is an "express declaration of a particular promise or stipulation in the contract itself" [*Friedlander v. Bank of Australia (HCA, 1909)*]. A term is expressly stated in a contract by reason of what the parties have written or said [*Nygh & Butt, 1158*]. The express terms of Cocoa Contract 1045 deal with the contractual goods, "cocoa beans", the quantity of beans required, 400 metric tons, the price charged and the currency of the contract, US$496,299.55 [*Request for Arbitration, 3*]. A precise date for delivery of the cocoa beans was not determined when MCA and ECE entered into their oral contract. However, ECE and MCA expressly agreed that, during the period of January to February 2002, ECE would fix a delivery date "that would be between the months of March to May 2002" [*Request for Arbitration, 3*]. Although the express terms of the contract only describe the "cocoa beans" in generic terms, the implied terms of the contract reveal that MCA contracted to purchase Equatoriana cocoa beans.

1.3 The implied terms of Cocoa Contract 1045 reveal that MCA *contracted to purchase Equatoriana cocoa beans*

35. ECE argues that the term "cocoa beans" referred to "Equatoriana cocoa beans". In contrast, MCA's contention, that it had "no special interest in where the cocoa beans came from" [*Claimant's Memorandum, para. 5*] because cocoa is a "generic good" [*Claimant's Memorandum, para. 29*; cf. *Claimant's Exhibit No. 4*], suggests that the cocoa could be sourced from any viable country. Further, MCA submits that, "When only one of the parties intended for the goods to come from one particular source, the other party is still entitled to delivery regardless of the source" [*Claimant's Memorandum, para. 6*]. As MCA and ECE "attach different meanings to the same contractual language" [*Lookofsky, 40*], Article 8(2) and Article 8(3) CISG should be relied on because they assist in resolving conflicting interpretations.

(a) An objective approach should be adopted in ascertaining *MCA*'s and *ECE*'s intention under Cocoa Contract 1045

36. Where there is insufficient evidence of the parties' subjective intent, Article 8(2) CISG provides that "statements made by and other conduct of a party are to be interpreted according to the understanding that a reasonable person of the same kind as the other party would have had in the same circumstances." Indeed,

Honnold notes that where there are "practical barriers to proving identity between the intent of the two parties . . . most problems of interpretation will be governed by paragraph (2) which follows the 'objective' approach" [*Honnold (1991), 164–165;* cf. *Junge* in *Schlechtriem, (1998) 143; Murray, 48; M. Caito Roger v. La Société française de factoring international factor France "S.F.F" (SA), (CA Grenoble, 1995)*]. Consequently, even if MCA maintains that it could not have been aware of ECE's subjective intent, it is the understanding of a reasonable person in MCA's position that is applicable in interpreting Mr. Sweet's and Mr. Smart's telephone conversation of 19 November 2001 [cf. *Schlechtriem (1998), 39–40; OLG Saarbrücken (1993), 1 U 69/92*].

37. Further, Article 8(3) CISG states that in determining the understanding of a reasonable person, due consideration is to be given to "all relevant circumstances of the case including . . . any practices which the parties have established between themselves". Article 9(1) CISG confirms that parties are bound by "any practices which they have established between themselves". In fact, MCA and ECE have established practices which indicate that the cocoa beans had to be sourced from Equatoriana.

(b) *ECE* and *MCA* have established practices regarding the origin of the cocoa beans in accordance with Article 9(1) *CISG*

38. MCA argues that it "would have [had] no objection to receiving cocoa from any other minor producer country" and that "It would have accepted cocoa beans from the countries listed in Group C NYBOT or in Origin Group 5 LIFFE" [*Claimant's Memorandum, para. 10*]. However, the established practices between MCA and ECE reveal that the cocoa beans had to come from Equatoriana.

39. In order for a practice to have been established it is necessary that "on previous occasions the parties have acted likewise" [*Bout, 3;* cf. *Perales Viscasillas, 22; Schlechtriem (1998), 78*]. In this context, "It is highly relevant that every sale of cocoa by Equatoriana Commodity Exporters, S.A. to Mediterraneo Confectionary Associates, Inc. has been of cocoa that was produced in Equatoriana" [*Answer to Notice of Arbitration and Counter-Claim, 5*]. Additionally, in Mr. Smart's written confirmation of the oral contract of 19 November 2001, he referred to the "usual terms" [*Claimant's Exhibit No. 1*], which are the terms for the sale of cocoa agreed upon by ECE and MCA "which had been used in all previous cocoa contracts" [*Procedural Order No. 2, Clarification 16*]. Hence, ECE and MCA "have acted likewise" [*Bout, 3*] on previous occasions.

40. MCA knew that the cocoa beans always came from Equatoriana because "it was the buyer's responsibility to arrange for the carriage of goods" [*Procedural Order No. 2, Clarification 19*] and the cocoa beans were packed "in original shipping bags" [*Claimant's Exhibit No. 2*], which indicated Equatoriana as the country of origin [*Procedural Order No. 2, Clarification 19*]. As there is "an expectation that in future cases parties will act in a similar manner" [*Bout, 3*], ECE reasonably assumed that MCA, in entering into Cocoa Contract 1045, had contracted to purchase Equatoriana cocoa beans. Hence, the application of Article 8(2), Article 8(3) and Article 9(1) CISG indicate that the cocoa beans had to be sourced from Equatoriana.

2. *ECE*'s late delivery of cocoa beans is excusable under Article 79 *CISG*

41. MCA argues that: (1) the "embargo does not qualify as an impediment because the contract between the parties is a contract for general goods and not specifically for cocoa from Equatoriana" [*Claimant's Memorandum, para. 11*], (2) even if the embargo is characterised as an impediment, the embargo is not "the direct and exclusive cause of [ECE's] failure to deliver the remaining 300 tons" [*Claimant's Memorandum, para. 12–13*], (3) "The storm and its consequences on the cocoa market were reasonably foreseeable and [there] are therefore no grounds to excuse" ECE's alleged failure to perform its obligations under Cocoa Contract 1045 [*Claimant's Memorandum, para. 16*] and, (4) ECE could have avoided the embargo or overcome its consequences. In this part of the Memorandum, ECE refutes each of MCA's contentions in turn.

2.1 *The embargo constitutes an impediment beyond* ECE*'s control*

42. Article 79(1) CISG states that, "A party is not liable for a failure to perform any of his obligations if he proves that the failure was due to an impediment beyond his control and that he could not reasonably be expected to have taken the impediment into account at the time of the conclusion of the contract or to have overcome it or its consequences." Article 79 CISG allows for an exemption only where the impediment is not within the defaulting party's sphere of control [*Bianca & Bonnell, 579–580; Magnus (1999), 489; Schlechtriem (1998), 610*]. This requirement is illustrated in *C. Czarnikow Ltd. v. Centrala Handlu Zagranicznego* where it was held that, as the seller was independent of the State sugar organisation, this organisation's embargo constituted an impediment beyond the seller's control [*HL, 1977*].

43. ECE was independent of the Equatoriana Government Cocoa Marketing Organization, which had a monopoly over the supply of cocoa [*Procedural Order No. 2, Clarification 11*]. As such, the embargo was an impediment beyond ECE's control. Moreover, ECE could not appeal against the export embargo because, "There was no legal procedure available" to protest it [*Procedural Order No. 2, Clarification 12*]. Therefore, the embargo constitutes an impediment within Article 79 CISG [cf. *Fox, 109; Rauh, 151; Schmitthoff, 121*].

2.2 *The embargo caused the delay in the delivery of the remaining 300 tons of cocoa beans*

44. MCA asserts that, in any event, the government embargo does not qualify as an impediment under Article 79 CISG because there was no causal connection between the embargo and ECE's failure to perform [*Claimant's Memorandum, para. 14*]. However, as soon as the Equatoriana Government Cocoa Marketing Organization released a small amount of cocoa beans, ECE shipped 100 tons of beans to MCA [*Claimant's Exhibit No. 6*]. This shipment is evidence that it was the embargo which prevented ECE from making a timely delivery of cocoa beans.

45. Furthermore, Enderlein and Maskow state that the causality element "depends on how much the goods have been *individualized*" [at *321*]. For example, if a contract requires the delivery of individualised goods "from a certain region . . . exemption will be granted when the . . . goods are affected" by an impediment

[*Enderlein & Maskow, 321;* cf. *Schlechtriem (1998), 614*]. The cocoa beans of Cocoa Contract 1045 are individualised, as opposed to generic goods, because the cocoa had to be sourced from Equatoriana [*Respondent's Memorandum, para. 35–40*].

46. Moreover, as Equatoriana cocoa beans falls under Origin Group C NYBOT, it must necessarily have a specific numerical "count" between 1200 and 1400 beans per kilogram as specified in Rule 9.18(b)(iii) NYBOT [cf. *Dand, 218–221*]. As such, it constitutes an "individualised" product. In fact, as MCA itself acknowledges, the goods were "of a particular kind or genre" [*Claimant's Memorandum, para. 31*] even within their alleged generic class. Hence, the government's embargo constituted an impediment under Article 79 CISG. This impediment was beyond the control of ECE and resulted in ECE's failure to deliver the 300 tons of cocoa beans.

2.3 ECE *could not reasonably be expected to have taken the storm or subsequent government embargo into account*

47. Article 79(1) CISG does not confer on a party an exemption from damages in circumstances where it could "reasonably be expected to have taken the impediment into account at the time of the conclusion of the contract" [cf. *Brauer & Co. v. James Clark (HL, 1952)*]. Where a party fails to take the impediment into account it exposes itself to risk and must carry the consequences of its actions [*AG Alsfeld (1995), 31 C 534/94*]. The phrase "reasonably be expected" in Article 79 CISG is based on the concept of foreseeability and requires that a party "neither knew nor ... ought to have been aware" of an impediment "because otherwise he would have had to take it into consideration" [*Enderlein & Maskow 323;* cf. *Honnold (1991), 542*]. The question of foreseeability is one of fact [*Perillo, 6; Sacco & De Nova, 675*] and "foreseeability should relate not only to the impediment per se but also to the time of its occurrence" [*Rimke, 216;* cf. *Schlechtriem (1998), 611*]. This is relevant because, whilst storms and embargoes are generally foreseeable, their occurrence at a particular time may not be. ECE argues that the severity of the storm and the subsequent government embargo were unforeseeable at the time of their occurrence.

48. Traditional *force majeure* events can include "unusually severe weather conditions" [*Rimke, 230;* cf. *Declercq, 233*]. The storm that struck the cocoa-producing areas of Equatoriana on 14 February 2002 was "unusually severe" and was more destructive than any storms in the past [*Procedural Order No. 2, Clarification 8*]. Similarly, in *Raw Materials Inc. v. Manfred Forberich GmbH & Co., KG*, a Russian seller was unable to fulfil its contractual obligations because the St. Petersburg port froze over during winter [*(US Dist. Ct Il., 2004)*]. The court held that while it was generally foreseeable that the Port could freeze over during winter, the severity and early onset of this particular winter were unforeseeable.

49. Although MCA argues that ECE should have foreseen the storm and its consequences because Equatoriana experienced a storm in 1980 [*Claimant's Memorandum, para. 20*], the severity of the storm on 14 February 2002 was unforeseeable because no other storm had caused extensive damage to cocoa trees [*Procedural Order No. 2, Clarification 8*]. In contrast, the storm of 14 February 2002 was unprecedented in its intensity, causing "extensive damage to the crop that was ready for harvesting" and, as such, was unforeseeable under Article 79 CISG [*Claimant's Exhibit No. 3*].

2.4 ECE *could not have avoided the embargo or overcome its consequences*

50. Article 79(1) CISG does not confer on a party an exemption from damages in circumstances where it could "have avoided [the impediment] or overcome it or its consequences". In this regard, MCA argues that ECE's failure to perform is not excusable under Article 79(1) because "RE could have overcome and avoided [the] consequences" of the embargo [*Claimant's Memorandum, para. 23*]. By way of response, ECE argues that (a) it could not have avoided the embargo, and (b) could not have overcome the consequences of the embargo.

(a) *ECE* could not have avoided the embargo

51. A determination of whether an impediment could have been reasonably avoided is a question of fact [*Enderlein & Maskow, 231*]. The CISG requires that the impediment is "reasonably insurmountable" [*Bianca & Bonell, 592*]. For example, military blockades and government prohibitions cannot reasonably be avoided under Article 79(1) CISG "although it may be possible to run a blockade or evade a law" [*Honnold (1991), 542*]. ECE argues that, as it was not reasonable to expect it to ship goods in defiance of domestic law, the embargo was "reasonably insurmountable".

52. MCA's argument, that ECE "was under the duty to apply for [an] exemption" [*Claimant's Memorandum, para. 24*] is flawed. First, there were no formal procedures available to ECE for protesting the Equatoriana Government Cocoa Marketing Organization's embargo [*Procedural Order No. 2, Clarification 12*]. Second, at law, ECE is only required to seek remedies against State restrictions insofar "as they have a chance of succeeding" [*Enderlein & Maskow, 324*; cf. *Rimke, 216*]. The futility of the process of protesting the embargo is illustrated by the fact that a number of cocoa exporters who applied for an exemption from the embargo, had their applications rejected [*Procedural Order No. 2, Clarification 12*]. Therefore, ECE could not have avoided the embargo.

(b) *ECE* could not have overcome the consequences of the embargo

53. The consequences of an impediment cannot be reasonably overcome where this will result in a significant change in the nature of the contractual obligation [*Burnett, 36; National Carriers Ltd. v. Panalpina (Northern) Ltd. (AC, 1981); VCLT, Art. 62*]. MCA argues that ECE "had the option of purchasing an equal substitute from a supply source outside Equatoriana" [*Claimant's Memorandum, para. 29*]. In contrast, ECE contends that it was required, under Cocoa Contract 1045, to supply Equatoriana cocoa beans [*Respondent's Memorandum, para. 35–40*], and that the delivery of substitute goods would have changed the nature of its contractual obligations so significantly "as to amount to performance of an obligation quite different from that contemplated" [*Nicholas, 4*].

54. Furthermore, "the party affected by impediments can only be obligated to deliver . . . substitute [goods] in exceptional cases" [*Enderlein & Maskow, 335*]. When "individualised" goods are contracted for, a demand for the delivery of "generic" goods would, in effect, allow one party to unilaterally alter the terms of the contract without the consent of the other party [*Bianca & Bonell, 582*]. ECE has argued that the implied terms of Cocoa Contract 1045 require the delivery of individualised goods because they had to be sourced from Equatoriana [*Respondent's Memorandum, para. 35–40*]. Hence, a substitute delivery by ECE from any other source would contravene the implied terms of Cocoa Contract 1045.

55. MCA suggests that there have been no UNCITRAL or ICC reported cases that have allowed an excusable breach under Article 79 CISG [*Claimant's Memorandum, para. 15*]. This is a selective view since there have been claims that have satisfied the elements of Article 79 CISG [*C. Czarnikow Ltd. v. Centrala Handlu Zagranicznego (HL, 1977); Raw Materials Inc. v. Manfred Forberich GmbH & Co., KG (US Dist. Ct. Il., 2004)*]. Furthermore, commentators have provided examples of hypothetically successful claims, which support ECE's contention that it could not have overcome the consequences of the embargo by making a substitute purchase [*Kimbel, 319; Secretariat Commentary on Article 79, para. 9*]. The Secretariat Commentary on Article 79 CISG provides an example of a contract for unique goods, which were destroyed before delivery. In this case it was deemed that the seller could not replace the goods contracted for by making a substitute transaction and was, therefore, exempted from liability for any resulting damage [*Secretariat Commentary on Article 79, para. 9*]. As such, ECE's failure to make a substitute delivery of the 300 tons of Equatoriana cocoa beans is excusable under Article 79 CISG.

III. *MCA* IS NOT ENTITLED TO CLAIM DAMAGES FOR *ECE*'S LATE DELIVERY OF 300 TONS OF COCOA BEANS

56. In Procedural Order No. 1, the President of the Arbitral Tribunal has requested a discussion of whether MCA can claim damages for ECE's late or non-delivery of 300 tons of cocoa beans, in the event that ECE's failure to deliver is not excused. MCA claims that it is entitled to damages since ECE's failure to deliver the 300 tons of cocoa beans "amounts to [a] fundamental breach because it substantially deprived CL of what it expected" under Cocoa Contract 1045 [*Claimant's Memorandum, para. 37*]. Consequently, MCA submits that it "validly avoided its contract . . . on 15 August 2002" and "is thus justified" to claim damages [*Claimant's Memorandum, para. 62*]. ECE specifically responds to these assertions by arguing that: (1) ECE's failure to deliver the 300 tons of cocoa beans does not constitute a fundamental breach under Article 25 CISG, and therefore does not entitle MCA to avoid Cocoa Contract 1045 under Article 49(1)(a) CISG or alternatively, (2) MCA was not entitled to avoid Cocoa Contract 1045 on 15 August 2002 in accordance with Article 49(1)(b) CISG because it failed to provide a *Nachfrist* period. In addition, ECE further argues that (3) MCA did not validly avoid Cocoa Contract 1045 in accordance with the relevant provisions of the CISG until 15 November 2002.

1. *MCA* is not entitled to avoid Cocoa Contract 1045 under Article 49(1)(a) *CISG*

57. While MCA makes no explicit mention of Article 49(1)(a) CISG to support its claim that it validly avoided Cocoa Contract 1045 on 15 August 2002 [*Claimant's Memorandum, para. 49*], it is this Article which provides the framework within which avoidance can occur. Article 49(1)(a) stipulates that the buyer may declare the contract avoided "if the failure by the seller to perform any of his obligations under the contract or this Convention amounts to a fundamental breach of contract".

"Fundamental breach" is defined in Article 25 CISG, which states: "A breach of contract committed by one of the parties is fundamental if it results in such detriment to the other party as substantially to deprive him of what he is entitled to expect under the contract, unless the party in breach did not foresee and a reasonable person of the same kind in the same circumstances would not have foreseen such a result." Therefore, two requirements have to be satisfied in order for a breach to be fundamental: (1) a substantial detriment and (2) the foreseeability of the detriment by the party in breach.

1.1 MCA *was not substantially deprived of what it was entitled to expect under Cocoa Contract 1045*

58. "Detriment", for the purpose of Article 25 CISG, focuses on the importance of the obligation to the individual parties to the contract in light of the relevant circumstances [*Babiak, 113; El-Saghir, para. 4; Honnold (1998), 206; Kritzer, 212; Melville, 308; Schlechtriem (1998), 177; Sutton, 286*]. The expectation of a party under a contract is a central element in the determination of whether the breach is detrimental [*Babiak, 120; Lorenz, para. 40; Schlechtriem (1998), 177*]. This is because the detriment must substantially deprive a party of what he is entitled to expect under the contract [*Enderlein & Maskow, 113; Michida, 281*]. The concept of "substantiality" in Article 25 CISG requires a real and considerable detriment, which depends on whether the breach can be cured without causing unreasonable inconvenience and delay [*Enderlein & Maskow, 115; Honnold (1998), 207; Radio 2UE Sydney Pty. Ltd. v. Stereo FM Pty. Ltd. (FCA, 1982)*].

59. MCA alleges that, "In failing to fully deliver by 31 May 2002 RE . . . substantially deprived CL of what it expected under the contract" [*Claimant's Memorandum, para. 40*] because ECE's actions resulted in a reduced production rate for MCA [*Claimant's Memorandum, para. 43*]. In this regard, a hypothetical case discussed by Kimbel is instructive. Kimbel explained that the seller's late delivery did not fundamentally breach the contract because the buyer was still able to perform its contractual obligations to its customers since its inventory was not yet depleted. Indeed, the buyer "was able to perform the re-sale contracts despite the delays by filling the re-sale contracts with [goods] from existing inventory" [at *319*; cf. *FCF v Adriafil (2000), 4C105/2000*].

60. In this context, MCA's assertion that ECE's late delivery "significantly affected CL's Production in 2002" [*Claimant's Memorandum, para. 43*] is baseless because at the time of MCA's alleged avoidance, its inventory had not been completely depleted and MCA could still fulfil its production needs with reserve cocoa. ECE would only have been in fundamental breach if it had not delivered by the time MCA had completely run out of cocoa, sometime at the end of November 2002 [*Procedural Order No. 2, Clarification 24*]. As such, no substantial detriment was suffered as a result of (a) ECE's failure to fix a delivery date or (b) ECE's late delivery of 300 tons of cocoa beans.

(a) *ECE*'s failure to fix a delivery date did not result in a "substantial detriment" under Article 25 *CISG*

61. Where delivery by a fixed date is required, the interest "in taking delivery on that date is so fundamental" as to constitute a substantial detriment when this obligation is violated [*Schlechtriem (1998), 177*]. However, there cannot be a fundamental breach for failure to deliver where the parties have not agreed on a specific date of delivery [*DiMatteo et al., 412; Karollus, 71; AG Oldenburg (1990), 5 C 73/89; OLG München (1995), 7 U 1720/94*].

62. The very nature of Cocoa Contract 1045 was unspecific as to the fixing of a delivery date [*Claimant's Exhibit No. 2*]. Indeed, no specific date for delivery of the cocoa beans was established in the contract, which provided for the fixing of a delivery date "between the months of March to May 2002" [*Claimant's Exhibit No. 1; Claimant's Exhibit No. 2*]. Furthermore, MCA, in its letter of 15 August 2002, merely requested the delivery of 300 tons of cocoa beans "soon", which does not constitute a specific date for delivery [*Claimant's Exhibit No. 7*]. Therefore, ECE's failure to fix a delivery date did not result in a substantial detriment for MCA.

(b) *ECE*'s late delivery of the 300 tons of cocoa beans did not result in a "substantial detriment" under Article 25 *CISG*

63. MCA argues that ECE's failure to deliver the 300 metric tons of cocoa beans by 31 May 2002 amounted to a fundamental breach of Cocoa Contract 1045 [*Claimant's Memorandum, para. 39*]. However, MCA's argument is erroneous because (i) late delivery does not constitute a fundamental breach under Article 25 CISG, (ii) MCA accepted ECE's part-performance, and (iii) MCA maintained an interest in the future performance of the contract [*Claimant's Exhibit No. 5*].

(i) Late delivery does not constitute a fundamental breach

64. "Late delivery does not generally constitute a fundamental breach" of a contract [*DiMatteo et al., 412*; cf. *Enderlein & Maskow, 114; Karollus, 71; OLG München (2002), 10 O 5423/01*]. In *OLG Düsseldorf* the court held that mere non-delivery or late delivery does not constitute a fundamental breach under Article 25 CISG provided that delivery is "objectively" possible and the seller is willing to deliver [*(1993), 6 U 228/92*]. Additionally, "A fundamental breach occurs if the seller declares seriously and definitely . . . that he will not deliver substitute goods, but does not occur if he only declares that he cannot deliver at the moment" [*Karollus, 72*; cf. *OLG Düsseldorf (1994), 6 U 119/93*].

65. ECE could "objectively" have performed its obligations as soon as the embargo was lifted. Indeed, ECE anticipated shipping "the remaining 300 tons in the very near future" [*Claimant's Exhibit No. 6*]. Furthermore, ECE only indicated that it could not deliver the 300 tons of cocoa beans at the moment. Therefore ECE's late or non-delivery did not constitute a fundamental breach under Article 25 CISG.

66. In certain circumstances "a delay in delivery can rise to a level of a fundamental breach when a timely delivery is in the special interest of the buyer" [*DiMatteo et al., 412*; cf. *Schlechtriem, 177; OLG Hamburg (1997), 1 U 167/95*]. However, the importance of a timely delivery date must be foreseeable at the time of the conclusion of the contract [*OLG Hamburg (1997), 1 U 167/95*]. At the time Cocoa Contract 1045 was concluded on 19 November 2001, there was no indication that time was of the essence [cf. *Enderlein & Maskow, 114*]. Furthermore, although Cocoa Contract 1045 stipulated that delivery had to occur by 31 May 2002, MCA was prepared to accept delivery after this date [*Claimant's Exhibit No. 7*]. Therefore, timely delivery was not of special interest to MCA and ECE's late delivery was not a fundamental breach of the contract.

(ii) *MCA* accepted *ECE*'s part-performance of Cocoa Contract 1045

67. In *HG Zurich* the court held that, where a seller failed to deliver the first instalment under a contract, the buyer may conclude that "a fundamental breach of contract was to be expected for further instalments" [*(1997), HG 95 0347*]. ECE performed Cocoa Contract 1045 in part by delivering 100 tons of cocoa beans on 18 May 2002 [*Claimant's Exhibit No. 6*]. This part-performance reinforced ECE's willingness to deliver the remaining 300 tons of cocoa beans and gave MCA reason to believe that ECE would perform its contractual obligations. Therefore, ECE's failure to deliver the 300 tons by 31 May 2002 did not amount to a fundamental breach.

(iii) *MCA* maintained an interest in the future performance of Cocoa Contract 1045

68. Furthermore, the purpose of the contract pursued by the aggrieved party must have been frustrated sufficiently for that party to lose interest in its contractual obligations [*Enderlein & Maskow, 113;* cf. *Koch* in *PILR, 245; Schlechtriem (1986), 59; BGH (1996), VIII ZR 51/95*]. MCA's acceptance of ECE's part-performance demonstrates that MCA did not consider the purpose of the contract to be frustrated. In fact, in its letter of 15 August 2002, MCA stated, "you continue to owe us 300 tons" [*Claimant's Exhibit No. 7*]. Hence, MCA had not lost interest in ECE's performance and the purpose of Cocoa Contract 1045 had not been frustrated.

1.2 ECE *or a reasonable person in the same position as* ECE *would not have foreseen the alleged detriment suffered by* MCA

69. Even if the Tribunal accepts that MCA suffered detriment within the meaning of Article 25 CISG, this detriment was not foreseeable. In determining foreseeability of detriment, an arbitral tribunal typically considers "knowledge of the facts surrounding the transaction" [*Babiak, 122;* cf. *Ziegel* in *Galston, §9.03*]. In particular, correspondence between the parties subsequent to the formation of the contract may be taken into account [*Flechtner, para. 4; Honnold (1998) 183; Lorenz, para. 51; Michida, 284; Schlechtriem (1998), 176*]. Furthermore, regardless of whether or not a seller could have foreseen the detriment which would occur as a result of late delivery to a buyer, the breach will still be fundamental under Article 25 CISG if a reasonable person in the same position as the seller would have foreseen such a result [*Enderlein & Maskow, 115; Schlechtriem (1998), 178*].

70. MCA claims that the detriment suffered "significantly affected CL's production in 2002" [*Claimant's Memorandum, para. 43*]. However, ECE and MCA's correspondence subsequent to the formation of the contract does not prove that the detriment was foreseeable by ECE. This stems from the fact that following ECE's part-performance, MCA never specifically stated when it would run out of cocoa and failed to stipulate the latest date by which delivery would be required [*Claimant's Exhibit No. 7*]. Additionally, MCA did not inform ECE of what the consequences of non-delivery would be for MCA. Therefore, neither ECE nor a reasonable person in the same position as ECE would have foreseen the alleged detriment suffered by MCA [*Respondent's Memorandum, para. 65*].

2. *MCA* was not entitled to avoid Cocoa Contract under Article 49(1)(b) *CISG*

71. MCA contends that if the Arbitral Tribunal were to decide that ECE's breaches were not fundamental, MCA is still entitled to avoid Cocoa Contract 1045 because

"CL implicitly fixed an additional period for RE to deliver the outstanding cocoa between 1 June and 14 August 2002" [*Claimant's Memorandum, para. 53*] and ECE failed to deliver within this additional period. MCA's argument is presumably based on Article 49(1)(b) CISG, which stipulates that the buyer may declare the contract avoided "in the case of non-delivery, if the seller does not deliver the goods within the additional period of time fixed by the buyer in accordance with paragraph (1) of Article 47 or declares that that he will not deliver within the period so fixed".

72. Article 47(1) CISG states that, "The buyer may fix an additional period of time of reasonable length for performance by the seller of his obligations." If there is no performance within the additional period or "*Nachfrist*", then the buyer may avoid the contract [*DiPalma, 43; Piliounis, para. 47; Schlechtriem (1998) 399; Van Houtte, 161*]. The buyer may also avoid the contract, under Article 47(2) CISG, if the seller declares that he will not perform within the additional period. ECE argues that MCA cannot avoid Cocoa Contract 1045 under Article 49(1)(b) because (1) MCA did not provide ECE with a *Nachfrist*, (2) even if MCA did provide ECE with a *Nachfrist*, it was not of a reasonable length, and (3) ECE did not declare that it would not perform within the alleged *Nachfrist* period.

2.1 MCA *did not set a* Nachfrist *period in accordance with Article 49(1)(b)* CISG

73. Where "a fundamental breach of contract cannot be established, the [buyer can] only claim damages for non-performance as a consequence of an avoidance of the contract according to Art. 49(1)(b) CISG, if the [buyer has] fixed a final deadline according to Art. 47(1) CISG in respect of the lacking partial delivery" [*OLG Düsseldorf (1997), 6 U 87/96*; cf. *AG Oldenburg (1990), 5 C 73/89; OLG Frankfurt (1994), 5 U 15/93; OLG Köln (1994), 22 U 202/93*]. MCA argues that it "implicitly fixed an additional period for [ECE] to deliver the outstanding cocoa between 1 June and 14 August 2002" [*Claimant's Memorandum, para. 53*]. However, at law, a *Nachfrist* period cannot be fixed implicitly. As such MCA's assertion that it fixed a *Nachfrist* is incorrect.

74. Enderlein and Maskow state that, "The buyer must *set an additional period, i.e. inform the seller accordingly either orally or in writing* ... It must be clear from the communication that it is an additional period of time for performance, i.e. fulfilment after expiration of that period is rejected" [at *183*, cf. *Honnold (1999), 314*]. If the *Nachfrist* notice is not of the clarity required by Article 47(1) CISG, avoidance must be based on a fundamental breach [*Honnold (1999), 315*].

75. In addition, it is generally accepted that the setting of a *Nachfrist* requires the fixing of a specific date for performance [*Schlechtriem (1998), 395*]. In *OLG Düsseldorf* the court held that "such an extension of delay must contain a precise request for performance that is combined with the fixing of a specific deadline" [*(1997), 6 U 87/96*]. Indeed, as Zeller states, "if the notice is not for a fixed period of time it may give the defaulting party the impression that it is free to postpone performance indefinitely" [at *5*]. Furthermore, he notes that the request for performance in the *Nachfrist* period "must not be couched in ambiguous terms" [at *5*]. Therefore, reminders that fail to fix a deadline and that contain "vague terms like 'soon' or 'promptly' do not suffice" [*Enderlein & Maskow, 182*; cf. *Honnold (1999), 315; Zeller, 5*]. MCA did not expressly provide ECE with a *Nachfrist* period as is required by Article 47(1) CISG and the terms of the alleged implicit *Nachfrist* lack specificity.

2.2 Even if the Arbitral Tribunal accepts that MCA *set a* Nachfrist *period, this period was not of a reasonable length*

76. A *Nachfrist* period fixed by an innocent party must be of a "reasonable length" [*Honnold (1998), 289*]. The buyer determines, in light of the surrounding circumstances, whether a *Nachfrist* is of "reasonable length" [*Enderlein & Maskow, 238; Honnold (1991), 371; Mo, 149*]. While a determination of whether a "period of time is reasonable must ultimately be left to the court" [*Zeller, 5*], several factors must be considered, including i) the period of time originally set for performance, ii) the need of the aggrieved party for quick performance, and iii) the event which caused the delay [*Will* in *Bianca & Bonell, 345; Enderlein & Maskow, 182*].

77. MCA argues that it had an interest in prompt performance of the contract [*Claimant's Memorandum, para. 45*] and therefore it was entitled to provide a shorter *Nachfrist* period. However, the need of the aggrieved party for quick performance is only relevant if this is apparent to the defaulting party [*Zeller, 5*]. This need was not apparent to ECE because MCA never clearly expressed when it would need to receive the replacement cocoa beans [*Respondent's Memorandum, para. 75*].

78. In any event, as Zeller states, "a party which has been prevented from performance by bad weather should be granted a longer [*Nachfrist*] respite than a party which merely forgot its duties" [at *5*]. ECE should therefore have been granted a longer *Nachfrist* period by reason of the storm over Equatoriana. MCA was aware of this impediment [*Claimant's Exhibit No. 4*] and ought to have provided ECE with a longer *Nachfrist* period as a result.

2.3 ECE *did not declare, under Article 47(2)* CISG, *that it would not perform within the alleged* Nachfrist *period*

79. MCA argues that it granted ECE a *Nachfrist* period, which ended when ECE failed to perform its outstanding obligations [*Claimant's Memorandum, para. 55*]. Article 47(2) CISG indicates that the buyer can avoid the contract where it receives notice that the seller will not perform within the additional period fixed. However, in order for Article 47(2) to apply, the notice must clearly express that there will be no performance during the *Nachfrist* period [*Enderlein & Maskow, 184*]. In *OLG Bamberg*, the court decided that a telephone call, during which the seller indicated that it could only deliver a portion of the total amount agreed upon under the contract, clearly expressed a party's intention not to perform [*(1999), 3 U 83/98*]. Conversely, ECE continually reassured MCA that it would deliver the remaining 300 tons of cocoa beans [*Respondent's Memorandum, para. 62*]. Therefore, MCA is not entitled to avoid the contract under Article 49(1)(b)(ii) because ECE's conduct comes within the exception in Article 47(2).

3. Alternatively, MCA did not validly avoid Cocoa Contract 1045 until 15 November 2002

80. If the Tribunal accepts that MCA was entitled to avoid the contract under Article 49(1)(a) or Article 49(1)(b) CISG, the letter of 15 August 2002 did not constitute avoidance as is claimed by MCA [*Claimant's Exhibit No. 7; Claimant's Memorandum, para. 55*]. At law, MCA did not validly avoid Cocoa Contract 1045 in accordance with the relevant provisions of the CISG until 15 November 2002. Article 26 CISG states that, "a declaration of avoidance of the contract is effective only if made by notice to the other party". While the CISG "does not provide any obligation concerning the form of the avoidance of sale contracts" [*FCF S.A. v. Adriafil Commerciale S.r.l (2000), 4C105/2000*], it should leave no doubts as to the avoidance of the contract [*OGH (2000), 1 Ob 292/99v*] and it must be conclusive [cf. *LG Frankfurt (1991), 3/11 O 3/91*].

3.1 MCA's *alleged avoidance in its letter of 15 August 2002 did not satisfy the requirements of Article 26* CISG

81. Under the CISG avoidance must be express and cannot be "ipso facto" or implicit [*Chengwei, para. 3; Schlechtriem (1998), 176; OLG Köln (2002), 16 U 77/01*]. As such, the wording of the notice of avoidance "must be unequivocal. In the case of doubt it should ... be interpreted as a mere threat of avoidance" [*Enderlein & Maskow, 243*; cf. *Honnold (1999), 215*]. ECE contends that MCA did not provide ECE with an express notice of avoidance within the meaning of Article 26 CISG because MCA never clearly or unequivocally communicated that it had avoided the contract.

(a) *MCA's* letter of 15 August 2002 did not constitute an express declaration of avoidance

82. MCA has argued that, "a declaration of avoidance can be made through implicit conduct" [*Claimant's Memorandum, para. 50*]. However, "Automatic or *ipso facto* avoidance was deleted from the remedial system in this Convention because it led to uncertainty as to whether the contract was still in force" [*Secretariat Commentary on Article 49, para. 2*]. As such, "conduct implying an intent to avoid a contract is not recognized" as an express declaration of avoidance [*Kazimierska* in *PILR (2000), 115*; cf. *AG Oldenburg (1990), 5 C 73/89; AG Zweibrücken (1992), 1 C 216/92*]. In *OLG Frankfurt*, the court found that a declaration of avoidance had to be unmistakably communicated to the seller [*(1991), 5 U 164/90*]. Thus, MCA was required to make an express declaration of avoidance to ECE.

83. MCA further argues that its letter of 15 August 2002, requesting ECE to set a delivery date "soon" [*Claimant's Exhibit No. 7*], became a notice of avoidance when ECE failed to comply with its request [*Claimant's Memorandum, para. 51*]. Thus, MCA's alleged letter of avoidance was dependent on the fulfilment of a condition by ECE. MCA relies on ICC Case No. 8128 to support its claim that avoidance may be conditional and only operates when its conditions are not met. However, at law "the declaration of avoidance cannot be conditional" [*Kazimierska* in *PILR (2000), 117*]. Furthermore, MCA is distinct from the buyer in ICC Case No. 8128, who "clearly indicated" to the seller that it needed to specify a delivery date before a given deadline. This stems from the fact that MCA, in its letter of 15 August 2002, never imposed a deadline by which ECE had to specify a date for delivery. As such, MCA's conditional avoidance was not "clearly indicated" or unequivocal [*ICC No. 8128, (1995)*]. Therefore, MCA's letter of 15 August 2002 did not constitute an express declaration of avoidance under Article 26 CISG.

84. In addition, "it would not be consistent with good faith and fair dealing for a party to rely on, for instance, a purely casual remark made to the other party" to claim avoidance of the contract [*Chengwei, para. 12*]. For example, in *OLG München* it was held that a comment on the possibility of a cancellation of a contract did not constitute a declaration of avoidance [*(1994), 7 U 4419/93*]. In its letter of 15 August 2002 MCA merely stated, "you continue to owe us the 300 tons" [*Claimant's Exhibit No. 7*], which implied that the parties were still in a contractual relationship. This statement was purely casual and was, at most, a comment by MCA on the possibility that it might avoid the contract in the future. As such, MCA's letter did not constitute an express declaration of avoidance.

85. In circumstances where the buyer makes a substitute purchase, an express declaration of avoidance is sometimes dispensable. However, this is only the case where it is certain that the seller will not perform its obligations at the time of the substitute purchase [*ICC No. 7645, (1995); OLG Hamburg (1997), 1 U 167/95*]. MCA was not entitled to dispense with a declaration of avoidance because ECE was still willing to perform its obligations by 24 October 2002 when MCA made its substitute purchase [*Respondent's Memorandum, para. 62*]. Therefore, MCA's argument that it implicitly avoided the contract by making a substitute purchase is flawed because it was required to make an express declaration of avoidance within the meaning of Article 26 CISG.

(b) A specific date of avoidance cannot be ascertained before 15 November 2002

86. Avoidance must occur on a specific date in order to overcome "the uncertainty as to whether, and possibly when, the contract is made void" [*Chengwei, para. 4*; cf. *Enderlein & Maskow, 116; OLG München (1994), 7 U 4419/93*]. MCA argues that the letter of 15 August 2002 [*Claimant's Exhibit No. 7*] became a notice of avoidance when ECE failed to fix a delivery date [*Claimant's Memorandum, para. 51*]. However, MCA has not clarified on which date this alleged failure occurred. The only communication that took place between MCA and ECE following MCA's letter of 15 August 2002 and before its substitute purchase on 24 October 2002 was a phone call on 29 September 2002 [*Procedural Order No. 2, Clarification 22*]. During this phone call Mr. Sweet simply "reiterated the concerns expressed in his letter of 15 August 2002" [*Procedural Order No. 2, Clarification 22*]. In this letter Mr. Sweet stated, "if we do not receive notification from you soon when you will be shipping the remaining 300 tons, we will have to purchase elsewhere" [*Claimant's Exhibit No. 7*]. This statement implied that the parties were still in a contractual relationship and therefore, Cocoa Contract 1045 was not avoided on 15 August 2002 or 29 September 2002.

87. In fact, ECE contends that MCA did not make an express declaration of avoidance of the contract under Article 26 CISG until 15 November 2002. This contention is based on the fact that MCA sent a letter on 15 November 2002 to the President of ECE, Mr. Albert Tender, stating that MCA "considers the referenced contract to be terminated" [*Claimant's Exhibit No. 11*]. However, this alternative submission that MCA validly avoided the contract on 15 November 2002 should not obscure ECE's primary argument that MCA is not entitled to damages as a result of a valid avoidance, following a fundamental breach.

IV. *MCA* CANNOT CLAIM ANY DAMAGES UNDER ARTICLE 74 *CISG*

88. In Procedural Order No. 1, the President of the Arbitral Tribunal requires a discussion in this Memorandum of the proper amount of damages. Although MCA has claimed that it is entitled to damages for ECE's alleged fundamental breach, it has not requested any damages for a non-fundamental breach of contract. Even if MCA had made such a request, it would not be entitled to any damages. In developing this argument, ECE contends that: (1) Article 74 CISG provides the appropriate legal framework for a discussion of damages, (2) MCA did not mitigate its alleged loss under Article 77 CISG, (3) MCA did not make a substitute purchase within a reasonable time and (4) MCA's purchase was not made in good faith. Alternatively, (5) ECE argues that damages amount to US$172,026.

1. Article 74 *CISG* provides the appropriate legal framework for a discussion of damages

89. MCA maintains that it is entitled to claim damages under Article 75 CISG for its substitute purchase [*Claimant's Memorandum, para. 36*]. However, ECE argues that MCA's reliance on Article 75 CISG is not substantiated. Indeed, Article 75 CISG, deals with the purchase of substitute goods following a legal avoidance [*Russia Arbitration proceeding (2000), 54/1999*; cf. *OGH (2000), 6 Ob 311/99z*]. As such, it is not applicable to this issue of damages because MCA's substitute purchase occurred on 24 October 2002, which is before its express avoidance on 15 November 2002. As Article 75 CISG is not applicable, Article 74 CISG establishes the legal framework for the calculation of any damages that might be awarded to MCA [cf. *Chengwei, para. 1; FCF S.A. v. Adriafil Commerciale S.r.l (2000), 4C105/2000*]. MCA cannot claim damages under Article 74 CISG because it failed to mitigate its loss as is required by Article 77 CISG [*Enderlein & Maskow, 299; Schlechtriem (1998), 586*].

2. *MCA* did not mitigate the loss caused by *ECE*'s alleged breaches of its contractual obligations

90. In accordance with Article 77 CISG, a buyer is obliged to take "such measures as are reasonable in the circumstances" in order to mitigate the loss stemming from a contractual breach [*Bianca & Bonell, 560; DiMatteo et al., 423; Sutton, 743; Arbitral Tribunal Vienna (2002) SCH/4366; Delchi Carrier S.p.A v Rotorex Corp. (2nd Cir., 1995); OLG München (1995), 7 U 1720/94*]. The reasonableness of the mitigation is judged by the standard of a prudent person under the same circumstances [*Enderlein & Maskow, 309; Schlechtriem (1998), 588*]. ECE argues that MCA did not take reasonable measures to mitigate its loss and, therefore, cannot claim damages for ECE's alleged contractual breaches.

2.1 MCA *did not take reasonable measures to mitigate its loss in accordance with Article 77* CISG

91. MCA claims that its "cover purchase is in itself a mitigation of loss" [*Claimant's Memorandum, para. 60*]. However, the purchase of substitute products is an adequate and prudent measure when mitigating losses only "as long as . . . it is certain that the seller will not perform its obligations at the time the substitute purchase is made" [*OLG Hamburg (1997), 1 U 167/95*; cf. *DiMatteo et al., 423; Sutton, 743; Budapest Arbitration (1999), VB 97142*]. ECE still expected to deliver the remaining 300 tons of cocoa beans at the time of MCA's substitute purchase and it was not objectively certain at the time that ECE would not perform its obligations [*Respondent's Memorandum, para. 62*].

92. MCA also submits that, "By making the substitute purchase, CL prevented a shutdown in production on cocoa confectionary products . . . [and] if CL had not bought from another supplier, it would have incurred even greater substantial losses" [*Claimant's Memorandum, para. 60*]. ECE argues that this claim is unfounded. In ICC Case No. 8574, the sole arbitrator held that the buyer would not have been able to honour its future contractual obligations if it had not entered into a substitute transaction [*(1996)*; cf. *Bianca & Bonell, 560; Schlechtriem (1998), 587; ICC No. 8128, (1995); ICC No. 8740, (1996)*]. However, MCA is distinct from the buyer in ICC Case No. 8574, because at the time of its substitute purchase, MCA was still able to perform its future contractual obligations [*Respondent's Memorandum, para. 66*]. As such, MCA's substitute purchase was neither prudent under the circumstances, nor was it a reasonable measure to mitigate its loss.

2.2 MCA *did not take the most appropriate action in the circumstances to mitigate its loss under Article 77* CISG

93. At law, measures taken by the buyer in entering into substitute transactions must be the most appropriate under the circumstances [*ICC No. 8574, (1996)*]. Even if the Arbitral Tribunal finds that MCA's substitute purchase was a reasonable measure, it was not the most appropriate action in the circumstances. A substitute purchase is deemed appropriate if the purchase is at the lowest price reasonably possible or if an increase in world prices is foreseeable [*Russian Federation (1995), 155/1994; Russian Federation (2000), 406/1998*]. MCA's substitute purchase was made on 24 October 2002 "at the then current market price" and "it is doubtful that a lower price could have been found" [*Procedural Order No. 2, Clarification 25*].

94. MCA concedes that it "knew of the quick changes in price that might occur on the cocoa market and anticipated that the price could only shift downwards before it would become in dire need to stock up" [*Claimant's Memorandum, para. 58*]. Therefore, it was not foreseeable to MCA that there would be an increase in world prices after October; rather, MCA expected a downturn in world market prices. Under these circumstances, it would have been more appropriate to wait for prices to drop, as happened in November, the month following MCA's substitute purchase on 24 October 2002 [*Respondent's Exhibit No. 3*]. Therefore, MCA's substitute purchase was not the most appropriate action under the circumstances.

3. *MCA* did not make the substitute purchase within a reasonable time in accordance with Article 77 *CISG*

95. "The timing of the non-breaching party's mitigation efforts is crucial to the ultimate calculation of damages owed" [*DiMatteo et al., 422*]. While a party is not required to mitigate its loss before the date of avoidance, mitigation must occur within a reasonable time [*DiMatteo et al., 422–423*]. In *OLG Düsseldorf*, it was held that a substitute purchase made nearly two months after avoidance was not within a reasonable time frame [*(1994), 17 U 146/93*]. As such, MCA's substitute purchase, made over two months after its alleged avoidance of the contract on 15 August 2002, was not made within a reasonable time. In fact, MCA waited for almost 5 months while it noted the rise in world market prices of cocoa before making a substitute purchase. In its letter of 15 August 2002 Mr. Sweet stated: "The market has been rising steadily . . . and there is some reason to believe it will" continue to rise [*Claimant's Exhibit No. 7*]. MCA then purchased substitute cocoa at the highest price since May 2002 [*Respondent's Exhibit No. 3*].

96. Furthermore, a Russian court found that the buyer had not taken the necessary measures to mitigate its loss, as required by Article 77 CISG because it had not declared the contract avoided [*Russian Federation (2000), 406/1998*]. Similarly, MCA only avoided the contract on 15 November 2002, after it made its substitute purchase [*Respondent's Memorandum, para. 89*]. Therefore, MCA failed to mitigate its loss under Article 77 CISG and MCA's recovery should be limited accordingly.

4. *MCA's* substitute purchase was not made in good faith

97. Article 7 CISG provides: "in the interpretation of this Convention, regard is to be had to its international character and to the need to promote uniformity in its application and the observance of good faith in international trade". The principle of good faith is not only applicable when interpreting the CISG itself; it also imposes a substantive obligation on the parties to a contract to act in good faith [*Bianca & Bonell, 85; Gabriel, 28; Gillies & Moens, 12; Honnold (1991), 146–148; Rosett, 290; SARL Bri Production "Bonaventure" v. Societe Pan African Export (CA Grenoble, 1995)*].

98. ECE argues that MCA should have known of the rumours that the embargo on cocoa was about to be lifted [*Claimant's Exhibit No. 10*] and that, therefore, the substitute purchase of cocoa beans on 24 October 2002 was not made in good faith. The rumours were "widespread" [*Claimant's Exhibit No. 10*] and MCA, as an industry participant, ought to have known of them [*Procedural Order No. 2, Clarification 29*]. In addition, MCA failed to contact ECE prior to making a substitute purchase, despite the fact that the parties' last correspondence occurred on 29 September 2002, which is more than three weeks before MCA's substitute purchase occurred [*Procedural Order No. 2, Clarification 22*]. This purchase, made without notice, when MCA should have been aware of the possibility that the embargo might be lifted, casts a legitimate suspicion over whether or not MCA's actions were exercised in good faith. As such, MCA is not entitled to claim damages.

5. In the alternative, the damages amount to US$172,026

99. MCA failed to mitigate its loss under Article 77 CISG and did not avoid the contract until 15 November 2002. The failure to mitigate results "in damages of an amount by which the loss should have been mitigated" [*Fisher, 51*]. Therefore, any damages MCA might be awarded under Article 74 CISG "should be measured by the difference between the contract price and the market price on 15 November 2002 and not by the larger difference between the contract price and the price paid by

Mediterraneo Confectionary Associates, Inc. in the substitute transaction" [*Answer to Notice of Arbitration and Counter-Claim, 18*].

100. Whereas MCA seeks to calculate damages under Article 74 CISG by analogy to Article 75 CISG, the correct reference would be to Article 76 CISG. Article 76 CISG provides that, "If the contract is avoided and there is a current price for the goods, the party claiming damages may, if he has not made a purchase or resale under article 75, recover the difference between the price fixed by the contract and the current price at the time of avoidance." Since MCA did not effect a substitute purchase in accordance with Article 75 [*Respondent's Memorandum, para. 87; UNCITRAL Commentary A/CN.9/264, 2*] "damages may be based on the 'current price' formula of Article 76" [*Honnold (1991), 512*] The price difference between the price in Cocoa Contract 1045 and the current market price on 15 November 2002 is US$172,026 [*Answer to Notice of Arbitration and Counter-Claim, 18*]. Therefore, any recovery MCA might be awarded should be limited to US$172,026.

ECE commends the arguments in this Memorandum to the Arbitral Tribunal to achieve "a just and effective resolution" of the dispute [*IBA Rules of Ethics for International Arbitrators, Article 1*].

BOOK REVIEWS

Cheong-Ann Png, *Corporate Liability—A Study in Principles of Attribution* (2001), The Hague: Kluwer Law International, pp i–xxvi, 1–191, ISBN 90–411–9846–6 (HB)

In the 18th century, Baron Edward Thurlow L.C. pointed out that corporations had no souls to be damned and no bodies to be kicked. At the beginning of the 21st century, much truth is still to be found in Thurlow's observation. However, the ever-increasing role of corporations in commerce and daily life has inevitably led to the need to develop clear principles governing their legal responsibilities, particularly in cases of alleged infringement or wrongdoing. It is in this context that the question arises whether, and to what extent, corporations—as legal persons—may incur personal liability for acts or omissions of employed individuals. Addressing this challenging and interesting topic, Dr Png seeks to demonstrate that principles of attribution (comprised of primary, general and secondary rules) provide a systematic and coherent way of determining corporate liability, and demonstrate that these principles are consistent with the historical and theoretical foundation of corporations rather than being a mere legal device to accomplish practical purposes.

The opening chapter of *Corporate Liability* provides an informative historical and theoretical background to modern corporations. It also presents a short introduction to different approaches to corporate liability. In Chapter 2, Png traces the development of the law of corporate liability from traditional concepts to the emergence of principles of attribution. He explains that the legal term "principles of attribution" was first introduced by Lord Hoffman in the Privy Council's decision in *Meridian Global Funds Management Asia Ltd. v. Securities Commission* [1995] 2 A.C. 500. The concept, however, can be seen as essentially derived from the "directing mind theory" established in the case of *Lennard's Carrying Co. Ltd. v. Asiatic Petroleum Co. Ltd.* [1915] A.C. 705.

Chapters 3 to 5 examine in detail the application of principles of attribution in civil, criminal and regulatory proceedings against corporate defendants and thus are of particular value to legal practitioners. One of the highlights of the book follows in Chapter 6 where Png addresses the highly sensitive problem of aggregation of individual knowledge or conduct in the perspective of principles of attribution ("problem of many hands"). On the one hand, it can be argued that "two innocent minds do not make a guilty one". On the other, as Justice Lightman points out in the book's foreword, it is questionable whether it is practical and or sensible to limit the doctrine of personal liability to situations where there is a single individual whose reprehensible conduct and state of mind is attributable to his corporate employer.

After identifying authorities that support the application of aggregation in civil cases, Png argues in favour of an extension of this concept to criminal and regulatory proceedings. Furthermore, Chapter 7 considers the relevance of Chinese Walls as barriers to the application of principles of attribution. Before drawing a conclusion in Chapter 9, Png sets out alternative approaches to corporate liability by examining recourses available against persons associated with corporate infringement or wrongdoing. The author specifically focuses on different circumstances where servants or agents may incur personal liability regardless of whether their conduct or knowledge is also attributable to the corporation.

This volume examines the concept of principles of attribution in both a practical and theoretical context and is therefore an important addition to literature on the law of corporate liability. Png's systematic and coherent analysis does not solely focus on English law but also provides a comparative perspective of developments in Canada, Australia, New Zealand and the United States. Unfortunately, Png's writing style is at times cumbersome and this tends to undermine the strength of his arguments. Despite convincing analyses, some passages lack clarity. Nevertheless, even with these weaknesses, the book makes worthwhile reading and merits the keen attention of corporate liability practitioners as well as scholars concentrating on comparative law.

Christopher Michaelsen

Pasquale Pistone, *The Impact of Community Law on Tax Treaties*, Kluwer Law International Ltd, London, 2002, pp i–xv, 1–405, ISBN 90–411–9860–1

The Impact of Community Law on Tax Treaties is about tax treaties of the member states of the European Union, and the impact that decisions of the European Court of Justice (ECJ) are having in regard to the treaties, both within the Community and in relation to third world countries.

Originally drafted in Italian, the author's doctoral thesis at the University of Genoa has been translated and adapted into English. Dr Pistone is a lecturer in tax law at the Faculty of Economics of the University of Salerno, Italy, and has lectured extensively in the area throughout Europe and South America. The author hopes his work will stimulate discussion among scholars and practitioners regarding the introduction of an EC Model Tax Convention and assists in the achievement of the integration of taxation within Europe.

Chapter I of the book analyses the Community law framework, on which the ECJ has based decisions that have developed taxation law in Europe. Chapter II follows with a systematic study of the 27 major tax decisions of the ECJ and the impact they have had on contemporary tax law in Europe. These decisions are analysed in chronological order from *Avoir fiscal* (28 January 1986) to the most recent case of *Hoechst and Metallgesellschaft* (8 March 2001).

Chapter III looks at the conflict between tax treaties and Community law, focusing on the system resulting from the interaction of tax treaties on income and capital with the domestic legislation of EU Member States. Chapter IV then considers six solutions which have been proposed to tackle the problems raised by the conflict between tax treaties and domestic legislation, and analyses each suggestion in light of the developing Community law.

Chapter V contains the author's proposal for an EC Model Tax Convention, drafted combining existing provisions of international tax law with the principles of Community law. In the proposed draft, the author has attempted to achieve a compromise between the competing elements of Community tax law, without undermining the cohesion of both tax treaties and Community law. Chapter VI considers execution of the proposed EC Model Tax Convention, and highlights a strategy of phased implementation.

The book is well written, and clearly conveys the author's enthusiasm for the subject matter. With a clear analysis of the case law being developed by the European Court of Justice and a well-drafted proposal for a EC Model Tax Convention, it is obvious that the author is very conversant with the subject, and it is very likely that his wish to stimulate discussion and debate on the topic of European Tax Treaties will be realised.

Peter Walsh

Christin M. Forstinger, *Takeover Law in the EU and the USA: A Comparative Analysis*, Kluwer Law International, 2002, 182pp. ISBN 90–411–1919–1

In its ambition to achieve a Common Market, the bold experiment that is the European Union (EU) has encountered many problems. These problems have largely arisen in its attempt to harmonise the diverse laws of its member nations. Corporate takeover law and takeover regulation is an area where these problems are pronounced. *Takeover Law in the EU and the USA* aims to look at the problems associated with EU-wide takeover law regulation and suggests solutions through a formula for the administration of this area. In particular, this text is concerned with contrasting a regime that fosters takeover regulatory competition with a regime that imposes harmonisation in takeover regulation. The purpose of this study is to see which regime, or elements of a regime, would lead to a more efficient EU takeover market in order to help realise the goal of the Common Market.

Forstinger examines the current corporate law and takeover law regulatory regimes from the United States (US) and some member nations of the EU (particularly the United Kingdom (UK) and Germany) in order to arrive at the formula referred to above. In particular, the regimes are held as working examples of how a particular regime could operate in the EU. For example, the US experience is used to analyse the features of takeover law regulatory competition as opposed to harmonisation, and to see how easily these features would transpose onto the European continent. In conducting this examination, Forstinger looks at the history, regulations, case law, statute and treaty law of the particular takeover regime being analysed.

The text begins this analysis by setting the scene in relation to takeover and corporate law generally. This initial explanation involved a basic overview of the various stakeholders usually associated with companies and the interests each of these groups have in takeover situations. This explanation is indeed quite basic and would be useful for those who have had limited contact with the dynamics of corporate and company law.

Following on, US general corporate law dynamics and their competitive aspects are outlined. Forstinger then delineates the limited corporate law jurisdiction of the EU and the problems this poses for harmonisation. Attention is paid to some other problems associated with the harmonisation of corporate law throughout the EU, for instance, the differing conflict of law rules in relation to the "home" of a corporation. This chapter also looked at the institutional corporate law differences between the US and the individual member nations of the EU. It is subsequently argued that these significant differences preclude a solution to the EU corporate and takeover law harmonisation problem as it involves a complete transplant of the US system over to the EU.

Proceeding from this analysis, the text begins to delve into the substantial issues that it aims to address. The examination begins with a closer look at the US system of corporate regulatory competition and then moves to a closer analysis of US takeover law regulatory competition. The US experience is used to show the benefits and dangers of regulatory competition. The US system is also used to highlight the limits of regulatory competition and where Federal intervention was deemed necessary to address these limits. The author argues that, especially in relation to takeover law, there are significant limits to the beneficial effects of regulatory competition due to the extreme conflict of interest between managers and shareholders in a takeover situation. Forstinger finds that in the US, state regulatory competition concerning takeover law (and indeed corporate law generally) has caused a convergence in the laws of the various states benefiting the interests of managers over shareholders and other stakeholders. The argument continues that the convergence is largely due to the financial incentives for states to attract corporations to incorporate and re-incorporate within their jurisdiction. Further it is argued that convergence is also due to the basic similarities of the legal systems within the states of the US.

Forstinger examines the takeover law regulation regime in the EU, in particular, the rejected proposed takeover directive of the EU. The author outlines the history of the directive, the contents of the directive and, finally, the reasons for its ultimate rejection. By way of contrast, Forstinger compares the effect of the directive with the relevant Federal legislation in the US and finds that the EU directive imposed more restrictions on target managements' ability to adopt defensive measures in the face of a takeover. The text then continues to look at European takeover regulation by examining the takeover regulation regimes in some member nations.

In conclusion, Forstinger hypothetically examines the EU situation and proposes a solution to the problem of EU-wide takeover law regulation, drawing on the US experience, the failure of the proposed takeover directive and the takeover regulatory regimes currently existing in the EU member nations. Forstinger finds that predominant regulatory competition, as found in the US, would not achieve the same convergence of laws in the EU as has largely occurred in the US because of the fundamentally different takeover law regimes present in the EU member nations. Forstinger also disputes the need for complete harmonisation of the takeover laws of the EU member nations but, rather, adopts a form of harmonisation called "reflexive harmonisation". This form would provide the member nations of the EU with a regulatory system that combines identical minimum standards in relation to takeover law with a degree of national autonomy at the implementation stage. This reflexive harmonisation of takeover law would help to preserve, to a degree, the unique corporate cultures of the EU member nations.

Takeover Law in the EU and the USA is a good theoretical introduction to the problems facing the EU regarding takeover regulation harmonisation. It is an excellent overview of the most important issues currently facing not only EU takeover regulation, but also US takeover regulation. This text is a good first point of call for anyone interested in the area.

Samantha Byles

J.M. Bennett, *Sir James Cockle: First Chief Justice of Queensland,* Lives of the Australian Chief Justices, Federation Press, ISBN: 1 86287 485 9

The widely published and well-respected legal historian, Dr J.M. Bennett, has added to the series "Lives of Australian Chief Justices", with the historical biography of Sir James Cockle F.R.S, the first Chief Justice of Queensland.

At first glance it is ironic that the last study in the present series of the foundation Chief Justices of the Australian States details the life of Sir James Cockle, given that he is more widely remembered for his mathematical and scientific investigations than as a lawyer. His passing on 27 January 1895 was barely noticed in Queensland, with most people having all but forgotten him. Dr Bennett elucidates Sir James Cockle's significant role in the transition of Brisbane from a "perfectly distressing" to a "commodious" town with "all the requirements of a capital for a fine and independent colony".

The recommendation of Chief Justice Sir William Erle and Sir James Cockle's subsequent appointment as Chief Justice of Queensland is contextualised by Dr Bennett's examination of the tenuous relations between the Queensland government and the Hon. Justice A.J.P. Lutwyche, the sole Supreme Court Judge. Prior to Sir James Cockle's appointment, the "troubled waters" between the legislative and judicial powers of Queensland were causing untold damage to the stability of the new settlement. James Cockle was sent to Queensland in the capacity of conciliator, succeeding within a few months to calm judicial tensions to the stage that a sense of fraternity was already evident between Bench and Bar. Sir James Cockle's conciliation permitted Mr Lutwyche's retention of his judicial tenure, to the advantage of Queensland.

The present judicial biography provides concise insight into how James Cockle's personality influenced the shaping of Queensland Courts, legal institutions and the law itself. The procedural functioning of the Supreme Court was undoubtedly affected by Sir James Cockle's preference for English practices and forms. Dr Bennett recounts difficulty in uncovering judgments of his Honour that have remained leading authorities, largely attributing this to Sir James Cockle's economic and scientific judicial style. The author relates James Cockle's trepidation in relying on the decisions of other judicial officers and hesitation to make pronouncements that traveled beyond the limits of the matter *inter partes* to provide principles of wide application, coupled with his Honour's preoccupation with relevance. In contrast to the class of judicial law reformers, Sir James Cockle saw responsibility for statue law as falling wholly within the purview of Parliament. It was stated by Dr Bennett that "[o]f his many excellent qualities a zest for law reform was not a conspicuous one". Sir James Cockle's strict literal interpretation of statutes and rules of court was reported by Dr Bennett as sometimes leading to jurisdictional awkwardness and reflecting an element of insecurity in managing the relatively new Supreme Court. Interestingly, Sir James Cockle, with clerical assistance, was the most productive of all the commissioners assigned to comprehensively consolidate the colony's statutes and to establish what law had effect in Queensland, accomplishing the entire laborious process of consolidation in little more than a year.

Dr Bennett gives long-overdue attention to the less than ideal conditions of employment borne by Sir James Cockle. Most would be horrified at the manner in which adequate remuneration for his services was delayed and rectification of the situation egregiously instituted. For the first eleven years of tenure as Chief Justice of Queensland he received an annual salary of £1500 in comparison to Justice Lutwyche's £2000. Politicians voted down an increase in his salary in 1865, and without his inherited means, he could barely have maintained his family and his judicial station on his salary. In May 1874, the Chief Justice's salary was settled at £2500 and puisne judges £2000. Similarly, Dr Bennett attends to the dilatory recognition afforded to Sir James Cockle, by way of a knighthood, a dignity then instantly accorded to all other Australian Chief Justices except in the Colony of Western Australia. It was not until Sir George Bowen's third recommendation, that this honour was bestowed upon Sir James Cockle. The judicial life of Sir James Cockle as the first Queensland Chief Justice ended on 24 April 1879. In an abrupt statement that gave no reasons he submitted his resignation of office as Chief Justice to then Governor Sir Arthur Kennedy of Queensland.

The book comprehensively examines Sir James Cockle's role in the controversies of early Queensland, both in relation to its political and judicial systems. This book is a recommended read for all those interested in early Australian legal history.

Zara Spencer

For Product Safety Concerns and Information please contact our EU representative GPSR@taylorandfrancis.com
Taylor & Francis Verlag GmbH, Kaufingerstraße 24, 80331 München, Germany

www.ingramcontent.com/pod-product-compliance
Ingram Content Group UK Ltd.
Pitfield, Milton Keynes, MK11 3LW, UK
UKHW022010180926
475701UK00003B/288

9780415419659